SOUVENIR

Margaret Truman's Own Story

SOUVENIR

920

BY MARGARET TRUMAN

WITH MARGARET COUSINS

McGRAW-HILL BOOK COMPANY, INC.

New York   Toronto   London

Appreciation to CBS Television, a Division of the Columbia Broadcasting System, for permission to reprint the transcription of Miss Truman's interview with her parents on Person to Person

Contents

Contents

Illustrations

FOLLOWING PAGE 144

MY FACE MARKS THE SUNNY HOURS.

WHAT CAN YOU SAY OF YOURS?

*Inscription on a sundial at
219 North Delaware Street, Independence, Missouri*

SOUVENIR

1: Down the ways

When I read in the paper not long ago that the USS *Missouri* was to be decommissioned, I experienced a pang above and beyond the call of duty. It seemed to me that the passing of the "Big Mo" set a seal of finality on an era in my life much more definite than the change of family address from 1600 Pennsylvania Avenue, Washington, D.C., to 219 North Delaware Street, Independence, Missouri. For the *Missouri* and I, in a manner of speaking, had started out together, and all her triumphs and vicissitudes were entwined in the strings of my heart. In many ways, she had been deeply involved in my affairs and whether she was serving as a setting for the signing of treaties or wallowing in a mudbank off the coast of Florida, I always felt as if I were her mother. When I pursued the news item to discover that the *Missouri* was headed for scrap, I was really saddened, but I decided at once that the connotation ended there! That's my platform and I'm sticking to it.

Still, the nostalgia brought on by my associations with that good gray battleship encouraged me to haul out the moth-eaten old suitcase trunk in which I had hastily stowed the scrapbooks, diaries, autographs, photographs, clippings, letters, telegrams, dance programs, place cards, ribbons, pressed flowers, and a few shreds of confetti, when I left the White House. (My father and I are incapable of throwing anything away!) When I had got it out in the middle of the living-room floor and located the key (although my father and I never throw anything away, sometimes we put things away so well we have great trouble finding them!) I sat staring at it—Pandora's box, full of so much that was glamorous, happy, exciting, and rewarding and so much that was not—undecided whether it was time to let it all roll over me again or to wait for a more distant perspective.

But I wanted to remember the *Missouri* on the crest of the wave, so I fitted the key to the lock and my life literally sprang out at me. The suitcase had always been a little too small to hold it.

૨૭ I was nineteen years old that winter. I was a junior in George Washington University, to which I traveled on a bus, hauling my heavy textbooks. I was a history major in the School of Government, and history books always seem to be larger and heavier than any other kind. I always had to do homework, so I was always carrying them. I wore sweaters and skirts and bobby socks and my hair was parted on the side and hung in a long straight pale mane slightly curled up at the ends. I had to put it up every night, and if the weather was damp it came uncurled. I wasn't too dissatisfied with my looks, since it seemed to me I looked pretty much like everybody else (which is desirable at nineteen), but I used to worry about my nose. It has since been described with many strange adjectives, even including patrician, but the fact is, it's better on one side than the other.

I was a member of Pi Beta Phi Sorority and was elated to have been elected to Phi Pi Epsilon, an honorary Foreign Service fraternity. I belonged to the Canterbury Club, an Episcopalian group on the campus, and I sang in the University Glee Club. My social life, while far from sophisticated, was satisfactory. Naturally, I would have preferred it to be more sophisticated. Jane Lingo, my best friend, and I double-dated on week ends and once in a while we got a drag bid to West Point, where I had cousins.

Jane was my first Washington friend. We were boon companions, the sharers of girlish confidences and participants in the usual number of fallings-out and makings-up that go with growing up.

At nineteen we were full of romantic notions, dreams of glory, distaste for homework, and struggles to live up to the high standards established for us by our affectionate and careful parents. Jane wanted to be a writer. I wanted to be an opera star. We thought about our lofty ambitions when we had time but mostly we buzzed around the campus soda fountain, where I indulged my passion for chocolate ice cream, or milled in the book and record and dress shops on Connecticut Avenue after school hours, gossiping and giggling. And we went to uncounted movies.

My father was the Junior Senator from Missouri. He had been a Senator half my life and while his name was often in the newspapers that year as chairman of the investigating committee, now known in the annals as the Truman Committee, I took his publicity as a matter of course. He had to travel so much in its behalf that it seemed to me I never saw him any more. We had always been great friends.

We lived at 4701 Connecticut Avenue in Washington, in a five-room apartment, where my mother was chief cook and I was bottle washer. I resented this because at home—our real home in Independence, Missouri—there was always Vietta, who was both. . . . Vietta Garr, the best cook in the world, begging your pardon, Mother.

I was still known in most quarters as "the little Truman girl," a designation for which I had the usual teen-age distaste, and I did not bulk large in any picture, official or otherwise. Mother was, is, and always will be a lady, reared in the traditions of the old school and intent on passing them on to me, come hell or high water. I was presumed to be *learning* to be a *young* lady, and my mother, the dearest woman alive and also the most forceful, was going to see to it. In this program, she was ably abetted by my father. Although fairly weak-willed where I am concerned, Dad was willing to take her word for the tenets of young ladyhood.

I had rarely been to the White House except as a tourist and my only official connection with state social circles had been the result of an accident. When I was eleven years old I had received an invitation to a White House dancing party. Nonplussed, my mother had investigated, only to discover that in some protocol bulletin or White House Directory there was an asterisk by my name which indicated that I was "an eligible daughter." I wasn't sure what this meant at the time but it sounded good. My mother, however, refused to consider my possibilities as a child bride and wrote to Mrs. Roosevelt, who was then First Lady, explaining that I was only eleven, and not eligible even for a dancing party.

When I was about fifteen I had set up a howl to go to a White House Reception. (It must have been because a movie star was sched-

3

uled to be there.) I started out to wind my father around my little finger, but it didn't work.

"But why? Why can't I go?" I whined.

"You're too young," Dad said. "You're only fifteen. And besides, your mother has decided against it."

That ended that.

But in December, 1943, my father received a telephone call in his office from Admiral Kelly, Commandant of the United States Navy Yard at Brooklyn, New York, requesting that I be permitted to christen the battleship *Missouri* at its official launching. As Senator from Missouri my father had been chosen to make the address on the occasion of the commissioning of the ship, the following June. Dad took my invitation under advisement and went into conclave with my mother. They agreed calmly that it was an honor that I had been asked and might be a pleasant thing for me to sponsor the world's mightiest battleship and give it a good name.

I was wild with excitement.

There was much telephoning back and forth between the Navy Yard and the Senator's office as details were relayed to me. I was invited to designate a sponsor. I immediately chose Jane Lingo as maid of honor, and we were wild with excitement together, which doubled the excitement.

I also asked Drucie Snyder to be a maid of honor. Drucie had been my friend since we were nine years old, and her father and mother, Mr. and Mrs. John Snyder of St. Louis, Missouri, and my father and mother had been friends before we were born. We met in Williamsburg, Virginia, where our parents had gone for a spring vacation combined with introducing their mutual offspring to colonial history, and we took an immediate shine to each other.

Subsequently Mr. Snyder left his banking business in St. Louis to come to Washington as an executive of the RFC, and our friendship progressed, although we never went to school together. Drucie attended boarding school in St. Louis, after her family moved to Washington, and went to Bradford College in New England when I enrolled in George Washington University, but our association continued to be close, and is until this day.

Drucie is a wonderful girl with dark hair and mischievous eyes, well-marked eyebrows and long lashes. Her face is oval with a generous, happy mouth and her nose is slightly retroussé. She has a pixie

4

sense of humor and a talent for having a good time. She can look as elegant and glamorous as a queen or as tousled and casual as a gamin, depending on the time, the place, and the situation. When you regard Drucie's portrait in her hyacinth-blue dress, with her fine shoulders and neck rising from it in proud serenity, it is almost impossible to believe that this is the same girl who used to stand behind a potted palm in the Blue Room of the White House and make faces at protocol!

Drucie was away at Bradford, but in view of the importance of the occasion, she was permitted to come down to New York for the day and stand behind me at the launching of the *Missouri*. This made my happiness complete.

As soon as the details were settled I began to worry about clothes, the weather, and my health. I had had a cold and I foresaw that the launching of the world's mightiest battleship would be as nothing if I happened to be running a temperature on the appointed day.

Fate was kind and nothing happened to postpone the occasion. The weather, while uncheerful, was not exactly a blizzard. I had managed to get rid of the sniffles in the nick of time. On January 28, the official party entrained in Washington on the Baltimore and Ohio, occupying a private car. I had never ridden in a private car, which seemed to me the height of all luxury. There was a large delegation from the state of Missouri, including my father and mother and many Navy and Government officials. (Jane, whose father was a naval officer, was Navy born and bred, and she was as thrilled as I was.)

We came into Jersey City in the early winter dusk and ferried the Hudson River. The panorama of New York City made a fabulous backdrop, though the lights were muted. Those were dim-out days. I remember that we saw a big white hospital ship, its red crosses scarlet against the unsullied white, brilliantly lighted but without a soul at any rail, gliding in dead silence down the river. It made a sharp contrast to the dimmed-out world—like some monstrous swan or a phantom ship above the dark water. It was eerie and melancholy, and remindful of the war.

But we couldn't stay melancholy for long. We were whisked off to the Waldorf-Astoria, which was alive with wartime bustle and confusion: men in uniform and women in evening clothes, flowers, furs, jewels; music from stringed orchestras; people sitting at little tables drinking tea; the clink of glasses; the hum of conversation;

5

Homburg hats, braid, gold lace. . . . New York! We sank in the red carpet, gaped at the chandeliers, and got lost in the lobby. When we finally settled in our rooms and unpacked we had to hash it all over, compare notes, and make observations. By the time we finished with that, it was almost morning.

&✷ The Great Day dawned cold, gloomy, forbidding, and smelling of snow. I had a moment of horrible depression, fearing that the weather might yet postpone my big moment, but then word came that we were to be dressed and ready immediately for the car that would take us to the Navy Yard. I had a new powder-blue suit which I fancied myself in, and all-black accessories, black shoes, bag, gloves, and hat. Over this I had to wear my old fur coat. I think it was muskrat. The curse was taken off it by the arrival of two enormous orchids which practically covered my chest. I was deeply impressed. When I think of the size, shape, color, and number of orchids that have shriveled on my left shoulder since that day, I sometimes feel I owe an apology to the orchid family. I have never been able to grow blasé about anything, much less orchids, but I *have* had quite a few and I have tried to take care of them under some fairly adverse circumstances. I can take orchids or leave them (honestly, I like violets better), but those were the fustest with the mostest, as the general said. Weighed down with orchids, I left for the Brooklyn Navy Yard.

As we were driven over the East River, we kept scanning the sky fearfully but when we got to the Yard, and there stood the *Missouri* in her ways, it was impossible to look at anything else. She was as tall as a fifteen-story building! This is not a figure of speech, but an actual fact. I don't know whether you have ever seen a ship as tall as a fifteen-story building standing up out of the water or not, but you can take my word for it—it's an overpowering sight.

There was another overpowering sight that day. The *Missouri's* Honor Guard of Marines was lined up the stair, from bottom to top, bristling with spit and polish and white gloves. Marines at attention always look as if they were carved out of enduring rock—not a flick of an eyelash, not a whisper of breath. Aware of the solemnity of the occasion and the responsibilities that devolved on me, it was impossible to stare, but I kept cutting my eyes around at them. They were marvelous.

6

Our party was met by Admiral Kelly and welcomed aboard. At the time of the launching, the *Missouri* was a shell, as all battleships are when launched. The motors, gun turrets, and other equipment had yet to be installed. The prow reared up so high you could scarcely see the top of it. A metal plate had been affixed to the side of the prow, against which the bottle of champagne had to be crashed to insure its breaking. I began to feel nervous. How could I hit such a tiny target in such a broad expanse?

The bottle had been scored by the United States Treasury and was encased in a beautiful silver container, perforated and filigreed so that the wine could escape. On it were engraved the details of the occasion, the name of the ship, the date, my name as sponsor, and the names of all the admirals in attendance. The bottle and the chalice were entwined with red, white, and blue ribbons.

At the end of the launching ceremonies, standing between my father and Admiral Kelly, I received the signal and let the bottle fly. "I christen thee USS *Missouri*," I cried, tremulously.

Fortunately the bottle connected with the metal plate and the champagne spurted. Beginner's luck! The ropes were cast off, but for some reason the ship did not move immediately down the ways. In my moment of exaltation, I apparently felt all-powerful, for I put my hand to the fifteen-story prow and gave it a good push! Nobody, least of all me, believes this had anything to do with it, but the *Missouri* suddenly began to move so rapidly that the bottle in its silver jacket went down over the side and had to be jerked up so unceremoniously that Admiral Kelly and I were baptized with wine, which sprayed out in every direction. My muskrat smelled like champagne all winter!

I scarcely noticed this extracurricular bath at the time, for as the Big Mo went sliding down the ways and hit the water, the sun broke through the lowering clouds for the first time that day and bathed her in luminous light. A great shout went up from everybody aboard, for in sailor lore, this is a good omen for a ship.

Well, the *Missouri* had good luck and bad, as most ships do, and most people, but to me there will never be another such ship. When she was commissioned, that is, made ready to go into battle, on June 11, 1944, my father delivered the commemoration address. My cousin, John C. Truman of Independence, Missouri, eventually became a member of her crew. I followed her progress in battle and out, until she was designated as the scene of the signing of the Peace Treaty with Japan—my father's personal choice. When my mother and Dad and I came back from Rio de Janeiro in 1946, where my father had gone to close the International Monetary Conference, we were aboard the *Missouri*, and on her hallowed decks, I crossed the equator for the first time.

But that day, all this lay in the future. When the launching ceremonies were over, Drucie, Jane, and I stayed aboard to watch the installation of the first gun turret. (The duty of maids of honor on such an occasion is simply to keep the christener company, as far as I could determine. I was untutored in the matter, but it tripled my pleasure to have them there.) I was quiet, sorting out my emotions. I had found the whole ceremony intensely moving. When Admiral Kelly presented me with the chalice, dented where it had crashed the side, I felt near to tears. It is still one of my most treasured possessions.

Wonders were not to cease. Drucie had to go back to school but Jane and I were invited to a cocktail party at the Plaza Hotel, given by Colonel and Mrs. August Busch. Demurely we drank tomato juice and chatted politely with the glamorous adults there. I remember standing in a corner in the beautiful white-and-gold suite and thinking, "Is this really me?"

That evening I realized one of my dreams. I paid my first visit to the Metropolitan Opera, as the guest of Major and Mrs. Thomas J. Strickler of Kansas City. We heard *Cavalleria Rusticana* and *Pagliacci* on a double bill. I had been especially excited at the prospect of hearing Lawrence Tibbett and when we got to the opera and discovered that his performance had been canceled because of illness, I had a twinge of disappointment. This disappeared when Leonard Warren began to sing. He was one of the Met's most promising young baritones and most personable actors. We were virtually carried away and I remember standing and beating my palms together, and wishing I had the courage to cry, "Bravo!" I number Leonard and Agatha Warren among my friends now.

Although the opera was less dressy during the war years, the audience that night seemed to me to be a blazing assemblage. Jane and I stared around the famous Diamond Horseshoe and wondered who people were. The old building exercised over me then the irresistible charm it has had for me ever since. I never sniff the faint mustiness of its red velvet and gilt without feeling that it is the epitome of romance. When the lights go down and the music swells and soars to the farthest reaches of the Family Circle and then the majestic curtains slowly part on some gaudy old story of love and intrigue, I find myself almost perfectly happy.

After the opera, Major and Mrs. Strickler entertained for us with a supper party at the Wedgwood Room of the Waldorf. By now the excitement of the days and the sleeplessness of the nights had done their work. We had less yearning to be sophisticated and more to be unconscious. I looked at Jane and she was glassy-eyed with fatigue. I tried to concentrate on something in the room to keep my eyes open, but every once in a while my head bobbled and I lost the trend of the conversation.

As a final fillip for *les jeunes filles*, Major Strickler had ordered crepes Suzette for desert. I had never had a crepe Suzette. In fact, I didn't think I had ever seen one. But I had heard about them and I knew how fashionable they were. I couldn't wait. But I had to wait. We waited and waited and waited. I became more and more sodden with slumber. I began to have an intense desire to put my head down in the plate destined for a crepe Suzette and go sound asleep. It took the Waldorf an awfully long time to whip up a batch of pancakes, and when they finally arrived, I had to be shaken by the shoulder to rouse me to welcome them. Then followed the elaborate ritual of the sauce. The headwaiter came over and began to pour things out of one bottle after another, a little bit here, a few drops there, and finally he doused the pancakes and set everything afire. While the crepes burned with a bright blue flame, I relapsed into oblivion. My mother might have been more exercised by my inability to stay awake at a party if it hadn't been that she took such a dim view of crepes Suzette to begin with!

At last, the *pièce de résistance* was served up and I took a bite. The warm brandy burned my throat, went up my nose, and made tears come to my eyes. I thought, "Is *this* what they kept me up for!" Needless to say, my opinion of crepes Suzette has been revised since then. I can cope with a crepe with the best of them, but I never see their little fires burning around a restaurant or hotel dining room without remembering my first meeting with them. The sight of a small blue flame always makes me feel slightly sleepy.

And so to bed. I don't remember how we got upstairs (I had lost my small black velvet hat and never saw it again!) or anything else that happened until morning. Then it was time to go back to Washington, back to George Washington University, back to Imperialism and International Law and Victorian Poetry, back to the sweater and the skirt and the simple ice-cream soda. Back to the bus!

I packed up all my souvenirs (I'm a saver of souvenirs)—the invitations and the place cards, the program of the opera, the matchbooks from the fancy places I'd been and the ribbons from corsages I'd worn, the dented silver container that had swung the wine against the great wall of the USS *Missouri*. Along with these I took my vivid impressions—the sight of the ship sliding into the future in a burst of sunlight, the sound of music from the brilliant stage, the memory of a young man's face.

These foolish things remind me of me.

2: I'm from Missouri

My father says that the first thing he remembers about life is chasing a frog around the back yard of his Grandmother Young's house in Cass County, Missouri. He was two years old at the time and the way the frog leaped tickled him so that he would have to stop his chase to slap his knees and roar with laughter. His grandmother noticed this and thought it pretty remarkable that a baby displayed such a keen sense of humor.

The first thing I remember about life was the hot-air register in the hallway of my Grandmother Wallace's house in Independence, Missouri, where I was born and grew up. I must have been a little past two at the time. It was in the spring of the year—that season of domestic chaos when the ladies of my immediate ancestry tore the house limb from limb, scrubbed, waxed, polished, painted, varnished, and enameled it and called it spring housecleaning. I had been noticing this register for some time. It had open grillwork, into which you could stick your fingers, and it obviously went somewhere that didn't meet the eye. As my father had been born with a sense of humor, I had been born with a bump of curiosity. I wanted to know what lay behind the register.

During the housekeeping holocaust that I speak of, old Frank, the handy man, under whose feet I could often be found, was required to remove the registers, take them outdoors and burnish them with

11

stove blacking, let them dry thoroughly, and replace them. When Frank took the register out of the hallway that day, I was lurking near. As soon as he got out of sight, I determined to investigate what I had long wanted to investigate—where it went!

I leaned over and fell headfirst into the hot-air pipe. I didn't get any farther than the first bend in the duct, which was just about large enough to contain my person. But I couldn't get out. I was stuck there with my short legs waving in the air. All this came as a great surprise to me and I began to scream bloody murder. Everybody in the house came running, for terror was mixed with rage in my lamentations.

Somebody pulled me out, red in the face, choking, and besmirched with soot and lint that collects in registers. Frank was horrified.

"I told her to stay away from there," he kept apologizing.

It was the consensus of opinion that it was nobody's fault but my own. My grandmother didn't think I was particularly remarkable and observed that curiosity killed a cat.

It may be that I remember this event so sharply because it was the first time everything hadn't given way before me. I was born into a world in which love and affection were paramount and babies were scarce. In one of his brief notes on his life and times, my father has written:

"When I was about six or seven years old my mother took me to Sunday school and I saw there the prettiest, sweetest little girl I'd ever seen. I was too backward even to look at her very much and I didn't speak to her for five years.

"From the fifth grade in school until my graduation from high school, we were in the same classes. If I succeeded in carrying her books to school or back home for her I had a big day."

My father's nature is rarely so well expressed as in his single-minded devotion to my mother from early childhood. They are the same age and were friends and companions for twenty-five years before they were married. Their courtship, at least my father's side of it, is legend. My mother, née Elizabeth Virginia Wallace, is a private person, and has remained so against great odds. She has maintained a decent reticence on the matter, as becomes a lady, and let Papa talk! But she had several hundred dates with him.

My father wooed her consistently—from a farm, where he had to commute twenty miles on Saturday nights by railroad train (in

1913 he bought a Stafford automobile to make commuting easier); from a trench in France, while shot and shell were falling, when he was Captain Truman of Battery D in World War I; from Kansas City, where he was working in a bank, and from wherever else he happened to be.

My mother, whose public façade has been unvaryingly sedate and whose public utterances have been unfailingly courteous but cryptic, is perhaps the least understood member of our family. She is a woman of tremendous character, which the public may sense, but in addition she is a warmhearted, kind lady, with a robust sense of humor, a merry, twinkling wit, and a tremendous capacity for enjoying life. From all I can gather—though not from *her*, as her modesty is so deep-seated that nothing can be done about it—she was an Independence belle. Her pictures show her to have been as slim as a willow wand, with large blue eyes and a cap of fair, wavy hair that fitted her head like a helmet. She loved games, was a crack tennis player, and distinguished herself in boarding school by winning the shot-put in a track meet. Her only comment on this last is that it has certainly come in handy as training for shaking hands with a thousand people at a time! It has also been reported that Mother could whistle through her teeth, play baseball, and beat all comers at mumblety-peg, but she has not been able to find later uses for these accomplishments.

Any hope on my father's part of being an athlete was cut off by the fact that he had had to wear those tremendously thick-lensed glasses from early childhood. He is hyperopic, having been born with a sort of flat eyeball, so that he is so shortsighted as to be virtually blind without his glasses. Although he rarely mentions this handicap and few people know it, it was responsible for one of the great disappointments of his life. He received an appointment to West Point in 1901 and passed all his examinations but was disqualified by his eyesight. While he was more at home with the keyboard of a piano than a tennis racquet, my mother could not seem to be satisfied with any other beau. If legend can be trusted, a good many young men proposed to her while she was waiting for Papa.

I have no way of knowing how many times Dad proposed, and my mother would certainly say that it is none of my business. Maybe it was only once. He's really a bashful man. They were married on the twenty-eighth of June, 1919, according to the local press, in

13

Trinity Episcopal Church in Independence, where I still sing in the choir when I am at home. Trinity is one of the oldest churches in our part of the country—a sweet little red-brick building—and the day they were married the chancel was banked with flowers from the gardens of friends and neighbors. In case you're interested, my mother wore a short white dress and a big hat and carried a bridal bouquet. Her cousins, Louise Wells and Helen Wallace, were her attendants. Daddy wore his new gray suit, and his war buddy, Captain Theodore Marks, was best man. Dr. John Plunkett married them and the reception was held at the home of the bride, after which they went to Chicago and Detroit on their honeymoon. They came back to live in our roomy old Victorian house on Delaware Street.

Nearly five years later, on the seventeenth of February, 1924, according to my first press notice, I was born there. The *Independence Examiner* carried this announcement on the bottom of page one, between a report of a high-school debate on the subject: "Should Kansas City Adopt the Commission Form of Government," and a news item on the visit to Independence of the dean of the School of Journalism at the University of Missouri. It read: "Judge and Mrs. Harry Truman announce the birth of a daughter at the home on Delaware Street Sunday morning."

I have always been glad that I was born in the house on Delaware, instead of the more impersonal confines of a hospital, where most people of my generation seem to have come into the world. I don't know why I wasn't born in a hospital. I would think, offhand, that Dad would have been so excited and worried that he would have insisted on it, but it may be that my mother made up her mind to stay at home and Dr. Krimminger humored her. I apparently arrived ahead of schedule because the bassinet or crib or whatever they planned to put me in wasn't there that Sunday when I put in my appearance. They had to take a drawer out of the dresser and put me in it on a pillow. Once in a while I have tried to tease my mother about this—indicating that she wasn't really expecting me or that she didn't make it to the hospital or why couldn't I have had a bassinet with ruffles and ribbons like other girls! My mother, who loves a joke, does not take kindly to such joshing. She does not consider the subject a matter for levity or even for discussion. When it comes up that I spent my early days in a dresser drawer, I can really start something by asking my mother if she kept the drawer pulled out!

I don't mind having been cradled in a dresser drawer. I always say that's the way many good actresses got their start in life and maybe that's the reason I have always been stage-struck. Anyhow, I think it will look charming in the program notes! Wait until Mother hears that.

I was christened Mary Margaret Truman, Mary after my Aunt Mary Jane Truman and Margaret for Grandmother Wallace. I never liked the double name and began to try to get rid of it as fast as possible. My father was named Harry S. Truman, after his uncle Harrison Shippe. The initial S. didn't stand for anything, however, and I think my father got tired of explaining that he didn't have a middle name, so he gave me two! Some people *still* call me Mary Margaret. I remain civil under such circumstances, but whoever calls me "Maggie" earns my lasting scorn.

My father calls me Marg (hard "g") or Margie (hard "g") and in moments of stress or sentimentality, he still calls me "Baby." I am trying to break him of this. When displeased with me, my mother calls me Margaret. I call her Mother and I call my father Daddy. When I was a little girl, I was permitted to call Mother "Mommy," but she prefers to be called "Mother." She has no cheer for the non-sense of calling your parents by their given names, and she doesn't like nicknames of any sort.

My father and mother both derived from close-knit families. While I have heard a lot about my ancestors from both sides of the house, I sometimes think genealogy is a bore to people who don't happen to be personally involved in it, so you may want to skip this. My only reason for mentioning it is that some of the family traits seem to keep cropping up in me!

My cousins, Miss Ethel Noland and Miss Nellie Noland who live across the street from us in Independence, were authorities on Daddy's ancestors and knew all the ins and outs of the family tree. Both sets of my great-grandparents on my father's side—Anderson Shippe and Mary Jane Holmes Truman and Solomon and Harriet Gregg Young—came to the Missouri frontier from Shelby County, Kentucky, around 1840.

My favorite ancestor when I was a child was my father's great-grandmother, Nancy Tyler Holmes. She was related to President Tyler, but that didn't mean as much to me as the fact that she was scalped by the Indians and lived. She always wore a fine lace cap to

15

cover the scar. Nancy is said to have pushed West alone, accompanied by her children and her slaves, armed only with a large sack of homemade teacakes and a beaver hat, a souvenir of her late husband, Captain Jesse Holmes, who had perished in Kentucky. Nancy is said to have been as stubborn as a mule and held to the theory that a woman never married but once—and once a widow, always a widow. In fact all the whole Truman clan hold strong views on the subject of marriage and there has never been a divorce in the family as far back as its lineage can be traced.

Another story I liked when I was a child was the one about Grandmother Truman's own mother, Harriet Young, a redheaded lady with a lot of spunk. In 1861 when she was a young wife in the border uprisings that racked Missouri during the War between the States, Jim Lane, the notorious raider and leader of the Union-sympathizing "Red Legs," rode into her barnyard, got off his horse, and ordered Great-grandmother Young to fix breakfast for his band of marauders. Great-grandpa Young was in California at the time, and she and her children were by themselves. Harriet Young got the children quiet, fired up the stove, and baked biscuits and fried meat until her hands were blistered. After a satisfying repast the Red Legs butchered four hundred of the Youngs' hogs, hacked off the hams, set the barns afire, and rode away. Neither Great-grandmother Harriet Young nor Martha Ellen Young Truman, my own grandmother, ever forgot this outrage or forgave the Union for it.

Once Daddy made the mistake of visiting his grandmother Harriet, wearing the blue uniform of the National Guard. She mistook him for a Yankee and ordered him out of the house. When Grandmother Truman came to visit us in the White House, I teased her, saying we proposed to honor her by letting her stay in the Lincoln room and sleep in Lincoln's bed. Mamma Truman announced that she was going right home to Missouri! Daddy made me stop teasing her because he was afraid she would do it. He'd been keeping the fact that Lincoln's bed was in the house a secret from her.

On my mother's side I was descended from George Porterfield Gates, a Vermonter, who was married to Elizabeth Emery of Rounds, England. Great-grandfather Gates emigrated to Port Byron, Illinois, and thence to Independence, where he established the Gates Milling Company, now the Gates-Wallace Milling Company, which continues to manufacture "Queen of the Pantry" flour.

16

The Wallace side of my mother's family came from Kentucky, like the Trumans. Grandfather David Willock Wallace was reputed to be a child prodigy. At the age of fourteen he was assistant docket clerk of the Missouri State Senate, and held a number of public offices, including county treasurer. Grandmother Wallace always said that he was the handsomest man in town. He died when my mother was a young girl and Grandmother Wallace took her and went back to 219 Delaware to live with her widowed mother in the house Great-grandfather George Gates had built. Great-grandmother Gates was still living there when I was born and for about six months there were four generations of us under that old roof.

I never knew either of my grandfathers, for they both died before I was born. Daddy's father, John, was a militant Democrat and a man of fierce pride and quick temper. He is reputed to have chased a big lawyer, who was cross-examining him in a lawsuit, out of the courthouse for calling him a liar. When my father was born, my grandfather nailed a mule shoe over the front door to bring his first-born luck. It was an old Missouri custom.

When I was a small child, all my immediate relatives lived almost within shouting distance. My mother's brothers—Uncle Frank Wallace and his wife, Aunt Natalie, and Uncle George Wallace and his wife, Aunt May, nicknamed "Beuf" by me—lived in Independence only a hundred feet from the house on Delaware Street. My mother's youngest brother, Fred, was unmarried then and lived at home. My Uncle Vivian and Aunt Louella Truman and their family, my only cousins at the time, lived on the farm not far from Independence and my Aunt Mary Truman and Grandmother Martha Ellen Truman lived at Grandview, Missouri, only a few miles away. I was the only grandchild in the Wallace clan and since I saw my young cousins only on visits, I existed largely in a world of adults, well disposed toward me.

Uncle Fred, who was still a young man-about-town, was especially well disposed toward me, and included me in whatever devilment he was engaged in around the house. I always thought of him as my own age, probably because Grandma Wallace called us both down with equal fervor. My father was also convinced that I could do no wrong, and I suppose I might have grown into an unbearable brat except for the strength of character exhibited by my maternal grandmother and her daughter, Bess. Both these worthies were convinced of the old adage that to spare the rod is to spoil the child. They were determined that I wasn't going to be spoiled. Child psychology didn't bother them! While my father was never able to bring himself to strike me, he could kill me with a sort of hurt look he has. I would have infinitely preferred a spanking to this look and I still would.

My Grandmother Wallace was a soft, gentle-looking woman, with large black eyes and heavy gray hair. She was educated at the Cincinnati Conservatory of Music and had a sweet voice and an air of great elegance. Although she had a whim of iron, she rarely raised that sweet voice. She must have had much to forgive me for. I was an active child and was always tearing around and around through a succession of doors in the house on my tricycle, knocking the patina off the antiques. She had grown unused to children, for it had been some time since Uncle Fred was a baby. But she forgave me everything.

On Sunday, after church and after dinner (Sunday dinner is in the middle of the day in Independence, Missouri—a groaning board— roast beef with the potatoes browned in the oven, or platters of fried chicken, apple pie, or homemade ice cream), we always drove out to Grandview to see my Grandmother Truman. She was a spunky little lady, an unreconstructed Confederate, and she used to tell me how, as a little girl, she had to jump into a feather bed for safekeeping when the Red Legs raided the farm. She had strong reactions to everything, and one of these was being called "Grandmother" or worse still "Granny." She preferred to be called "Mamma" spelled with a double "m," and what Mamma preferred, the members of her family did. They did it out of respect and love, but they did it.

Early in life I became aware that she loathed "Granny" and the thought of calling her that became irresistible to me. I had a healthy respect for her temper and I never really managed it but once. One Sunday afternoon when I was about four years old I was feeling especially full of myself. I waited until I was safely ensconced in the back seat of the car and Daddy had already started the motor. Then I rolled down the window, stuck my head out, and shouted, "Good-by, Granny!" at the top of my lungs. Fortunately at this juncture the gears meshed and we rolled away, or I daresay Mamma Truman would have yanked me out of the car and given me what-for then and there. She didn't hesitate to do so later, but by that time

18

she had lost some of her steam, and also she had been heard to admit privately that I seemed to be a chip off the old block.

Mamma Truman was a remarkable person. It was impossible to know her and not be influenced by her marvelous code, which was based on justice, honor, integrity, and the rights of the individual to pursue his own destiny. Everybody knows the story of Mamma approached by a reporter who asked her if she wasn't *proud* of her son Harry, who had just become President of the United States.

"Of course I'm proud of him," Mamma Truman said, "but I have other children I'm just as proud of. I have a daughter and another son who are just as fine as Harry."

Although Mamma Truman lived on the farm most of her life, and preferred the country and little towns, she was a woman of sagacity and wisdom. Her opinion on matters of all kinds was sound and vehement and my father often had recourse to it. Her life didn't alter in any outward particular after my father became President. I imagine she prayed for him more fervently because she thought he needed it. So many people were depending on him. She was devoutly religious and was a lifelong member of the Baptist church, as my father is. (My mother and I are Episcopalians, but my father has remained a Baptist.) Mamma Truman was what she called a "light-foot" Baptist, as opposed to the "hard-shell" variety. She did not believe in the restrictions laid on some Baptist congregations. She loved to dance and play cards and in her youth, rumor has it, she was quite a dancer.

If Mamma Truman was for you, she was for you, and as long as she lived I always knew that there was one person who was in my corner. Mamma Truman was my loyal cohort, who accepted me without praise or blame, as long as what I wanted to do seemed right and made sense. When we held a family conclave about my pursuit of a musical career, Mamma Truman, who was already past ninety but unfailingly modern in her viewpoint, was all for it. She took a more lively interest in the fact that I was struggling to learn to sing than in the fact that I was living in the White House.

The fuss and feathers of public life never impressed her in any way. When she visited us after we were living at 1600 Pennsylvania Avenue and was met at the plane by the press corps and the photographers, her reaction was testy dismay.

"Fiddlesticks," said Mamma (her strongest oath). "If I'd known

19

everybody was going to carry on like this, I wouldn't have come!"

I will never forget those long Sunday afternoons at Grandview when I was a little girl, and I am happy that I have them to remember. My Aunt Mary made a pet of me. Aunt Mary is a real musician and has always been a special friend of my father's, who used to look after her when he was a little boy and she was a baby. Aunt Mary remembers that he could braid her hair and would rock her to sleep and sing to her. They had studied piano with the same teacher when they were growing up and they loved to play duets. As soon as we had got off our wraps in Grandview and passed the time of day, Aunt Mary and Daddy would hustle over to the piano and start going through the music. They preferred the classics and some of their duets were quite technical and difficult. Daddy said they enjoyed them more than we did.

Sometimes Aunt Luella and Uncle Vivian and some of my young cousins would be there and then I would have a field day. Aunt Mary knew my penchant for oatmeal cookies and there would always be a big plateful of round drop cookies, spiked with nuts and tasting deliciously of molasses, for the children. Aunt Mary would play with us, cutting out paper dolls or reading the funny papers. Or Uncle Vivian would show us things around the farm. Uncle Vivian did not play the piano. Mamma had tried to drive him to it, but he said she couldn't find a lasso big enough!

I wish I could re-create the rhythm of those early days of mine in Missouri for you, for it seems to me that I was completely happy and that I lived in the center of the world. The house on Delaware Street is nearly a hundred years old and it was built at a more spacious time in history. The rooms are enormous and the ceilings high, wide, and handsome. The long living room runs across the front of the house with a little parlor or music room and a study. The dining room is big and the pantry is huge and the kitchen is a real kitchen, always smelling deliciously of Vietta's cooking. A long porch runs the length of the house in the back and that was where we used to eat supper on summer evenings. The dark trees leaned over the house and you could smell the lilacs and Grandmother's roses.

In some of the faraway corners of the world where I have found myself—in jouncing Pullman berths and mediocre hotels or in the vaulted bedrooms of embassies and palaces—I have tiptoed around the rooms of the house on Delaware Street in my mind, and felt warmed and comforted.

When I was a little girl the floors were dark and polished, so that I could see my face in them, and covered with oriental rugs. Grandmother Wallace loved antiques and there were many family heirlooms in the house. Her pride and joy was the fine old secretary in the living room which Great-grandfather Gates had brought out from Vermont in a wagon train.

I suppose that the grown people must have had problems and troubles then, as grown people do, but no breath of them ever touched me. It was many years before I knew that my father lost the only election he ever lost in his life the year I was born. He was defeated for the county judgeship. I remember only the sound of laughter, for I grew up in a family of jokers and teasers on both sides of the house. In fact, my first connection with political affairs was a joke and occurred when I was four years old. It was 1928 and Herbert Hoover was running for President against Al Smith. My uncles were listening to the election returns on a crystal radio set in the study. Mother and Daddy were upstairs.

"I want you to do something for me, Tuffy," Uncle Fred said, and called me over and gave me detailed instructions.

I entered heartily into the conspiracy and ran upstairs shouting happily, "Hoover was elected! Hoover was elected! Hooray!"

You can imagine how well this went down in a Democratic household. I guess that's the last time I ever rooted for a Republican!

One incident which might be considered political happened prior to this. My father was already involved in politics when I was born and since, as a family, we were always together, my mother used to take me to speeches and gatherings; also, politicians came to the house for conversation and hospitality. Once an old-line politician, a typical baby-kisser and ward heeler, running for governor of Missouri, insisted on taking me in his arms. He was a big man with an enormous red nose. Just as he was about to give me the immemorial buss, I reached up and gave his nose such a tweak that he cried out in pain. He put me down in a hurry.

Mother was unable to exhibit proper chagrin at my manners on this occasion, as she opposes baby-kissing in politics.

"Served him right," she said tartly.

21

∾ There were always jokes, and once I got into the spirit of the thing and almost pulled the chair out from under my mother as she started to sit down to dinner. It was the consensus of opinion that I was too young for humor.

The days ran by in even tenor, and the year always came to a climax at Christmas. All the Trumans and all the Wallaces have a passion for Christmas and nothing ever is or ever has been too much trouble at Santa Claus time. From earliest memory, for me Christmas has been a season of sugar and spice and everything nice and myself on tiptoe with excitement. The big tree always stood (and still does) in the large bay window of the living room, covered with dear and sentimental decorations. The cardboard snowman and one red ball that decorated my first Christmas tree are still on our tree every year.

One of my earliest recollections of Christmas on Delaware Street is concerned with the year I was three. I talked early and talked long, but I had an odd speech idiosyncrasy when I was a small child. I got words backward. Instead of saying butterfly, I said flutterby. That year the whole family had decided to give Aunt May Wallace one of those elaborate dresser sets she had set her heart on. Each member of the family planned to give her one piece. Uncle George would give her the mirror; Mother and Daddy would give her the comb and brush, and so on. I demanded to give Aunt May something, so they told me that I could give her the nail file, but that I mustn't tell anybody, that it was a secret.

This was the first secret I had ever had and I thought highly of it. I was full of responsibility. However, as the days wore on and the secret weighed on me, it became a veritable burden. Every time I saw Aunt May, which was daily, I thought I would burst. Finally I did burst.

"I've got a Christmas present for you," I confided.

"Oh?" said Aunt May.

"I can't tell you what it is," I said. "It's a secret!"

"It is?" said Aunt May.

"No," I shouted, overcome. "It's a filenail!"

Aunt May, who was aware of my cart-before-the-horse idiosyncrasy, was able to translate this into a dresser set, and the surprise was spoiled.

Everybody was quite put out with me, but I experienced a sense of deep relief. I still don't much like secrets.

22

When I look back on those Christmases, it is like looking through the isinglass windows into one of those wonderful panoramas in an Easter egg. The smell of cinnamon and cedar and spruce and the waxy smell of burning candles; the thirty-pound turkey, brown and smoking from Vietta's oven; the fruit cakes and the chocolate cakes; the preserves and pickles and creamed onions and the striped peppermint and oranges; the grandmothers and the uncles and aunts and Daddy and Mother around the groaning table; the nickel-plated tricycle under the tree and the sleepy doll that came in my stocking!

Oh, little town of Independence circa 1927, how still I see thee lie.

3: Make me a child again

One of my father's biographers, Jonathan Daniels, describes me in childhood as "a little girl of taffy and snow." This is a pretty compliment, but if Mr. Daniels had ever seen me around that time, he might have made it "chocolate and tow"! My hair was as white as cotton, but this depressed nobody, as any hair is better than none. I was a bald-headed baby and I remained hairless so long that the family almost gave up. If my hair had come in blue, they would have welcomed it. My predilection for chocolate was as strong then as it is now, and traces of it usually decorated my face and hands, in spite of there being so many grown people to wash it off. Aunt Beuf Wallace was a superb contriver of homemade chocolate ice cream and I was usually hanging around when the dasher was removed.

I was meticulous only on state occasions, but then I could be as serious as the next one. When I was four years old, I was a flower girl at Cousin Jody's wedding. I was got up in a peach-colored taffeta dress with a bonnet to match and provided with a basket of rose petals. A certain amount of apprehension on the part of my elders accompanied this sally into public life at such an early age, but I had my instructions. I was to scatter petals in the path of the bride and I did it in the most fastidious manner. I scattered them one at a time and while people soon lost their fear of a fiasco, they eventually began to wonder if we would ever get to the altar!

A certain amount of apprehension on the part of my elders has accompanied most of my days. After my father became President and the usual quota of Secret Service men was assigned to the family, people used to say to me, "Doesn't it bother you to be *watched* all the time?"

My answer to this was, "What's new about it? I've been watched ever since I can remember." This familiarity with watchfulness did make this facet of life in the White House less onerous for me than it might to somebody my age who had grown up more wild and free.

There was a reason for watchfulness beyond parental fondness. I started to public school in Independence when I was five years old. The year I was in the first grade, a strange man with his hat pulled down over his eyes arrived at the school one day and said that he was calling for "Mary Truman, Judge Truman's daughter." I had never been called "Mary" and the man was such a suspicious-looking character that my first-grade teacher, Mrs. Etzenhauser, notified my father and mother, instead of turning me over to him. Detectives were summoned and the man fled. Nothing ever came of it but a short item in the paper, which I couldn't read, so I actually never knew anything about it for years. But it instilled a fear of kidnapping in my parents which haunted them for a long time. I was always escorted to and from school in Independence by some reliable person and for several years after we want to Washington I was accompanied and called for. This routine was so much a part of the pattern of my life that I didn't resent it, and when a Secret Service man began following me around I felt right at home.

I don't know whether this had any bearing on the matter or not, but I was never too enthusiastic about school. I had the best time at home. My fun and excitement were always there. While it seems to me that I have been going to school and studying most of my natural life, I could take school or leave it from the very beginning, and would have preferred to leave it!

This may have been aggravated by the fact that I had delicate health as a little girl. I had an early and bitter tonsillectomy and one of the tonsils grew back. It seemed to be host to a succession of infections, and I had the flu which went into pneumonia which went into rheumatic fever. I was down with rheumatic fever for six months one winter and my father bundled up my mother and me and a nurse and sent us off to Biloxi, Mississippi, for several months, hoping that a blander climate would improve my health and build me up for a second tonsillectomy. I don't know whether it did or not, but I remember the strain of separation in Biloxi and wishing to be back home in Independence.

The Christmas of 1932, when I was eight years old, I was bedded down, as usual, with the flu. (It seems to me that every Christmas and every birthday for years I was bedded down with something.) The only thing I wanted in life (besides being able to get up) was an electric train. I insinuated loudly that I wanted an electric train and I insinuated it often. The day before Christmas I was aware that there was considerable commotion going on downstairs and visions of miles of track, automatic switches, signal towers, and I don't know what else, danced in my head.

On Christmas morning when Daddy came to wake me his face was shining like a new moon.

"Wait until you see," he rhapsodized, wrapping me in a blanket. "Wait until you see what you've got!"

In my mind's eye I saw the darling little train, running madly through miniature villages and over tiny bridges, headlight aglow and whistle blowing. I grinned and snuggled into his shoulder. He carried me down to the parlor.

"Well, there it is!" Daddy cried proudly and set me down in front of a shiny new baby grand piano.

"Where?" I asked stupidly, looking around for the train.

"Right in front of you, Baby," Daddy said.

Out of disappointment and sheer weakness, I burst into tears and wouldn't touch the keys.

Poor Daddy! It was certainly the most important and expensive present he had ever bought. He was earning a modest salary as presiding judge of the Jackson County Court. The time was the depths of the depression and nobody was buying baby grands. Mamma Truman had an old upright, and I doubt if my father, an ardent music lover, had ever played on anything else. To him this piano was the most luxurious and wonderful present on earth, and his cantankerous offspring didn't react properly at all.

27

Most fathers give their girl children electric trains because *they* want to play with them, but my father gave me a piano!

It was some time before my health mended sufficiently for me to pursue the art of this piano, but I finally grew up to it and it has given us many happy hours. It has followed me from pillar to post and has listened to more of my outpourings than any other inanimate object. When Dad was elected Senator it went to Washington, and when we moved into 1600 Pennsylvania Avenue it moved with us. I was given the suite on the West Pennsylvania Avenue corner and the piano had to be heaved up the side of the White House with a block and tackle, into my sitting room. When the White House began to disintegrate physically during Papa's tenure of office, guess what went first! Dad went into my sitting room one day and the baby grand was about to fall through the floor. It was a good, solid piano, but I never did have an electric train.

Dad was my first piano teacher. By the time I was six, he had taught me *The Little Fairy Waltz*. On Sunday afternoons at Mamma Truman's he would show me how to pick out simple airs on the old upright and he also taught me to read music, using F-A-C-E for the treble clef spaces and "Every-Good-Boy-Deserves-Fun" for the lines. Formal music lessons began when Mrs. Joseph C. Story, the organist of Trinity, our church, consented to give me an hour a week. It is necessary to report that I abhorred practice and used to be fairly inventive when it came to getting out of it. In this I took after my mother, who had abhorred practice to such an extent that Grandmother Wallace had stopped her music lessons. Mother was grateful at the time, as she preferred the tennis racquet to the metronome. I *wanted* to play the piano. I just felt that I didn't have time to learn how. But when Mother threatened to stop *my* lessons, I fell to and practiced. I was a quick study, due to my early training in sight reading, so I managed to get by.

Papa and I used to play a few duets, *Chopsticks* and the *Jenny Lind Polka* he had taught me, but I never measured up to Aunt Mary Truman as a duet player. I never measured up to Papa as a pianist either. I learned to play the piano well enough to attack Chopin and Beethoven's *Pathétique*, but my father is more than a talented amateur; he is a real pianist.

It has been reported that Dad accompanies me on the piano when I sing in private. This is absolutely untrue. My father is not and never

28

has been an accompanist. He is a soloist and he has never accompanied me in my life. Chopin and Mozart are his favorites. Given the opportunity and the economic resources requisite to a musical career (and nobody knows how requisite they are better than I do), I think my father could have been a concert pianist. He has been mercilessly kidded about his piano playing, but people of critical judgment who have heard him play have come to scoff and remained to praise. His musicianship is sound and true and his technical proficiency, after years of being deprived of time for practice by his exhausting labors, remains remarkable.

Although I was an only child, I never lacked for children to play with. The house on Delaware Street was fortunately surrounded with other houses containing assorted little girls. There were nine in our block. Our house was a good place to meet. It had a big yard, an attic, and a basement and, in an effort to keep me within bird's-eye view, swings and a sliding board had been installed on the lawn.

These mechanical contrivances were too neat and circumspect to interest us much. We had a graveled driveway which offered more charm. I was young during the long years of the dust-bowl drought, and in summer the foliage was usually burnt to a crisp and the Missouri dust was always rolling. Most of my friends—Betty and Sue Ogden, Jane Berridge and the Allen sisters: Marie, Harriet, Mona, and Barbara, who made the nucleus of our little group, along with Mary Shaw—were equipped with wheel toys and we made complicated networks of roads and highways out of the loose gravel of the drive.

At the time, my father was president of the National Trailways Association and keenly interested in roads. He used to take me with him on tours of inspection of new highways, so that I was road-conscious and the highways we constructed out of gravel were engineered in the newest designs. The tricycle and scooter traffic in the driveway was intense. As soon as we had raked up hills, valleys, hollows, and highways in the drive, we set about riding them down. Whoever lacked a wheel was the traffic cop, provided with a whistle, so that there was much screeching, piling up of vehicles, falling down, and fights. From this melee clouds of dust arose in the hot summer drought. The house had to be dusted three times a day and there were loud complaints from both my womenfolk.

29

We also discovered that the half shells of English walnuts, stuck with a pin for a mast and fitted for locomotion with tiny triangles of paper for sails, made boats in those arid summers. Given boats, there had to be waterways. We lacked the streams and ponds that beautify so many parts of the United States, but nothing daunted, we dug a waterway. It was a kind of canal, beginning at the drip-faucet at the side of the house and running muddily through the mint bed, tumbling with waterfalls downward through Grandmother Wallace's lilies of the valley (which were ruthlessly uprooted), and on into the rose garden where further depredations took place. It looked, indeed, as if a bunch of moles had got on top of the ground and continued their architecture. It was quite a problem to raise flowers in that weather and at this vantage I have a better under-standing of the wan looks of my grandmother when she regarded the fallen petals of her treasured Talismans.

We, the Ogdens and the Allens and Jane Berridge and I, lived within calling distance and we were rarely separated except to be washed, fed, or put to sleep. We resented these occasions deeply. We were required, as most children are in hot climates, to take after-noon naps. Since nobody had any hopes of our sleeping if we were together, as soon as lunch was over we were marshaled upstairs in our separate domiciles, arrayed in nightgowns, and ordered to slum-ber. We never were sleepy.

Our sleeping porch was just across the treetops from the Ogden sleeping porch, and in order not to lose contact, Betty and Sue and I first worked out a system of communication by rapping a code. This seemed unsatisfactory, so we rigged up an elaborate and cumbersome network of strings and wires between the two sleeping porches by which we could exchange not only messages but such articles as doll clothes, cookies, and lollipops. This was all fine except when the strings got tangled or went awry over the alley, leaving our private and personal correspondence trapped in a tree or hanging in midair or fallen to earth where any passer-by who happened to be ambling along the alley could read. I would have to depart my alleged nap by stealth, sneak downstairs through the quiet, shaded house, and rush out into the blazing sun to retrieve the missives before they were pounced on by alien eyes. When this was discovered I would be removed from the sleeping porch and put down on a pallet where some adult could keep a drowsy eye on me. I remember those long, lazy summer afternoons in that old high-ceilinged house. All the ladies "lay down" after lunch in those days and sometimes when I am racing from one afternoon appointment to another in New York, I wish the custom had carried over!

There was an old outbuilding in a back yard near us which had started life as a quartering place for slaves, deteriorated into a henhouse and finally into an empty building when the chickens flew the coop. My friends and I discovered this shack one day and decided to organize a club with the shack for headquarters. We called ourselves the Henhouse Hicks and began to annoy our families for bits and pieces of cast-off furniture to decorate the clubhouse. Here we kept our files of movie magazines and pictures of Nelson Eddy, Clark Gable, Spencer Tracy, and Robert Taylor, which we sent off for, and stashed away a few oatmeal cookies and soda pops against hunger. Our meetings were largely composed of these items, though we had a constitution, bylaws, rules and regulations, and a house organ—a newspaper which we wrote, edited, and had mimeographed. This weekly gazette, which persisted for five whole weeks, was not a triumph of literature but reported neighborhood happenings with serene honesty.

One day Uncle Frank leaned over in the garden and split his trousers. The *Henhouse Gazette* reported this incident in suitable or unsuitable detail. Uncle Frank was horrified and, more in sorrow than in anger, attempted to buy up the whole edition. It was on this occasion that the paper reached its highest circulation figure. It was in demand all over town!

&~ We also read omnivorously, both together and separately, all the books in the school library. Once we became so fascinated with a book that Betty Ogden decided to write a play based on it. It was called *The Clever One*, and while my memory of its content is hazy, I know that it was about a Mexican bandit and was full of blood and thunder.

When the dramatization was complete, we decided that we had to produce this masterpiece. It was too wonderful to blush unseen.

Every summer the Henhouse Hicks gave a show for the Penny Ice Fund, a project whose charitable purposes escapes me at this late date. We usually gave a circus, where friends and family were sandbagged into paying a dime for tricks and fancy riding on bicycles, low-wire walking, and other typical entertainments, but with the script of *The Clever One* in hand, we became more ambitious.

I obtained the leading role in this opus, that of the dashing bandit, not by virtue of any histrionic ability but because I happened to possess a Mexican costume. However, I was gratified, as I have been stage-struck from earliest memory and a natural-born ham. At the age of seven or eight I was playing in the school orchestra and we made a public appearance before the Parent-Teachers Association. We were all keyed up and when we finally navigated the piece successfully, the rest of the orchestra filed gladly off the stage. I didn't. I remained right there, accepting the applause. Finally I noticed I was alone on the stage and people had stopped clapping and begun to laugh. I wandered into the wings, got lost, and had to be retrieved by the school principal.

The production of *The Clever One* was, by all odds, the outstanding achievement of the Henhouse Hicks. It was a swashbuckling script and we played it to the hilt. The show was naturally held outdoors, and we had it in our yard because we had a pingpong table which could be used as a back flat. We rigged up sheets and blankets on ropes for curtains and drops. It showered a little that day and I had to lug in all the props and put them all back out!

The Mexican bandit made his entrance over the top of a high wall according to the script. This meant that I had to leap the back flat, once over lightly, and land on the stage. This necessitated my hoisting a ladder against the back of the pingpong table. At the opening performance, I, the debonair bandit, scrambled up the ladder, and under my weight the pingpong table began to sway precariously back and forth and seemed in imminent danger of falling forward and flattening the other actresses. I drew back to steady it and the ladder wobbled wildly. For a minute I thought I was going to break my neck, but this was *my* entrance and I was bound and determined I was going to make it! By main strength and awkwardness I clambered over the top of the flat and landed on the stage on all fours, holding the pingpong table up with my rear. I have never made such a dramatic entrance from that day! It brought down the house.

The show, which received excellent notices in the Independence paper and had a phenomenal run of two performances, accomplished two things. It accumulated the remarkable sum of thirty dollars for the Penny Ice Fund, and it broke the drought. Exhausted from tri-

32

umph, we left the scenery and props all outdoors and at 5 A.M. the next morning the deluge descended. I had to get up and race downstairs to bring in the family blankets.

⁊❧ I made a few other public appearances in those years. Mrs. Story used to present her pupils in piano recitals in the spring—a whirl of organdy dresses and sashes and squeaking patent-leather Mary Janes. I remember relishing these occasions, particularly if I had a showy piece in which you crossed one hand over the other. When I was about ten years old I was selected to pull the rope that unveiled a statue of Andrew Jackson in front of the new Jackson County Courthouse, which Dad had been instrumental in having erected. I approached this event in the manner of Katharine Cornell.

Life ran on in its even tenor. Mother and I drove around the country with Daddy, looking at roads. Jackson County still has one of the finest road systems in the United States, inaugurated during my father's judgeship. Daddy would look at the old hog-backed macadams and sigh and Mother and I would pick wildflowers or bittersweet to take home. I developed my passion for the movies and had trouble with my allowance.

The movies and my allowance always seem intertwined from natural causes. I spent my allowance on the movies. I got a dollar a week spending money and I was always running out of it. My mother was very firm on the subject and would not permit anybody to augment my regular stipend. One night I was teasing for a quarter to see a movie I had already seen a couple of times. I was broke, as usual, and my yearning became so persistent that Uncle George and Aunt Beuf finally asked Mother if they could have the pleasure of escorting me to the film just to reestablish peace and quiet. Mother said no.

I was not in the mood to take no for an answer and I kept looking wistful out loud. Finally Dad called me over and slipped me a quarter surreptitiously. I scuttled out before anybody could change his mind, but I could hear Mother taking Daddy to task.

"Harry," she said, "how am I ever going to teach this child the value of money without your cooperation?"

Dad protested feebly, grinning, and I went to the movies.

I also got in money trouble for using slang. I love slang and still find myself using uncouth expressions like "dopy" and "flip my lid."

As a child I picked up all the slang I heard and had one spell of calling everybody, from Grandmother Wallace to the family dog, "Dearie." Even Dad got bored with this. He finally announced that every time I used the word "dearie," a fine of ten cents would be levied on me. One night at the dinner table I committed this crime four times and had my entire capital of forty cents wiped out, with allowance time days away. For the rest of the week I had no money at all, and having no money is no fun. This broke me of the word "dearie" and every time I hear it to this day I flinch! The daughter of one of my friends called me "dearie" the other day and I reprimanded her out of all proportion to the seriousness of the crime.

"Don't you ever let me hear you call anybody 'dearie,' " I said censoriously. The child looked so surprised that I had to explain about my lost forty cents.

But these were minor irritations and most of the time I was entirely happy. Once Mother and Dad went off on a trip to Washington with William Southern, Jr., publisher of the *Independence Examiner*, and "Mom" Southern, and left me with Grandmother Wallace. I was against this and as the car drove away I stood at the door bellowing, with streaming eyes. As soon as they were out of sight I turned off the tears like a spigot and forgot all about it.

The Hicks, needless to say, had a few altercations. Betty and Sue Ogden, as became sisters, fought like cats and dogs, and there were other private vendettas and feuds among the membership. Barbara Allen was the baby of the crowd and her sisters found it irksome to have her tagging along, too young to comprehend what we were doing. But I hated quarreling and I still do. I couldn't bear for anybody to go off mad. I held this circle so dear that I couldn't face the thought of anybody leaving it or anything breaking it up.

In the end, I was the one who went away.

I was ten years old the year my father ran for the United States Senate. I was a scrawny, gawky kid, running to long arms and legs and knobby knees—my straight bob was just turning from tow to blond. If I lost sleep I got dark blue circles under my eyes, and Dad was calling me "Skinny" that year. I was vaguely aware that he was making speeches and immersed in important business because he was gone a lot and preoccupied when he was at home. Sometimes Mother and I went with him when he campaigned.

People were always asking me, the way they will to make conversation with a child, "How would you like to go to Washington to live?"

My answer to this was prompt and invariable: "I wouldn't!" I didn't pay much attention to these rhetorical questions because, honestly, it never had occurred to me that there was any place to live *except* Independence, Missouri. I could not imagine myself separated from the house on Delaware Street—coming in at sundown to see the last rays of the sun striking the old rubbed mahogany of the furniture and the faded colors in the carpet; watching the lightning bugs holding convocation in the garden in the summertime; eating supper on the back porch; playing with the Hicks.

8> The night Dad was elected to the Senate the house was suddenly filled with people and excitement. All my father's and mother's relatives, friends, and neighbors came by to offer congratulations.

"Well, how does it feel to be the daughter of a United States Senator?" a strange man asked me.

"What's a *Senator?*" I inquired fearfully.

That night after I'd gone to bed, Daddy came in to say good night.

"How do you think you'll like to live in Washington?" he asked me proudly.

I flounced over and began to kick my feet in the bedclothes, with all the earmarks of a tantrum.

"I don't want to go to that mean old Washington!" I howled, and began to weep.

It was then borne in on me that the old threat about going to Washington to live was coming true. From January to June—six whole months, half the year—I was going to be gone. I was disconsolate. I went around with a long face, touching things. The news had got to the Hicks too. One night after supper we gathered in solemn conclave at our favorite meeting place, a big old tree in the corner of the yard just over the fence. We stood around awkwardly for a minute and then simultaneously burst into tears. We put our arms around each other and cried until our eyes were gummy, convinced that nothing would ever be the same, that we would never see each other again! Finally we rallied and swore vows of eternal friendship as long as we all should live.

These friendships have persisted as we swore they should. All

35

the Hicks are married now except Mary Margaret. They have scattered in many directions but they come home again at Christmas and we have a reunion and clatter away, a mile a minute for hours, catching up on husbands, babies, and careers. It's hard to believe that that conclave in the garden happened more than twenty years ago!

Before we left Independence, some of Papa's friends gave a banquet in his honor. This was interesting to me chiefly because it brought on my first visit to the hairdresser. Mama took me to Mrs. Pearl Wood, who always did her hair, and Mrs. Wood curled up my straight flaxen Dutch bob with the curling irons. I still remember that curious, acrid smell of the irons in my hair, making my nose crinkle.

I took my favorite doll, Raggedy Ann, a rather tired specimen, to Aunt Beuf and asked her if she would make it a new dress so it would be fit to appear in Washington society. Shortly thereafter we packed our trunks and set out for that city which had hitherto been merely hearsay, a dot on the map in the geography book, a ten-letter word.

4: The long visit

My earliest memories of Washington were concerned with a feeling of transiency. I had never traveled very far, and going to Washington was like going on a visit. You came and you stayed and you were polite and then you went home. I found myself clinging to that. In June I would be back on Delaware Street, but the space between stretched like an endless plain.

I suppose any child who is uprooted in the middle of a school year and faced with the necessity of making new friends and new associations suffers apprehension. I think this apprehension may have been shared by both my parents. My father was working at a new job —a job so complex and intricate and full of nuances that only the passage of time and the most studious application could make it simpler. My mother, who had lived in the same old house all her life, was now installed in a small furnished apartment at 3016 Tilden, just off Connecticut Avenue, which appeared cramped and nondescript to her. Everything in Washington seemed expensive and difficult. The glamorous life of the capital (I presume it was glamorous) swirled past us. My father brought home mountains of work and long after I was in bed he would be reading and studying his problems, so that he could learn to cope with them.

I hated being cooped up on the upper floor of an apartment house after my easy-come, easy-go life in Independence. I could never

37

go outdoors alone and the apartment was like a prison. I have never learned to like apartment life. In an apartment there seems to be no way of putting down roots.

Everything was strange. When I was taken to the Senate Gallery to witness my father's swearing-in, even Dad didn't look familiar. As he came down the aisle with Senator Bennett Clark to take the oath he was wearing unaccustomed striped pants and a morning coat, and his face was so serious and grave that I scarcely recognized him. I still wasn't sure what a Senator was and I wasn't sure I wanted Dad to be one. But I knew I didn't want to live in Washington.

Although I had always gone to public school in Independence, in Washington I was entered in Gunston Hall, a small private school for girls, on the theory that it would be easier for me to keep abreast of my divided life if I went to a school in Washington which would afford more individual attention. From the time I was eleven until I graduated from high school I went to public school in Independence (first Bryant School, then Independence Junior High, and then William Chrisman High) from September to January and to Gunston Hall from January to May. While this system had its difficulties, it did provide me with an opportunity of attending coeducational public school and a private girl's school, with the advantages of both.

Gunston Hall was a school for young ladies in the old Southern tradition. It was housed in four beautiful old Washington houses which had been converted into classrooms and laboratories with modern wings added for dormitories. Gunston accommodated both boarding and day pupils. I was a day pupil. There was a big new gymnasium with a stage and the campus was a green acre of lawns and old spreading trees.

I entered the fifth grade at Gunston at midyear. Everybody already knew everybody, except me. Some of them had always gone to Gunston and the crowds and the charmed circles and comradeships had already been set up. I had come from a place where everybody had known me since I was born and I had never had to exert myself to make friends. For a while there I certainly wandered lonely as a cloud. Sometimes when I thought of the Hicks I was so homesick I couldn't swallow. I wanted to run away or hide or just crawl into a shell.

I guess those early days at Gunston were good training for me. I finally realized that it was sink or swim and I struck out against my own shyness. I began to linger around the fringes of activity and take at least a public interest in what was going on.

At the recreational periods between classes all my fellow students attempted to dazzle each other with their special talents. Nancy Stover was a brilliant performer on the horizonal bars in the gym. Helen Bull was the most accomplished rope skipper. I had never been an athlete and I knew that I couldn't show off in feats of strength or daring. I was feeling more and more forlorn about it all when one day there was a contest to determine who could screech the loudest and longest. Screech I could! Even then I could hit F above high C. I shut my eyes, inhaled deeply, and hit F on the button. I held it until I was blue in the face and everybody else dropped out of the contest. For the first time, they all turned and noticed me and I witnessed a dawning respect in their eyes. After that I began to make friends. When there was any singing or screeching to be done, I was invited.

⧂ In those first years at Gunston Hall, Mother usually took me to school and picked me up when school was out. We wandered around looking at things, like tourists. Relieved of the regular activities she had enjoyed in Independence, Mother was probably as lonely as I was. Sightseeing was fun. We went everywhere—to the Lincoln Memorial and the top of the Washington Monument. (I wanted to walk down, but Mother said it gave her the bends.) We went to Mount Vernon and to the Lee Mansion and the Tomb of the Unknown Soldier.

We went to the Smithsonian Institution exhaustively. Years later when the Gunston girls were taken to the Smithsonian on a field trip, I staggered them with my knowledge of that confusing and wonderful old place. When they couldn't find "The Spirit of Saint Louis," I led them promptly to it. When they were hunting the Pyramids and the annals of the Phoenicians, I took them there. I was practically a guide. Mother I went to the Corcoran Art Gallery and the Library of Congress, and when spring came we wandered up and down the walks along the Tidal Basin under the drifting snow of cherry petals, and went to the open-air concerts at Watergate.

We also went to the White House and stood in the slow-moving queue that wound through the East Room and the Blue Room and the Green Room and the State Dining Room. That turned out eventually to have been a waste of time!

My mother and I became great pals in those years. I felt as if I knew her as another girl. She was more lenient with my childish foibles than she had ever been in Independence, probably because there were fewer people spoiling me. In fact, nobody was spoiling me in Washington, so she relaxed. When we weren't sightseeing, we would traipse through the stores and shop a little and sometimes we would indulge ourselves in a little treat, though treats were rather few and far between.

There was an old-fashioned ice-cream parlor out on Connecticut Avenue where they had the most marvelous ice-cream sodas and rich chocolate fudge sundaes, but my mother considered it rather expensive. One afternoon I began to plead for a chocolate soda at my favorite spot, and she finally gave in. We drove out there and put in our order. And then my mother happened to look in her purse.

"Heavens," she said, stricken. "I don't think I have any change!"

Naturally I didn't have any change. I never had any change. I always went to the movies with it.

She raked up the nickels and dimes in her purse and the total came to thirty-four cents. About that time the order arrived and we didn't know whether to eat it or not. But chocolate overcame scruple and we fell to, waiting fearfully for the check. The sodas turned out to be fifteen cents each, so we thankfully paid the bill and got home with four cents between us. It made us feel like real conspirators.

One afternoon when we were shopping, one of those sudden rainstorms that sometimes descend on Washington descended on us. I was wearing a new crepe dress which got soaking wet. As it got wet it began to shrink and soon was way above my knees. I was horribly embarrassed. As a matter of fact Mother had to spirit me into Woodward & Lothrop's and buy me a new dress before I would go home. This is symptomatic of my early agonies of shyness.

While Mother gave me a lot of her time, she did have things to do. In addition to her duties as a Senator's wife, Mother worked for my father as an assistant part of the time he was Senator. My mother is a vigorous and energetic person with a good business head, and my father and I both continue to consult her on matters

40

relating to our careers. (The first person to read this book in manuscript was Bess Truman!) When Mother was busy, I was allowed to ride the streetcar from Gunston to the Senate Office Building and get off and go upstairs. I was usually ravenous and sometimes Reathel Odum, one of Dad's secretaries, would treat me to a ham-on-raisin-bread sandwich in the Senate Cafeteria.

Dad would also contrive to send me on errands so that I would get a chance to ride the Underground Railway which connects the Senate Office Building with the Senate Chamber. This railway is maintained for the use of Senators and their staff members, but it was a standing rule that I couldn't ride it just for fun. I had to be going somewhere and doing something. Dad could usually think up something for me to do if he wanted to get me out of the office. Sometimes I would go over to the Library of Congress and read or have lunch in the Senate Dining Room, though it never appealed to me much for its cuisine except for the bean soup which made it famous. Then we would ride up in the elevator reserved for Senators and this always made me feel pretty special.

There were often visitors in Dad's office, constituents from Missouri and sometimes famous Democrats like John Nance Garner or Sam Rayburn. I was instructed to keep quiet and stay out of the way. I knew how much my father respected these men and I did as I was told, but they were among my earliest friends in Washington, and never too busy to speak kindly to a little girl.

The first time my father ever presided over the Senate, I happened to be in his office. Mr. Garner, who was then Vice-president of the United States and President of the Senate, called my father to take the chair. I raced up to the gallery reserved for the families of Senators to watch the proceedings. Dad was sitting in the big chair on the dais, looking dignified and serious. I was aware that he considered this a historic occasion, and I wanted him to know that I was there.

As soon as I got up in the gallery I began to try to attract his attention. I waved and he didn't pay any attention. I stood up and gesticulated and leaned over the gallery rail and did everything I could think of to catch his eye, but he continued to ignore me.

Daddy has several public mannerisms. One of them is sitting with his hand over his mouth. He usually does this when he is feeling tense. That day he was sitting with his hand over his mouth. As I continued to cavort around in the gallery, he must have come to the conclusion that I was going to fall over the gallery railing and be catapulted to the floor of the Senate and break my neck. Without changing his expression one iota or removing his hand from his mouth he fluttered his fingers at me as a signal of his awareness. I collapsed with the giggles. I certainly lent no dignity to his first experience as presiding officer.

When the sessions of the Senate were over, on rare occasions I would meet Daddy downstairs and he would take me on the floor. I would stand there staring around at the empty desks and all the panoply of public office while he finished a conversation. One night there was nobody left in the Chamber but Daddy and me and Mr. Garner.

"How would *you* like to preside over the Senate?" Mr. Garner asked and hoisted me to the big chair where I sat, looking around owlishly.

"I don't think I would," I said and began to struggle to get down. By now I *know* I wouldn't.

When he was a Senator, Daddy, and Mother of course, used to be invited out to various dinners and parties. They would get dressed up and go, leaving me in the apartment with Reathel Odum. Daddy hated to leave me behind and as a sop he would bring home his place cards and give them to me, all autographed by the celebrities who had attended the dinners. He was quite an autograph hound and I had a large assortment of these place cards, signed by the famous, without knowing in the least who they were.

❧ As time went on the strangeness of Washington receded. It was then that I made a friend of Jane Lingo, the daughter of Commander and Mrs. B. Harrison Lingo (Commander Lingo has since died). Jane was and is a beautiful, dark-eyed, dark-haired gypsy of a girl, full of fire and fun. In many ways besides the difference in our coloring, we are opposites, but this seems to have lent strength to our friendship. Jane was born in Washington—one of the few Cave-Dwellers (as native Washingtonians are called) I have ever known, and that made the city seem less transient. First we were friends on the campus at Gunston Hall, and then we began to have Saturday lunch together and go to the movies, always chaperoned by Mother or Mrs. Lingo. This was my first social life in Washington. Sometimes we went to the Shoreham for lunch or the Mayflower and felt very elegant. Jane could talk more and faster than anybody at the age of ten, and she giggled as much as I did. We had the same taste in movie stars, and Jane was a connoisseur of ice-cream sodas. We had a great deal in common.

After Jane and I became such fast friends, I began to feel warmer toward Gunston Hall and eventually fell in love with it. (Dear old Gunston—gone with the wind! It did not survive World War II.) It was at Gunston that I first began to do things. There was always something exciting going on there and you had to make an effort to be part of it.

Mrs. Kuntz, my mentor there, was a charming, forthright woman, somewhat advanced in her thinking and her educational methods for the time. We began to study Shakespeare in the fifth grade at Gunston and there was none of this nonsense about watered-down or condensed versions. We read Shakespeare in the original version and figured out what he meant according to our lights. At Gunston I also fell in love with Shakespeare, a romance that has persisted down the years.

All the classes of students who were old enough to read Shakespeare gave a Shakespearean play every year, and when I was eleven years old and in the fifth grade I acted in *Julius Caesar*. I played the part of the Third Citizen, a minor role, whose sides were not numerous but made up for their lack of number by being dramatic. My favorite was "Oh woeful day!" which I brought out in ringing tones with a suitable expression of dismay.

During the long weeks when we were whipping *Julius Caesar* into shape we all became so fascinated with both Shakespeare and Caesar that they became indistinguishable. For some time a good many of us thought they were contemporaries and that Shakespeare was an inhabitant of Rome. We also identified ourselves with the characters to such an extent that we used Elizabethan English at home when we asked somebody to pass the butter.

Mary Calvert, who played the Second Citizen, and I were constantly engaging in our dialogue at off hours. We also heard that there was a movie short of *Julius Caesar* playing at one of the neighborhood houses and we hied ourselves there and sat in tense expectancy. When the Second and Third Citizens flashed on the screen we were boiling with excitement.

"Mary," I squealed. "There you are!"

43

"That's *your* line!" Mary cried when the Third Citizen bewailed the day.

We sat through it several times.

While Mary's and my roles weren't important, we got the most out of them. The girl who played Caesar had been chosen because she was a good actress, but she had been giving herself airs and we decided she was a stuck-up snob. When Caesar was stabbed, in our play, the Second and Third Citizens were pressed into service to remove him from the scene. We took care of *her* but good! Rarely has the corpse of Caesar been treated so roughly.

I have always been grateful for the early grounding in Shakespeare's works that I received at Gunston Hall. I learned to read him as a friend, the way you read Dickens or Kipling, and not as a scholarly project. I never cease to rejoice in him, on the boards or in the book. Indeed, the most beautiful lines in the English language to me occur in the first scene of the first act of *Hamlet*: ". . . the morn, in russet mantle clad/Walks o'er the dew of yon high eastward hill." But these words became dear to me much later.

&ᴥ I made other friends in Washington. Due to the fact that Papa was a Senator, I was automatically a member of the "DOTS"—Daughters of the Senators. While I was really too young for their weekly luncheons and annual dances, I knew Imelda and Gloria Chavez, Marilyn Wherry, and Mimi Langer, who were near my age.

&ᴥ Before June rolled around, Connecticut Avenue was as familiar as Delaware Street and I had learned to appreciate at least certain portions of Washington. It is a beautiful city and when I saw Paris, I realized how much the original French architect and planner of Washington had impressed his nationality on it. Washington is different from every other American city, because it was actually planned and properly laid out, and maybe that's why you never feel entirely at home there. It didn't grow up higgledy-piggledy like most American towns.

It was a sleepier place in my childhood. Everything moved at a lackadaisical pace. There weren't as many automobiles and the traffic ran measured and slow. Everybody rode the Washington trolleys and buses. I remember sitting on the bus one afternoon with my nose in my homework. Suddenly I was hit on the head with a folded newspaper which had been thrown at me. I looked around furiously and there sat Dad, laughing his head off.

When Congress adjourned that June and we packed up and started the drive to Independence, we all felt a jubilant sense of relief. "Going home! Going home!" I thought, looking back at Washington until its white buildings receded into the horizon. It occurred to me then that it was really a nice place to visit.

Well, it turned out to be quite a long visit. It lasted around twenty years.

5: Years between

During that twenty years I always felt a little like a split personality. From January to June I was the little Truman girl in Washington. From June to January, I was Mary Margaret in Independence.

In Independence there was our happy old house on Delaware Street with the damask wallpaper and the petit point chairs; the sound of Grandmum's soft voice, running on, and the music of Vietta, beating things and singing in the kitchen. There was the grind of the ice-cream freezer turning and the voices of aunts and uncles on the long back porch, raised in laughter or teasing or argument, and the swish of the bridge cards being shuffled. (Uncle Fred had married by now and Aunt Christine, better known as Chris, was a welcome addition to the family circle.) There was the twitter of birds and the high, sweet calls of the children in the block. There was the grassy square with the Williamsburg-style courthouse in the center (always called Uncle Fred's courthouse, because he had designed it) and Mayor Sermon's grocery store and Brown's drugstore. There was the movie theatre, where we went when we had the wherewithal and the Tasty Soda Shop where we went later if we had a dime left!

When September came there was junior high school, just a block from home, where I enrolled with my old friends and sat in the same rooms that both my father and mother had gone to school in. (The old building finally burned and my father is not above insinuat-

47

ing that they had to burn it down to get me out of it. As a matter of fact I had graduated from junior high before this conflagration occurred, but I would have relished a good fire while I was wrestling with algebra there!) There were Friday night mixers in the gymnasium, where we used to go and dance so we could get accustomed to boys and social life. It was there my first date with a boy was made. We went to a high-school football game, heavily chaperoned by a jocular uncle.

Christmas was always a little bittersweet from then on, because right after the first of January we had to pack up and go to Washington. In Washington there was the furnished apartment on Connecticut Avenue and Gunston Hall and Shakespeare! Shakespeare helped a lot. At Gunston my class was embarked on *As You Like It*. I played the part of Charles, the Wrestler. My costume, a tunic of sorts, was so short that it made me nervous. Mother insisted that I wear a pair of black bloomers under it. I didn't really want to wear the bloomers but there didn't seem to be any help for it, so when I delivered my deathless lines, of which I can only remember "There's no news . . . , sir, but the old news," I was always afraid I would come out with "There are no bloomers, sir, but the old bloomers"! Years later, when I saw Katherine Hepburn in *As You Like It* and Charles' line came over the footlights, I burst out laughing.

&> At Gunston we were graded not only on our courses, but on deportment and initiative. After I had been there a couple of years, Mrs. Kuntz took me aside one day and told me that I ought to think about the latter.

"You must make more of an effort, Margaret," she said. "You are a nice, intelligent girl, but you insist on effacing yourself."

It had never occurred to me that you ought to push yourself. In fact, training for ladyhood hinted that you should eschew such a program, but after Mrs. Kuntz's gentle hint I thought about it quite a lot. I must have been a little past twelve at the time, and I believe that this was the first time I really ever thought seriously about myself. Mrs. Kuntz's words had a marked influence on my whole life.

The sum of this brooding resulted in my making up my mind which role I wanted to play in *Twelfth Night* when it was being cast. I decided to be Maria. Mary Ogden had already been cast as

48

Maria but I knew that Mary yearned to be Sir Toby Belch. I figured out a three-way switch and then I went to Mrs. Kuntz.

"I want to be Maria in the play," I said.

"Well," said Mrs. Kuntz, "that's a big part and somebody already has it."

"But I want it," I said, "and I can do it, too." I explained my plan for the switch.

"If everybody else is satisfied, it's all right with me," Mrs. Kuntz said.

The plan was carried out with great diplomacy and I went into Maria's part. I worked like a Trojan, and I brought it off, too. I'll never forget one small triumph I had the night of the performance. The teacher of rhythmic dancing at Gunston had never thought much of my rhythmic dancing. In fact, she could not believe I was rhythmic in any way, and, let's face it, I hadn't thought much of her either. But she came backstage and congratulated me on the way I had handled the role.

I was drunk with power, although the performance had been slightly ragged. At one point Jane Lingo had been due to sing an Elizabethan ditty and as Jane has never been known for her voice, Helen Bull (better known as Puddin') and I were cued to carry the air for her from backstage. Just before Jane's song, Puddin' and I had a big scene and when we finished it we were supposed to disappear into the false trees to wait for Malvolio. Off stage, we were to dub in Jane's song.

Puddin' and I received a big hand at the conclusion of our scene and we were so overcome with the sound of applause that we waltzed off the stage, patting each other on the back. We forgot all about Jane, who finally quavered out her tune in solitary helplessness. Puddin' and I were still congratulating each other on being great actresses when Jane burst into the wings, fit to be tied. We never heard the last of it.

Jeanne Miles, the best drama student Gunston ever had, was playing Malvolio that night. Malvolio was described in the book as wearing "cross garters" but nobody could find any cross garters in Washington. The drama coach and prop woman solved this by painting cross garters with oil paint on long yellow stockings, while Jeanne was standing in them. Jeanne had one rapid change of costume and

49

while she made it I was on stage. My cue for her entrance was, "Yonder struts Malvolio in the sun!" I sang out the line and paused, waiting for Malvolio to strut. Nothing happened. I repeated my line and still nothing happened. After the third repetition, I looked frantically into the wings and there was Jean, squatting on her haunches, trying to tear the stockings off her legs. Her cross garters had stuck to her skin and she couldn't get out of the stockings. She was making wild gestures and looking at me piteously while somebody ran for a bottle of turpentine. For two whole minutes I ad-libbed Shakespeare and became the heroine of the evening.

I studied piano at Gunston and also Music Appreciation. This course fascinated me, largely because it was taught by such a pretty teacher. Her name was Miss Lowe and she also taught voice. I yearned to take voice, because Miss Lowe taught it. She was the darling of the school, and we were disconsolate when she left to get married. Her Music Appreciation course was unusually sound. I never hear a symphony orchestra tuning that I don't think of her.

Those were among the joys of Gunston. There were also horrors—mathematics and chemistry. I couldn't bear them. I couldn't *do* them! In this hideous little category, I will also include Latin. Latin was required. We all hated Latin and found it a terrible chore, except for Ann Bryan. Ann was an honor student, referred to as "the Brain," and she seemed able to translate Latin as easily as she spoke English. Ann was a generous girl and every morning in study hall she would hand around her translations of the day's lesson (concerned with some more of Caesar's depredations in the province of Gaul), and we would faithfully copy it.

One day this came to the attention of the Latin teacher, who took it up with me.

"Margaret," she said, "your paper this morning seems to be an exact replica of Ann Bryan's, including the mistakes."

Honesty has always seemed to me the best policy and certainly it's the only policy when you've been caught red-handed.

"You didn't think that *I* was that smart, did you, ma'am?" I asked wistfully.

I was rewarded with an interminable piece of Latin, dealing with one of those ubiquitous bridges of Caesar's, to translate. I don't know whether I or the Latin teacher was happier when Caesar and I parted company. Alas, I never got on to the philosophies of Cicero

50

or Virgil's graceful verses. I folded up at the end of the two years' requirement. I have often regretted, when trying to learn French and Italian as part of my musical education, that I didn't hang on. It would have made everything much easier.

We had teas and garden parties in the spring of the year at Gunston and it was at one of these functions that I wore my first long dress. It was a pale-blue organdy with a full skirt, and my father had sent me a corsage. The first real dance I ever went to was one given by the *As You Like It* Club, of which I had become a member, at the Country Club. I had a long white crepe dress, with a red bolero, and a date with a boy whose name I cannot remember at all, which seems a pity!

There was one period in my wearying for Independence when it seemed fairly likely that I might get to go back there and stay the rest of my life. I was too young to realize that my father's job as the Junior Senator in Washington had been none too easy. I only knew that he worked day and night. But as the fortunes of politics go, when his term was about to expire and it became necessary for him to run again in Missouri, many of his erstwhile political associates saw no chance of his being elected. In fact, his most loyal friends feared that he would not even be nominated. My father announced that he would run, even if the only vote cast for him were his own.

As soon as he made his announcement, a handful of stalwarts rallied to him. Mayor Sermon of Independence and General Harry Vaughan were among them. The campaign opened in Sedalia on the fifteenth of May in 1939. (It was the day after Hitler's troops had marched on Paris.) Mamma Truman was there and sat on the platform. She was already eighty-eight years old but she was uncannily able to tell who was really for my father and who pretended to be for him. Dad made his speech and everybody said, as usual, that he was a terrible speaker. He made a lot of the same sort of bad speeches in that campaign and nobody gave him a chance of winning. Everybody was in despair except Daddy, but when the votes were counted he had a suitable majority. Once before 1948 he went to bed defeated and waked up elected. The next morning he flew back to Washington.

The summer I was twelve, I joined the choir of Trinity Church. Mrs. William Sermon, the choir-mistress, told Mother I had a promising voice, but she added that she thought it was not advisable for me to start voice lessons until I was sixteen. I sang in the choir in Independence and I sang with the Gunston Glee Club in Washington. I loved to sing but I didn't think much about it at the time, for I was concentrating my musical efforts on the piano. In 1940 Mrs. Sermon urged my mother to begin my vocal training.

Various people claim to have "discovered" my voice and there is one story to the effect that a friend who happened to ride from Independence to Washington in the car with us was overwhelmed with my vocalizing as we rode along. I doubt it. Mrs. Sermon was certainly the first to call attention to its possibilities, but I don't think anybody discovered it—like Topsy, it "just growed."

Due to Mrs. Sermon's urging, Mother and Dad discussed voice lessons and we had a family conference. In addition to the expense involved (and there's always expense in a musical career), there was the problem that arose from living in two places. Where should I study singing—in Independence or in Washington? And with whom?

They finally agreed that I had more time in Independence than in Washington, so it seemed reasonable that I should begin at home. The choice of a teacher was simple. One of my father's old war buddies, Major Thomas J. Strickler, was married to a singer. Mrs. Strickler heard me sing and agreed to give me lessons. I had one lesson a week all that summer and I studied with Mrs. Strickler until 1947 when I began to coach for my professional debut.

Due to my divided life, the circumstances were often trying. Mrs. Strickler obviously could not commute to Washington, but occasionally she would come through there going somewhere else and we would go out to a room at the Wardman Park Hotel or the Shoreham for a session. At the same time I was always staggering under a heavy schedule of courses in school and trying to fit together the educational systems of Independence and Gunston. Due to the family leaning for music, I went to all available concerts and my interest in singing deepened and became steadily more serious. The satisfaction I obtained from singing began to outweigh the pleasures of the piano and almost before I knew it I had entered on the long hard road of the soprano.

When my father began his second term as Junior Senator from Missouri in 1940, the European war was at the crisis stage. France was occupied and in May began the heroic retreat of the British armies from Dunkirk, followed by the bombing of Britain in July. I was sixteen years old and while I read the papers, and thrilled to Winston Churchill's magnificent voice, rallying the English, and cringed at the horrible stories of bombed and burning London, and wept over Greer Garson as *Mrs. Miniver*, the war still seemed remote to me, as it may have to you.

However, it was very close to my father. His concern over the burgeoning arsenal that the United States was becoming may not have seemed especially dramatic at the time, but he was appalled at the waste and inefficiency in defense measures he had seen as a veteran and a citizen and a Senator. Not many people know that my father has always been a student of military maneuvers. He had hoped for an Army career and had seen much active fighting in World War I. He and Mr. John Snyder used to go out and study old Civil War battlefields around Washington when I was young. As a student of military history, my father did not go off half-cocked and jump into an investigating committee operation without cause.

As soon as he got back to Washington he began to voice his opinions on the errors in the defense efforts of the United States, and in February, 1941, he proposed the investigating committee which eventually came to bear his name and first attracted nation-wide attention to him. The accomplishments of the Truman Committee, which acquired great prestige and considerable power, are unlikely to be forgotten by history, but my reaction to it at the time was that Daddy was always gone!

He was gone one gloomy Sunday in December that year, though Mother and I had remained in Washington all winter instead of going home to Independence, hoping to catch a few more glimpses of him. We were all planning to meet on Delaware Street for Christmas and Daddy had called Saturday night to say that he planned to spend Sunday in a small hotel in Columbia, Missouri, just resting and sleeping, after a week of rugged daily schedules.

It was a cold, forbidding day in Washington. I had one of my interminable colds and was housebound. I was listening to the Philharmonic broadcast from New York and trying to persuade myself to attack my homework. Mother was in the other room, writing letters. Suddenly an announcer broke in to say that Japanese planes had attacked some port or other. Japan and China had been at war so long that I didn't pay any attention to it. Japanese planes were always attacking *something*. A few minutes later the same thing happened. But the announcer seemed unusually excited and his voice kept breaking. When the brief announcement was over, the music continued and I sat listening to it dreamily. After two or three more reports of the same bombing, I regret to state that I felt annoyed (my cold made me cantankerous), but what is more shocking is that my geography was so weak that I didn't recognize the name that has since been written in American history in letters of fire. I got up and went into the other room.

"They keep breaking into the symphony," I complained to my mother, "to say something about the Japanese attacking Pearl Harbor, wherever that is."

"What did you *say?*" my mother asked, rising and scattering her letters.

"Somewhere in China," I said irritably. "Pearl something. Sounds like Pearl Harbor."

"Pearl Harbor!" my mother cried. "Pearl Harbor is in Hawaii!"

It was then borne in on me that Japanese planes had attacked the United States.

My mother ran to the telephone and put in a call to the Tennant Hotel in Columbia, Missouri. She woke my father out of a sound sleep and gave him my echo of the opening guns of World War II.

Daddy said later that he was frantic. He knew that he had to be back in Washington immediately but, pining for isolation, he had taken himself far from established airlines. He leapt into his clothes and walked across the fields to a little private airport on the outskirts of Columbia and stated his predicament. The owner of the airport borrowed a private plane and flew him to St. Louis where he managed to get on a plane for Washington, arriving in time for the convening of Congress.

I will never forget that morning. Congress met in joint session with a solemn pall over both Houses.

I had begun to keep the diary that I have written in almost every day since and this notation appears for December 8, 1941:

"At eleven o'clock this morning the United States declared war. There was a madhouse on the floor. The galleries were packed and cheered the President to the echoes. Planes have been sighted twenty miles from San Francisco!"

I remember that I was sitting in the photographer's gallery at the session and just before it was over, I dashed down the back stairs, for I was familiar with every nook and cranny of those chambers, hoping to catch up with my father. (When Congress meets in joint session, the President leaves first, followed by the Vice-president, the Cabinet, the Supreme Court, the Diplomatic Corps, the Senate, and the House of Representatives.) I got down on the level of the House floor in time to hear the vote by the Senate. They voted by roll call—Aye for the affirmative; opposed, No. The vote was over in five minutes—82 Ayes in the Senate; 381 Ayes in the House of Representatives and one No. I missed my father and walked out with Senator Brooks of Illinois.

We were at war! I felt I ought to *do* something, but I didn't know what to do, so I went home to lunch. I had been moved and awed by the tremendous solemnity of the session and by the declaration, but the full significance did not break over me for a long time. It did not break over many of us, I suppose—the long years of struggle and separation and death, the dislocations and the disorientations and the suffering and loss that will never be entirely mended in our time.

We were at war but I had a cold and a temperature and what was vastly more important—a date with a boy. I remember my mother taking my temperature that afternoon and the way I fudged on her—leaving my mouth wide open so the thermometer wouldn't register, for fear she wouldn't let me go out.

How picayune are the personal memorabilia of the days of history. When I paw through this stack of diaries that carry a day-to-day record of some of the most cataclysmic moments in twenty centuries of civilization, I am chagrined to observe that my entries ran more to the bloody horrors of mid-term examinations than to the bloody horrors of battlefields. I was in the exact center of the maelstrom of a nation entering upon the greatest war in its history, but it seemed more exciting that I had a new hair-do, and was rehearsing in *She Stoops to Conquer*, the Gunston senior class play, and that Jane and I had been to one more Jeanette MacDonald–Nelson Eddy musical!

There were rumors of enemy planes over New York—over Baltimore—over Washington itself. People began to pour into Washington. The sleepy, lackadaisical atmosphere vanished and was replaced by the hivelike activity of millions of figurative bees. Gas rationing came in and I began to travel to school on the bus. The buses were very crowded. Washington was full of hundreds of new government girls and swarms of uniforms. Sugar rationing came in and shoe rationing and rationing of all kinds. Meat and butter were hard to come by. The cherry trees bloomed forlornly along the Tidal Basin and we looked at them askance, as if we expected some sinister oriental significance to emerge from their delicate blossoms. There was talk of chopping them down, but reason prevailed and the bright plume of their beauty was spared. Still, they didn't seem so pretty that year.

My father was very busy. He always looked exhausted and grave. My mother always looked worried.

My mother was working in my father's office at this time. Due to the ever-increasing pressures of work brought on by the Truman Committee operations, he had to have more help. Due to her involvement in the office routine, she knew and thought a great deal more about the war than I did.

Then suddenly it was the end of May and Commencement was upon us. We, the senior class, marched into St. Margaret's Church in our bright summer hats and pale dresses for the baccalaureate sermon and went to the traditional luncheon tendered the senior class by the junior class. June first was immemorially Class Day. I sang a song that Jeanne Miles had written about dear old Gunston at the Class Day exercises. That night I went to the traditional dinner tendered the senior class by the alumnae of Gunston Hall at the Sulgrave Club, and in the midst of everything I thought sadly, "Now I'm an alumna!" I sang three songs that night as part of the entertainment and had a date with a new beau. My diary reports ecstatically, as of June 1, 1942: "And then we went to the *Shoreham Terrace* to dance. He has a new gray convertible that rides like down!"

On June 2, 1942, I wrote in my journal: "Today I graduated from Gunston Hall. I had a long white dress of net and pique. Dad made the Commencement address and Miss Mary B. Kerr, the headmistress, gave us our diplomas. I won the English Prize, the Spanish Prize and Honor Roll for the year. Wow, what a day! We all stood around and cried." So much for youth's sweet-scented manuscript.

෪ Summer rolled over us and I went to Independence and reverted to type. I forsook Nelson Eddy and fell in love with Charles Boyer! My diary is composed largely of lists of movies I attended and if the movie industry ever needs to know exactly what pictures were getting the vote in 1942, they have only to consult me.

On the sixth of September that year, Daddy gave the dedicatory address at the unveiling of the American Legion monument in St. Louis. Mr. Snyder and Drucie were there on a War Bond selling tour. I met them in St. Louis. Edward Arnold and Frances Dee were members of the bond tour, and Drucie and I were introduced to them and were overwhelmed. In the heat of the bond selling, Frances Dee got so excited that she offered to auction off her shoes. They brought a big price and Edward Arnold picked her up bodily and carried her, shoeless, off the platform. This struck Drucie and me as the epitome of patriotism and romance!

I had decided to enroll in George Washington University in Washington, due to the fact that it was famous for its history and government departments, subjects in which I planned to major. Mother and Dad were pleased since I would be able to live at home. (George Washington is in the city of Washington, available by bus to Connecticut Avenue.) Jane Lingo had also decided to go to GW, as it is affectionately called. I felt somewhat morose at the breakup of the old Gunston crowd which was scattering in many directions, some to Hollins College, some to Stephens and others to universities all over the country, but Jane and I were being rushed by several sororities, so we didn't have time to mope.

My diary reflects such earth-shaking comments as those that follow:

"I went to the Pi Beta Phi Preparational Dinner tonight. I like them *best*. Now to see if they like *me!*"

"Received a box of brownies from Aunt Mary. Goody!" (I neglected to observe that Aunt Mary Truman had probably sacrificed a week's sugar ration to me.)

"Dad brought home a shoe heel made out of synthetic rubber.

57

He said it was a secret but soon we would have a lot of things made out of synthetic rubber. I wonder." (Look at who was wondering!)

"I had a voice lesson today in the Shoreham Ballroom. Mrs. Strickler was in town."

"I went to lunch with the Chi Omegas. Nice."

"The Kappas have invited me to tea."

On September 23 I took time out of my social life to register for college. The first thing that happened was that I was forced to strip, wrap myself in a sheet, and take a physical examination. I hated it. I was required to take some course in athletics and I despised that. I am no more an athlete than my father was or is. The only physical exercise I favor is dancing. Dad likes to walk, but I even hate to walk. In spite of George Washington University athletic requirements, I never became proficient in any form of athletics. I can play a fair game of tennis if I absolutely have to, but my mother can always lick me, even now. It is impossible for me to return her serves, as she has one of the fastest, hardest serves I ever saw. The balls come over the net with the speed and accuracy of bullets. She can play rings around me. I couldn't learn to swim then, and I still can't swim. I am terrified of water, and I don't *want* to swim.

On September 28, I observed in my diary:

"College is as bad as high school!"

(I don't know what I had expected it to be.)

On September 29, I wrote:

"I was pledged Pi Phi at 7:30 A.M., but it was worth getting up for!"

(Coming from slugabed me, this was quite an admission. I have always loathed getting up early and cannot think before twelve noon!)

October 1, 1942, I checked college off.

"I had two classes today. I am *sick* of the whole thing. School on *Saturday!*" Obviously I had reached the ultimate horror.

On October 5, 1942, I took new hope.

"I was formally pledged Pi Beta Phi today. Now I'll have a golden arrow to wear when and *if* I make my grades."

Jane Lingo also pledged Pi Phi and we entered happily upon our pledgedom. In a later entry in the diary I reported:

58

"The pledges gave a dinner for the Grand Secretary of Pi Beta Phi. I cooked it!"

(Alas, poor lady. I dread to think of what she ate. Cooking has never been my strong point.)

That winter was enlivened by a good theatrical season in Washington. Playgoing opened up a whole new world to me and I thought it vastly superior to college. At the time, almost anything would have been superior to college. I was restless and bored and suddenly I determined to get into the war effort.

"College is not interesting," I announced to Mother. "All those old dead and dusty history books! I'm going to join the ATS!"

"You'll make a great pilot," my mother scoffed.

"I don't see why I wouldn't!" I bridled.

"Well," said my mother, "you can't subtract two from three without making a mistake, and you can't add two digits without carrying the one! You'd never get the ship off the ground."

"Do you have to know *math?*" I demanded.

"Haven't you heard about navigation?" my mother inquired.

That was the end of the ATS. Mother knew best, so it was back to government and history and school, even on Saturday. This was ameliorated by the fact that Jane and I had discovered the double date and recurrently I find in my diary the names of Jack Washington and Bob Hiffler and the legends of bridge games and singing around the piano and supper in our apartment.

The war was nearly a year old. Washington was dimmed out and occasionally blacked out. The Truman Committee was growing in importance and Dad was flying all over the map—to Charleston, West Virginia, to inspect the ordnance plant there and to New Orleans and on to Kansas City. The Germans sank the French fleet at Toulon, and we were all depressed.

I had joined the Glee Club at George Washington and we were practicing the Christmas cantata. I had a solo part and felt very proud. In December I also sang at the Red Cross Serviceman's Canteen in Washington. I was wrestling with psychology at school and trying to do my Christmas shopping and get ready to go home. The African invasion began and on the eighteenth of December the gas shortage became so alarming that all gas ration cards on the Eastern seaboard were called in. I remember how eerie the city seemed, without a car on the streets. There were only the buses and a few cabs for official use and the Christmas shoppers had to foot it.

Mother and I finally got ourselves together and headed for Independence. Dad was in New Orleans and proposed to join us at home, and he got there on the twenty-second. In spite of the pressure of his duties in New Orleans, he had had time to go shopping in the French Quarter and had brought me two beautiful antique bracelets. Christmas was quiet that year, but we were all grateful to be at home together.

ᘒᔍ The beginning of the second year of the war was distinguished by the fact that I finally dropped Psychology and took up Public Speaking, a great relief to all who knew me. I survived my first year of college without actually altering my early opinions of it, but as a matter of fact, I had a wonderful time. The boys were just beginning to be called up that year and there was a constant round of parties and dances and singsongs. There was something going on all the time and Jane and I were always in the big middle of it. By the spring term the ranks of men had thinned appreciably and when school was out, George Washington University was practically a girl's school.

Summer in Independence was dull that year. I was going with a boy there whose idea of a big date was a pound of chocolates and the porch swing. In my assay of him in one of the more intimate passages in my diary, I wrote that "he just couldn't seem to get off the ground." I got hay fever and my singing lessons went badly. Dad got to Independence periodically, but he was always dog-tired and inclined to be grouchy. The war was dragging on and nobody could predict its end. August was, curiously, a cold, disagreeable month and we had to have the furnace on in Missouri, an unheard-of thing.

My diary is illuminated with such brilliant events as:

"Turned up the hem of a dress today."

"Played solitaire with Aunt Beuf."

"Had a date with ——. He brought me *another* box of candy!"

I dreaded going back to school with a passion out of all proportion to the cause, but the black day rolled around. There I was immersed in history instead of living it, or so I thought. On November

60

26 of that year, Dad made his first coast-to-coast broadcast in Washington on the findings of the Truman Committee. He spoke on the *March of Time* program and Mother and I went down to the studio to hear him. I was introduced to Earl Godwin, who was very nice to me. He was the first radio personality I ever met.

The committee hearings were in progress in Washington at that time and I went to one of the sessions. Mr. Jeffers reported on the rubber situation. Leon Henderson discussed rationing and Mr. Eastman spoke about supply lines. Harold Ickes also testified, and I remember how excited I was to meet so many celebrities in the flesh. I was truly proud of Dad.

It was about this time that I had the happy opportunity of meeting one of my heroes. As chairman of the Truman Committee, my father gave a dinner honoring Douglas Southall Freeman, who had been an adviser, at the new Statler Hotel in Washington. I was ordinarily not included in such affairs, but when I heard that General George Marshall was going to be there, I began to tease my father to let me go. He finally gave in. The dinner was held in a private dining room and I remember that we were all seated at small tables. Mine was rather remote and I was sitting there feeling lonely and out of my depth. Suddenly I looked up and there was General Marshall, smiling down at me. I instantly gave up Charles Boyer and fell in love with General Marshall. He is one of the kindest men alive, and to my thinking one of the best-looking.

"May I sit down?" he said.

I nodded, for I was tongue-tied.

He then engaged me in conversation for nearly half an hour. Some people have the knack of talking to young people and others simply do not. General Marshall has it. Though I was just a schoolgirl, he made me feel like a brilliant and scintillating woman of the world. *He* seemed to be interested in *me*. It was almost more than I could bear.

"What are you studying in college?" he asked.

I told him about history and government and all the rest of it.

"How do they teach history these days?" he asked.

I gave him a rough idea.

"I have a theory about the teaching of history," General Marshall said, and began to expound his marvelous theory. I wish General Marshall could have taught me history!

61

About twenty minutes later, my father walked over to the table. "Now see here, Margaret," he said. "You can't go on monopolizing our famous guest."

"I've enjoyed our little talk," General Marshall said to me, though my end of it had been composed largely of monosyllables. "I hope I'll see you again." He bowed over my hand, as if I were a personage.

I have always loved him for that and for his everlasting kindness to me. At the inauguration of President Eisenhower, I was standing off to the side, feeling lonely and left out. Someone came softly up behind me, bent over my shoulder, and kissed my cheek. It was General Marshall—saving the day again.

That night I knew I was in the presence of a great man. In the years to come I was to see him often and it was one of the happy aspects of all that came to pass.

There are two sides to the ledger of any life, and mine has been no different. It is still a moot point in my father's mind whether or not residence in the White House in my girlhood was the best thing that could have happened to me. It is true that along with the good things that come of such a situation, there are heartaches and disillusionments and limitations, which a young person not so situated might avoid. But it cannot be gainsaid that the opportunity to associate with great men and women who rise to the top in a democracy, is the most superb advantage. They make a lasting impression on any open mind and heart. These friendships are my jewels.

6: The tail of the comet

In the various articles and interviews that have been written about me since I became an object of public interest, writers have passed several interesting judgments on me. This may have resulted from a search for angles. (Tallulah Bankhead, questioned about me by one journalist, said, "She's a nice girl, darling, a terribly *nice* girl. When you've said that, what else can you say?") At any rate, a number of people have said that I am *ambitious*.

This word has several connotations and many of them do not apply to me. My besetting sin has always been a lack of initiative, and way back in Gunston Hall, I never could seem to get A for effort. But it is true that since I was a small child, I have cherished a wish to make my father and mother proud of me. I dreamed of achieving fame in some vague way and bringing it to lay at their feet like a trophy. This desire may have served as an incentive for my musical plans.

In 1944, my father entered on a phase of his career which enveloped me in reflected light. His star rose with the sudden brilliance of a comet and I traveled irrevocably in its wake. If he had reservations about his appointments with destiny, they were concerned to a degree with me. He is a thoughtful man and did not wish to deprive me of the opportunity of making a life on my own terms.

63

My father did not consciously plan the course his life took. Early in 1944 he was urged to run for the Vice-presidency.

"I talked it over with Bess," my father is reported to have said to his sponsors, "and we've decided against it. I've got a daughter and the limelight is no place for children."

Early in 1944 my only ambitions were to get rid of my perennial cold and to survive the mid-term examinations at George Washington University. It was a dank, wet spring. Washington was full of crises. The war was at its most critical stage—the United States was readying the invasion of the European continent. My father's work on the investigating committee was growing in importance and public appreciation, since it had saved the country billions of dollars. "The Doghouse," the description of the private office where admirals, generals, factory managers, and Cabinet members met in informal conferences with the members of the investigating committee, had become a national byword. Here many of the serious problems of the war were attacked and solved. But Dad still found time to take Mother and me to the movies.

"Harry likes any movie that Margaret wants to go to," Mother said.

Dad said my penchant for movies gave him a good chance to catch up on his sleep. He couldn't work in the dark, and he could sleep right through any picture that bored him, and usually did. This was about his only relaxation at the time.

On June 6, 1944, the Allied Armies established a beachhead on the coast of France. My contribution to history in my diary on this great occasion were some notations of news flashes on the landings and the salient fact that I had a date with Joe Crowe who bought me, at my request, an Italian dinner!

At the end of the school session at George Washington, I was awarded an Associate of Arts Degree, which is granted to students of GW who have completed two years of study. Since I was committed to two more years this didn't impress me very much, but I was thrilled at the convocation exercises. Bidu Sayao sang *The Star-Spangled Banner*.

I greeted the end of school with my usual enthusiasm, but was somewhat bored that I couldn't settle down on Delaware Street and go native. The National Democratic Convention was to be held in Chicago in July, and we had to go. My father was naturally more interested in the convention than I was! He had work to do.

There were rumors everywhere, and certainly in the confines of the Democratic party, that if President Roosevelt should insist upon Vice-president Wallace's nomination for a second term, the Solid South would bolt the ticket. I knew and admired Vice-president Wallace and his daughter Jean was a good friend of mine. I didn't really understand the political situation, but the Washington grapevine, which usually works overtime, had consistently hinted that National Democratic Chairman Robert Hannegan was still promoting my father for Vice-president in spite of his refusal.

My father was promoting Speaker Sam Rayburn and made no bones about it. Speaker Rayburn himself finally persuaded my father to give up the campaign in his behalf, as the Democratic party in Texas was so seriously split that he felt he could not be a candidate. My father then switched his support to Senator James F. Byrnes of South Carolina, the Democratic whip in the Senate. My father departed for the convention, charged with making the speech nominating Senator Byrnes as Vice-president.

We had come home to Independence as soon as school closed but it seemed to me that we barely got unpacked before we packed up again and started for Chicago—Mother, Dad and I. It was terribly hot and dry. Chicago was stifling. Daddy was a member of the Resolutions Committee and was staying by himself in a suite on the seventeenth floor of the Stevens Hotel, so that he could conduct business. Mother and I were at the Morrison Hotel, and most of the wild confusion which preceded the nomination and the weighty decision that accompanied it were spared me.

For several days my father flouted every suggestion that he should be nominated and was finally overpowered only when Mr. Hannegan showed him a penciled note in President Roosevelt's handwriting: "Bob, I think Truman is the right man. FDR." News of these developments came to me in bits and snatches. Marion Montague, a friend of mine from Washington, had joined me for the convention and we ran around the way a couple of girls in a big city will. I took so little stock in the matter that Marion and I rarely attended the sessions but inspected all the Chicago department stores.

65

I append here a verbatim copy of my diary during those few days to show you the sort of Cassandra I am!

July 17, 1944
We are on our way to Chicago. Hope it will be fun but probably not very exciting.

July 18, 1944
Arrived in Chicago. Staying in suite at Morrison. Went to Edgewater Beach Hotel for dinner with the Eddie McKims. It was lovely.

There is talk of Daddy for Vice-president. Just a rumour I'm sure.

July 19, 1944
Ye gods! The Missouri delegation has decided to nominate Dad for V-P. Vice-president Wallace is very strong so I doubt if we win, although the South doesn't want Wallace at all.

Marion Montague arrived from Washington this morning. She is so nice.

July 20, 1944
Pres. Roosevelt was nominated for a fourth term.

We went out to the Convention for a while. The galleries tried to stampede the Convention into nominating Wallace. They are CIO men who want Wallace. We need time. Had dinner at Blackstone with Col. Snyder and the Fred Bowmans. Marion and I went shopping at Marshall Fields and got lost!

There has been a revolt in the German Army!

A big July 21, 1944 day
All I can write after such a day is *whew!!!* Daddy has been nominated for Vice-president to run with President Roosevelt. Mr. Wallace led in the first poll 429½ to 319½ for us. Then in the second poll Maryland switched and the whole South got on our bandwagon and then all but 105 or 66 votes were ours (1,076) and the Convention went wild. I autographed papers and the cameras were all turned on Mother, Dad & me. Mr. & Mrs. Souter were with us, also E. McKim & J. Snyder.

Actually, my father had finally made up his mind to accept the nomination about midnight on the night of July 19, after the most trying day of his life. He telephoned Senator Byrnes his honest chagrin, and Senator Byrnes (whom Roosevelt had *not* thought the right man) showed his long-lasting disappointment. I am sure this situation was most difficult for my father, for he cannot bear to hurt a friend. Dad asked that Senator Bennett Clark, his colleague from Missouri, put his name in nomination. Senator Clark accepted, but he had very little time to prepare a speech he had never expected to deliver. The choice of my father was a complete upset, and the supporters of Wallace made a stringent effort to stampede the convention, even to having the organist in the convention hall play *Iowa* over and over and over.

The convention recessed on the twentieth of July without the nomination of a Vice-president. Mayor Kelly of Chicago demanded an adjournment, because forces behind Mr. Wallace (few people believed that he himself condoned the mob tactics) had issued counterfeit tickets and the stadium was crammed with one-third more people than it could lawfully accommodate.

The next day, Vice-president Wallace led on the first ballot, as everybody expected. On the second ballot, Senator John H. Bankhead of Alabama, who had been nominated for Vice-president as a favorite son, proposed to switch the votes of his state to Daddy. Alabama is the first state to vote, due to its alphabetical position. However, the Alabamans missed the cue and voted for Bankhead again on the second ballot. Maryland, followed by Senator Kerr of Oklahoma, who was a favorite-son candidate himself, switched to Dad and started the famous avalanche, with one delegation after another rallying to our bandwagon.

Daddy had been sitting in Mr. Hannegan's office, under the convention platform most of the day, but hunger finally drove him out and he availed himself of a hot dog smeared with mustard and joined the Missouri delegation, just before the second ballot. Mother and I were in a box, on the sidelines. Mother looked tired and worried and as if she had been crying all night. I don't know how I looked, but I was pretty excited. Anyone who has witnessed a convention on television knows how exciting they can be, and I was certainly personally involved in this one!

When the nomination became an actuality on the second ballot, Dad was working on another hot dog. The floor went into wild confusion and the cheering delegates stormed the platform to press around him and shake hands. Snake dances started all over the house and the relief of tension which had been built up for two days gave way to fantastic pushing, shoving, and shouting. Mother and I got up and started for Dad, who was finally shouldered up to a microphone, where he delivered the shortest nomination-acceptance speech in the history of the United States—ninety-two words. The roars redoubled. Mother and I finally reached Dad in the pandemonium.

Reporters, cameramen, radio broadcasters, and guards converged on us. The building was illuminated and reverberating with the popping of hundreds of flashlight bulbs.

Police and Secret Service men surrounded the three of us.

My mother said almost piteously to my father, "Are we going to have to go through this all the rest of our lives?"

Dad was too tired to say anything, and he had a nomination he didn't want.

It required ten policemen to get us through that yelling, screaming, clawing mob. Suddenly I was stricken with real terror. The people ceased to be individuals and became a frightening mass of pink faces, animal roars, and plucking fingers. It was at that moment that I conceived a fear of crowds that has never left me.

The next morning a writer named Margaret Alexander, now an editor of the *Kansas City Star*, began to follow me around. I simply couldn't understand what it was she wanted of me. That afternoon, to my intense relief, we started back to Independence. My diary gives a cryptic and typical report of the next few days:

July 22, 1944

Mother had a press conference this morning and we left in the car for Peoria, where we spent the night at Père Marquette Hotel.

July 23, 1944

Got home this evening. Aunt Natalie fed us. I left *seven orchids* in the refrigerator at the Père Marquette. What a dope! I'll never have that many again. (Hah!)

July 24, 1944

Tonight we had an open reception in the yard. Shook hands with our 3,000 fellow townspeople and out-of-towners. Major and Mrs. Strickler were here and Dr. & Mrs. Hess. All of us are dog-tired.

July 25, 1944

I slept today. I have a touch of ptomaine. Too much excitement.

July 26, 1944

Today I feel better. Went with Mother, Beuf & Aunt Nat to tea for Mrs. Roger Sermon. He is running for Governor.

It looks as if Hitler's rule is cracking and the army is getting control. I have telegram from Pres. Roosevelt to Dad on the night of nomination. Dad gave it to me. It says: I SEND YOU MY HEARTIEST CONGRATULATIONS ON YOUR VICTORY. I AM OF COURSE VERY HAPPY TO HAVE YOU RUN WITH ME. LET ME KNOW YOUR PLANS. I SHALL SEE YOU SOON.

FRANKLIN D. ROOSEVELT

July 27, 1944

I stayed by myself all afternoon as Mother and the Aunts went to a luncheon. I went down to Aunt Nat's and played on the piano and sang.

The war is going well and the Russians are just 30 miles from Warsaw.

I have received so many nice congratulatory notes but so tired from answering them.

July 28, 1944

International News Service and *Life* magazine photographers spent an hour or so taking pictures of us today, then went to city, shopped and met Mrs. Strickler.

Our forces are working hard in Pacific. I hope all goes as well as in Europe.

I had letter from a friend, Lt. Ed. Brennan. He has Purple Heart for wounds in France. He's getting well now in England.

July 29, 1944

Tom Twyman took me to dinner and a show. I had fun but am so tired.

July 30, 1944

We drove to Mamma Truman's this afternoon. Went to Beuf's & Daw's for supper with Mr. Mel and Miss Thelma (Mrs.) Pallette. We had loads of fun.

The Germans are retreating in Normandy.

August 1, 1944

Today is Primary Day and everybody in the family except me is voting. Daddy left for Washington tonight. All the old gang, Betty Ogden (Flora), Sue Ogden, Jane Berridge, Harriet Allen, Mona Jean Allen, Dorsy Lou Compton (Warr), Lucy Lane Compton, Jane Short and Jeanne Scott came over this evening. We played cards, then we ate and talked over old times. Jane Berridge spent the night. I had so much fun going over old times. None of us has changed radically.

August 2, 1944

The results of the primary were mostly good except Sen. Bennett Champ Clark was defeated and Roger Sermon was beaten for Governor by Donnelly. We wanted them in. Sen. Clark's isolationism stand at the beginning of the war went against him I'm afraid.

August 6, 1944

I sang a solo part in Merbecke's plain chant at church today. *Life* magazine is writing an article on the religious affiliation of all the candidates and a writer followed me all morning gathering material.

We tried to relax the rest of the summer, but there wasn't much opportunity. Nomination is not election, and Dad had to get ready for the campaign. On the eighteenth of August he went back to Washington for a few weeks. I went back to my music. I made several records that summer at the Kansas City Music Hall. I got accustomed to singing in halls before I made my musical debut.

I had been invited by the Pi Beta Phi chapter of the University of Missouri at Columbus to attend rush week, and on September 16 Mother and Daddy drove me down there. I was so excited at the prospect that Daddy said later when I got out of the car, I forgot to tell him good-by!

&⁓ I think I had the best time that week I ever had in my life. The girls were wonderful and the boys were marvelous. I had a new short, black evening dress trimmed with jet, which I adored, because I believe it made me look sophisticated, and a lovely, long, pale-blue evening dress. My cousin, Anne Louise Wells (now Mrs. Norman White), was enrolling in the University of Missouri that year. I went there to pledge her to Pi Phi. I let the sisterhood down because Anne Louise pledged Kappa Kappa Gamma, but even that didn't extinguish my pleasure. My godmother, Mary Paxton Keeley, was also a Kappa who was back for rush that year. She came over and took me to a Kappa party. A few minutes later a delegation of Pi Phis arrived and took me back to the Pi Phi house. They said they didn't like the idea of my giving tacit consent to the Kappas!

There wasn't anything I didn't do that week, from Kemtoning the walls of the chapter house, cozening rushees, cooking and dishwashing, to sitting in the window in my nightgown while the Sigma Chis serenaded us. There's nothing quite like the sound of young male voices raised in the time-tried but lovable sentimentality of *The Sweetheart of Sigma Chi*, on a moonlight night in early autumn, when you don't have anything on your mind but tomorrow's pleasures.

We would work and slave and rush like mad all day and then we'd go to Gabler's, the college hangout, for dinner and to the movies and then back to talk and giggle all night long. I don't think I slept a wink for five days and nights. It was the only time I ever lived in a sorority house and I'll never forget it.

When the family picked me up to take me back to Independence, I was practically comatose. About the only thing my diary has to report for the next few days was the fact that I sang my first solo at church and slept and slept and slept.

The only contretemps I remember that month was *l'affaire* laundry. I was always required to do my personal laundry (a habit I cannot break—I am often found washing my white orlon coat in the bathtub at the Hotel Carlyle, and one thing I pine for is a portable washing machine!), but at that point I hated the whole idea and thought Vietta ought to pamper me in this. This was an opinion my mother could not bring herself to share, even if I was the daughter of the Vice-presidential nominee.

I let the laundry pile up and pile up, thinking Fate might take a hand or that if I ignored it, it would go away. It finally got to the place where I not only had nothing left to wear, but you could scarcely get in my room. Mother read the riot act to me, and one fine September morn I put out a tremendous wash. As soon as I got my clothes all washed and ironed, I couldn't bear to mar their pristine freshness by putting them on, so I went around looking like a ragamuffin for several days.

Near the end of September, Dad and Colonel Harry Vaughan came to Independence to help us move. Colonel Vaughan and Daddy started for Washington in two cars, with our belongings packed inside and some of them lashed to the roofs of the cars. They looked like pioneers on a trek. Mother and I went on the train. The wartime trains were so crowded there was hardly room to move. We stood in line for hours trying to get into the diner and finally gave up and ate candy bars for dinner.

As soon as we got back to Washington, my mother's housewifely soul decreed that the apartment had to be cleaned from stem to stern, an operation for which I had no cheer but in which I must, perforce, take an active part. School yawned before, slightly mitigated by the rush week festivities that inaugurated it. On September 30, my diary notes: "Senator Kilgore's daughter is going through rush. I want *her!*" As a bristling veteran of the art of annexing new members to Pi Phi at Missouri, I was all over the place. Eleanor Kilgore pledged Pi Beta Phi and became my first Pi Phi daughter.

I registered for college and began to feel tired.

Dad was gone on a month-long speaking tour. He was campaigning again, but this was part of life. On October 5, I obtained tickets for Ethel Barrymore in *Embezzled Heaven.* Although school had the ability to exhaust me completely, I seemed able to stay up all night any night to go to the theatre. The night I saw Ethel Barrymore first, I had a sore throat and felt absolutely awful but I was carried away, according to my journal: "Tonight I saw a performance I'll never forget! Ethel Barrymore! She was magnificent!"

Later on that month, Mother and I went to New York to hear Dad speak in behalf of the Democratic ticket at Madison Square Garden. It seemed the most enormous place in the world to me and was jammed with wildly enthusiastic Democrats. Dad was wonderful, I thought. Mother and I had our photographs made, heard Alec Templeton in a concert, and went to the opera.

On November 1, we boarded the special train to take us back to Missouri. I have become a veteran of such tours since that day, but then it was all wonderful and exciting and I will let my diary take over for a few pages to give you a girl's-eye view:

November 1, 1944
I am on the special car. It has a private dining room & kitchen, lounge and shower bath and 5 compartments. It's beautiful. We have our own chef & two boys to do all the work! We stopped at Parkersburg for a parade and meeting tonight. Grand meeting!

November 2, 1944
What a day. We started in Pittsburgh and with 26 police on motorcycles and sirens we went through many towns and to luncheon at McKeesport to Uniontown and back to Pittsburgh. It took 2 hours once to go 18 miles! The crowds were terrific. There were 10 cars in the parade. Orson Welles had dinner with us and then spoke on same platform with Dad. On the go from 8:45 to 10:30 tonight. Daddy made about *10* speeches today.

November 3, 1944
We're in the Penthouse in the Muehlebach Hotel, in Kansas City.

November 4, 1944
People are coming and going. Our apt. here is beautiful! We went to Liberty for a meeting and tea and then a parade at home and a dinner and then a meeting at home where Sen. Maybank spoke for Daddy.

November 7, 1944
I had a voice lesson and spent half the day with Mrs. Strickler listening to Galli-Curci records and singing. Robert St. John was waiting for me

when I got back. I am going on the radio with him in the morning if we win.

I stayed up all night and WE'VE WON!

November 8, 1944

Broadcast with Robert St. John at 9:15. He is *so* nice and it was fun to be with him on the radio. My first time on the air.

Robert St. John was marvelous to me and sent me the following note which I still cherish:

"I wish you were going into radio. You're that good. But I hope you will do a bigger and more important job."

ᓚ While I have noted that my father did not want the nomination for Vice-president and gave in only after he had heard Mr. Roosevelt's sentiments, and that my mother was bitterly opposed to it, because she understood the burdens it would lay on my father's shoulders, I have never expressed my own reactions. I suppose these were superficial at best, since I did not know much about the ramifications of public office, in spite of having been exposed to it all my life. I naturally thought it was wonderful. I was proud of my father and it didn't seem to me that being the daughter of the Vice-president would bother me at all. I looked forward to it.

I wasn't aware, as most of the people of the United States were not aware, of the fairly precarious state of President Roosevelt's health. I didn't even think about the future. I just thought it was grand that people appreciated my father enough to tender him a high office in the government. I had known a couple of Vice-presidents—Mr. Garner and Mr. Wallace—and they seemed to lead normal lives and people looked up to them. Jean Wallace's existence as daughter of the Vice-president hadn't seemed too different from mine as daughter of a Senator. I didn't expect any drastic revision in my days. Anyway, I was only twenty years old and not given to profound speculation. The hysteria of the convention floor had frightened me but I didn't expect a repetition of anything like that. I rather liked seeing my picture in the papers. Who doesn't?

One aspect of public life rolled over me at this juncture. The mail began to pour in, from everybody, from everywhere—from long-forgotten friends and associates and from perfect strangers. I

73

had been taught to answer all letters, and added to the burdens of homework was the tyranny of the mail. I must have written a million letters in my time.

On Thanksgiving that year, Colonel and Mrs. Vaughan took Mother and me to the Army-Navy game in Baltimore. We went on the train and when we got off we had to walk miles. It was freezing cold and I think I actually would have given up if the parishioners of some kindhearted Methodist Church on the route hadn't served hot coffee to the freezing footballers. As we stood in line and waited to get into the stadium, we warmed our benumbed hands on the paper cups of hot coffee. Army won that year—23 to 7—but I was almost too cold to care. The next time I went to the Army-Navy game, things couldn't have been more different! I was the same girl, but the comet was in ascendancy.

෫෫ On December 16, we left for Christmas on Delaware Street. I sang a solo at Trinity on Christmas Eve, and made a wistful little note in my diary:

"Everything and everybody looks so good! Tonight I decorate the tree. I thought I might miss it this year. The fates are good!"

After Christmas, Mother and I rushed up to Kansas City to buy dresses for the Inauguration. We shopped madly—you know how it is. My dress was a simple gray-green woolen with a hat to match and I had a fur scarf. We got back to Washington on December 30, in time for Mother and Daddy to go to a big party given by Evalyn Walsh McLean at her fabulous home, Friendship.

I had a feverish cold, so I had to stay at home, and spent the evening playing my records. This is the way the momentous year ended, not with a bang but a sniffle!

7: Unofficial history

As a sometime student of history, I am aware that the events of the year 1945 will be chronicled in enormous and official detail for generations to come and schoolboys and schoolgirls unborn will be memorizing its dates and racking their brains for motivations, causes, and effects to write down on examination papers, unless things change radically. As an innocent bystander with a front-row seat, I can contribute little to the official record. But perhaps there is a place for unofficial history—for the wayward thoughts and the vagrant yearnings that beset the minor figure on such a stage; for the little disappointments, the unimportant fears, the mothlike anxieties that make us kin to the future and the past; for the small pleasures that make a girl in one century like a girl in any century.

For instance, it always seemed an irony to me that while I was living through that year of multiplied crisis, I was always busy with the crises of other places, other times. Until I graduated from college in fateful 1945, scarcely anything happened to me that did not coincide with a final examination!

The day my father became Vice-president of the United States was no exception. I intimated to Papa that they ought to change the date of the Inauguration, since it conflicted with my midyears, but this witticism did not make much of an impression. I took it up with my professors at George Washington, and while they did manage to let me out of an exam on Inauguration Saturday, they could not rearrange the college curriculum to suit my engagements. It was incumbent on me not to fail. Papa was going to be Vice-president and that would have made it so public. Vice-president or not, my father took a dim view of anything less than a B average.

The net result was that throughout the Inauguration festivities, with the possible exception of the time I stood on the Portico of the White House, I was weighed down with a big old blue book of English literature, required reading in Dr. Shepard's course in Victorian Poetry. Whenever an uncomplicated moment presented itself, I buried my nose in the book, endeavoring to fix in my memory some of the utterances of Matthew Arnold and his contemporaries. While the mid-twentieth century engulfed me, I was also wandering around in the mid-nineteenth. While the elected representatives of the people took office, Macaulay's Horatius was holding the bridge over the Tiber in iambic pentameter. While I was walking in the train of the Government of the United States, I was wrestling mentally with the Governments of Europe, one of my major courses.

On January 19, 1945, the day before the Inauguration, I had a heinous final. It took practically all day and our guests for the Inauguration were already arriving. Two of my friends from Kansas City, Harriet Allen and Mary Shaw, "Shawsie," were in town. The Truman and Wallace clans were gathering from all forks of the creek. We were still living in our smallish apartment on Connecticut Avenue, so that our friends and kinfolk had to be spread around. All the aunts and uncles stayed at the Carlton House. Grandmums Wallace and Shawsie stayed with us and Harriet Allen stayed with our next-door neighbors, the Davises. (Annette Davis Wright, their daughter, was and is one of my best friends.) However, our apartment was the meeting place and it was like Grand Central Terminal. People were popping in and out and sitting down to a sandwich or a cup of coffee at all hours of the day and night. There were all sorts of official and unofficial entertainment going on and we were going to receptions and luncheons, dinners and parties, and running home to change clothes for the next event. It would have been awfully exciting if the Governments of Europe or Victorian Poetry or Far Eastern Affairs hadn't been leering over my shoulder.

ફ્ On the morning of January 20, Inauguration Day, we were up at the crack of dawn. Religious services were held at 10 A.M. and protocol and good manners instructed that you did not keep people waiting. It was a cold, wet, miserable morning. As I got into my new dress it became apparent that I would not be able to get away with my new fur scarf, as planned. Mother put her foot down on that. I had to cover my glory with my school coat because it was the warmest, and no amount of complaining did any good. I tried to be philosophical, but why is it that when history is being made, something generally goes wrong with your clothes! When I met the present Queen of England I lost my petticoat. The night I was dancing with the President of Chile, my first strapless evening dress collapsed in the front!

The Inauguration of the President of the United States is by invitation only, and I cherished my invitation. I have it among my souvenirs. Only 7,800 people were invited to President Roosevelt's Fourth Inauguration—many of them disabled veterans. (This is considered a very small crowd.) Due to the fact that we were at war and President Roosevelt had unusual demands on his strength, festivities were kept at a minimum. Nevertheless, the city put on a gala appearance. There is nobody in Washington who is not affected by an Inauguration. The city just turns inside out. While the oath of office is usually taken on the steps of the Capitol, President Roosevelt chose on this occasion to be sworn in on the Portico of the White House.

Tickets of various colors had been issued by the committee in charge, to indicate where you stood. I had a blue ticket, which meant that I had a place on the Portico. Annette and Shawsie had red tickets, which meant that they had to stand on the lawn in ankle-deep slush. The weather was so bitter it's a wonder we all didn't come down with pneumonia!

As soon as the religious ceremonies were over, Mother and Dad went over to the Carlton House to round up the family and get them started. Then they were driven to the White House. A car had been ordered for Shawsie, Annette, and me, but we were never able to find it. I had to leave them and make my way to the Portico to be on time. I was standing between Mrs. Woodrow Wilson and Senator Byrd of Virginia.

I stood there shivering and trying to catch a glimpse of Shawsie or Annette in the crowd on the lawn. I was never able to locate them, or anybody else I knew in that sober and damp crowd. I felt lonely and sad while I waited, and every now and then I would be jabbed by an anxious thought of tomorrow's examination.

When the moment arrived, President Roosevelt came through the long French windows of the White House, onto the portico, in a wheel chair, propelled by his son James. He wore a dark suit and no overcoat and kept pushing back the long blue cape draped around his shoulders. James Roosevelt was in his dress uniform. President Roosevelt looked tired, and he made several impatient gestures to James and the people around him. He finally flung aside the cape when he stood up and was assisted by James to the podium. He stood there in the freezing wind, bareheaded and without a coat.

I suddenly felt horribly depressed. All the world seemed to me to have turned to gray ice. Even now, when I think of that day, a film of gray ice slides before my eyes. It was drizzling and freezing on the slippery streets, the sky was lowering and the cold, wet wind blew ceaselessly, but it was more than the weather. While I was preoccupied with these melancholy musings, President Roosevelt began his brief address of which I remember only the last line: "We have learned the simple truth, as Emerson said, 'that the only way to have a friend is to be one.'"

After the ceremonies, there was an official luncheon for the honored guests. The whole first floor of the White House was turned into one vast luncheon party, with the buffet in the State Dining Room. There must have been about 1,500 people present at this luncheon. President Roosevelt's physical condition was not equal to this festivity, but Mrs. Roosevelt and Mother and Daddy stayed through the whole thing, shaking hands with all 1,500. The luncheon was followed by a reception for a still larger group. Dad ducked out and went to his office and telephoned Mamma Truman in Grandview.

"Did you listen to the radio?" he asked her.

"Yes," Mamma Truman said. "I heard it all. Now you behave yourself up there, Harry. You behave yourself!"

Daddy had to promise his mother to behave.

I left and went home to take a nap, but Mother, that sterling character, and Mrs. Roosevelt, that stalwart woman, stayed all after-

78

noon and shook the hands of thousands. Mother didn't even get a chance to sit down, and dragged herself home just in time to get dressed for Mr. and Mrs. Robert Hannegan's reception. Mr. Hannegan was National Chairman of the Democratic party and this party was held at the Mayflower Hotel. I had a new, long, black dinner dress and a date for the evening with Joe Crowe from Independence. Joe came by after me and we went to the Blue Room of the Shoreham for dinner.

჻ The next day was Sunday and the Trumans had an old-fashioned Sunday dinner at the apartment, for the family. They were practically hanging from the rafters, but we made do. That afternoon the Stuart Symingtons and the John Snyders gave a reception for Mother and Dad and our guests. All my girl friends had been invited and this was the best party of all to me.

After the reception we girls went off by ourselves and had dinner, which gave me a chance to act natural. I was about to fall apart from poise and dignity. Jane Lingo, Annette Davis Wright, Mary Shaw Branton, Harriet Allen, and Caroline Turner made up the party and we hashed over everything that had happened during the week end. The best story was Annette's, and I felt slightly relieved to find that other people had trouble with their clothes in moments of history! While Annette and her mother were waiting in line for the reception on Inauguration Day, a strategic button had popped off of Annette's dress. Nothing daunted, her mother had whipped a needle and thread out of her purse, and sewed the button back on in full view of the assembled multitude. We all agreed that there is nothing like a mother!

The next day, Monday, was very busy and crowded. I had a luncheon for my girl friends. Daddy swore in his successor, Senator Briggs of Missouri, in a ceremony in the Senate Chamber. I took various members of the family on a sightseeing tour of Washington. Mrs. Lingo and Jane gave a tea for us and our guests and Grandmother Wallace took us to Hogate's, Washington's famous fish restaurant, for a fish dinner.

The next day everybody went home, and I folded. I came down with a sore throat—*e pluribus unum*—and was confined to my couch, where I improved each shining hour by writing the first of hundreds of thank-you notes. This industry has never closed down. There's hardly a day I don't have a shoal of thank-you notes to write, which means that I still have much to be grateful for.

My life did not change appreciably after Dad became Vice-president. (I got one break. The Vice-president is provided with a car and driver, so I could usually hitch a ride to school.) Mother and Dad were plunged into a social whirl, which they had avoided in the past. My father felt that he ought to meet as many people as he could in his new capacity, and my mother is a game girl. She kept her sense of humor and laughed in private at the pretentious and the social climbers and the publicity hounds. Nothing changes my mother. She is that independent lady from Independence— dignified, reticent, and unpretentious and busy keeping me the same, not to mention giving Dad a few sidelong glances.

We continued to live in our five-room apartment on Connecticut Avenue and we did not add frills or furbelows to our living stand-ard after my father became Vice-president. I am sure Dad's ex-penses increased, but he was a firm believer in living within his income.

If Dad had served his full term as Vice-president, he and my mother would certainly have had to do a certain amount of official entertaining. Our apartment was too small for this, but I presume they would have solved that problem when they came to it. When he was Senator from Missouri, Dad and Mother usually gave big dinners at a hotel. As far as I know, they never considered moving to a larger place.

In February and March Mother and Dad were busy going to functions, which seems to be part of the Vice-president's job. My father is gregarious and loves people, and while my mother has never courted social life, she is socially gracious and adept. I think they had a good time during the two-and-a-half months my father was Vice-president.

I used to be very proud of them when they were all dressed up for a party. My mother has the most beautiful blue eyes I ever saw, clear and sparkling and very direct. Her skin is fair and fine and her curly blond hair was then beginning to turn silver. It is now com-pletely gray. Dad has blond coloring and hazel eyes, which seem to change color, depending on the light or the color he is wearing. Mamma Truman used to say that she couldn't say exactly what color his eyes were herself. He had brown hair and there's still quite a lot of it left, but of course it's gray now. Mother had pretty clothes that year and it was exciting to see them both in full evening dress, or in the dignified party clothes of official afternoon functions. Once when they were standing at the curb waiting for the car to take them to a garden party at the British Embassy I could not resist leaning out of the window of the apartment and taking a snapshot of them as they set off.

The next big event of the year was President Roosevelt's birthday on January 31 and the March-of-Dimes campaign which drew an unusually juicy assortment of movie stars to Washington—Alan Ladd, Joe E. Brown, Jane Wyman, Kay Kyser, Linda Darnell, Suzanne Foster, Sue Carol, and Danny Kaye. It was my first close-up look at movie stars and, as one of America's leading movie fans from the age of four, I really enjoyed it. Dad, who knew my penchant well, brought home all their autographs on his place card from the official dinner.

Having survived my examinations and entered on the final leg of college, I was permitted to go to New York over the George Washington's Birthday holiday with Mary Jane Jacobs, the daughter of Admiral Jacobs. Mary Jane and I had the marvelous distinction, on this occasion, of going to dinner with eight men. There is nothing like having four escorts apiece to make a couple of girls feel comfortable. We went to the Stork Club, which was also new to me, so I was already in seventh heaven when we walked in and Mary Jane said to me, "Psst—don't look now, but there's Clark Gable!"

"Where?" I scoffed cynically. "Hanging on the wall?"

"Don't be a dope," Mary Jane hissed. "He's right over there—in the solid flesh!"

I looked, and so help me, he was. My jaw dropped, the way it does when you see Clark Gable in the solid flesh. I couldn't keep from staring at him. My four dates were unable to attract my attention the rest of the evening. All I could do was rivet my gaze on Gable. I can understand people rubbernecking. I tried to remember, when people started gaping at me a few months later, that I am one of the worst offenders.

I've never met Clark Gable to this day. Well, it's good to have something to live for!

A photographer came over to our table that evening and asked if he could take a picture. We thought it was a nice gesture and gave our permission. The week President Roosevelt died, a cropped version of it, showing me and one of the escorts, was published in a New York newspaper, captioned "Margaret Truman Night-clubbing"! The implication was that I was out having a gay old time while the rest of the nation was in mourning. Nothing was said about the picture having been made on February 23. That hurt my feelings.

In March I met Mrs. George Mesta for the first time. She invited me to a dinner at the Sulgrave Club, and Rosa Ponselle sang. I was introduced to the artist and she asked me to come to see her. I did not think much about the invitation, but a few days later she called and made a definite engagement, for the week end of March 17. Miss Ponselle lived in Baltimore, at Villa Pace. Mrs. Mesta was also invited for the week end and I went with her. The people at the house party were mostly much older than I but Betty Farley, Jim Farley's daughter, was there, and we roamed around together and had a pleasant time.

While I was at Villa Pace, I discovered that Rosa Ponselle had arranged for her voice coach to hear me sing. I sang for him and he was very encouraging. I found myself surprised to have such new friends take an interest in my voice. As a matter of fact, I was bewildered by it all, but Monday morning I was back at George Washington with the Governments of Europe and soon forgot it.

Mother and Dad and I went to a dinner that week honoring General Stillwell, and I met the General and also Mr. John Gunther. The last of March Dad had to go to New York to make a speech and he took Mother and me along. As a treat Dad took us to lunch at the 21 Club. This was my first visit to 21 and Mr. Kriendler gave me a conducted tour through the famous wine cellars of the place, which stretch far underground along 52d Street, almost to Fifth Avenue. All the machinery that had been part of the operation during Prohibition was intact, and the buried wine cellars are entered by what looks like a blank wall. A wire thrust into an invisible hole in this wall turns the mechanism and the wall folds back to display a great cavern of cobwebbed bottles of marvelous vintages. I bought my Easter hat in New York and we went back to Washington.

On Easter Sunday, April 8, Mother, Dad and I were invited to

Sunday luncheon by Evalyn Walsh McLean at her home. We went to early services at church and then set out for lunch. I loved Mrs. McLean. She was a genuinely kind, gracious person and gave the most marvelous parties in Washington. Her house, on M Street in Georgetown, was absolutely beautiful, one of the most beautiful houses I have ever seen. Her guest list was always composed of congenial people and she was a hostess who yearned to make everybody happy. She did not seem to entertain for a *reason* as some people in Washington did, but only because she was gregarious and loved a party.

That day, however, I thought I would starve. At these big affairs I was never seated anywhere near my father and mother, whose places were designated by protocol. Often I did not know anybody around me. On this particular day, the first course was a cold poached egg *en gelée*, surrounded by cold rice. I am sure this was a gourmet triumph, but I took a dim view of it. When the meat course came around, for some reason the service missed me, so I didn't have any lunch.

ॐ The following week I had a lot of plans. April 12 was Annette Wright's birthday and Mrs. Davis was having a birthday party for her. On the same evening I had a date with Marvin Braverman for dinner and the theatre, and we were going by Annette's party. I had a new dress and a new beau. I was happy and full of myself. Life was just a bowl of cherry blossoms.

I was already flying around the apartment getting dressed, when the telephone rang. I answered it. It was Dad.

"Hi, Dad," I greeted him jovially.

"Let me speak to your mother," he said. His voice sounded tight and funny.

"Are you coming home to dinner?" I inquired. "*I'm* going out!"

"Let me speak to your mother," Dad repeated, not rising to my bait.

"I only asked you a civil question!" I pouted into the phone.

"Margaret," my father said, "will you let me speak to your mother?"

"*Mother!*" I called, offended, and went back to making up my face.

Grandmums Wallace was staying with us at the time. I was

83

aware that after my mother had hung up the receiver, she had said something to her. But she had spoken in such a low voice and so quickly that I hadn't heard it, and I didn't pay much attention. I went into her room and Mother was standing there in an attitude of dejection with the tears running down her face.

"Mother!" I cried. "What's the matter? What is it?" I put my arm around her.

"President Roosevelt is dead!" Mother said.

"Dead!" I echoed stupidly.

The silence fell on the three of us like lead.

I am ashamed and guilty to remember that the larger implications of the tragedy did not occur to me immediately. It is the nature of unofficial history that grief and awe come later. I looked at the pouf of my dress and my dancing slippers and my white gloves and I thought about the play and the man who was going to take me to it and the birthday party and I felt like a child denied. It was simply that I, like a good many other people, I suppose, couldn't encompass the disastrous news. Nothing of its far-reaching effect on the world or its eternal effect on my own life communicated itself to me. I just wanted everything to be the way it had been ten minutes before!

"You had better change your clothes," Mother said crisply. The tears still stained her face.

I did not analyze her emotions at the time. I was too busy with my own. My mother is a mature and serious and private person. Along with her grief for a great man and a good friend, she must have looked down the unknowable future and shuddered. If I had had any perception, I might have been some comfort to her. But I couldn't collect myself.

"Call Marvin," Mother said. "But ask him not to mention it. No one knows. Then get dressed."

I dragged over to the telephone and put in the call.

"Marvin," I said. "I can't go tonight."

"What's the matter? Don't you feel well?"

"President Roosevelt is dead!"

I could almost see him rock back on his heels. His voice came over the wire in a whisper, after a shocked silence.

"Dead!"

Marvin told me later that it was several hours before the news

84

made any impression on him. He was standing in the lobby of the Statler returning the theatre tickets to the broker when the impact broke over him. He laid the tickets on the counter, went out, and walked aimlessly around the streets for hours and hours. This sort of thing happened to people all over the world that night—even to people who had never seen Mr. Roosevelt's face or heard his voice.

After I had spoken to Marvin, I began to dig around in my closet for something to wear. I got out a brown suit that seemed to be the only thing pressed. I didn't know what was going to be required of me, so I didn't know what to put on. I was standing there in my slip, trying to make up my mind, when the doorbell rang.

I was so confused that I opened the door in my slip.

A woman was standing there.

"Miss Truman?" she asked.

"Yes," I said.

"I'm from the Associated Press," she said. "I would like—"

Rage flowed through me. "I can't talk to you now," I cried and shut the door in her face.

That was the beginning.

When I opened the door in my slip to that press girl, it was the last time I ever opened a door without finding out who was there. It was at that moment that I ceased to be a free agent.

I finally got into the brown suit. Mother told me that a car was being sent for us. Dad had received the news in Speaker Sam Rayburn's office—the "Board of Education," they called it, where Democrats used to meet. Dad had gone straight to the White House and called Mother from there. We were to join him at the White House. I had been thinking of Daddy and his feelings about Roosevelt. It hadn't occurred to me that he was about to become President of the United States.

When we were ready, the Secret Service men took Mother and me out the back way. A crowd of curious people had already swarmed around the apartment building and the lawn was covered with photographers. As we came through the door, a glare of flashlights exploded in our faces. I had had an inkling of this sort of thing in Chicago, but now it seemed ugly and distasteful when President Roosevelt was lying dead in Georgia. I looked at Mother. Her face was grave and sad and also stoical.

"Come on," she said, and I followed her into the car.

85

When we got to the White House, Mrs. Roosevelt and her daughters-in-law were there. Mrs. Roosevelt looked white and strained but composed. Justice Stone and the members of the Cabinet and some of our old friends were waiting. My father was sworn in at 7:08 P.M. on April 12. The United States had been without a President for several hours, so my father was sworn in as the thirty-third President in a matter of minutes. Dad's face was grief-stricken and worried. I had a rush of compassion for him. I prayed my wordless prayers. "Give him the strength. Let everything be all right. Let him be equal to it. Let him live through it."

After that, Mother and I left the White House and went back to the apartment. Daddy followed us later. He seemed stunned, almost in a state of shock. General and Mrs. Davis and Annette were there when we got home. They had brought most of the food from Annette's canceled birthday party. Mrs. Davis fixed Dad a ham sandwich and a glass of milk and that was his first dinner as President of the United States. None of us had had anything to eat, so we nibbled the party food and the neglected birthday cake. Then everybody went away and, worn out with our emotions, we went to bed. My father says he went to bed and went to sleep and did not worry any more that day.

But it is the nature of unofficial history that a woman has to put cream on her face, pin up her hair, and lie staring into the dark, wondering.

8: The end and the beginning

The death of President Roosevelt cast a blight on the whole earth, but in Washington, grief was unusually personal. Many Washingtonians actually knew Mr. Roosevelt and most of them felt they did. He had lived there for twelve years. As soon as the news was known, aimless crowds began to walk disconsolately around the streets or collected in Lafayette Square to stare across at the White House. The radio poured out the progress of the funeral train, en route from Warm Springs, Georgia, and reported the stunned reactions of the world.

My father went to his new office for the first time on Friday, the thirteenth. We were at the crux of the war and there was certainly no time to lose. The Secret Service men came to the apartment and spirited him down the back stairs. The indefatigable press— reporters, cameramen, and microphones—were set up outside the office wing of the White House to meet him when he arrived. But I am sure the average person felt less interest in the living than in the dead that day.

It must have been a very difficult morning for my father. Many of the members of Mr. Roosevelt's loyal staff, who had suddenly become members of the staff of a different man, were in tears. Some of them had reasonable difficulty remembering that my father was President. He had a great many things on his mind—the reaction of the nation, our armed forces, and our allies to the death of a man they had literally worshiped . . . what might happen to the war effort, to war production, to our relationships with other countries. His first official act as President was the signing of the proclamation for Mr. Roosevelt's funeral—not a happy duty.

The funeral train arrived from Georgia about ten o'clock on Saturday morning. It was a hot, steamy day, unusually warm for April. Spring had come early that year. The grass was already green and the tulips blazed in the parks and gardens. The hot sun beat down on the massed thousands who lined the streets, and added to their discomfort. My father went to the station, accompanied by Secretary of Commerce Henry Wallace and Senator James F. Byrnes, to meet the Roosevelt family and ride back in the procession.

The funeral procession was an impressive sight. The Army Band, playing a slow march, was followed by the Guard of Honor, composed of men selected from all branches of the armed services, preceding the caisson which was drawn by six white horses. The people were packed into Lafayette Square, as far as the eye could see, but the silence was incredible. There wasn't a whisper. The only sounds were the muffled drums, the clop of the horses' feet, and the drone of Air Force planes over the city as the cortege crept along.

At three-thirty that afternoon Mother and I joined Daddy at the White House to attend the state funeral which was held at four o'clock in the East Room. The East Room is enormous—wide, deep, and high-ceiled—but every inch of the four walls, from ceiling to floor, was covered with flowers. Floral offerings were heaped and stacked around the catafalque, which bore the bronze casket, in wild profusion. The scent of jasmine, tuberoses, and lilies came in suffocating waves through the humid atmosphere. The room was jammed with people, standing in close proximity, and this intensified the heat of the day. Many of them were dignitaries. I remember seeing Crown Princess Martha of Norway; Mr. Anthony Eden; Emir Faisal of Saudi-Arabia; the Earl of Athlone, Governor General of Canada; Mr. Bernard Baruch; Mr. James A. Farley; Governor Dewey, Mr. Harry Hopkins, and Mr. Henry Wallace.

No breeze stirred the long red curtains of the East Room and it was almost impossible to breathe. The perspiration ran out of my hair and trickled down my neck in a steady rivulet. Occasionally above the melancholy music there would be the sound of muffled sobbing. My old feeling of claustrophobia, induced by crowds, began to settle on me. To maintain my poise I concentrated my attention on Bishop Dun, who was conducting the simple Episcopal service. He was wearing the traditional vestments and he was very warm. His face was flushed scarlet from the heat and one single droplet of perspiration had run off his forehead, down the bridge of his nose and was now balanced precariously on the end of it.

I hesitate to report that I stared at the drop of perspiration, thinking, as one will in moments of almost hysterical solemnity, the kind of idiotic thoughts for which one feels immediate shame: "Will it fall off? Will it stay there? Will he wipe it away?"

Bishop Dun didn't even notice it. The drop of perspiration on the Bishop's nose was presently joined by another, larger drop, and they fell off of their own dead weight, on the front of his vestment. I was stricken with guilt and stared up at the little rainbows created by the prisms of the chandeliers. The waves of jasmine continued to roll over me and I thought with compassion of President Roosevelt's children—Anna and Elliot, who were in the room, and James, Franklin, and John who were all away in the war. I knew what a good father meant. Finally it was over and the people filed out.

I accompanied my father and mother on the funeral train to Hyde Park that night. The reports of the state funeral had only intensified the crowds along the streets. They were still packed, shoulder to shoulder, in Lafayette Square at 9:30 P.M. when the cortege left the Portico and moved along the East Drive. Down the length of Constitution Avenue the people were crowded to the walls of the buildings and they were massed by the thousands around the Union Station. Over all there still brooded that curious, heavy, almost tangible stillness. They never uttered one sound when the flag-draped casket was placed in the glass-walled, illuminated railroad car, surrounded by a fantasia of flowers. The Army Band played *Nearer, My God, to Thee* and the train moved slowly off into the hot, damp night on its mournful journey to Hyde Park.

I will never forget that ride. Of course it was impossible to sleep. We were all too strung-up and nervous and miserable. We had begun to recover from our numbness and to experience the deep sense of personal grief that the loss of President Roosevelt occasioned. My mother made me go to bed, for I was practically stumbling with

89

weariness, but I lay sleepless in the dark. The train moved with the slow solemnity of the funeral march, pausing at many intervals. When we made our first stop I raised the shade a fraction to stare out into the starless night.

I stared straight into the serried ranks of faces, packed along the side of the track—thousands of them, motionless and soundless, seeming to press against the very panes of the windows. It was as if they had ceased to breathe—row on row on row of impassive, solemn faces—devoid of curiosity, but bowed down in mute sorrow or uplifted in mute reverence. It seemed an intrusion to look on their naked grief. I lowered the shade.

When we stopped in Philadelphia, I raised the shade to the top. Not only were the people pressed into every available foot of space in the railroad yards, on the station platforms, ramps, and tracks, but they ran like a silent river up that great bridge that overlooks the North Philadelphia Station and were massed on the bridge in a motionless phalanx, patient as dumb animals.

As we moved along the flare-lit track, I never roused during the night and looked out that the faces weren't there. And there seemed to be no sound in the world, not even in nature—not a night bird's cry or a cricket's voice. When I remember the death of President Roosevelt, I always think of that preternatural quiet.

We arrived in Hyde Park about nine-thirty the next morning and drove in the funeral procession to Mr. Roosevelt's childhood home by the Hudson. There, in the rose garden, a simple and beautiful ceremony took place and Mr. Roosevelt was buried in the place he loved best. I stood between the Honorable Mackenzie King, the Prime Minister of Canada, and the Earl of Athlone. Mr. Mackenzie King, a paragon of kindness, kept smiling at me to give me courage.

In my diary I wrote:

Sunday, April 15, 1945 (Clear)
The ceremony at the grave was simple and very impressive. Cadets from West Point were there and fired a salute. He is buried in the garden as he wished to be.

We left Hyde Park at noon to return to Washington. The train was crowded with national leaders, elder statesmen, and dignitaries. Dad spent the afternoon working on the speech he proposed to deliver to Congress on Monday morning, which he felt was the most important one he would ever utter. His chief concern was for the armed services. He wanted, in some way, to reassure them that all would be well.

A great crowd of people met the train when it pulled into Washington. Silence had given way to tears. My father pointed out an old Negro woman to me. She was sitting on the curb, crying as if her heart would break. Most of the men and women on Constitution Avenue were weeping. They had come to welcome my father, but they could not cease to mourn at once. Nobody understood that better than he did. I shared the general emotion, and I felt depressed.

Mamma Truman summed it up when she said, "I cannot really be glad that my son is President, because I am sorry that President Roosevelt is dead. If he had been voted in, I would be out waving a flag, but it does not seem right to be happy or wave flags now."

&⤳ The next day was Monday and we had to move.

I noted in my diary:

Monday, April 16, 1945
We are moving to Blair House across from the State Dept. today. It is perfectly beautiful. All old and priceless. Visiting dignitaries stay there. Dad is the first President to do so.

It often seems to me that I have been packing and moving all my life. For a string saver and accumulator of trivia, as I am, this can be quite a problem. All our furniture had to be emptied, crated, and shipped back to Independence, with the exception of my piano, which I could not get along without. This meant emptying drawers and chests and stowing things away I thought I wouldn't need.

In order to afford Mrs. Roosevelt leisure in the dismantling of her personal possessions, Dad chose to move into Blair House, and I think this was fortunate for me. I have always adored Blair House and I spent about three years there before my father's administration was over. I hope it will not seem like heresy when I say that I prefer it to the White House. It was more like a home, and I was never one for the grand manner.

Blair House is located on Pennsylvania Avenue (a stone's throw from the White House), an old, square, yellow building, four stories high, with long windows and beautifully proportioned rooms. It is well over a hundred years old, begun in 1824, I believe, by a Dr. Joseph Lovell, an Army surgeon in the War of 1812 and subsequently Surgeon General of all the armies. It was sold, on the death of Dr. Lovell in 1836, to Francis Preston Blair, a newspaperman and member of President Jackson's "kitchen cabinet." It remained consistently in the Blair family until 1942 when the Federal Government purchased it as a residence for the entertainment of visiting kings, nobles, foreign ministers, and other distinguished visitors.

Blair House is steeped in the history of the United States. General William Tecumseh Sherman was married there. It was there that Abraham Lincoln offered Robert E. Lee the generalship of the Northern Armies and Lee made his decision to stay with Virginia. Captain David Farragut was visiting at Blair House when he was apprised that he had been chosen to command the Union forces at the Battle of New Orleans, during the Civil War. He went on to become the First Admiral.

The house has the greatest charm. The first floor comprises a pair of beautiful drawing rooms, elegantly furnished with fine Early American and French pieces, Aubusson rugs, crystal chandeliers and gilt-framed mirrors, and a wood-paneled dining room. On the second floor there is a library, looking out over the small back garden. There are seven bedrooms on the upper floors, mostly provided with their own sitting rooms and baths.

Mrs. Victoria Geaney, who presides over Blair House as housekeeper, is a delightful woman whose life work is to make the guests in the house comfortable. She maintains an excellent staff, including a cook named Jane, whose culinary art surpasses everybody's—with the possible exception of Vietta's. We settled down to being cherished in short order.

The next morning I had to go back to school. No matter what transpired in those days, school awaited me at the end.

It now became necessary for me to ride to school in a car. I did not find this particularly onerous! It was a great improvement over the bus, and I was placed under the jurisdiction of a Secret Service man, John Dorsey. Mr. Dorsey trailed me for years and we became good friends. That first morning I felt a little stiff about being protected, but otherwise things seemed normal. I was unprepared for the swarm of reporters and photographers who converged on me at school. In fact, I was on the point of tears when I was rescued by some of my professors at George Washington and given sanctuary in a room until I could collect myself.

I have made it a rule never to try to run from photographers or to prevent their taking their shots. Taking pictures is their business and they mean to take pictures, with or without the victim's cooperation. If you act coy or antagonize them, they may take bad pictures—and, I sometimes feel, on purpose!

I have the misfortune to photograph badly. I usually look twenty pounds heavier and ten to fifteen years older than I actually am. I do not say this out of vanity, nor did I arrive at the conclusion on my own. The people who know me have said it consistently. My coloring, which is light (I refer to it as washed-out), disappears in the lens. My green eyes fade and any circles that happen to be under them accentuate. My hair is generally described as ash-blond (it is naturally pale) but in photographs it becomes a drab no-color. My face has a bad side and a good side in profile, and I look much better full-face, but I am rarely photographed thus! All my photographs are deceptive. Some have flattered me and others have been so unattractive as to furnish grounds for libel, but none of them really looks like me.

By cooperating with photographers, I have come out less a scarecrow than I might have done. In turn, photographers have cooperated with me. When I have asked them not to photograph me in shorts, slacks, or bathing suit, or in situations that might embarrass my family or me, they have desisted. Only one photographer ever took advantage of me this way and he was belabored by his fellows, so that I didn't have to chastise him. I never quite forgave him. I'm not vindictive, but I don't forget.

Unaccustomed as I was to being photographed, I decided to let the photographers have at it that day. I was photographed in the car, out of the car, on the steps of the School of Government, in the corridors, in the classroom, with my classmates, with my professors, alone, drinking chocolate ice-cream sodas, and from whatever other angles the photographers thought up.

We didn't get much education done at George Washington but I thought the only sensible thing to do was to give them a field day, after which, presumably, they would let me alone. My professors were sympathetic to my problem, with the possible exception

93

of Dr. Shepard of the English Department, who wanted to get on with his subject without benefit of popping flashbulbs. After the pictures, in which Dr. Shepard's scholarly face loomed, were printed in newspapers far and wide and he began to hear from his old students from all over the world (many George Washington graduates go into foreign service), he was slightly mollified.

The effect on my college career of being my father's daughter was less difficult than might be supposed, because my friends and professors understood the situation and were willing to keep the status quo. It is true that my opinions on world affairs, uttered in the cloistered classroom, were sometimes reported in the newspapers. Since my opinion didn't amount to a hill of beans and had no more background than anybody else's, this was ridiculous, but I did have to think twice before I said anything about anything, even when the teacher asked me a direct question.

Outwardly the chief change in my routine derived from being under constant surveillance of the Secret Service. Mr. Dorsey was a discreet and thoughtful bodyguard and I often forgot he was there. (This is the highest compliment I can pay a bodyguard.) My friends were less accustomed than I to being trailed. Gone were the days of loitering on Connecticut Avenue, shopping and dawdling with the girls. I had to ride home in state.

As I have said, watchfulness wasn't new to me—an only child—and there were times when it seemed to me that Dad could easily have qualified for the Secret Service! I'll never forget the time I was bidden to a dance at West Point and Daddy decided that it would be a good time for him to go up there and inspect the place. He was the Senator from Missouri then, and I don't suppose there is any way to prevent a Senator from inspecting West Point if he takes it into his head to do so. At least I couldn't think of one!

Senator Truman entrained for West Point and put up at the Thayer Inn, but it seemed to me that he was more interested in where I was going, with whom, when I was coming back, and what I was going to do, than he was in the ramparts of the fortress. I had a terrible time with him. He wasn't being difficult; he was just interested. If I had been more mature then, I might have realized that one of the dreams of his life had been to attend West Point, from which he was prevented by his bad eyesight, and that maybe he only wanted to know what one of those dances was really like. Anyway, I was accustomed to being guarded.

The Secret Service is a brave, useful, and tactful organization, endlessly efficient, and there were times when it was a relief to have them roll up, change a tire, summon a cab, catch up with the milk train to Washington so I could get home, and otherwise look after their footless charge. I suppose it was human nature that made me take a fiendish delight in trying to cross them up occasionally or enjoying it immoderately when they made one of their few mistakes. It was because they were so relentlessly perfect, tireless, and—like Mother—knew best! But Mr. Dorsey and I got on famously.

One of the problems of continuous surveillance in the case of a person like me is the handicap the Secret Service offers to escorts and beaus. As everybody who can read English or any number of foreign languages must know, the press (and I don't know how many of the general public) yearned to get me married, or at least engaged, while I was a tenant of the White House. It would have given the news a romantic fillip and been good for business! There were times when I may have felt wistful to go along with this program, if it would only offer the chance of becoming a private citizen again, but actually, I had made up my mind early in the game that I would not marry while I lived in the White House.

While I am not silly enough to suppose that being watched over by the Secret Service had any real effect on romance, I ask you to consider the effect of saying good night to a boy at the door of the White House in a blaze of floodlights, with a Secret Service man in attendance. There is not much you can do except shake hands, and that's no way to get engaged!

One of the unexpected things about my new life was the interest that was suddenly generated in my romantic affairs, which up to then had bothered nobody but me and maybe Mother! Even the *George Washington Hatchet*, my school newspaper, and hopefully friendly to me, plastered the front page on April 17 with a story headed: "Boss' Daughter Great Catch for Anyone." This embarrassed me and hurt my feelings, but it was only the beginning. There is scarcely a periodical in existence which has not speculated at some time or other, ad nauseam, on my spinster state and how to put an end to it. I have learned to ignore this sort of thing and laugh the rumors off, but some of the men whose names have been coupled with mine (usually erroneously) have got into real tizzies.

&⤷ We had dinner that first night, *en famille*, at Blair House, reporting the cares and excitements of the day to each other. Mrs. Geaney had done us proud. It was a wonderful dinner. I am always glad to remember how well-nourished we were during those pioneering weeks, which were crowded and bedizening, as this excerpt from my diary will show:

Wednesday, April 18, 1945 (Clear)
Things are beginning to take shape and routine.
 The Lingos, Mrs. Davis, Mrs. Ricketts, Mrs. Miekelsen and Annette came over. Mr. Board was here to dinner. Reathel Odum is now Mother's private secretary. Blevins Davis came to call with Mr. Steward.

Thursday, April 19, 1945
People called all afternoon and right up to dinner time. We had to put them all on a schedule to make connections.

Saturday, April 21, 1945 (Clear; cloudy; rain)
I had a fitting with the tailor at 11:30. I went over to the White House to see the rooms and I will have a sitting room and a bedroom and bath. The White House upstairs is a mess and looks awful. I was so depressed when I saw it. The furniture is so old. They are painting now.

Sunday, April 22, 1945 (Clear)
Mother, Dad and I went to the Walter Reed chapel to church today. Then we called on General Pershing! Such *excitement!*

In that brief sojourn at Blair House we tried to orient ourselves and prepare for the experience before us. I hardly need to repeat that my father reiterated his hope that we could remain a private family in the middle of public life or mention my mother's fears that we might not be able to do that. Although we had breakfast, lunch, and dinner together, there was usually somebody with us all the time now and we were all so intensely busy that we had very little time to discuss the future except for a quiet word here and there when we found ourselves alone for a few minutes.

Even if things had been different, I don't think we would have had any long-drawn-out conversations on the subject, because we have never done that as a family. All three of us take things as they come, cope with them, dispose of them the best we can, and go on to the next thing. I have never looked far ahead or set my heart on something in the future. It has saved disappointment. I don't look far ahead now. I keep an open mind and try to remain as flexible as possible since this seems to me to be the best philosophy for survival.

As a family, we had a code, which was to do the right thing, do it the best we could, never complain and never take advantage. When my father became President, our code did not change. We clung to it, and that is the way we lived. I never brooded on my prerogatives or sacrifices as the President's daughter. I tried not to think about it at all. If I had let myself think about it, the enormity of it would have swamped me.

If my father and mother discussed these matters between themselves, they did not bring them to my attention. I dare say they talked about it in the modicum of privacy they had left, but fathers and mothers rarely communicate such conversations to their children. My father did not change in any way when he became President. Neither did my mother. Neither did I. Everything around us changed, but we were exactly the same people we had always been.

On April 20, Mrs. Roosevelt, who had been working night and day, had supervised the loading of the thirteenth truck of the Roosevelt's personal possessions, said good-by to her staff in the East Room, and returned to private residence. The following morning Mother and I, as noted, went over to inspect the President's private quarters on the second floor of the White House and to decide on decoration. The White House is a very old building and while the public may feel that the President is supported in luxurious comfort from viewing the public rooms on the first floor, the furnishings of the private quarters leave much to be desired. They are frazzled from years of use by families in transience.

The second floor looked unusually barny and gloomy that day. I was determined to have something cheerful. As a special concession to me, a corner closet was built in my bedroom to replace one of the old wardrobes which pass for closets in the White House, which was built before clothes closets came into general use. I chose Wedgwood blue for the walls and woodwork of my sitting room, which had a pretty marble fireplace. In this room I decided on curtains of flowery chintz and rust-red sofas, to flank the fireplace. My piano was put in this room, along with my record player and record collection. Eventually a spinet piano was added to the musical equipment, so that Annette and I could go on playing our piano duets.

Mother's suite was done in lavender and gray—lavender in the bedroom and gray for the sitting room—and Dad's bedroom was painted cream-colored, while the walls of his study were off-white. His desk was at a window overlooking the Washington monument, and he had a piano in his study. The large central hall was painted a light Nile green. When the painting and refurbishing were finished the place looked much refreshed, but it was impossible to make these rooms cozy or homelike. Their size and shape prevented this and the atmosphere of the institutional somehow hung over them.

We moved into the White House on the eighth of May, my father's birthday. We didn't do much in the way of celebrating his anniversary—we were too busy straightening out our dresser drawers!

The month of May whizzed by in a swarm of activity, interspersed, as ever, with exams. The general details are reflected in my diary:

Tuesday, May 8, 1945
We're still moving in. My bedroom is pink with antique white furniture. Deep pink draperies and white window curtains. Flowered chintz on 2 chairs. It also has a fireplace and mirror. High (25 ft.) ceilings. The bath is eggshell white and is enormous.

Tuesday, May 15, 1945
Mrs. Bob Hannegan gave me an Irish setter puppy and he arrived today. He is adorable. I have named him "Mike." He is *so* cute and red and has long floppy ears.

[N.B. Mike was a dear, but didn't have a grain of sense. He promptly fell in one of the fountain pools and Reathal had to go after him in her clothes to keep him from drowning!]

Wednesday, May 16, 1945
I had an exam in Governments of Europe. It was a very fair exam. I wrote *seventeen pages!*

Thursday, May 17, 1945
I had an exam in Philosophy. One question! Don't think I did so well in this.

Friday, May 18, 1945
No exam, slept late, thank goodness.

Saturday, May 19, 1945
I had exam in Victorian Poetry. Was a catalogue of poems and poets. Lousy exam!

The photogs took pix of Mike today for ½ hour. He did nobly.

Marvin Braverman took me to see *Sing Out Sweet Land*. Then to Statler to eat and see late floor show and dance.

Sunday, May 20, 1945 (Clear)
Mamma Truman, Grandmums, Aunt Mary, Dad, Mother, Rea and I all went down the river for a short jaunt on the *Williamsburg*.

Tonight Rea (Reathel Odum) & I went to Evalyn McLean's for dinner. I sat by Justice Frank Murphy.

Monday, May 21, 1945
Tonight Capt. Everett Walk called and we went to Mrs. Goodwin's to practice the Virginia Reel for the Pan-American Day show on Friday. My feet are worn to a nub.

Tuesday, May 22, 1945 (Clear)
Marvin Coles took me to dinner at Army-Navy Town, then to see a play: *Snafu* (Situation Normal All Fouled Up). It was very funny. I had a very good time.

One great discovery that I soon made about the White House was that you could *command* films. You could see any movie you wanted, past or present, simply by expressing a wish. As one of the most confirmed movie-goers of the twentieth century this broke on me with sheer delight. I began to see that there was some small virtue in being the President's daughter. While not given to command, I instantly began to make a list of all the pictures I had loved, containing all the heroes I had adored, and to ask for them.

If a picture was good, seeing it once merely served to whet my appetite. I could see it over and over again and the operators of the White House projectors must have got rather weary of *Naughty Marietta*, which ran a marathon with *The Scarlet Pimpernel*. *The Scarlet Pimpernel* won. I saw it a total of sixteen times. I'm sure this is a world's record.

Other benisons of White House living emerged and I began to

99

feel more cheerful. On May 13, the period of official mourning for President Roosevelt came to an end, and the following day my father invited Bob Hope and his traveling troupe to the White House. They gave the show they had been performing for GI's in all the war zones. It was screamingly funny—a marvelous production—and there was Bob himself, in the flesh, not just a shadow on the screen.

I was introduced to him and he stood there chatting with me— as delightful off stage as on.

"If I'd known you were coming"—I began.

"You'd have baked a cake," he said.

"No," I said. "I'd have brought my whole sorority!"

That was the beginning of many happy acquaintances in the theatre which I continue to treasure. Theatre people have fired my love for their art and kept it blazing. My penchant for charming mummers once caused my mother to adjure my chaperone, when I started on a concert tour, "Whatever else you do, don't let her marry an actor!"

The settling-in process at the White House was often confusing, often exciting. Once more I had about Washington the feeling of being a visitor. The transition from a five-room apartment, where I often washed the dishes and ironed my own clothes, to that great antiquity with its vaulted ceilings, enormous bathrooms, no closets, and an enormous staff of servants, fresh flowers from the greenhouses every day, cars and chauffeurs, housekeepers, butlers, maids, valets, gardeners, ushers, guards, social, private, press, and several other kinds of secretaries, aides, protocol experts was bedizening. It was a while before I realized that the demands made on the nation's highest public officer make all this machinery necessary in order to enable him and his family to accomplish what they have to get through every day.

At first it was like having a suite in an old-fashioned luxury hotel (I *couldn't* be actually *living* there, I thought) except that at a hotel you could pay your money and take your choice. Here the social calendar was handled by elaborate channels. Invitations were studied and conferred on, replies were dispatched, and you kept appointments which were often formidable. Service, even in the family dining room, was formal and elaborate and while this did not ameliorate the institutional quality of the food, it was most impressive. One's rooms were tidied and kept in order. One's clothes were pressed and cared for. One's every wish was considered with the greatest courtesy—even one's whims—and yet the feeling persisted that one was a reluctant guest of the state with appropriate sacrifice of freedom. In such large establishments, impersonality cannot be avoided and the atmosphere simply could not rise to the casual and carefree spirit which had always illuminated my home. One must conduct oneself with dignity. One was forever on stage.

I used to escape to the Davises', to spend the night with Annette in our old apartment house, with such a sense of relief and release that it amounted to pure bliss. I was interested—I was often enthralled—with my new life, but I missed what I had always had. I missed the spur-of-the-minute dates, the relaxed conversation, the icebox raiding, the easy give-and-take of home life, the phone calls, the boys who just dropped by, the spontaneity of living. Since I had really done nothing personally to deserve the luxury in which I found myself embedded, I felt required to be extra considerate and grateful. I was, but I missed *home*.

9: 1600 Pennsylvania Avenue
— National 1414

Shortly after we moved to the White House Leonard Lyons reported in "The Lyons Den" that I had called some of my sorority sisters and said, "I hope that my father's becoming President won't affect our good friendship." I don't remember this, but if Leonard said it, it must be true. I am forced to admit that 1600 Pennsylvania Avenue is a forbidding address for somebody who is twenty-one. I always felt awkward about giving it to a salesclerk as a place to deliver a package, and I did say to some of my friends in the early stages, "I hope you won't forget all about me now that I'm living in the White House." People do feel shy about running spontaneously into that imposing structure with their hair done up in pin curls and the like.

I got around this hazard as fast as possible. I made it known to the telephone operators that I was available when my friends called National 1414 and gave their names. Of course, this was after I found out the telephone number myself. The day after we moved to 1600 Pennsylvania, I was doing some chores for Mother in town and had to telephone her. When I got into the phone booth I realized I didn't know my own phone number. It wasn't a number you just look up and I felt embarrassed to ask an operator for it, so I went home and found out what it was.

The White House guards soon got accustomed to the sight of Jane Lingo, Annette Wright, Drucie Snyder, and a number of other girls and rarely challenged them. When I had a new beau or a first-time caller, I would leave the name at the gate. I encouraged my crowd to meet in my suite, if we were going out in the evening, or to come back there after the party was over. It was central. My sitting room was the scene of numerous hilarious occasions when we played noisy card games, such as "Michigan" or "Spit," down on the floor on our hands and knees.

In an effort to give my life some semblance of home, Daddy and Mother would often come into my sitting room when I was expecting people and stay to greet them, as they would have done in Independence. There was a small kitchen on the third floor for our family use and I kept this stocked with cheese and cold meats, bread and butter, soft drinks and the makings of hot chocolate, so we could raid a normal-size refrigerator.

The state affairs that went on on the first floor of the White House were endlessly fascinating to me whether I was personally involved or peering, like a child, over the balustrade at the party swirling below. The public rooms of the White House, which many of you must have seen at one time or another, are gracious and dignified. The first floor comprises a five-room suite, which is entered through a white marble foyer.

The East Room is the largest reception room. It is dominated by great marble fireplaces surmounted by gilt-framed mirrors that reach to the ceiling, flanked by branched candelabra. Magnificent crystal chandeliers hang from the ceiling. The wainscoted walls and ceiling have elaborately decorated moldings and the massive windows are hung with damask, falling from gilt cornices. The parquet floor is kept waxed to a high state of perfection and an enormous concert grand piano, supported by three gold eagles and decorated with a frieze of golden figures, occupies one corner. The East Room is actually the ballroom of the White House, where most of the dancing is done.

The Green Room has walls of green damask, damask chairs, a rug in which the Great Seal of the President is woven, and portraits of past Presidents on the wall—notably John Quincy Adams and

James K. Polk. (When we were in the White House we moved these portraits around to afford the Democrats the most prominent positions!)

The Blue Room is a graceful oval in shape, with a huge crystal chandelier in the center. It has a curved marble mantel, to conform with the curving walls, surmounted by a French clock. The walls are hung with blue silk brocade, above a white dado, and the hangings are patterned brocade, with heavy valances spangled with gold stars. The furniture is white and gold, with brocaded upholstery in blue, and there are gold stars on most of the decorations. The floor is bare, to display the fine parquet and because the Blue Room is largely used as a reception area.

The Red Room is also walled with damask and has a fabulous chandelier, a marble mantel with a portrait of Grover Cleveland hanging above it, comfortable sofas and chairs.

The State Dining Room has paneled walls, massive furniture, and a great table. The floor is carpeted and the chairs are high-backed and imposing. Above the marble mantel is the portrait of Abraham Lincoln. When the table is laid for a State dinner with the gold plate, crystal, flowers, and great branched candelabra, it is a sight to see. I always slipped downstairs before the guests came to look at it.

That always pleased Fields, the head butler, who was the major-domo of the State Dining Room. Where all the housekeeping executives and ushers left off, Fields took up. He was the veteran of several administrations and had probably served more kings, queens, princesses and princes, prime ministers and diplomats than anybody in the United States. Fields was proud of the quality of his service and was an imposing figure in the State Dining Room.

While it was impossible for me to think of the public rooms of the White House as home (and no reason to do so, since they belong as much to all the citizens of the United States as to the incumbent tenants), they had a splendor, especially just before a party, that unfailingly awakened a thrill. When the Marine Band, in their red coats, were massed to play and the flowers and greens were newly arranged and the light refracted from the beautiful chandeliers and the gold plate there was a festiveness about it all that I will never forget.

Still, I loved best the private parties we sometimes had at the end of the second-floor lounge, which was furnished and arranged in some semblance of a living room. Here we entertained our personal friends and were able to relax and be ourselves.

My own room was admittedly girlish—I was a girl when I went there—and the newspapers were always mentioning the stuffed animals and dolls on the bed. I used to keep a little clutch of donkeys there in honor of the Democratic party, and a French sailor doll which had been given me by a group of French school-children. The Gunston alumnae used to stuff animals for Christmas toys for one of their altruistic projects, and I was disquieted to note once that I also had a clutch of stuffed elephants who looked very Republican on my bed. Fortunately, the papers never photographed that! I kept my collection of demitasse cups and Meissen and Dresden china in a vitrine in the sitting room, and when my pictures were hung, my personal photographs and souvenirs scattered about, and the piano in place, my rooms had a feeling of home or as much of that atmosphere as could be transmitted to a transient situation.

One of the first official entertainments in the White House after we moved there was given in honor of the Prince Regent of Iraq. He came on the twenty-eighth of May and was invited to tea, which was poured in the Red Room. The Prince's arrival was treated with great pomp and ceremony. He got there on the dot of 5 P.M., accompanied by his entourage. The Guard of Honor saluted with many ruffles and flourishes and the Navy Band played the Iraqi National Anthem, followed by *The Star-Spangled Banner*. My father met the Prince on the Portico, to greet him and offer the hospitality of the house, surrounded by a battery of photographers. Mother stood just inside the door. Mrs. Helm, the White House social secretary, and I waited in the Red Room.

I was naturally overwhelmed with curiosity and kept peering through the door.

"Which is the Prince?" Mrs. Helm whispered.

"I think it's the one wearing the lace curtain!" I piped up.

My mother gave me a monumental frown and shushed me.

The party advanced with measured tread, and I was presented and received his Royal Highness's greeting. He was young and very good-looking—modest to the point of shyness—and spoke beautiful English. We all had tea and stood about chatting and then I noticed that my father had spirited the Prince and Ali Jawdat, the Iraquian Ambassador, Captain Harry Vaughan, and Captain Vardamon to his private quarters upstairs. I got the impression that someone had expressed a wish for a beverage slightly stronger than tea!

The Prince was entertained at a State dinner that evening to which no ladies were invited. The table was decorated with mirrors, the gold candelabra and gold plate and was so gorgeous it almost put your eyes out.

Subsequently Reathel Odum and I went to a reception for the Prince Regent at the Shoreham Hotel, where he gallantly recalled our tea-party talk.

&. A constant stream of requests for my mother and me to appear at public functions and do things had begun to pour in. One of Mother's first official entertainments was a party for all the Washington newspaperwomen who were anxious to see our private quarters on the second floor. We gave them a guided tour and tea and conversation. They were very pleasant and I made many friends among the ladies of the Washington press. My mother did not hold press conferences and has never given an interview to this day, but she enjoyed entertaining the press girls, as she would have done at home, and attended their social functions.

Mother was shortly invited to christen two new Air Force bombers at Washington Airport and I was selected as maid of honor at this launching. Unfortunately the Air Corps hadn't seen to it that the Treasury Department scored one of the bottles of champagne and it simply wouldn't break. Ah me! I thought we never were going to get that plane christened and off the ground. I don't know whether you've ever tried to break a champagne bottle by slamming it against the side of an airplane or not, but it's not easy.

After about six failures I announced audibly, "If Mother can't break that bottle, nobody can!"

"Be quiet!" Mother hissed in my direction, furious at the recalcitrant bottle.

"Fine thing for a shot-put champion!" I told her later.

My mother declared I could never be maid of honor for her again.

Around that time (it was the twenty-seventh of May to be exact), I decided to sleep in Lincoln's bed. When we moved into the second floor, all the Monroe furniture reproductions, which had been added to the White House private apartments by Mrs. Herbert Hoover, were moved back into the Monroe sitting room and Lincoln's bed was returned to the old Lincoln study, where President Lincoln had signed the Emancipation Proclamation. It's an overpowering old bed—bulbous, carven, gloomy, dark, and—I'm here to tell you—lumpy!

I don't know why I wanted to sleep in Lincoln's bed, except that there was a legend around the White House that Abraham Lincoln's shade sometimes reappeared in his room. The maids and butlers were always claiming that he came back and it was rumored that Mrs. Calvin Coolidge had actually *seen* his apparition.

I wasn't so brave in the end that I wanted to conduct this experiment alone. I finally enlisted two cohorts who were as eager and willing as I was. Jane Lingo and Annette Wright brought their toothbrushes and nightgowns and after a happy, lachrymose evening with Jeanette MacDonald in *Springtime*, we three repaired to Lincoln's study and retired.

We retired but not to sleep. It wasn't Lincoln's ghost that bothered us. It was simply impossible to get comfortable in that bed. While it was certainly large enough to hold the three of us, no matter which way we tried it, it was more uncomfortable than the last. We slept up and down, lengthwise, crosswise, and catawampus. We tried sleeping at the foot and in the middle and at the head. Nothing worked. We got the giggles, wound up on the floor and talked all night. I'm sure this was the only slumber party ever held in Lincoln's bed.

The next day we discovered that my father had made elaborate preparations to scare the wits out of us by having Lincoln appear. He had chosen one of the six-foot-two butlers, Mayes, who dated from Theodore Roosevelt's time and looked a bit like Lincoln, and was going to dress him up in tail coat and stovepipe hat and send him into the room to deliver a sepulchral lecture from the shadows. He was foiled because Mayes was sick that day, and we were saved a seance with Lincoln's alleged spirit. If Dad's prank had worked, we'd probably be running yet. It might have been a relief, at that, as we could at least have fled to a twentieth-century mattress. I don't know how Lincoln survived the Presidency as well as he did, saddled with that couch.

ʘ◙ On Saturday, June 2, 1945, I wrote in my diary: "We are on the way *home*, underlined, four exclamation points." (I had never got around to thinking of 1600 Pennsylvania as home, so I meant Independence.) "In a private car, *yippee!*" I appended inelegantly. Private cars were brand new to me then, but I saw plenty of the inside of that one before it was all over!

In spite of my enthusiasm for departing Washington, both Mother and I always hated to go off and leave Dad, who was capable of the most abysmal loneliness when we were out of town. He enjoyed being picked on about his loud shirts and neckties and used to wear them to get a rise out of us. When we were gone, I'm told, he wore the most circumspect haberdashery, because there wasn't anybody to complain. He looked so forlorn when he saw us off that we were ready to turn around and go back, knowing he would be eating dinner in solitary state and wishing for us. A President has a lonely job.

When we got to Independence the next day, the station presented a mob scene. We could scarcely find the family in the seething crowd of well-wishers who had come to welcome us. Mother and I were astonished. It had never occurred to us that this frenzy would extend to people who had known us always. Practically the entire population of Independence was on the platform. The next Sunday I sang at church, as usual, just the way I had since I was old enough to carry a tune. It was in all the papers all over the country as something special!

Everybody seemed to expect me to be different, but I couldn't *be* different. I was just the way I always had been. I relapsed into a seersucker dress and didn't do anything for a solid week. I don't know *when* I'd had such a good time. When a schedule gets as involved as mine had been in Washington, the thought of having no plans was sheer heaven.

The big excitement that month was that I met General Eisenhower for the first time. He had just returned from the European Theatre and there was a parade in his honor in Kansas City. I was conducted to the reviewing stand and introduced to him.

Dad flew out to Independence on June 27 and we went to the

109

Fairfax Airport to meet him. If our welcome had been sizable, his was stupendous. The crowd was so thick that it took more than an hour to drive in from the airport—a trip that usually requires about thirty minutes. Dad rode in an open car and greeted the cheering crowds. He spoke at Kansas City Auditorium to a packed house and was entertained at a luncheon by his law class at Kansas City University.

That night the Merchants Association of Kansas City gave a dinner in his honor at the Muehlebach Hotel and he received an LL.D. degree from Kansas City University, the first honorary degree the college had granted in ninety years. That day Mary Shaw had given a luncheon for me at the Kansas City Club. We walked around town afterward and you could always tell where Dad was by the crowds milling and standing about the streets. They had to wait for hours for him to appear once, because he folded up and took a long nap, but they waited.

He left for Washington on July 1 and ten days later he was on the flagship *Augusta* headed for Potsdam. He hadn't been to Europe since he went on a troopship in 1918. His presence on the ship was naturally top secret, since we were still at war. When the *Augusta* arrived at Antwerp, an old friend and sometime beau of mine who shall be nameless—a lieutenant j.g. in the Navy—was in charge of the Antwerp port. The *Augusta* was drawing too much water and my bold friend refused her admission to the harbor. Dad said he presumed he should have taken *me* to Potsdam with him in order to get into Antwerp. When my friend discovered that he had refused the President he was covered with confusion. This was a family joke with us for a long time.

Dad telephoned us when he got to Potsdam and reported that Stalin hadn't arrived. He was a day late to the conference and was rumored to be in poor health. Mr. Churchill was already there, impeccably prompt, and had called on Dad in Berlin. Subsequently I had a letter from Daddy, written in Potsdam, in which he described the dinner Stalin gave in considerable detail—the bewildering assortment of exotic foods and the incredible number of toasts, during which all hands stood and drained their glasses of vodka. It must have been quite an evening.

Dad had previously entertained for Stalin and Churchill at dinner where Sergeant Eugene List played the piano as entertainment and my father wound up by personally rendering the *Minuet in G*. He brought me a menu of the dinner that Churchill tendered Stalin and himself, inscribed to me by both Stalin and Churchill. This is one of my most valued souvenirs. It came naturally to Daddy to do this. He's been bringing me inscribed menus and place cards since I was nine years old.

ॐ Dad was in Europe almost a month. He left Germany on August 2. En route home the *Augusta* put in at Plymouth, England, and my father inspected an honor guard and had lunch with King George VI, aboard the *Renown*. Dad had a fine time with the King and told me all about the luncheon party, which also included Lord Halifax, Admiral Leahy, and others. King George served soup, fish, lamb chops, and ice cream with chocolate sauce, just like anybody else. There was considerable ceremony involved in the meeting, however, and as soon as Dad went back to the *Augusta,* the King returned his call and boarded our ship. He inspected *our* honor guard, complimented *our* sailors, and collected a couple of autographs for *his* daughters!

"But what did you talk about?" I wanted to know.

"Oh, the conference," Dad said, "and a lot of other things." I found out subsequently that one of the topics of conversation had been the atomic bomb, which had not then fallen on Hiroshima. (The next day at 7:15 P.M. Washington time, August 5, 1945, it fell.) King George had heard about the "great explosion" at Almagordo, New Mexico, on the sixteenth of July, which the Army, in the interests of secrecy, had reported as the explosion of a munitions magazine.

People have often asked me whether I knew anything about the atomic bomb in advance but of course I didn't. The decision to use it against Japan was made at the Potsdam Conference in a meeting which included several of our military leaders and two or three Cabinet members. My father had to make the final decision. As troubled as he was, he did not hesitate to give the order to use it and he has said that he has no regrets, for it ended the war and saved many lives. He received the news of Hiroshima aboard the *Augusta*. Mother and I never knew anything about it until we read it in the papers.

Mother, accompanied by my dog, Mike, left by train for Washington to meet my father on the eighth of August. I stayed behind in Independence with Grandmother Wallace. On the tenth, while Dad was still trying to get his speech together on the Potsdam Conference and trying to decide how much to tell the press to tell the people about the atomic bomb, he received the Japanese offer of surrender. Our terms were unconditional, but they wished to make the condition of keeping the Emperor. That night Dad delivered his speech on Potsdam over the radio. It was unusually well received, though he had been convinced it was a bad speech and had rewritten it four times.

Four days later the Japanese capitulated. Such a day! The war was over! Dad announced the receipt of Japan's terms on the radio. Independence went wild. Horns, whistles, bells, and mobs of people. Mother and Dad were photographed on the Portico of the White House, greeting the surging crowds. Of course, *I* would be in Independence! I have a faculty for being somewhere else at the dramatic moment.

We didn't have a fence around the house in Independence in those days and I walked out in the yard that morning to cut some roses. John Cameron Swayze was standing there.

"Do you have anything to say?" he asked.

"What about?" I asked, dumbfounded.

"The war's over!" Mr. Swayze said. "I would like a statement."

"Peace, it's wonderful," I said.

᠊᠊ Compared to the surging momentum of world events at this time, my little triumphs bulk extremely small. That was the summer I was elected Lamda Chi Sweetheart, by the Lamda Chi Alphas of the University of Missouri. They gave me a party and presented me with a gold plaque. We rode in a big parade in an open car under the hot sun with a strong wind blowing, and oh, my hair! I didn't look like anybody's sweetheart. The car finally broke down and the Secret Service men had to retrieve us.

My church choir sang over the radio in Kansas City and we had to practice and rehearse all summer for this—get up at six A.M. and rush to the studio. We were all so excited about it. I had been taking voice lessons all summer and working like a dog, and I was rewarded by being allowed to make a few personal recordings.

On the fourteenth of September, Mother and Dad flew in from

Washington. It seemed to me that I hadn't seen my father in years. It seemed to him that he hadn't seen me in years. He didn't even mind my talking his ear off. "Tell me about Potsdam," I demanded and before he could get a word in, I told him about Independence.

He had brought me the most beautiful present, which General de Gaulle had given him to give me as a token of friendship from the people of France. It was a Cartier piece and started a whole new trend in Cartier jewelry. I still wear it with joy—a heavy gold bracelet, studded with rubies, emeralds, sapphires, and diamonds with a tiny watch in the center, surrounded by diamonds. It is one of the dearest presents I ever received.

In two weeks I was on my way to Washington and on September 29 I registered for my last year in college. My comment on this ugly fact in my diary was contained in one short word: "Ugh!"

Music remained uppermost in my mind, though I was still plowing through college, replete with homework and seminars. That fall I went to New York and called on Estelle Liebling, the famous voice coach, in her West 55th Street studio, using the name of Margaret Wallace. Miss Liebling consented to hear me sing and I sang for her for about twenty minutes. I am convinced that she did not know who I was at the time.

"You have a lovely soprano," Miss Liebling said. "But you must definitely put time and work on it."

I felt grateful for her encouragement, which I believe was objective.

I was introduced to Edward Johnson, then director of the Metropolitan Opera. He took me up on the big stage of the Met and I sang from that eminence to the great empty Golden Horseshoe. Shortly thereafter I met Lawrence Tibbett. He was singing *Rigoletto* and I went backstage. He was marvelous to me and we had a long chat and had our pictures made. Tibbett also listened to me sing—with considerable trepidation, I think. When I finished he said, "Thank God, you've got the voice. Now all you need is more work!"

So I worked.

I listened to music at every opportunity. I attended the opera throughout the Washington season. Bobby Stewart, one of my favorite beaus, took me to hear Grace Moore in *Tosca*. There was a real Tosca. I have never seen her like again—she had all the passion as well as all the sophistication the role demands. We had a wonderful time.

Music always made us hungry. I often invited the men who took me to the opera to the White House for supper afterward. They were usually servicemen who had been deprived of the delicacies of home for a long time. I always ordered ice cream in great silver bowls, so they could scoop out as much as they wanted. One night there were two extra silver bowls of ice cream through some mistake in the kitchen. Bobby and a brother officer sat down and demolished a bowl apiece, intended for eight servings!

There were many blandishments offered by 1600 Pennsylvania Avenue. My friends enjoyed it, and I soon learned to tell the difference between friends and people who just wanted to be invited to the White House.

There were drawbacks, too. I'll never forget one night Annette and Irv Wright, who had been off traveling, came by to spend the night with us. Irv decided that he had to run across the street to the drugstore to get some toothpaste. He went off without his coat and while he was out the White House guard changed. When he got back, there was a brand new guard on the gate who had never seen or heard of Irv Wright in his whole life.

"I'm Mr. Wright," Irv said confidently. "I'm staying here."

"Run along, buddy," said the guard. "Don't give me any trouble."

"But I *am* staying here," Irv said.

"You and who else?" asked the guard.

"Me and my wife," Irv said, getting hot under the collar.

"Tell it to the Marines," said the guard.

"If you'll just let me use the telephone," Irv said, "I will."

The guard had his instructions regarding suspicious characters. He said no.

"But I haven't even got my wallet!" Irv pleaded. "I haven't got my luggage. I haven't got a coat. They're all inside."

The guard refused to relent.

The upshot of it was Irv cooled his heels at the gate until somebody came along who recognized him and got in touch with the head usher. Finally they called me.

"Where in the world is he?" Annette and I chorused. "He's been gone two hours."

The food at 1600 Pennsylvania Avenue also left something to be

114

desired. Although matters improved after my mother took over the menus, some of the early provender was rather grim. Shortly after we were ensconced in the White House, my mother had to go out of town. She left me in charge of the household and we seemed to be existing on a perpetual diet of Brussels sprouts. My father won't eat Brussels sprouts and I pointed this fact out to the housekeeper. That night for dinner we had Brussels sprouts again. (We had just had them for lunch.) This went on for a couple of days, until I was on the verge of losing my temper. In fact, I got so mad my father threatened to send me away from the table.

I had had some advance warning on this particular housekeeper from a former resident of the White House—Elliott Roosevelt.

"Has Mrs. —— succeeded in starving you yet?" he asked, when I met him at a party.

"Not yet," I said wanly.

"She will," Elliott told me cheerfully. "If you need any help with her, just call on me!"

After *l'affaire* Brussels sprouts I found that the housekeeper seemed to take special delight in thwarting any suggestions I made about my father's preferences or the menus I planned. Finally I called Mother and advised her that she had better come home as I was on the point of firing the housekeeper. This struck my mother as out of my province, but she did shorten her visit. Fortunately, this housekeeper moved on, sparing us the necessity of unpleasantness and possible mayhem on my part, a project in which Elliott Roosevelt would have been a willing collaborator.

The White House kitchens are so enormous that the food is perforce institutional. When there are six or eight cooks with their fingers in the pie, it's apt to taste that way. There are the cooks for the executive wing who feed the people who work in the offices and there are the cooks for the White House incumbents and guests. There was great rivalry between these two groups and once a year Pye, the head cook of the office-wing group, gave a luncheon at which he entertained the White House staff. I often attended these parties and they were a lot of fun.

The demands made on the White House kitchens are so fantastic that it is difficult to understand how they do as well as they do. The White House staff has been known to be called on to produce a luncheon for fifty or sixty, a tea for twelve or fifteen hundred, a state dinner and a large reception in one day. At large mass teas there was never any way of really knowing how many people would arrive, and since the White House operates on a budget, the staff could not afford to overbuy or waste food.

Every detail of these entertainments was worked out, listed on "poop" sheets, and passed out to all the ushers and staff members, so that everybody knew exactly what was required of him. When foreign dignitaries were invited to lunch or dine, every effort was made to compliment the guest with food for which he might have a special inclination and to take cognizance of his nationality.

Royalty and important diplomats usually passed at least one night in the White House before returning to their own embassies or to Blair House. The pretty bedroom on the second floor with the canopied four-poster continues to be known as the Queen's room, since the Queens of England and Holland slept there. There were a half-dozen bedrooms available for guests, and our relatives and friends were permitted to occupy these when they came to visit us.

Our family circle in the White House was completed by Grandmother Wallace, who lived with us most of the time we were in residence there, and Vietta, who was an invaluable help. Not many people knew that my beautiful and delicate grandmother of the large dark eyes and soft voice was there. She was in failing health and rarely appeared at official functions. She lived very quietly there and I know how she hungered for home. Vietta looked after her, as she had done for two dozen years, and when my own mother managed to salvage an hour of leisure, she usually spent it with Grandmums.

It is difficult to describe the regimen that my mother entered on at the White House. While the corps of domestic employees at the White House were excellently trained and many of them had served there through several administrations, my mother was charged with the management of the establishment and took an interest in the gardens and everything that concerned it, as she had in Independence. The domestic details of any house take up a lot of time, and running the White House was akin to running a hotel. Along with this were the many entertainments which accrued to her official position and the functions she had to attend. Then there were Daddy and me and Grandmother.

People always seem curious to know what life was like in the private quarters of the White House—to catch a glimpse of the President in his house slippers! I have been reading over this book and it sometimes seems as if Dad was always making a speech or working in the office or traveling; that Mother was always presiding at some official function and that I was always going to a party! To some extent, that's the way it was. On those infrequent occasions when there wasn't something we all *had* to do (and I can't tell you how infrequent they were), we sat around the upstairs lounge like any other family. Dad and Mother read the papers and engaged in the desultory conversations common to husbands and wives long and happily married—news about the relatives or old friends, opinions on this or that, current events, what we had to do next. Perhaps we discussed the political topics of the day and talked less about national and world affairs than most people. If you are in these things up to your neck all the time, you don't discuss them when you have a little leisure.

My mother never cared for handwork, so I cannot present you with a picture of her knitting or making petit point. She often read the sports pages of the newspaper, because she likes baseball. When Dad read for pleasure, he usually read history. I talked about school and what Jane or Annette or Drucie and I were up to, or my new beau or where I was going tomorrow. We rarely dealt in personalities, but if I expressed an untoward opinion of some public figure, I was usually shushed. My father and mother are never mean about people.

My mother's personal friends remained the same. I suppose her dearest friends were the members of her Independence bridge club, but she had made friends among Washington ladies and she met with them whenever there was time. One of these was Mrs. Davis, Annette's mother, who had been our neighbor in the apartment on Connecticut Avenue. She was fond of Mrs. John Snyder and Mrs. Fred Vinson. She had also made friends with the mothers of some of my school friends. Mother loved to have lunch with Mrs. Davis and Annette and me on one of her rare free days, or to drive around with me, looking at the windows of Washington shops, without benefit of a limousine or chauffeur.

Though we had a proper respect for the White House and all it stands for, it never managed to overawe us completely. As far as we could, we lived the way we always had, and my father felt the same responsibility for the White House that he felt for the house in Independence. He was always going around checking the windows and doors to see if they were properly locked up for the night. Once when Mother and I were out of town, Washington had a torrential rainstorm, which reached hurricane proportions. It came in the middle of the night and Dad got up to see whether it was raining in. It was—coming in around the windows in buckets. He sprinted to his bathroom and grabbed a load of Turkish towels and began to mop. This went on for about half an hour before one of the ushers was attracted by the lights and came to his rescue. It had never occurred to Dad to call for help. He wrote us a vivid account of his heroic swabbing and it always seems endearing to me to think of my father in his striped pajamas and probably barefoot, loping from room to room of the White House, mopping up the rain.

When we had dinner alone we ate in a smaller dining room which adjoins the State Dining Room. It's a handsome room, with a portrait of President Tyler, my ancestor, on the wall, and Chippendale furniture. It was nice to be alone in a room scaled almost to human size. Though it was called the "small" dining room, it was pretty big, but the State Dining Room always looked to me as if it were a place in which you signed treaties!

One night in early summer we were having dinner in the "small" dining room and the *pièce de résistance* was watermelon for dessert. There is nothing in life on which my father and mother agree more wholeheartedly than watermelon. I can take it or leave it (I'm a chocolate-ice-cream girl), but that night I was taking it.

In the middle of the dessert course, Dad flipped a watermelon seed at Mother off his thumb and she responded in kind. I joined the fray and we had a classic watermelon-seed fight at the table. In the middle of this battle one of the butlers came in to remove the plates, but retreated in short order, in a rain of melon seeds. Through the swinging door we saw the help goggle at us once and then bend double with laughter. I don't remember who won, but I think it was Mother. She's pretty good at watermelon-seed fights.

Any old house profits by its association with human beings, and the White House is a very old house by American standards and has known some amazing human beings. It was first built in the eighteenth century, almost completely destroyed in the early nineteenth, and if its walls could talk, how fabulous are the tales they would unfold. So

118

many figures of our history had occupied it and sometimes when I climbed the stairs late at night, I could not keep from thinking of the other women who had lived under that roof—Mary Lincoln, storming up and down; Dolly Madison gathering up the silver plate to hide it from the British before she fled! I thought of the girls who had lived there too, whose problems were all so different from mine and yet had much in common. I would feel almost lightheaded at the idea of being a member of this great tradition, and humble and a little eerie. Then I would be grateful to reach my room, return to the twentieth century, and find Mother—solid and contemporary—waiting up to ask me all about the party.

10: The accidental belle

I have cherished no particular social ambitions in my life, nor ever aspired to belleship. Belles have often bored me, and insistence of older people on belleship for a girl has bored me more. The members of my family have deplored social high jinks even more than I have and have never failed to remind me that pretty is as pretty does; that there are good people in all strata of life; and that there is never any reason for a person to give herself airs.

I never wanted and certainly never expected to be a belle in any sense of that word, and yet, as the months wore on, it became apparent that my situation as the first girl in the history of the United States to be the only child of the President was going to have an irresistible influence on the course of my life, at least for a while. I began to be the recipient of much undue attention on the part not only of the press but of diplomats, hostesses, and people in commerce (who were reasonably looking for an angle), simply because I was twenty-one years old and I was *there*.

I can claim no credit for this popularity, which accrued to me as a symbol of something, and not because I was prettier or more charming or witty or desirable than any other girl. I did not encourage it, past trying to please (as I had been brought up to do), and exerting a determined effort to make everybody happy, at the expense of sleep, physical health, and peace of mind. In fact, I resisted it in whatever quiet ways I had at my command. I think I might have resisted it even more strongly if I had not felt that my willingness to appear at public functions might ease the burdens of my father and mother. But I preferred my old friends and clung to them with a tenacity that was sincere and earnest.

Still, I began to be bidden to stand in the receiving lines of embassy receptions, to attend dinners where my partners ranged from a General of all the Armies to atomic scientists, to go to balls where I was swung out by the presidents of foreign powers, princes, prime ministers, and movie stars. I became the recipient of fabulous gifts, and people named hats, colors, and flowers after me. Musicians composed scores and lyricists wrote words that were for me alone. A convertible was provided for my personal use at the White House and I began to get hundreds of letters containing advice, suggestions that I browbeat my father into doing something, and proposals of marriage. I had regiments of beaus, who squired me hither and yon and made me pretty speeches. I was invited to christen boats, planes, and products and to attend race meets, hunts, cruises, cotillions, fairs, breakfasts, lunches, teas, cocktail parties, dinners, and receptions. I rode in private cars, private limousines, private yachts, and private planes, but had no privacy. A fantastic fuss was made over me out of the yearning of the American people for a figure of glamour, and I endeavored steadily to appreciate it all, but to remember how it came about. Whenever I got a little full of myself, my father was quick to remind me that I was the recipient of a public responsibility; my mother was quick to remind me that she had brought me up to be a lady, and so I must remain; and everybody was quick to remind me that the main objective was to finish college and get on with my music.

Nevertheless, I became, in a manner of speaking, a belle. I say this with humility and with full recognition of the motivations of those who accomplished it. I did what I could to conceal it. Most of my friends in Independence had no inkling of the regimen I embarked on and if Mamma Truman had known, I don't doubt she would have sniffed.

I do not think this unwarranted adulation or attention changed my basic nature. I remained mulish, pigheaded, curious, romantic, hero-worshiping, loyal, affectionate, procrastinating, slangy, amiable, wistful, high-tempered, frank, loquacious, and nonstudious. I would also have remained lackadaisical and lazy but I didn't have time.

The airs and graces of society fell on my preformed personality like glancing arrows and did not improve it much. Neither did they undermine it, for while I experienced a number of things that might have permanently embittered me, I learned only to shrug them off and laugh. I lived in a giddy whirlwind, but I was always able to stand off and view my personal cyclone with a certain amount of objectivity. The iron of this sort of ambition has never entered my soul. For this I am grateful, as it can be as fatal as a disease.

I have a taste for pleasure, admitted, and a certain talent for enjoying myself. I strive to give these full rein where it is possible, but I have never failed to prefer society on quiet terms in small groups with people I love and trust. I like to have a good time and to see other people have a good time, but I can have a good time sitting on the porch at Independence or sipping a soda in Blue Springs, Missouri, as well as drinking vintage champagne at El Morocco or waltzing with a celebrity.

It was only necessary for me to remember when I was cut in on before I could take two steps with a partner on a dance floor that the men in the white ties and tails, the men in the brilliant uniforms with the decorations, the men in the native costumes or what have you, chose to break in because they wanted to tell somebody next morning that they had danced with the President's daughter (not plain Margaret Truman from Independence, Missouri), to keep everything in proportion. It would have been nice to think that my face or my smile or my manners or my ball gown or the way I hoofed (I love dancing and I'm pretty good at it, if I say so myself) had drawn them to my side, but I have never been able to fool myself. Of course, there were a few—tried and true friends—who actually liked my sense of rhythm or my quips, and I welcomed these, no matter how badly they danced.

Anyway, there I was—a belle, not only accidental but reluctant.

Belleship, no matter whose or how arrived at, exacts certain penalties. The most devastating of these is the limelight that suffuses every social occasion, no matter how private, personal, or unimportant. Rumor breeds and travels fast. If I was observed eating a hamburger with a man and a month later I happened to speak to him on the street, romance was in the air.

123

Another problem, once I had become public property, was the tendency of the world at large to observe my defects with the frankness of a mother. I read that I was "phlegmatic"; that I had a "hunchy" carriage; that my nose was "crooked" and ought to be "fixed"; that my figure was "matronly"; that I had "heavy" legs; that I was too "mature" for my years; that I was too "immature"; that my dates were not "romantic"; that I had no "taste"; that I had no "style"; that my hair-do was "messy"; that my clothes were "wrong"; that I favored "washed-out pastels" instead of the strong maroons, blues, and golds that became me; that I had no "escorts" and somebody should assign some to me; that I was "ambitious"; that I was "not ambitious"; and, of course, that I could not sing. Faced up with these brutal appraisals, you sink or swim. I chose to swim. I found some of them uproariously funny. I ignored some or I just considered the source.

There is also the tedium of constant grooming and dressing attached to belleship. The minute a girl arrives at this exalted place, she ceases to have time for its most requisite chores. I could not spare the hour that almost any woman is allotted for the hairdresser and was often washing my own hair in the dead of night, which added to the number of colds I had. This problem was partially solved when Mother and I got a hair dryer installed in our private quarters.

The wardrobe was even more disturbing. As a schoolgirl I had had the necessary complement of suits and sweaters and woolen dresses with one or two formals, but since I must constantly submit to photographing and often attended four or five occasions a day the problem of what to wear amounted practically to crisis. If I was seen too often in the same costume, there was certain to be talk. "Hasn't she got but one dress?"

My father was not a rich man and the White House has never been noted as a place to achieve a competence. In addition, shopping for clothes requires time and attention that I was ill-equipped to give. Between going to college, studying singing, and attending functions I barely had time to put on clothes, much less hunt for them.

Under the circumstances, I did the best I could. My taste in clothes is conservative and durability is one of my mother's watchwords. I had to wear the same things from one season to the next. I did not go in for high-style numbers, not only because they did not suit my temperament but also because people are more apt to spot and remember the spectacular. The classic can go on for years. Thrift and prudence had to be considered. I am still wearing some of the clothes I had in the White House.

There was one other aspect of this situation that might not have troubled other girls if they had been in my position. In addition to being accidental and reluctant, I was also a part-time belle. The beauty sleep was not for Margaret, who was bidden to grace the breakfast table no matter what time she got in, including Sunday. My mother liked to attend early services at St. Margaret's Church, and generally in what seemed to me to be dawn, I was crawling into my Sunday clothes. This was usually followed by eleven o'clock church with Dad, who remains a Baptist. On weekdays there was forever school, so I lost quite a lot of sleep. I have heard it said that some girls do not arise until noon. What bliss!

As far as we were able, we kept my activities out of the papers. My mother detests publicity. Still a tiny legend began to struggle up and, in Washington, at least, I had the prerogatives of a princess, through no fault or inclination of my own.

There were little stories that went around such as the milk story. One Sunday night a crowd of us drove to an inn near Chevy Chase for a fairly late dinner. It had been a busy day at the inn, and the owner was frantic when she saw us come in, because she had run out of milk. A whispering ran through the restaurant, for I was a well-known milk drinker. The waitress poised with bated breath at the table while we ordered and, of course, I ordered milk. So did everybody else at the table. The simple and logical thing to have done was to say that the milk was all gone. But the owner hated to disappoint us. She set out herself to garner milk. As she started out the driveway, a couple of State Troopers who drank coffee at the inn rolled up on their motorcycles. She told them her dilemma and they decided to escort her to the nearest delicatessen. With sirens wide open, they swept down the road and returned in a blare of whining noise with a gallon of milk for our party. I do not think this anecdote will bulk very large in history, but it gives you a rough idea of the sort of thing that might turn one's head if it isn't pretty carefully fastened on.

ॐ On the fifth of October we all drove down to Berryville, Virginia, to a wedding. My father's former senatorial colleague, Senator Bennett Clark of Missouri, was the bridegroom. This struck me as a glamorous occasion, not because I had ever thought of Senator Clark as glamorous, but because he was being married to an actress. Violet Hemming was the bride and she was very pretty and gracious. I never thought that Senator Clark felt very warmly toward my father, although he introduced him to the Senate and nominated him for Vice-president, and my father appointed Senator Clark to a Federal judgeship. Still it's always nice to have the President of the United States as a best man.

Two days later, Evalyn Walsh McLean gave a dinner party at Friendship for General Omar Bradley. I had always loved her parties, even when I used to be solitary at them among the older people, but this one was quite different. I sat right up with the big folks. General Bradley himself was my dinner partner. Afterward we danced and danced. I do not know that it will burnish his military reputation, which scarcely needs it, but I would like to say that General Bradley is a marvelous dancer and a wonderful dinner partner.

჻ Belleship, of the nature I describe, offers a great training ground for talking to all sorts of people, and by and large, I can manage to make conversation with anybody who speaks English, and I have limped along in a few foreign languages. I have on occasion met abject defeat, however. I was once the dinner partner of an atomic scientist, whom I sincerely admired. He was a youngish man, rather nice-looking, and I was prepared to be humble and respectful. I couldn't talk to him. I suppose he felt as bewildered as I did and was probably thinking, "What can I say to a silly young thing like this?" Anyway, he didn't help me at all.

Sitting in silence at a large dinner party can be sheer agony, and after I had tried everything in my little bag of tricks, I turned to my partner on the other side. "He won't talk," I said out of the corner of my mouth. "What'll I do?"

"Talk to me," Admiral Nimitz said, so I did.

I was slightly cheered to note that the lady on the other side of Dr. Oppenheimer, who was older and undoubtedly more adept than I, was having the same difficulty. He presented an absolute wall of silence. Since he was engaged in secret projects, maybe he feared to give them away if he opened his mouth. More likely he was just bored by the social requirements that accrue to people of importance, no matter how abstruse the work they do.

I sat beside some of the greatest figures of twentieth-century history and heard some of the most remarkable conversations—often my partners talked over me to each other—but this was the only time I drew an absolute blank. The President's daughter has no position in protocol and at a state dinner, if I were invited at all, I would be number 56. I never minded sitting "below the salt." Hostesses on less formal levels were kind. I had spectacular partners.

∂~ In October we went up to New York for the celebration of Navy Day, which was Saturday, the twenty-seventh of October. Drucie Snyder and Jane Lingo went with me and we marched into Cartier's to have the watch General De Gaulle had sent me regulated. This provided a good excuse for looking at the jewelry. They were very courteous to us in Cartier's, addressed us in French, which we answered in what passed for French (Gunston's best), and they inquired whether we would like to try some of the jewels. Drucie, Jane, and I hastened to say that we were just looking, but the minions of Cartier pointed out that you could look better if you were wearing it. Nothing loath, we tried on several million dollars' worth of diamonds and pearls and then went giggling out and bought a pair of $2.95 gloves at Saks. We met Howard Chandler Christy that day and he expressed a wish to paint my portrait. Since nobody had ever expressed such a wish before, I was bowled over.

The next day was Navy Day, all day long. It was bitterly cold for October and I thought I would freeze. The entire Atlantic fleet was anchored in the Hudson River, stretching from the Battery to an area far beyond the George Washington Bridge. It was a sight that made your heart turn over, and in the big middle was my ship, the *Missouri!*

We left the Waldorf at eight-forty in the morning. When my father boarded the *Renshaw* to review the fleet, the twenty-one-gun salute broke from every ship in the harbor. The noise and vibration of the salute always makes me flinch, and between shivering and flinching, I looked like a person taken with chills and fever. Admiral Ingersoll, an old British sea dog who was aboard the *Renshaw*, noticing my quivers, said, "Rahly, my deah Miss Truman, they are only *blank* shots!"

It was impossible for me to explain to him that I didn't expect to be killed, only permanently deafened.

Governor Dewey, Mayor La Guardia, and Mrs. Woodrow Wilson

were also on the *Renshaw*. Dad commissioned the *Franklin D. Roosevelt* aircraft carrier that day and then we went to lunch aboard the *Missouri*, where the President's flag was flying. Of course we had to examine the exact spot where the Japanese surrender was signed and also renew old acquaintances.

That afternoon Dad spoke to a vast meeting in Central Park, and while he made a fine speech, I was beginning to feel more and more tired. That's another one of the problems of belleship. Sooner or later you get so tired that you get sick. I folded up with the flu. Penicillin had just come into use and the wonder drug was administered to me in peanut oil, over and over. The doctors were afraid the infection would go into my lungs and result in pneumonia, so I was practically a guinea pig for penicillin. At the time I felt the dose was almost worse than the disease, but I was lucky that it had been invented in time to ward off another bout of pneumonia.

I was determined to recover as fast as possible as on November 3 Jane Lingo and I had a bid to a West Point Hop at Pelham Hall. The last time I had been to a dance at the Point, I had been having so much fun that I missed the train to New York. When I finally got back to New York I had missed everything but the milk train to Washington. This was a sort of freight train with one alleged passenger car, made of corrugated iron and immovable plush seats that faced each other. It was a car fit only for the Smithsonian and it took the train that hauled it all night long to get to Washington. When I got off at the Terminal at daybreak in my evening dress, Dad was there. He had almost worn a track in the marble floor, pacing up and down. He was furious and I was in disgrace.

This time when we went to the Point it was all very sedate. The Secret Service drove us there and drove us back to New York, reminding us in ample time to get back for the regular Washington train. They settled us in the parlor car, practically pinning our handkerchiefs to our coats and telling us not to speak to strangers! When we arrived in Washington more Secret Service were on hand to drive us home. Gone were the wild free days!

On the tenth of November, Clement Attlee, the Prime Minister of Great Britain, came to the White House. My father entertained him at luncheon, and that afternoon, Jane Wells, who happened to be spending the day with me, and I were presented to him at tea. He was a dear—witty and brilliant—with a real talent for drawing out young people. He told Jane and me a string of funny jokes and stories and had us in stitches. As I have said before, some people are able to converse with young people and others simply are not. Or perhaps I should say that young people find it easier to talk to some celebrities than to others. Clement Attlee was unusually adept. He had daughters of his own and endeared himself to Jane and me by seeming interested in us.

There was a State Dinner for Mr. Attlee that evening, to which I was not invited, but I ran down and looked at the table in its gleaming array and left the door of my living room open so that I could hear the music of the Marine Band.

On November 22, I was back in New York for the week end. Saturday night, Bobby Stewart and I went out on the town. We went to the theatre and then had supper at the Maisonette of the St. Regis and danced for hours. It was such fun that it was three o'clock before I knew it. We were scheduled to attend services at the Cathedral of St. John the Divine the next morning. Bishop Manning conducted the service and Bobby and I sat with his daughter, Miss Manning, in a very prominent pew high up in the chancel. I am sorry to report that both of us went sound asleep in the middle of Bishop Manning's sermon while sitting beside his daughter, in full view of an enormous audience! One of the prices of belledom is that the time arrives when you can't stay awake another minute no matter where you are.

On the twenty-seventh of November that year, Mother and I were invited to attend the opening of the Metropolitan Opera in New York. It was the opera's sixty-first season and the first night was exceptionally gala now that the war was over. We were the guests of the opera committee and sat in Box 35, held by Mr. and Mrs. Thomas Watson. It was the first time in the history of the opera that the President's wife had honored opening night with her presence, and quite a lot of splashy publicity came of this.

In deference to the occasion, Mother and I had done ourselves up in our best. Mother had a royal blue gown with a brocaded coat in a matching color and I had a brilliant green taffeta dress with cap sleeves, a faintly plunging neckline and, glory be, a bustle and a short train. It was actually a big bow that looked like a bustle and I didn't know exactly how to sit on it. A detective stepped on the train in the crush between acts, and nearly sundered the bustle from the dress. It made me so mad. I had gold slippers and a blue-green wool coat trimmed with gold braid around the shoulders. I had a pair of long white kid gloves and a string of pearls. After looking around at the blazing jewels, the ermine, white mink, and chinchilla in the audience, I could have wished to be slightly more inconspicuous, but this was out of the question. We were sitting in the exact middle of the horseshoe in a box draped with the American flag.

We were invited to dine before the opera in the Opera Club, as the guests of the Opera Committee. We arrived at the old Met about 6:30 P.M., which saved us from the wilder crush of curiosity seekers, and were welcomed by George Sloan, the president of the Metropolitan Opera Company, Cornelius Bliss, chairman of the board of the Metropolitan, and Miss Lucrezia Bori, chairman of the Opera Guild. There we were presented with great bouquets of orchids.

The Opera Club is just off the grand tier and we had dinner at a beautiful table laden with flowers. There was mousse of lobster, guinea hen, and ice cream frozen in the shape of musical instruments. Even the cakes had a chocolate treble clef and notes running over them.

When our party entered the box just before the curtain rose, the orchestra burst into *The Star-Spangled Banner*. It was a tremendous thrill. I was fascinated to see that the people in the parquet had turned around to level their opera glasses at our box, until I happened to catch my mother's warning eye. She gave me a sardonic glance and I realized that I was preening, and would probably never hear the last of it from the Teasing Truman.

The opera was *Lohengrin,* and after it began, I forgot all about myself.

Between the acts we went backstage to meet the cast. Backstage of any theatre always affects me like a draught of wine. Backstage in the ancient Metropolitan is fairly grim, to tell the truth. One is always tripping over boards and properties, but the chorus running about in their costumes and the stars coming to the door to receive telegrams and flowers made it exciting.

Torstan Ralf, the Swedish tenor, sang the Lohengrin role and Helen Traubel was Elsa. Fritz Busch conducted and gave a superb rendering of the score. The opera was unusually good for a first night and I was carried away.

When it was over, the police had to beat a path for us through the crowd. This made me feel silly. I felt as if I should have been there on the sidelines trying to pick out Lily Pons to stare at, not walking along and being stared at myself. As a matter of fact, I kept craning my neck to see whether I couldn't locate some real celebrity.

    ॐ On December 1 that year, we went in style to the Army-Navy game in Philadelphia. My father and mother had an entourage of about two hundred people, including General Marshall, General Arnold, Admiral King, Admiral Nimitz, and Admiral Leahy. I had Jane Lingo, Nancy Anderson, and Mary Calvert as my personal guests. We were driven right up to the gates of the stadium and our seats were, naturally, on the fifty-yard line. This offered a marked contrast to a year before when we had stood in line for hours, freezing and shivering, and were only revived by the hot coffee proffered by the Methodist Church. I regret to state that I thought to myself, "This is living!" and felt slightly smug.

My father undertook a strict neutrality—sitting first on Army's side and then on Navy's side and cheering both sides equally for good plays. I was unable to be so broadminded. I was a hot rooter for the Army and was a picture of dejection every time they lost a yard or had to give up the ball. When Blanchard or Davis, Army backs, plowed through Navy's line, I could not contain my squeals, pounded my mother into a pulp, and jumped up and down. I wouldn't leave Army's side at the half and turned out to be thoroughly partisan.

"She double-crossed me," my father stated.

    ॐ As soon as this excitement died down, I plunged into a wedding furor. I was a bridesmaid at the wedding of Jane Wells, one of my Washington friends, and on the twelfth of December I had a luncheon for her in the State Dining Room. I invited all the old Gunston gang and there was a great deal of gossiping and catching up to be done. The table looked beautiful, but the dining room was freezing cold. The White House, at least in those days, was a drafty old place and it was hard to heat that enormous room. It was never quite warm in the winter. We all giggled and shivered through lunch. This was my first bridesmaidship, but eventually I became a veteran. I was often a bridesmaid.

On the eighteenth of December Mother and I left for Independence. The temperature was five below zero. Dad followed us in the *Sacred Cow*, flying just ahead of a storm. The press plane got caught in it and there was a wave of hysteria about the President risking his life, intensified probably by the fact that the United States had no Vice-president at the time. Dad would have walked through the drifts to get home to Independence for Christmas, but after that he always had trouble from his advisers when he attempted to fly in bad weather.

෪ Christmas was, as ever, real Christmas in Independence. On Christmas night, since time immemorial, the family has always gone down to Uncle George and Aunt Beuf's house to eat what Aunt Beuf terms "leftovers." Aunt Beuf is a wonderful cook and her leftovers are unique—whole baked hams, whole cold turkeys, mounds of jellied salads and savories, pies, cakes, and homemade ice cream.

I went to parties all week and saw all my old friends. On the thirtieth of December I had a date with an old beau. He took me to dinner and a hockey game. In my diary I wrote ungraciously, "That's a great date!"

Then I swiveled around and looked at myself. "Hold your horses, Mary Margaret," I said to myself. "This belle thing can go *too* far!"

The tendency to believe your own publicity is a pitfall for any belle, accidental or otherwise. As late as 1952, I went down to Washington for the week end, and it apparently seemed to my father that I was feeling my oats a bit too much. He sat down and wrote me a letter after I left. When the letter arrived, I knew by looking at the outside of the envelope that I was due for a lecture. He had addressed it Miss Mary Margaret Truman.

It was such a wonderful letter that I want to include it here, for it seems to me to be an excellent commentary on belleship and good advice for anybody.

Letter from Dad, January 28, 1952:

Dear Margie:

It was a most happy week-end. It always is when you are with your Mommy and Daddy. Your Pop has been carefully watching the progress and change in his daughter, just as he watched it from five to fifteen. You've never had any advice from your Dad except in your interests. When you were anxious to be a singer at fifteen your Dad told you to be sure you had an education first. You took his advice. Now you're faced with a successful career. Be very careful that you remember your background and bringing up. I want you to succeed in whatever you undertake. To do that you must give it all you have. Keep your balance and display all the Truman-Wallace mulishness where right and wrong are in the balance. Right must always prevail. Do not let the glamor get you. There are decent, honorable people among the very rich, just as there are among the very poor. Honor knows no class. It is just as great and as necessary at one end of the scale as at the other. No one can say which is the top. Jesus Christ was the son of a carpenter (foster son) and was one himself. He was looked down upon by the socially great of his time. So were Martin Luther, John Knox, Wycliffe, Thomas Jefferson, Andrew Jackson and Abraham Lincoln. Remember always to keep your balance no matter how great you may become in your own time. Great men and women are assayed in future generations. Your Dad will never be reckoned among the great but you can be sure he did his level best and gave all he had to his country. There is an epitaph in Boothill Cemetery in Tombstone, Arizona, which reads, "Here lies Jack Williams; he done his damnedest." What more can a person do? I hope that will be yours and your Dad's epitaph.

Love,
Dad

11: *School's out!*

The year 1946 dawned with special significance for me, since it portended the end of my college career. There was a little matter of two sets of final examinations to be got through—one in January and one in May—before freedom could set in, but if I had arrived at the home stretch, I didn't propose to be felled by an aggregation of true or false.

I got back to Washington from Independence the day after New Year's and school began promptly the next morning. In fact, I had to get up and leave a seminar in order to hear Dad deliver his speech to the nation on "Our Year of Decision," on January 4. Dr. Ragatz, the professor of the seminar, thought this was wisdom. He was one of the greatest teachers I ever had, and aside from his courtesy to me on such occasions, never took the slightest notice of my exalted address. Once, when a crowd of reporters endeavored to storm his seminar, he drove them off with a fine display of dignity. He had no interest in the press or publicity or anything but the subject on which he was engaged, and saw no reason for the invasion of his seminar by the fourth estate, unless they were enrolled in George Washington University and paying tuition!

While school was always there, it continues to be a matter of wonderment to me that I got around to it. When I think of that year I hear music and I remember dancing—the harmony of strings, the moody saxophone, the cacophony and beat of the rumba and the samba, and the endless slide of my thin soles around some polished perimeter. Frank Handy often took me dancing. Frank was the best waltzer I ever knew, and when he married another girl from Missouri, I gained a new friend and lost my best partner.

I continued my avid onslaught on the theatre. I saw Alfred Lunt and Lynn Fontanne in *O Mistress Mine* twice in the same week. Sue Bugby, a friend of mine and a niece of the Lunts, was working for them at the time and we went backstage on both occasions. I was, as ever, enthralled by the whiff of grease paint and the mystery of dressing rooms and the stimulating conversation of real troupers. I remember the Lunts sending Sue and me out to buy them a pound of sweet butter. They kept it on the windowsill of their hotel room, out of old habit. A Wisconsin gourmet couldn't abide the taste of hotel butter on his breakfast toast!

I went to concerts and heard Lauritz Melchior sing for the first time. I was invited backstage and met him. He was charming to me and gave me his autograph. Lauritz is a dear and has a natural affinity for having his picture made. When a flash bulb pops Lauritz rises like an old fire horse to the scent of smoke and begins to pose. And when Lauritz moves into the range of the lens, anybody else around is apt to get covered up, for he has the figure of a Viking. We had our picture made together and I came out sort of peering around Lauritz, on whose face is spread the smile of a happy child.

On January 11, I note in my journal, I went to a dinner given by Mrs. George Mesta, with whom I had not then arrived at a first-name basis. It was a party for Washington newspaperwomen, and was very pleasant. The next day I had a dinner for my Gunston Hall friends and showed them a new Clark Gable movie. This ability to produce the latest opus of the schoolgirl's delight added greatly to my popularity in those days.

The same day Mother, Dad, and I sat for official photographs for what seemed like hours on end. There were forty photographers taking pictures at once. I wished that Lauritz could have been there to substitute for me! I dread official "sittings," where I invariably freeze and emerge in the negatives looking like the Great Stone Face. On the other hand, I love to *take* pictures, and went around with a camera in my hand a large part of the time I was in the White House until my father finally complained, "It's not enough that my homely countenance is at the mercy of the press—I have to have a photographer in the family!"

I also like to *look* at pictures—my own and other people's—professional, commercial, and amateur—still or moving. The movie projector got scant rest during our tenancy of the White House. Dad always looked over all the newsreels of the week's events on Thursday afternoons and I was an interested observer at these sessions. There is nothing like your own private Trans-Lux.

Washington was a whirlwind of gaiety that year after the war. Secretary of Commerce Henry Wallace and Mrs. Wallace announced the engagement of their daughter, Jean, to Les Douglas, at a beautiful tea at the Wardman Park Hotel. There was a command performance of *The Glass Menagerie* for the President and the whole cast of the play came to tea at the White House. I remember that Laurette Taylor arrived thirty minutes late and Dad was fit to be tied. Not only is he a punctual man, but the schedules at the White House are so rigidly fixed that a deviation of thirty minutes can wreck the whole day. The recollection of Laurette Taylor's superb performance in the Tennessee Williams play, however, encourages one to forgive her anything.

Movie stars swarmed on the capitol for the March of Dimes campaign. They too came to the White House for tea. (Van Johnson was thirty minutes late.) Mother and I made spot appearances and short speeches at all the hotels on January 29 to launch the campaign. I went to a concert by Vivian Della Chiesa and to see Maurice Evans in *Hamlet*. He invited me backstage and I was so overcome with the privilege that I stumbled on the stairs leading to his dressing room and practically fell in. He gave me tea and I had a wonderful, tongue-tied time.

The announcement of the engagement of Gloria Chavez, daughter of Senator and Mrs. Dennis Chavez of New Mexico, to Lieutenant Jorge Tristani was the signal for a round of parties. Gloria was an old friend of mine from the DOTS (Daughters of Senators) and she invited me to be a bridesmaid in the wedding. In the final stages of a long series of fetes, Imelda Chavez Miller, Gloria's sister and matron of honor in the wedding party, gave a glamorous luncheon for the bridesmaids and I gave an evening party for Gloria and Jorge, the first dance to be held at the White House since before the war. The wedding party came for dinner in the State Dining Room, im-

137

posing if drafty, which was banked that evening with feathery ferns and red carnations. (Gloria's wedding colors were red and green, which suited her dark beauty and the wintry season.) Everybody else came at ten, to the East Room, where the Marine Band in their scarlet coats were tuning up. Mother and Dad came and stood at the door with me for thirty minutes, greeting my guests. Unfortunately, my father does not dance—says he *can't* dance, which seems strange for one so musical.

Madame Helle Bonnet, the wife of the French Ambassador Henri Bonnet, had brought me the most beautiful dress from Paris, which I wore for the first time. It was green silk with scoop neck, in which a big pink silk rose was nestled and yards and yards of skirt. I had a new, sleek page-boy hair-do. Jim Davidson and Roderick O'Connor were my dates, and I went in to supper with Colonel Robert Dahlstrom.

The music was splendid, especially the rumbas and the sambas, which the Marine Band reeled off with the aplomb of veterans. Jorge was a native of Puerto Rico, so that Latin rhythms were favored to do him honor. Gloria was radiant, bubbling like champagne, and scarcely lost a thing all evening. Gloria was famous for losing things. She lost her engagement ring in a hotel dining room. She lost her wedding gloves just before the wedding, and she lost her lime-colored going-away suit too. This was found in the nick of time, locked in a closet. Getting into the spirit of the thing, Jorge had lost his hat that day. In view of the tendency of their possessions to get misplaced, Jorge proposed to have four wedding rings on hand on the morrow, so as not to be caught short.

There were sixty-four guests and we danced until midnight and then adjourned to the State Dining Room for supper, which was served at small tables. We had the immemorial chicken salad and hot rolls and ice cream and cake and then they trooped down the stairs singing *Good Night, Ladies*.

Gloria was to be married in St. Matthew's Cathedral by Monsignor John Cartwright and a large part of the next afternoon was spent in rehearsal. It was fairly complicated for me, since I had to learn when and where to genuflect.

On the day of the wedding a scheduled vote to end a Senate filibuster on the FEPC had to be delayed in order to permit Senator Chavez to give his daughter away. It was a beautiful wedding. The

138

bridesmaids (there were six of us) wore long gowns of full-skirted emerald green velvet, with green lace mantillas and fingerless mitts of matching lace and we carried great sheafs of long-stemmed American Beauty roses. Imelda, who was matron of honor, wore a rosy red velvet dress and carried yellow roses. Gloria wore traditional satin with a magnificent real lace veil. Even the flower girls wore lace mantillas.

The wedding went off without a hitch, nobody having lost anything after we got into the Cathedral. An enormous wedding reception was held at the Shoreham. We stood in line almost two hours, shaking hands. Unless you've done it, you don't know what murder this can be. I finally came across Mother in the crush.

"Haven't we met somewhere before?" I asked her.

"Your face is familiar," Mother said.

ॐ The next day I attended the Annual Dinner of the National Woman's Press Club. Eugene List, the brilliant young pianist who had played for Dad's dinner at the Potsdam Conference, was my dinner partner and one of the evening's entertainers. He told me that Dad had turned the pages of his music for him at Potsdam.

Bess Furman, one of our favorites of the Washington newspaperwomen's corps, was president of the Press Club that year and mistress of ceremonies for the dinner. Mother and Dad were also there, along with Lord and Lady Halifax. Dr. Lise Meitner, the great physicist who received an award from the Press Club, was seated by Dad. Dad leaned out and peered down the table through his thick lenses to locate me and wave, and Mother sent up a note to Bess Furman to remind Dad who Dr. Meitner was! Dad said he *knew* who she was but he didn't feel equipped to discuss nuclear fission with such an authority. What he did discuss with her was the terrible responsibility which had descended on him when it came to dropping those two atomic bombs on Japan—a decision he had never regretted, since it had served to hasten the war's end and save lives on both sides. Dr. Meitner said that the thought of an atomic bomb had never entered her head when she was striving to find ways to split the atom and release more energy than the earth had ever seen.

Dad spoke "off the cuff" at this dinner and made a plea to the press to do what they could to persuade America to tighten her belt and not let fifteen million Europeans die of starvation. The Greek

139

famine was at its height and he was fighting for relief for the Greeks and the Turks.

The next day, February 9, Sir Winston Churchill arrived and I met him. He was, as expected, a charmer. En route to Washington by plane from London, he had been instructed to keep his seat belt fastened, but he hadn't paid much attention to that. The plane hit a pocket and threw him against the ceiling with a resounding thwack resulting in a laceration of his head. But this accident didn't dampen the spirits of the lion of Great Britain. That week end he went to Fulton, Missouri, and delivered a verbal shot heard round the world.

On the fifteenth of February, the celebration of my twenty-second birthday began. It went on for about five days and threatened to age me beyond my years! My old school fellow from Gunston Hall, Lillian Samoza, daughter of President and Señora Samoza of Nicaragua, and the Nicaraguan Ambassador gave a charming reception for me that day, followed by Mrs. Mesta's dance in my honor at the Sulgrave Club. This was a fabulous affair, the flowers flown from Florida and an enormous cake, decorated with my name in sugar roses, flown from New York. My escorts were Drew and Bob Dudley, but I didn't see much of them. I danced every dance, with a minimum of six different partners for each dance, and I didn't get home until a quarter of three.

The next evening, Madame Henri Bonnet gave a small and enchanting buffet supper and dance for me at the French Embassy. I had a new pink dress trimmed in black and I went with Bobby Stewart and Jim Batte. The music was beautiful; and at midnight, when my birthday actually arrived, a birthday cake, alight with twenty-two candles, was borne in. Madame Bonnet gave me a bottle of Nina Ricci perfume straight from Paris, and as sophisticated as my new age demanded.

On the morning of February 17, I had to get up as usual. Growing old did not alter the routine of family breakfast. Or the presents piled on my chair. My father, in the midst of his busy life, had planned a birthday party for me. He gave me a luncheon aboard the *Williamsburg*, the Presidential yacht, with all my favorite food. (This certainly added up to quite a conglomeration, but we had it all.) Dad wrote out the menu and asked the guests himself. We had a pleasant sail and got home to the White House, where Vietta had made me the immemorial birthday cake—dark chocolate with candles, just like home—the best birthday cake of all.

The next day the Daughters of the Senators gave a dinner dance for me at the Sulgrave Club, with a charm bracelet from all the members—my first charm bracelet. I had got so in the habit of celebrating my birthday that the next week when I went to a reception at the Russian Embassy, celebrating the birthday of the Red Army, for a confused moment I expected to see a birthday cake arrive with twenty-two candles! This wasn't forthcoming, but the wine flowed and there were fantastic bowls of caviar to commemorate the anniversary of the birth of the Red Army. The Congressional Club Associate Members gave a dance for me the next night and soon after I took off for a week end in New York.

I got back to Washington on March 5 and found that Mother was giving an official luncheon for Mrs. Winston Churchill. Her daughter, Sarah Churchill Oliver, was also there and they were both darlings. When I met Sarah, she giggled and said, "Don't look now, but I've got a dress exactly like the one you are wearing. I started to wear it today."

Hildegarde was holding forth at the Statler in Washington that spring and Marvin Braverman took Jane Lingo and Bobby Stewart and me to dinner and the show. Hildegarde gave me one of her famous red roses. Dad took me to the Jackson Day Dinner at the Mayflower Hotel and I sat at the head table.

Shortly thereafter, to the surprise of no one, I folded up with influenza and a temperature of 104, with the doctors lurking in the corridors all night. I had had a wisdom tooth out and, for obvious reasons (I don't think I had had eight consecutive hours of sleep since the first of January), I had begun to feel awfully tired. I was in bed a week and barely staggered up in time to take over the housekeeping problems when Mother left for Denver, Colorado, to act as godmother at the christening of Freddy and Chris Wallace's new baby.

Running the White House, with all that help, may seem like a simple trick, but I didn't find it so. My mother's orderly management maintained things for a few days and then Dad began to ask unexpected people home to supper and the kitchen would act as if a crisis had occurred. However, I would rattle around and give or-

141

ders, making like Mother, and sooner or later supper would arrive. Actually, nobody paid much attention to what I said, but I felt called on to make the effort.

On March 20, Mrs. Sissal Bratz, Miss Guri and Miss Mette Lie, the three daughters of Trygve Lie, Secretary General of the United Nations, were officially invited to tea at the White House. I was jittery at the thought of all the duties of hostess-ship devolving on me and terrified that they would not be able to speak English. Needless to say, I didn't speak Norwegian. I called up Jane and Drucie and rallied them around to help out.

I learned subsequently that the Lie girls were as frightened as I was. They had met few American girls and didn't know what to talk to me about. Worse, they were staying at Blair House and they weren't sure how to get to the White House. They inquired, and everybody said, "But it's just across the street. You can walk over there." But they didn't know how to get into the White House and had a horrible feeling they might knock at the back door or the office wing. Finally, they hired a car and were driven across the street to the White House, a ruinous extravagance, but they were so afraid they would do something wrong. It cheered me to discover that girls of all nations have the same kinds of problems.

They spoke beautiful English and the stiffness lasted about sixty seconds when we all began to chatter like magpies—and have never ceased to do so when we are together. Guri Lie lives in New York and has taken out her first papers for American citizenship. She is one of my good friends and we used to sit up half the night talking about men, music, politics, and what we were going to do next, in the order named, before she became Mrs. William Zeckendorf, Jr.

My application to the waltz, the fox trot, and the late supper had been more marked than my application to Modern Art, and this was emphasized when I found myself struggling with some hideous examination questions at George Washington University. Fortunately, Mother got home from Denver and I was able to fold up and be sick in bed for another week and to give up what passed for my management of the White House.

I revived sufficiently by the first of April for a session of piano duets with Annette Wright, and then began another frenzied month. Mother had an official luncheon for Madame Gouin, the wife of the President of France, and Madame Bonnet. I went to a dinner for the

Cuban Ambassador at the Mayflower. I saw *Blossom Time*, though why I thought I had to crowd this in I don't know, for I had seen it eleven times and could have doubled in brass for any participant.

On April 5, Drucie and I went with Dad to Chicago for the celebration of Army Day. We went out one night in the Presidential car and came back the next. Dad spoke to a big crowd at Soldiers' Field and we rode in parades and attended a luncheon and a dinner and heard speeches. All the way out and all the way back, Drucie and I read Shakespeare, taking the various roles and cuing each other. We were embarked on a rereading of all the plays, and as the train roared through Ohio and Pennsylvania, we were declaiming *Hamlet*.

On the twelfth of April, Dad went to Hyde Park to pay his respects at the tomb of Roosevelt. It was impossible to believe that only a year had passed since that cataclysmic other April twelfth. Sometimes it seemed like a moment and sometimes it seemed like a century. Things happened too fast for me and they kept on happening.

Jim Batte, one of the White House aides, took me dancing at the Army-Navy Country Club, and at home we were getting ready for the arrival of Mother's famed Independence Bridge Club. They came on April 15 for the week end and the White House was full of feminine chatter and the click of high-heeled slippers. Mother was as happy as a girl, catching up on all the gossip, and it was bubble and squeak from morning until night. They must have played some bridge, but I don't know how or when.

Mother entertained at dinner for "the girls" in the State Dining Room, followed by a visit to the Shrine Circus on Saturday night. Dinner ran on and it got later and later. Finally they all had to get up and run and I never heard such a clatter in the marble halls of the White House as they sprinted for their cars. At the circus one of the clowns singled out their party for his special attention. He got bolder and bolder when they responded to his antics and finally he sat down in Mother's lap. This struck her as a bit too much and she just looked at him with one of her lady looks. He got up and fled without any urging from the guards or the Secret Service men!

ᘒ On the sixteenth of April, I went with Dad to the opening baseball game of the season, where he threw out the first ball. In spite of our lusty rooting, the Washington Senators lost to Boston, 6 to 3. On two successive nights that week, I went to see Maurice Evans in *Hamlet*, and would have been happy to do so every night. On both occasions my party was invited backstage to see Maurice, who entertained us royally.

On April 21st, I attended a luncheon party given by Evalyn Walsh McLean at Friendship and my luncheon partners were Ambassador Bonnet and Justice Fred Vinson. I was privileged at this time to hear a long discussion of the United Nations between the two men, much of it secret. It seemed to me to be better education in history than I could get at school. I kept my mouth shut and listened, and I kept my mouth shut after I had listened. One of the things I had learned to do was to keep my mouth shut.

The next evening I entertained my Pi Beta Phi chapter from George Washington University at a dinner in the State Dining Room, followed by a showing of *Henry V* in the movie theatre. I continue to think that this is the best film I have ever seen, and by now you must know how many I've seen!

Easter Sunday dawned bright and clear and Mother and I went to early service at St. Margaret's. The day was made memorable for me by the receipt of three beautifully decorated Easter eggs from Jan Masaryk, with the following letter in his own hand.

Ministerstvo Zahranicvich Veci
Easter Sunday, 1946

My dear Miss Truman,

Air American crew landed in Prague the other day, bringing 50,000 hatching eggs from U.N.R.A. to our farmers.

They were most welcome. They are flying back today.

May I present you with these special eggs made by our peasants. They are interesting—the gilded stuff is plain straw. I hope you enjoy looking at them.

With respectful greetings to your father,

Sincerely yours,
(signed) Jan Masaryk

I have often brooded on this letter, written in its strong, bold script, and wondered if the story of Masaryk's untimely demise has ever really been told.

Major and Mrs. Strickler came through Washington and Mother and I joined them for a couple of days at Atlantic City. The day we arrived there were thousands of people sunning themselves on the boardwalk. Actually, I dislike strong sunlight, which parches me,

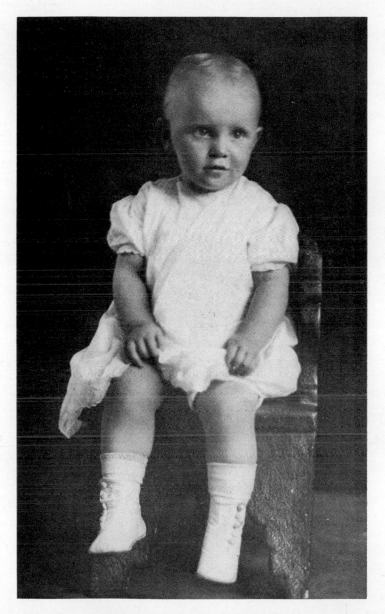

*This is my mother's pet picture of me, made when I was
about eighteen months old. The fuzz on my head is parted!*

Here is a picture of
Mother and me, made
when I was three months
old. So far I had no hair
whatsoever.

Here I am at the age of four months on the gallery at
219 Delaware Street, Independence, Missouri, sound asleep.

This picture of Mother, Dad, and me was made in May, 1928. I can't imagine how I happened to turn my back on a camera!

In 1928 I was an active child and a demon tri-cyclist; but Mother feared I would be knock-kneed for life then.

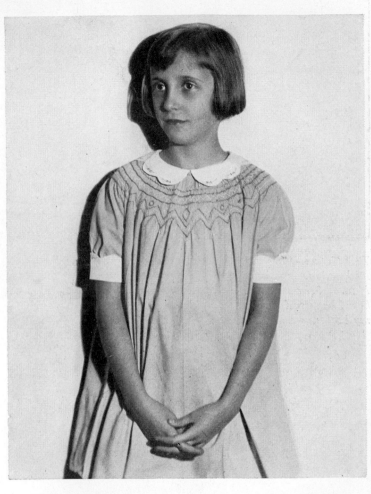

*This was made about the time my father was elected to
the Senate and we went to Washington. I was ten years old.*

I posed in my cap and gown for Uncle George Wallace in the back yard of the White House. Note the big magnolia.

Vietta Garr has been part of my life since I was three years old. Her fine character is written in her face.

Martha Ellen Young Truman, my father's mother, was always my ally. She encouraged me in my musical career.

Margaret Gates Wallace (called Madge), my maternal grandmother, influenced my life strongly. I was her namesake.

There's no business like show business when you're taking another bow! From the wings, Kiel Auditorium, St. Louis.

*Though we led such busy lives we managed family reunions.
Here we all are on the* Williamsburg *one Sunday in 1946.*

*I take pardonable pride in this photograph of the President
and me and the only sun tan I ever managed to acquire.*

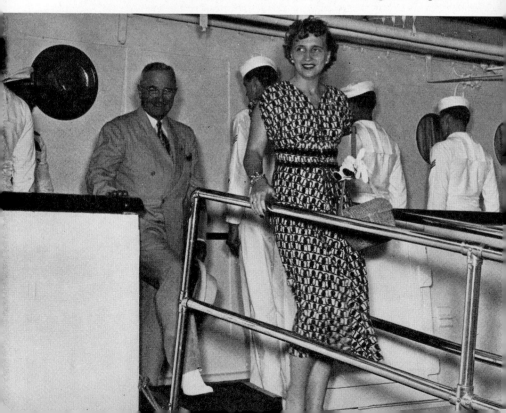

All the family came to the White House for Christmas in 1947. Here we are at dinner. I am sitting on Dad's left.

Here is a hot Canasta game between Mother, Aunt Natalie, Aunt Beuf, and Uncle Frank in our second-floor quarters.

Commodore Harry T. Manning, captain of the SS United States, *tries to teach me navigation on the bridge.*

I took this snapshot of Mother and Dad in a rare moment of relaxation one summer afternoon at Blair House.

Dad was the cameraman for this picture of Mother and me in the garden at Blair House. He jiggled it slightly.

This is one of my favorite pictures of Mother, because it really looks like her. I wish it could have been in color.

The future Queen Elizabeth wears the Order of the Garter here. I hadn't been decorated. That's just my Dior dress!

*This is my favorite picture of myself, a professional
photograph made by NBC. I fondly think it looks like me.*

beaches, which make me gritty, and close communication with the ocean, which scares me. I can't swim and I don't even want to learn.

The next day it was raining cats and dogs and beastly cold. We made one foray along the boardwalk in covered basket chairs, but I was cheered when Mother decided that we ought to drive back to Washington. Believe it or not, I had some homework to do. I had to give my oral report at Dr. Ragatz's seminar and I didn't want to go off half-cocked.

A pressing invitation had been sent to me to attend the Kentucky Derby the following week and while my interest in horse races is not overpowering, the thought of the company persuaded me to go. On May 2, I set out for Louisville in a party with Ambassador and Madame Bonnet and Mr. and Mrs. Fred Vinson. We traveled in a splendid private car, which had been tendered us by the president of the C. & O. Railroad, in a train composed entirely of even more splendid private cars. All the splendid private cars in America had been gathered in to make up this train and they were almost overpowering. We walked through the train, just for the experience, and I believe the most spectacular car belonged to Miss Barbara Hutton.

When we arrived in Louisville, we were taken on an automobile tour to Calumet Farms where I made the personal acquaintance of Man o' War, an old darling if I ever saw one, and as a special favor to me, we drove to Shelbyville, Kentucky, where my father's grandmother, Harriet Young, had been born. Shelbyville came out to meet me and made a big fuss. I signed the guest book and thought of Great-grandmother Harriet, who had eloped to marry my great-grandfather, pioneered in Missouri, reared a large family, withstood the raids of the Kansas Red Legs and lived to a ripe old age.

Back in Louisville, we attended a dinner party given by Mr. and Mrs. Barry Bingham. The next day was Derby Day and the excitement in Louisville was indescribable. Mr. and Mrs. Mark Etheridge gave a beautiful luncheon at their home preceding the race and then we all set off for the track. Some of my friends favored Assault, the Texas horse, and kept nagging me to bet on him. I favored Lord Boswell, the favorite (how could all those experts be wrong?), but to keep the peace, I put $5 on Assault's snub nose. He looked like an old farm horse to me, but he romped in ten lengths ahead of his nearest competitor and I became $46 richer. From this I

145

had to subtract the $5 I had bet on Lord Boswell, just in case! Cautious Margaret, they call me. I spent the $41 with wild abandon.

I made numerous pleasant friends in Louisville, predominantly Mr. and Mrs. Bingham and Mark and Willie Snow Etheridge, who had no axes to grind and could not have been more courteous or warmhearted toward me. But there were a few people in Louisville with politics on their minds and I am always offended and resentful when I receive political proddings under the guise of social life. I do not know whether the gentlemen who persisted in pressing me about this sort of thing believed that I was too stupid to know what they were about or not. There is no more hopeless approach to my father than through me. I would never dignify such attempts by discussing them with him.

We spent the following day at the Homestead in Hot Springs, Virginia, as the guests of the C. & O. Railroad. That night a dinner dance was given in our honor at the Homestead. At midnight we left for Washington. I had had a good time with my charming companions but I was anxious to get home. Exams were staring me in the face. From the end of that trip until the moment my exams began on May 13, I boned, breaking my vigil only to buy Mother a box of Fannie Mae chocolates and a pair of gloves for Mother's Day and to spend Sunday with the family at Shangri-La in the Pennsylvania Mountains. Shangri-La was actually a Marine Corps Center—a rough-hewn log lodge with three guest houses, surrounded by heavenly woods, heavenly peace, and heavenly quiet. Chocolate ice cream was provided for lunch in my honor, in spite of the fact that it was Mother's, not Daughter's, Day.

Concurrent with my exams, a coal crisis arrived in Washington. Dad went around looking as lugubrious as I did. On May 13 I had a horrible exam. On May 15 I had a more horrible exam which I was afraid I hadn't passed. On May 17 I had an exam in Far Eastern Affairs which ended in writer's cramp for me. On May 18 the railroad strike set in. While Dad was struggling with that he had to fly out to William Jewell College in Missouri to make a speech and receive an honorary degree. I stopped studying for my Modern Art exam long enough to run out on the balcony and watch him fly over the White House. You could see him as plain as day, and it didn't look safe to my mother, who has never got over her distaste for flying.

146

On May 20 I had my examination in Modern Art. Murder!

One of my graduation presents was a trip to New York to see the Old Vic company, which had arrived from London to perform a week of plays. Drucie and I were the guests of Louise Stewart at River House, who gave us a dinner party and then we rushed off to see Olivier in *Oedipus Rex*. It was beyond description, so I won't try. After the theatre that night, Blevins Davis gave a supper party for us at the Persian Room of the Plaza Hotel.

The next day we went to the theatre to see Part I of *Henry IV*. Afterward we were invited backstage to meet Ralph Richardson and Laurence Olivier. Vivien Leigh was also present, and she was as beautiful as you've heard.

The railroad strike had set in in dead earnest by then and we had to drive back to Washington out of necessity. This turned out to be fun, if wearing, and when I had to go to the Rosemary Ball the following night I almost fell asleep, in spite of its being a fine party. Dad delivered his speech to the nation on the subject of the railroad strike that night and he looked as tired as I felt.

On Sunday, May 26, graduation festivities began with the Baccalaureate Sermon at the National Cathedral. We all marched in, two by two, and were adjured of our responsibility to the world. I took time out to wonder if I had passed my exams. On Monday night, Dr. Marvin, president of George Washington, gave a huge reception for the graduating class. Hundreds of presents poured in for me from friends, family, and perfect strangers. It isn't fair—I said so then and I say so now—for one person to have so much.

Mother and Dad gave me a diamond-and-sapphire dinner ring. I had been pining out loud for one, and my natural bump of curiosity was driving me crazy. I kept trying to find out if my heart's desire was in the offing. Finally I tricked my poor mother into telling me before the presentation.

"I hope you've got me a diamond ring," I said. "Set in yellow gold!"

She looked at me in consternation. "Why, no," she said. "It's platinum—"

I just looked smug. Platinum was what I had had in mind.

On May 29, I was graduated with the degree of Bachelor of Arts, in Constitution Hall. My father made the Commencement Address. When I walked up on the stage in the regular procession of graduates to receive my sheepskin, Dr. Marvin announced that he would like to invest his prerogative temporarily in the President of the United States.

Grinning broadly, my father handed me the hallowed sheepskin that represented so many frenzied hours. I have always wondered if it was really legal! The procession had paused and I was alone on the vast stage. I didn't know how to get off. It was like the time I was left behind when the school orchestra played. I looked around frantically for the provost, but I couldn't locate him. Finally somebody came to retrieve me and lead me away.

Something always happens to me in Constitution Hall!

The rest of the exercises proceeded without a hitch. Dad was awarded an honorary LL.D.

"It took Margaret four years," he chuckled. "But it took me only four minutes."

"There's no justice," I told him.

After the exercises, Dr. and Mrs. Marvin entertained at a supper party for us. They presented me with a priceless book—one of the first folios of Benjamin Franklin's *Autobiography*. There was a cake for Dad, Jane Lingo, and me—the graduates. So my school days drew to a close.

The next morning I waked feeling incredibly light and free. School was out! I felt like a child, with a long happy summer stretching ahead, except that the summer would never be over. I didn't have a thing to do but write about five hundred thank-you notes. I went down the river on the *Williamsburg* to celebrate the end of school forever. I dallied about, savoring the thought that there would never be homework again. I felt as if the world were mine.

It was too early for me to realize that your education never ceases as long as you draw breath.

12: Soprano

Ever since I can remember, I have wanted to be on the stage, but my ideas about how to get on it or what to do when I got there were appropriately nebulous. When I was nine years old and learning to play the piano, I dreamed of being a concert pianist. When I was twelve years old and singing in the Trinity choir in Independence, I saw myself in a long, beautiful dress with a rose in my hair, warbling like Galli-Curci. When I began to study singing and learned some of the arias of the great operas, I went on to imagine myself acting and singing at the same time. This was immensely satisfying, for, I think, in the recesses of the subconscious, I have always yearned to be an actress.

Although my father and mother have unvaryingly wished me to pursue my own destiny there was a certain amount of dissension about my choice of a career. My father is a musician and could have no objection to the study of music, but even after I had made my debut as a singer, he stated within the hearing of reporters, "I had rather have grandchildren in my family than a prima donna!" My mother, a fair-minded woman, thought I had selected a long, hard road and could have wished that I had chosen something less complex, difficult, and public, but she did not try to dissuade me. Mamma Truman, who believed that you ought to do what you felt called on to do in this world, as long as your principles were sound and

149

your aim high, encouraged me and thought I should go at it, hammer and tongs. Aunt Mary Truman, a really fine musician, agreed, and she told me how excited she was when she was driving along the road in her car one day, and my voice came to her on the radio—out of the blue.

But my Grandmother Wallace, that gentlewoman of the old school, held the stage anathema, and remained convinced that no real lady could bring herself to be associated with the sock and buskin or tainted with the smell of greasepaint, in any way, shape, form, or fashion. She was a musician herself, but she had learned music as one of the polite arts of ladyhood, like water-color painting or embroidery, and not as the crass means of earning a living. Grandmother Wallace not only disapproved of the stage; she expressed herself on the matter periodically and in no uncertain terms, long after I was in it up to my neck.

People have hinted that after my father became President, I took an opportunistic advantage of the fact, and launched myself on a career to make money while the iron was hot. This is signally untrue. I would have pursued both music and the stage, no matter what route my father's life had taken. When I began to study voice seriously, he exacted a promise from me to finish college before I made any other plans. He may have set more store by formal education than the average father because his own education had been difficult to obtain and often interrupted.

As far as my career was concerned, my situation as the daughter of the President had disadvantages that balanced off the advantages. If I was able to obtain important engagements early, without the trial-and-error experience of the typical young singer, I was also exposed to the first-string critics and to demanding audiences. If some critics condoned or overpraised me because of my political position, others accused me of trading on my father's prestige. Whatever they said, it was hard to be sure that I was being judged on performance alone, and I wished, at all times, to be judged on performance. I yearned to sing under an assumed name, but was convinced this would add fuel to the flame.

The ramparts of music are troublesome to scale, whoever you are. In my case, there were dozens of people who wished or proposed to help me. Everybody needs all the help he can get at such a time, and in many instances I accepted it gratefully. Most of these people were professionals and many of them honestly and selflessly tried to help me and did help me. Others simply took advantage of my youth, inexperience, and amateur spirit to further their own interests. In at least one instance, this had fairly serious consequences as far as my singing was concerned, and the corollary disillusionment which comes with the discovery that you are being used. However, I managed to survive and keep on singing both with the head and the heart. If I became wary, I have never become actually suspicious.

As soon as I had fulfilled my father's stipulation regarding the B.A. degree, I was ready to go off to New York and start climbing the long hill. I was in such dead earnest that I couldn't think of anything else and I observe a notation in my journal on June 6, 1946, concerning one of my favorite beaus: "—— came tonight, and I thought he would *never* go home. Phooey!" I can only ascribe this inelegant comment to my lack of interest in everything but music, since the next entry concerns a long session of piano duets with Annette, described in the most enthusiastic terms. The President of Colombia came to lunch and brought me sixty wildly variegated orchids, flown from his native country for the occasion, and while I was appreciative and interested, I didn't seem to be as stunned as I should have been, for my mind was somewhere else.

However, it was the consensus of opinion that I should rest from my college labors for a while and in the middle of June I went home to Independence, started polishing silver, watering the lawn, cooking dinner on Vietta's day off, and driving around with Mary Shaw, Roger Sermon, Tieman Crowe, and other friends. Mother went back to Washington on the twenty-eighth of June and I stayed on in Independence with Grandmums Wallace, who was eighty-four that year. I also visited Mamma Truman a good deal. She was ninety-four, so I had the benefit of mature advice all summer. Uncle Fred's son, David, arrived from Denver to spend the summer and I was divided between the old and the young.

But my career continued uppermost in my mind. I had two projects. One was a sensible study of Shakespeare. I read a historical play every night, in order of their sequence, to familiarize myself with them on my own terms. I enjoyed this, because all my life I had been reading Shakespeare and having it interpreted for me by somebody else. That summer I made my own interpretations. The

151

other project was the recording of operas. I was studying voice regularly with Mrs. Strickler and practicing every day, but the recording sessions were good experience. I could play the records back to myself and observe my faults and try to improve on them.

Mother and Dad flew home in the *Sacred Cow* on the third of August, to vote in the primaries which were held on August 6. They landed in Grandview, as Mamma Truman was not well and Dad was anxious to see her. They were met by a welcoming delegation, twenty-five hundred strong. This may not sound like much of a crowd, but it is larger than the population of Grandview.

Primary Day was August 6, and I cast my first ballot. Needless to say, I voted the straight Democratic ticket. I was pretty excited at the thought of exercising the franchise for the first time until I got to the polls. Here I was so besieged and badgered by photographers that I couldn't possibly enjoy myself. Also, the Democrats were losing all over the place. As long as they were in town, the photographers continued to haunt us and I posed one whole day for newspapers. The pictures were dreadful and I couldn't keep from feeling resentful that they had to intrude on my vacation.

Dad went back to Washington. At this particular time he was in the middle of the growing dissension between Secretary of State James F. Byrnes and Secretary of Commerce Henry Wallace. This was like being between two hot fires, since both of these men felt that they should have been President instead of my father. (Each had expected to receive the nomination for Vice-president when Dad was nominated.) Mr. Wallace, whom my father liked but found difficult to understand (many other people have felt the same way about him), had been criticizing the foreign policy of the government, for which Mr. Byrnes was responsible. Mr. Byrnes took umbrage at this and the crisis arrived when Mr. Wallace delivered a speech at Madison Square Garden on September 12, which was subsequently interpreted in the light of appeasement toward Russia. This speech, as it was delivered, led to a revision of all speech clearances in the White House.

In discussing the matter with my father, Mr. Wallace is said to have made this statement: "I think there are times when the end justifies the means." Since this was a denial of my father's most basic principle, Mr. Wallace shortly left the Cabinet and Averell Harriman became Secretary of Commerce. Dad thought of both

Mr. Wallace and Mr. Byrnes as friends, and this increased his dismay. Mother went back to Washington with him.

I stayed on with my voice lessons and my grandmothers, reveling in the lazy fall days and rejoicing that I didn't have to get back and register for college. On November 4, Mother and Dad came home to vote. Dad and I voted together in my first national election. Mother had got up at the crack of dawn and gone to the polls as soon as they opened, to escape the reporters and photographers, but she reckoned without those worthies, who were already on hand and followed her around. Dad and I went at a normal time of day and some of them had drifted off, so we didn't have much trouble.

It was about then that the newspapers first erroneously announced my engagement. Some columnist published a rumor to the effect that Marvin Coles and I were to be wed. Such a thing had never entered my mind or his, but he called me up in great agitation. It struck me as ridiculous, but I managed to remember in time not to laugh. My mind was still focussed on New York and dreams of glory.

On November 6 I flew to Washington and the next day I left for New York, accompanied by Mrs. Strickler, to begin the groundwork for the most important launching I would ever experience. I stayed at the Waldorf, and honesty forces me to admit that it was a dismal month and the longer I stayed the more confused I became. I all but lived at the Metropolitan Opera and heard as much music of all sorts as I could and I talked to countless people. One of the nicest was Frederick Jagel, who tried very hard to help me. I would never minimize the difficulties that anybody has breaking into concert music. I seemed to be abysmally ignorant on every subject except music itself, and there were so many dozens of people offering advice, criticism, suggestions, and instructions that I didn't know what I was doing half the time.

Finally, after Thanksgiving, I couldn't bear it another minute. I got on the train and went to Philadelphia alone. I made my way to the Army-Navy game and hunted up Dad, who seemed glad to see me. After the game was over he let me go back to Washington with him. Once there, I tried to sort out my jumbled impressions and decide what to do next.

I stayed in Washington two or three days before I could muster courage to go back into the fray. Jan Christian Smuts, the South African Premier, was visiting this country at the time, and Dad gave a state dinner in his honor. The dinner was stag, but Mr. Smuts came to the White House to tea and I spent some time with him. He told me a wonderful story about Churchill. He said that during the Boer War Sir Winston had come to South Africa as a newspaper correspondent and made the mistake of being captured with a detachment of British soldiers and thrown into prison. Churchill was incensed at the failure of Boers to discriminate between a journalist and a soldier and kept shouting that he was a reporter and therefore immune from capture. But Churchill was British and seemed to be with the British Army, so the Boers couldn't tell the difference. Churchill appealed to Smuts in a few of his well-chosen words, from prison camp.

Smuts immediately set the machinery in motion for his release, but before he could accomplish this legally, Churchill escaped from prison. Long after, Smuts met Churchill on some state occasion and recalled the incident.

"If you hadn't been so slow," Churchill told him, "it would have cost me nine thousand pounds!"

"Nine thousand pounds!" Smuts said.

"I wrote the story of my escape and sold it for that!" Churchill chortled.

Prime Minister Smuts was a very elegant and dignified old gentleman when I met him, but he had a wonderful twinkle in his eye. He asked me if I were studying domestic science.

"What's that?" I asked.

"Why," he said, "the most important thing in life for a woman —cooking, cleaning, washing, ironing, and caring for a home."

"I'm not studying it," I said, "because I don't need to. I've been doing it all my life. Besides, I loathe it."

He was aghast. He said no woman worth her salt would fail to study domestic science. When he left, he gave me his card, autographed, "To the domestic scientist!"

After such pleasures, it was even more difficult to get on the train and go back to New York and try to cope with my non-existent career. I knew if I didn't go back at once I never would, so on the second of December I headed again for the big town. Frank Handy came to town and took me dancing at the Roosevelt Grill. I danced to the music of Vincent Lopez, who told me I was a good dancer, and this cheered me a little.

I spent most of the month of December in New York, going to Washington for week ends. Though I had always loved New York, and been doubtful about Washington, these week ends loomed on the horizon like a lamp in the window. One week end Mother and Dad had a reception for disabled soldiers. It was very ceremonious, with the Color Guard lined up and down the stairs and the Marine Band playing. Mother and Dad came out and marched down the stairs, followed by the Cabinet. I talked to the men and tried to make myself useful and amusing. There was an enormous crowd. The ushers used to have a private pool around the White House when there was a big reception coming on. The problem was to guess how many people would put in an appearance. They could win up to fifty dollars in this pool, but the newspapers got wind of it and Dad had to put a stop to their innocent gambling.

On Pearl Harbor Day anniversary Dad and I went to see the exhibit of Dutch paintings which had been retrieved from the salt mines in Austria by our armies, and the day was also made notable by the fact that John L. Lewis called off the impending coal strike. Hallelujah! This was a great relief to my father. A President has to get rid of one crisis as fast as possible so he can be in shape to meet the next one.

On December 11, I was back in New York and sang for Lawrence Tibbett at Steinway Hall. He was, as ever, kind and encouraging and urged me to keep working and to keep fighting to get started. But at the end of that week, I called it a day for 1946 and went home to Independence for Christmas. Dad was so involved that he didn't get to Delaware Street until noon on Christmas Day. I had saved my presents to unwrap with him. As usual, he opened his with speed and precision. At the end of thirty minutes his presents were all laid out with the proper cards in them, the holly papers smoothed and folded and the ribbons wound into neat hanks. Two hours later I was still tearing into mine with screams of appreciation, in a welter of paper and ribbons, with most of the cards lost. I told him I didn't know why I waited for *him*.

That was a gala Christmas. Everybody was up and about and able to take nourishment. Independence and Kansas City were both buzzing with parties. I didn't have to think about my career for a

155

whole week. It was quite a relief. On New Year's Eve, Joe Crowe took me to a ball at the Mission Hills Country Club in Kansas City, and when the clock struck twelve, all I could think of was: "What a year!"

The next day I slept until I waked up. This, to me, is one of the most enchanting occasions in life, but if New Year's Day sets the pattern for the year, something went wrong. I don't think I slept until I waked up again for at least 364 days.

I got back to Washington in time for Dad's State of the Union speech on January 6. The Cabinet gathered at the White House and we drove in state to the Capitol. The occasion was distinguished by the fact that I was wearing a bunchy muskrat coat and a pair of platform-soled shoes! In the photographs made that day, my dress looks too short and I seem to be freezing.

Dad made an excellent speech, applauded by both parties, which is unusual but nice.

The next day Mother and Dad gave their first big diplomatic reception. It was in honor of Premier De Gasperi of Italy, who was visiting Washington, accompanied by his daughter, Maria. There are few American social events more colorful than a diplomatic reception, to which all the ambassadors in Washington and their entourages are bidden. They usually appear wearing splendid uniforms or full evening dress, blazing with decorations. The assemblage is always spattered with scarlet and gold coats, epaulets, sashes, and jewels. The members of the Cabinet and their wives met in Dad's study for the De Gasperi reception. The Guard of Honor—composed of one officer and four enlisted men from the various services —arrived and requested permission to take the colors. When Dad had granted permission, the Color Guard seized the flags—the American flag and the President's flag—and in precise, military formation, marched to the head of the stairs, shaking the floor as they went. I was afraid they were going to knock down one of the chandeliers.

Mother and Dad then left the room, followed by the Cabinet members and their wives, in the order of precedence. Drucie and I waited until everybody had got downstairs and then sneaked out to peer over the stair railing.

Mother and Dad went into the Blue Room, which was divided in half by the receiving line. The diplomats who were gathered

156

in the East Room were convoyed through the Green Room and at the door of the Blue Room were announced by the aides. They were received by Mother and Dad and passed on to the Red Room where the members of the Cabinet received them. Then they went to the State Dining Room where tea, coffee, sandwiches, and cake were served. (No liquor is served at diplomatic receptions in the White House.) After all the diplomats had left the East Room, the Marine Band struck up and played for dancing until midnight.

Drucie and I met Premier De Gasperi, and he kissed our hands with all the grace and gallantry of Italy. The chief topic of conversation at the reception was the resignation of James F. Byrnes as Secretary of State, and the appointment of General Marshall to the post. I regretted Mr. Byrnes' ill health, but General Marshall was a special friend of mine, and it was impossible not to be happy about his appointment.

While I kept telling myself that I had to get on with my life work, one thing followed another in such rapid succession that I was hard put to practice, much less get back to New York. On January 9, Mother had two teas in one day. I have drunk a lot of tea and made a lot of small talk in my time. White House teas are pretty much like teas everywhere else, I suppose, except that the guest list always runs into the hundreds, the sandwiches and cakes into the thousands, and the handshaking into exhaustion.

That same evening I went to Constitution Hall to a concert of the Boston Symphony Orchestra. Koussevitsky was conducting and I was invited backstage to meet him before the concert. Koussevitsky was late to the podium but came in to a tremendous standing ovation. When we got to the President's box, the orchestra burst into *The Star-Spangled Banner*. It was such a thrill.

On the fourteenth of January, Mother and Dad entertained at the traditional Supreme Court Dinner. Oscar Levant was my dinner partner and the entertainer of the evening. Mr. Levant was extremely nervous—in fact, he was so nervous that I was concerned about him. But when he got up to play, the assembled company was enthralled. The next day I made a speech at the Capitol to open the Mile-of-Dimes Campaign for the National Association for the Prevention of Infantile Paralysis. *I* was extremely nervous. Like Levant, I muddled through, but I can't say the populace was enthralled.

Among my pleasantest friends in Washington were Mr. and Mrs. Curt Schiffeler, who owned the Raleigh Hotel. They were cosmopolitans and had a wide and fascinating acquaintance. They used to give Sunday evening parties at the Raleigh, where I met many important people in the world of music, art, and literature. That week end they entertained for Andre Kostelanetz and I was invited. I sat at a table for four, and my table mates were Madame Henri Bonnet, Admiral Nimitz, and Thornton Wilder. Needless to say, I just listened.

On January 20, General Marshall was sworn in as Secretary of State. Afterward I had lunch with Madame Bonnet at the French Embassy and that evening Mother and Dad entertained at a reception in the White House for all the people who worked in the government.

On January 21, His Royal Highness the Crown Prince of Saudi-Arabia and the Princess came to dinner. The next day Mrs. Roosevelt came to lunch, and Mother gave two more teas that afternoon. On January 25, Mother had a tea for the Democratic Women's Organization and that night I gave a dance for the White House aides and their girls, in the East Room. There were about twenty aides, drawn from all branches of the armed services, and they are a great institution. Aides have to be personable, attractive, and unmarried! They had eased my path in the pitfalls of protocol on many occasions and waltzed me endless miles.

When this party was over, I decided that I had to get back to my scales. I had had several conversations with Mother and Dad on the subject and we had agreed that it was time for me to set up a more permanent habitation in New York, if I was to make progress. Mother had investigated possibilities and we mutually agreed that an apartment in the Carlyle Hotel was an ideal solution. On January 29, I moved into my New York home overlooking Central Park. The apartment had a big living room, two bedrooms, a bath and kitchenette. Mrs. Strickler stayed on with me as chaperone and I was working with a new accompanist, Collins Smith. When I was not practicing I was listening to music, at Carnegie Hall or the Metropolitan. I heard Bruno Walter and Rubinstein and many others. Alec Templeton called on me and played operas by the hour.

On February 14, Mamma Truman fell in the house at Grandview and broke her hip. Dad flew home and I went to Washington to be on call. My birthday was imminent and Vietta had made me a chocolate cake. Vietta has made me a chocolate cake for my birthday every year I can remember in my life and I don't think I could celebrate this anniversary without it. I was glad to be back in Washington, for New York was still lonely and discouraging. Dad came back in time for my birthday celebration on the seventeenth with satisfactory reports on Mamma Truman and took Mother, Jane, and me to see *Pinafore*.

We sat in a front box, and John Charles Thomas, the star of the show, came out and announced that he would like to dedicate a song to me. He sang *I Saw a Lady Passing By* and at the end of it, the whole cast of *Pinafore* burst into *Happy Birthday*. It was such a surprise and such a touching gesture I was almost overcome. What a wonderful way to grow older!

The next evening Mother and Dad entertained at a Congressional Reception, attended by all the members of the Senate and the House of Representatives and their wives. I spent the evening dancing with Senators and Congressmen. They were all good men and true but they gave my feet a workout! Ouch.

On the twenty-first of February I returned to New York, feeling gloomy. My mood was lightened only by the fact that Lucrezia Bori had invited me to tea and I was going to Voisin's to dinner. I spent the Washington's Birthday holiday practicing and making up for lost time, and it was just as well, for on the twenty-sixth of February came the first break in the wall of nonchalance presented by the world of music.

Karl Krueger, conductor of the Detroit Symphony Orchestra, invited me to make my singing debut with his orchestra over a nationwide radio hookup on Sunday, March 9. I was frenetically excited and began to redouble my practicing efforts. Mrs. Strickler had rejoined me and I tried my voice in Town Hall and Carnegie Hall. One of the wise things that she insisted on was that I work in auditoriums to accustom myself to large areas and various acoustics.

I put in long hours that week and on March 2, two days before I was to entrain for Detroit, I waked up with a dull headache and a sore throat. I wanted to weep. A sore throat had never arrived at a convenient time, but now—of all times, I couldn't afford it.

159

My diary for March 3, 1947, reads as follows:

"I spent the day in bed and I feel better. I am going on that train tomorrow if it kills me or I have double pneumonia. I must sing on Sunday if possible and be on my way to a career."

Well, I went. After a miserable train ride, I checked in at the Book-Cadillac Hotel in Detroit. My throat was practically closed by then, but I had decided to ignore it. I looked as badly as I felt and I went to bed to try to mend this. The next day I sang for Dr. Krueger, who seemed enthusiastic, in spite of the fact that all my top tones had vanished in the heavy cold. He wanted me to sing on Sunday and I was determined to go through with it.

The next day the news was noised abroad that I was going to make my debut and the photographers arrived in legions. Dr. Krueger and I were photographed endlessly and Mrs. Strickler and I were entertained at a big dinner at the Detroit Club. My chest had begun to feel tight and funny.

The next morning it felt tighter and funnier. I could scarcely breathe. Word of this state of affairs had sifted back to Washington and presently Dr. Graham flew into Detroit, taking my pulse and temperature in spite of all I could do. I knew I was in the soup when I looked at his face.

"You have bronchial pneumonia," Dr. Graham announced accusingly.

"But I have to sing Sunday . . . ," I croaked.

"No," said Dr. Graham. "You don't."

"But I *want* to," I protested.

"But you can't," he said.

I turned over and began to cry. "Now everybody will say I was just too scared," I wailed. I was scared, but not that scared. After all that slaving I didn't like the idea of being felled by a virus.

But the next morning when Hank Meyers, the pilot of the *Sacred Cow*, and the crew arrived, I loved every one of them. I never saw anybody look so good. They bundled me into the airplane and flew me home. God bless them every one.

Announcement that my debut had been postponed a week was given out, and I suppose a good many people did think I was too scared. I was sheltered from what anybody thought by being in bed with a high fever. The room reeked of the benzoin kettle and

160

I was taking penicillin every few minutes. Some of the time I was afraid I was going to die and the rest of the time I was afraid I wasn't!

On the fourth day, I struggled up and got out of bed and began to try my voice. It sounded terrible and I was so weak I could hardly stand up. But I kept at it. On Saturday, March 15, I was back in Detroit, with a regular entourage. Mother had dispatched Reathel Odum to be with me. Dr. Graham was along and Major Strickler had also arrived to do what he could. The odor of benzoin continued to cling to my person. My nose was red, my eyes were watery, and my hair had that lifeless look that comes of a bad cold and fever and a delayed shampoo.

As soon as I arrived I went into a practice session with Dr. Krueger. I can remember very little about it, except that he was sweet to me and gave me a big pep talk. I was numb from so much penicillin and all I remember is that I was determined to go on the air on that Sunday, no matter what happened.

When the fateful day dawned, I had to get up early and start practicing. I rehearsed with Dr. Krueger until noon and then went back to the hotel to rest until 2 P.M., when I had my first rehearsal with the orchestra. I managed to get through this and Dr. Graham checked me over. He decided to put me under a sun lamp for a few minutes and left me in charge of a Medical Corps attendant, who apparently did not understand his instructions. The intense light of the sun lamp scorched the back of my legs so that they broke out with water blisters. I felt stiff and feverish, the way you do when you get a painful sunburn.

Finally it was time to get dressed. I was wearing a long chiffon dress in pale blue, with a velvet bodice in a darker shade of blue and a billowing skirt in many layers. Something broke while I was putting it on and Reathel had to sew me into it. By this time, it seemed to me that nothing else could possibly go wrong. I felt hysterical but I refused to permit myself to give way to it or to pamper my nervousness. I just talked myself out of it. Grandmother Wallace had sent me an orchid, which seemed like a good omen.

At 8:28 Eastern Standard, Sunday the sixteenth of March, 1947, I went on the air. I sang *Cielito Lindo*, an anonymous Spanish folk song, in an arrangement by Manuel Padilla; an aria from Felician

161

David's *La Perle du Brasil,* familiarly known as *Charmante Oiseau,* and *The Last Rose of Summer.*

Perhaps sheer naïveté saw me through. I was possibly the first unevaluated singer to make a debut with a major symphony orchestra to a radio audience estimated at twenty million persons—a gamble that would have turned a more sophisticated musician gray. I had had little experience singing with orchestra. Unlike a singer who walks in from the wings to make a debut before an audience, I was forced to sit on the stage for twenty-five minutes before I sang, with the music of the orchestra ringing in my ears. Instead of singing into the auditorium, I sang into a microphone, which requires a special technique and made my voice difficult to hear in the balconies where a battery of newspaper reporters and critics were ensconced. I was aware that my father was glued to a radio in the Navy Commandant's quarters in Key West; that my mother was listening in the White House, that Mamma Truman was listening from her bed in Grandview, and that Grandmother Wallace, who didn't have much use for the stage, was listening critically in Independence. I couldn't let anybody down.

(Of course, I was scared. I'm always scared just before a concert. I have stage fright yet when I am going to sing, and if I didn't have it I'd be worried. It usually sets in a couple of hours before a concert, and I spend so much energy disciplining my stage fright before I go on that when I reach the stage, I've worn it out in advance.)

I took off my fur jacket and I stood up, smoothing my skirt, walked to the microphone and began to sing *Cielito Lindo.* I forgot all about my pneumonia and my blistered legs and the fact I was sewn into my dress and that the critics were lined up in the gallery, and the family hanging on every note. I sang—because I love to sing.

As soon as the broadcast was over, Dr. Krueger made me a little speech in which he said I was a real trouper and he was glad to have had a part in the launching of my career, and gave me a sheaf of roses. I thanked him and the members of the orchestra. Then hordes of photographers sprinted down the aisles. I made only one request and that was that they not take any pictures of me with my mouth open. This was a long, grueling session but when we had fought our way out of it and back to the Book-Cadillac, I had a

162

telephone call from Daddy, who told me that I had performed wonderfully, but of course he's *prejudiced*. Mother called from the White House and said that she was satisfied and flowers and telegrams poured in in an avalanche. I had received five hundred wires before midnight and the broadcasting station's switchboard, as well as the White House switchboard in Washington, were engulfed in phone calls and had to close down temporarily.

There was a press reception at the hotel after the concert, given by NBC, and suddenly I felt wonderful. I felt light and free—as if I had survived a tough exam in Victorian Poetry. This was the biggest and hardest exam I had ever had, but I wouldn't know whether I had passed until the notices were in.

By and large the critics were very kind to me. They may have been more kind than I deserved but I will always be grateful to them. Many of them mentioned my youth and inexperience, and one Chicago critic announced that my voice was immature, unremarkable, and unobjectionable! Robert Merrill said I had given a fine performance, and Al Jolson said I would make a singer. Two Hollywood writers who had previously offered me $5,000 to appear in a film named *Las Vegas*, raised the offer to $10,000!

I finally went to bed but not to sleep. I don't think I closed an eye all night and for once in my life I didn't mind having to get up early. I got my first pay check on Monday, the seventeenth of March. It was for the staggering sum of $1,500 and I already had it spent.

We went back to Washington that day and I went right down and bought a mink scarf. I selected the very best. Mother was with me and approved of my choice.

As I gave the charge address, my mother said, "Oh no you don't."

"Why?" I asked.

"You bought it," she said. "You pay for it."

This came as a distinct shock to me. If I'd thought about that, I don't think I would have selected anything quite so fine.

"You're making your own money now," my mother said.

After years of trying, she finally convinced me of the value of money!

A fantastic number of telegrams and letters continued to pour in and I signed mail and wrote thank-you notes for days on end. Drucie and Jane came to dinner and they had to hear all about it. Alex

163

Radford took me to the Toll House for dinner and he had to hear all about it. Annette and Irv Wright came and spent the week end at the White House and they had to hear all about it, all week end. I held a press conference and thanked everybody in the world.

On April 1, I opened my first bank account at the Hamilton National Bank. All I had to put in was what was left after buying those three mink skins to wear with a suit. I got a lot of instruction in finance that day. Finance confused me and still does. This may come of not being able to add or subtract very well.

Almost the nicest thing about the whole debut were the perfect strangers who stopped me on the street to congratulate me and say nice things . . . little old ladies and messenger boys and teen-agers and policemen and all sorts of people. They were the ones who made me want to go on singing.

About a week after the debut, Betty Buchanan had a luncheon at the Statler. When I came in, the orchestra struck up but I didn't pay any attention to it—went right on talking. Suddenly Jane punched me in the ribs with her elbow.

"Do something!" she hissed.

"Why?" I asked.

"They're playing *your song!*" Jane said.

"Which one?" I asked dumbly.

"*Cielito Lindo!*" Jane said. "Don't you remember it?"

"Just barely," I said, and smiled on all the thoughtful people there.

13: Traveling troupe

With my first public appearance out of the way and with the notices at least promising, I began to have serious hopes for a concert tour. Machinery had been set in motion for me to take to the road around the middle of May, and since many of the critics had hinted that I needed to work, I worked as hard as I could while trying to manage the various obligations that descended on me—to family, friends, and public.

I had no regular concert manager at this time. Mrs. Strickler, my teacher, made my first bookings. While her experience in this part of the music business was limited, she did the best she could and she did set up several engagements for me.

We spent a quiet Easter Sunday. Mother and I attended early Communion at St. John's and then we set off for the celebrated old Pohick Church in Virginia for eleven o'clock services. The drive through the blossoming Virginia countryside was so beautiful and peaceful, I wished for a fleeting moment to be a lady of leisure, but my work was cut out for me.

The next day was Army Day and there was a big parade in Washington. I have a passion for parades and the sounds of bands and marching go to my head, whether I'm in it or standing on the sidewalk. I finished up Army Day by seeing a show—Maurice Evans in guess what—*Hamlet!* I saw Maurice in *Hamlet* a total of five times, which must be a record for that production. I counted the month lost when I didn't see Maurice in *Hamlet*.

The big event of that April was the marriage of my dear friend Mary Shaw, better known as Shawsie, to Coleman Branton in Kansas City. I was maid of honor. The wedding took place on April 12 and I went to Missouri on April 8. Between visiting Mamma Truman and the aunts and uncles, I sandwiched in a lot of parties for Shawsie and had a group of photographs made by Iris Palmer. The day before the wedding I had a frenzied day. Dad arrived at Fairfax Airport to visit Mamma Truman and I went to meet him. Then I had to pick up all Shawsie's trousseau luggage. Then we all posed for pictures and went to the wedding rehearsal, which was followed by a dinner party.

It was a lovely wedding and the bride looked beautiful in a gown of ice-blue brocade and lace. This was my first stint as maid of honor and I was more nervous than the bride. They were married with a double-ring ceremony, and I wore the ring that Shawsie had for Coleman on my thumb as I walked down the aisle and all during the ceremony, for fear I would misplace it at the critical moment. There was a big reception after the wedding at the Junior League Clubhouse, which went on most of the afternoon. I finally managed to drag Shawsie away from her friends and well-wishers and get her into her going-away outfit. Then Coleman's brother, who had been best man, and Shawsie and Coleman and I went to the train and we saw the honeymooners off to Ponte Vedra.

I had been the President's daughter for two years that day.

I spent the next day with Mamma Truman and then embarked with Dad on the *Sacred Cow* for Washington. The following day I was in New York to reactivate my career. It was more of the same—studying, practicing, singing, making records, going to opera. I heard *Traviata* at City Center. The soprano was a buxom girl and the tenor was a small, slight man. In one of the big scenes the soprano went down on the floor and dragged the tenor with her. I had always expected this to happen on an operatic stage and when it did, I am ashamed to admit, I almost burst in an effort to keep from laughing.

I was engulfed in the excitement of preparing for the concert tour. On the twentieth of April, Mother came up to New York to consult on clothes. All my concert dresses have always been made

166

by Madame Pola. Kosbukoff, her husband, is the conductor of the Don Cossack Chorus, and she has lived in the atmosphere of the concert hall and the theatre and understands the sort of gowns which are suitable and comfortable for singers.

Possibly the most spectacular concert dress was the one Madame Pola made from sari cloth. The fragile, gold net fabric, posed over pink taffeta, was embroidered with little birds in golden thread in an all-over design. My other favorite was an off-shoulder white chiffon, trimmed around the neckline and bodice with a tracery of sheer black lace, which stood up on the shoulders like small wings. The dress was tucked all over and had twenty-eight yards of white chiffon in multitudinous layers in the skirt. It had a muff of tucked white chiffon, trimmed with black lace, and made a marvelous stage dress. Greta Kempton eventually painted my portrait in this dress and it hangs in the front hall in the house on Delaware Street. There were other dresses but these stand out. I stood for endless fittings on them and this whacked hours out of my crowded days.

I had asked Mrs. Henry Gossard of Kansas City to be my business manager, and on May 5 I signed my original contracts. My first engagement was scheduled for the Syria Mosque in Pittsburgh, Pennsylvania, on May 19. I managed to get to Washington for Dad's birthday on May 8 and then rushed back to New York to meet my accompanist, Mrs. Carleton Shaw. The next week was taken up with the endless details of concert planning and with publicity pictures and releases for the tour—with practice and more practice.

I was already feverishly packing when Mother telephoned me to say that Mamma Truman was on the point of death and Dad had flown to Independence. He had left word that I was not to alter any of my plans until he advised me. But of course I was depressed and torn between getting on with it and getting to Independence to be with my father. I couldn't concentrate on a concert when Mamma Truman was so sick.

Nevertheless, on April 18 I did as instructed and entrained for Pittsburgh, in company with Mrs. Shaw and Vietta, who had been sent on by Mother to act as my dresser, comforter, guide, and friend. Vietta kept me pinned together that week. Not only did she get me into my clothes but she made me laugh. Something had gone wrong with our reservations (this is basic in a concert tour) and Vietta had to sleep in an upper berth. The spectacle of her getting

167

into it and out of it made us laugh until the tears rolled. Vietta can be as much of a ham as I am.

On the morning of May 19 we were in Pittsburgh and received word that Mamma Truman was not expected to live through the day. I immediately canceled the concert in Pittsburgh and also the scheduled engagement in Cleveland, Ohio. What a wild time that was. As soon as I had made my peace with the concert managers, I got on a plane for Independence. The plane developed engine trouble and one of the motors conked out. For a while I didn't know whether I would live to see Mamma Truman. I finally got home and out to Grandview. Mamma Truman was very ill, but her mind remained crystal-clear. She brightened when she saw me.

For the next five days Mamma Truman became progressively worse, weaker, more frail, and eventually developed a high fever. We had no hope. But on the twenty-fourth of May she waked up and demanded a slice of watermelon in a clear, firm voice. Dr. Graham said she should have anything she wanted and we scurried around and got the watermelon, though it was not in season. Mamma Truman ate most of it!

The next day she was greatly improved. Four days later she was sufficiently on the mend for us all to take off in the *Sacred Cow* for Washington. It was incredible. Her powerful spirit had risen above the weakness of the body and she sent us off with calm assurance. There I was, back in Washington as if nothing had happened—kiting around in the convertible, stopping at the Hot Shoppe for sodas, and going to the circus with Chief Justice and "Mommy" Vinson.

On the ninth of June, Mamma Truman was healthy enough for Dad and Mother and me to take off on our first official visit to another country. We had been invited to Canada and we left Washington that evening for Ottawa in the Presidential car, accompanied by an entourage which occupied the whole train. Dad's entire staff went with him, and I called us the Traveling Troupe.

I love Canada, and the city of Ottawa, with its massive Houses of Parliament and Government House in the Tudor style, was brilliant with flowers and greenery. The first day we were there I wrote in my diary:

Tuesday, June 10, 1947

The Canadian Minister of External Affairs M. St. Laurent, Chief of Protocol M. Measures, and our Ambassador Mr. Atherton got on the train at Rouses Point, also the Governor General's aides. The first three had lunch with us and we arrived outside of Ottawa at Island Park Drive. There was a pavilion and red carpet and oh! those Mounties. I rode in the parade with Prime Minister MacKenzie King and Admiral Leahy. There was quite a crowd gathered to see us arrive.

Outside the gate to Government House (Rideau Gate) Dad and his Excellency the Governor General Lord Alexander of Tunis inspected the Guard and there was a salute—fired over a hill, thank goodness.

We had tea inside and then went out in the garden where Mother and Dad each planted a tree. A short—very short—rest and then to dress for a State Dinner.

My room is big and done in blue and a big splashy print. The bath is miles down the hall. I wore my pink and gold lamé dress from India and it caused quite a lot of comment, especially from the Prime Minister. He is so sweet.

A big reception followed, but I didn't have to stand in line, thank Heavens.

᭜ What I didn't go into in my diary was *L'Affaire* Bathroom. As I have noted—it seemed miles away from my room. I got unpacked and got into a robe and took my little cosmetic kit and my toothbrush and started to make the trek. When I opened the door of my bedroom, I was flabbergasted to see two or three liveried men standing at rigid attention at intervals along the long hall. Hastily I shut the door and retreated. I waited about fifteen minutes, thinking that as soon as we were settled they would go away. Then I peered cautiously out the door and there they stood, impassive as marble. I poked my head out the door two or three more times, but they were always there, and finally I realized that they were *guarding* us . . . that this was the precaution taken by a foreign government when the President of the United States was in residence.

I didn't know what to do but I had to get dressed, so finally I sailed out in my negligee, with my head up and my eyes front, and marched down the long hall between the guards and gained the bathroom. It was a shattering experience!

The state dinner and reception were unusually splendid and Prime

Minister Mackenzie King, whom I had met on numerous occasions, was especially nice to me. He was a dear man and had that happy faculty of talking to young people that I have often mentioned with appreciation in these memoirs. In fact, he had a whole battery of ladylike jokes with which he regaled me. He asked me if I had heard about the poor chameleon who made the mistake of climbing onto a piece of Scotch plaid.

"What happened?" I asked.

"He burst!" said the Prime Minister, proud as Punch that I had bitten.

Our days in Canada were full of excitement and fun as my diary attests:

Wednesday, June 11, 1947

Had breakfast on a tray in Mother's room. Then we walked in the garden. Gorgeous sight. All colors of tulips, red, purple, white, are planted in a huge square with green carpet in the middle. It's an enormous garden. There's a pool in the middle of a lovely rock garden, falling from terrace to terrace.

We drove to hear Dad address a joint session of Parliament—like England's. He made a good speech.

We drove to the War Memorial where Dad placed a wreath. The band played three national anthems, ours, Canada's, and the British. Most impressive and hot as H!

We drove back to our Embassy for lunch with Mrs. Atherton and Mia [our ambassador's wife and daughter]. It is a huge house on a high hill with acres of ground. Our flag was out and it looked wonderful. Government House is big and rambling, over a hundred rooms. It was fascinating to stay there but I am so glad to be here. The bath is *by* my room.

Took a short nap and then there was a dinner of young people here at the Embassy for me. Mother and Dad went to the Prime Minister's for dinner. It was Mia Atherton's birthday. I had a song dedicated to me, very clever, by a man named Saul Rao.

Julia [one of the White House maids] has come with us and Mother and I couldn't dress without her.

Thursday, June 12, 1947

I had breakfast in bed. Such luxury. We all drove to the Seignory Club outside of Ottawa fifty miles. It is in the Province of Quebec. All the signs and advertisements are in French. It was a lovely luncheon. I sat between Mike Pearson [now Foreign Minister] and our Ambassador.

Back at the Embassy, Dad pinned a medal on General Hodges, Canadian Chief of Staff. We had a Mountie escort on motorcycles both ways and we almost flew getting back in time.

Tonight there was a formal dinner at the Embassy. Here, in Canada, the ranking guests (Lord and Lady Alexander) come last, naturally. And they are taken around and introduced to all the other guests. It is apt to wind up in second introductions and confusion. I like our way of the guests and host standing in line.

We drove straight to the train after dinner and I had the Prime Minister all to myself. He is charming and told me so many jokes. He is 72. You'd never guess it. Has been P.M. for 20 years—longer than any other P.M. in the British Empire.

There were more Mounties at the train and a stand and red carpet again. I won't be able to board any ordinary train any more, I'll want scarlet carpets and scarlet-coated Mounties!

Friday, June 13, 1947

I got up to take a glimpse of Niagara Falls and then went back to sleep. We had a grand visit and built up, I think, a lot of good will. Everyone was so hospitable and gracious to us. The country looks so fresh and not so closely populated as the USA. Ottawa is quite small for a Capital city. It is all beautiful and looks very old-world and, at the same time, modern. The picture I shall always carry in my mind of Ottawa and Canada are the big gray buildings of Parliament, the green grass and the splashes of red color in the coats of the Mounties.

Got in safe and sound, but late.

&> The next day we arose to greet a whole contingent of summer visitors—several relatives from Missouri came to spend a few days. And Jane Watson came down from New York to spend the week end with me. Drucie was sailing for Europe on the SS *America* in a few days and I had a luncheon for her in the State Dining Room. The centerpiece was a silver galleon loaded with flowers, on the side of which we had put the legend SS *America*. I was happy that Drucie was going to Europe but I was so envious of the trip I could scarcely contain myself. I had never been abroad and I wanted to go.

On June 17, the Traveling Troupe set out for Princeton, New Jersey, to take part in the celebration of the two hundredth anniversary of the founding of Princeton University. General Eisenhower, Chief Justice and Mrs. Fred Vinson, and Admiral Leahy

171

were in our car. Lord and Lady Alexander had come down from Ottawa to attend the ceremonies. President and Mrs. Dodd entertained at a luncheon, and my luncheon partner was General Eisenhower. Before lunch I was chatting with a delightful lady, the late Mrs. Preston, once the wife of Grover Cleveland, when General Eisenhower came up to claim me. I introduced him, but he apparently did not know who she was. I didn't get a chance to tell him. We were talking about Washington, and the General joined politely in our conversation.

"And where did you live in Washington, ma'am?" he asked.

She looked up at him demurely. "In the White House," she said.

The General's face fell. I'm sure he wanted to murder me, but he hadn't given me time to brief him. Well, such things happen to all of us.

The Princeton Academic Procession on this occasion was the longest in history. It was extremely colorful. The French participants wore brilliant green uniforms; the English wore long scarlet robes; most of the black gowns were surmounted by the brilliant hoods that denote various degrees. I enjoyed it thoroughly, since I didn't have to take a degree!

We got back in time to tell our departing relatives good-by. After we had made our farewells and were standing on the Portico to wave, they all piled in the car and it wouldn't start. This was a real anticlimax. Finally the car had to be pushed round and round the White House grounds and in the end a mechanic was summoned. They didn't get off until two-thirty in the afternoon.

On the twentieth of June we held a reception for the disabled veterans from the Service Hospitals. A vast number of them came. I devoted my attention to the wheel-chair cases, serving them refreshments, supplying them with autographs, and running errands for them.

My father was feeling especially depressed at this time, as the Eightieth Congress had just presented him with the Taft-Hartley Act, which he had vetoed as "a shocking piece of legislation." I do not have to tell you that the veto was overridden in both houses. But my father believed that he was right, no matter how lonely this action made him feel.

On Sunday, June 3, Mrs. Roosevelt came to a luncheon with

172

us on the porch of the White House. She and Dad were scheduled to make speeches that afternoon at the Lincoln Memorial, and we had a long leisurely lunch, during which Mrs. Roosevelt reminisced about her days at 1600 Pennsylvania and regaled us with stories of President Roosevelt. She remarked on the friendship of Roosevelt and Churchill and said they could spend a long evening together without once mentioning politics.

Soon after this I went to Independence. I couldn't wait, but the thought of having to pack almost deterred me. In my long war with luggage, I feel qualified to say that I have packed and unpacked as much or more than any woman my age, but then I was only beginning! I didn't know! I spent a peaceful Fourth of July, picnicking and watching fireworks. Dad made a speech at Monticello, which I listened to on the radio, in which he called a spade a spade. The maritime strike was just over and he had many other worries.

The happy pattern of Independence repeated itself. I polished the woodwork, took a singing lesson, practiced, and gallivanted around at night with dates. Mother took Grandmother Wallace to Denver and deposited her with Uncle Fred and Aunt Chris and came back home. I had a postcard from Drucie in which she was so madly in love with Paris that she couldn't leave it for five more days! I gritted my teeth and installed a badminton court in the back yard to improve my figure.

On July 26, I lost one of my best friends. I wrote in my diary:

Saturday, July 26, 1947
Mamma Truman died today at 11:05 A.M. Mother and I drove out there and then on to the Grandview Airport to meet Dad at 3:30. He had been told while flying over Cincinnati. We all stayed out until dinnertime and then came home.

Sunday, July 27, 1947
I got up early and went to Grandview with Dad and talked to people who came to pay their respects. I finally got up my nerve and went in to see Mamma Truman. I'm glad I did because she looks much better than she has the past few weeks. She looks very natural except her eyes are closed and I've never seen her asleep before. I keep hearing her voice and when everything is quiet I could swear I can hear her talking. It doesn't seem possible she's gone. She did mighty well to live 94 such good years. I'll never forget her.

Monday, July 28, 1947

The funeral was at home in Grandview. It was brief, as Mamma Truman wished. The house was covered with flowers and the basement floor was carpeted with floral tributes. The Cabinet sent a huge wreath of red roses and President Aleman of Mexico a huge wreath. One of gardenias came from Cuba and one of glads from the Senate. Mother got an enormous spray of red roses, Mamma Truman's favorite, for the casket. All the other flowers were sent to hospitals. We all drove to Forest Hills Cemetery for the services and they were short too. She is beside Grandfather Truman now.

With the loss of Mamma Truman, death struck for the first time at my intimate circle, but perhaps people are alive as long as they are remembered. I thought a lot about Mamma Truman and the tremendous span of time her life had encompassed. She was born when Fillmore was President, early in the reign of Queen Victoria, when the population of the United States was less than twenty-five million. She had witnessed the raiding parties of the Civil War. Everything had changed around her, but Mamma Truman had never changed. Her life had had its share of disappointments, hardship, and loss, but she had lived it to the hilt and she had never been confused or frightened. Her philosophy was simple. You knew right from wrong and you did right, and you always did your best. That's all there was to it. That's about all you need, too. I hope that strong and simple integrity rubbed off on me.

߷ On the fifth of August I received an invitation to sing in the Hollywood Bowl on August 26, from conductor Eugene Ormandy. Mother had brought Grandmother Wallace home from Denver in time to celebrate her birthday on August 4 and had gone on to Washington to join my father. I called them at Shangri-La and discussed the concert engagement. They were all for it and I began to make plans, redoubled the practice sessions, and took more lessons every week. Lib Knowland, the flutist, worked with me. On the sixteenth of August I entrained for my first trip to California on the Super-Chief. I was accompanied by Major and Mrs. Strickler, Mrs. Gossard, and Margaret Alexander, a reporter for the *Kansas City Star*.

We arrived on the morning of the eighteenth and were met by the usual press detail and welcoming committee. This was followed by a trip to the Bowl, the very thought of which terrified me. When I saw it, I didn't feel nearly so afraid. Of course, it is gargantuan, but the acoustics are so marvelous that you can hear a pin dropped on the stage all over the canyon.

I found that it would be necessary for me to join the American Guild of Musical Artists before I could appear at this concert, so I joined, and still carry my union card.

The happiest thing possible happened then. I got word from Shawsie and Coleman Branton that they were in San Francisco and proposed to come down and hear me sing. I couldn't have been more thrilled. Shawsie was invaluable. She not only served as holder-upper but went out and combed the stores of Los Angeles and Beverly Hills for some long underwear to go under my white chiffon dress! The California nights were so cold that I knew I would freeze and probably wind up with bronchial pneumonia again.

Shawsie had a terrible time finding the necessary article in Southern California. The salesgirls were indignant when she asked for winter undies in that tropical paradise, but she persisted. She finally got a suit and we cut it up so that it wouldn't show and I wore it gratefully. It probably saved my life. I was cold enough that night with it on. I wore the white chiffon and black lace dress Madame Pola had made for me and the ridiculous muff came in handy.

I refer you to passages from my diary for a description of the concert:

Friday, August 22, 1947
Had my first orchestra rehearsal at 12:15 with Mr. Ormandy and the orchestra. It was a real thrill. He is a nice sandy-haired gentleman and has such a grand sense of humor.

I had my second rehearsal with him and orchestra at 4:00. I feel very secure about my songs.

Saturday, August 23
The big day! Had a dress rehearsal with Ormandy and orchestra at 1:00. Then came back to the hotel and ate lunch and rested. At 6:00 I had a steak and potato and went to the Bowl. I was cold and glad of my winter underwear. I saw two men outlined against the moon way up on the hill when I was singing and they looked about an inch high. It was an odd sensation to sing to 20,000 people all at once and be able to see them. Mr.

Ormandy was a love. He talked to me between numbers very sotto voce on the stage and relaxed me completely. He said after it was all over if I weren't such a big shot he'd kiss me. So I told him I wasn't a big shot and he kissed me. He is my favorite conductor of all time. He sent me an orchid for good luck. I was also presented a bouquet of 144 orchids flown from Hawaii for me by the Bowl Association.

The reception at the hotel was awfully long. I talked to Mother and Dad before going to it. Ezio Pinza came to the reception, also Jeanette MacDonald and Gene Raymond and Nelson Eddy, Risë Stevens and Lauritz Melchior. They were all most kind and cordial. Nelson came up and said I was on my way, and good luck.

The concert seemed to have gone well. At least, the papers were complimentary and it seemed to me that I had gained confidence since my last appearance. I actually had had a good time and felt immensely grateful to Eugene Ormandy, who had seen me through it.

I left California the next day in the *Independence*. It was my first trip aboard this great airship. I had to hurry home because the Traveling Troupe was now headed for South America on a diplomatic mission. In a manner of speaking, I was excess baggage on any diplomatic mission, but other countries like a chance to look over the youthful members, just as we loved it when foreign diplomats brought their sons and daughters to the White House. I couldn't have been more pleased to make up this unnecessary cargo, and began to brush up on the samba.

14: The South American way

My father's official purpose in going to Brazil was to attend the Monetary Conference in session at Petropolis. He had also been invited to address the Brazilian Congress and to review a parade in honor of Brazil's Independence Day, September 7. We flew out of Washington on the *Independence* on Sunday, August 31, 1947, and we were gone six weeks—one of the longest absences from the White House my father permitted himself while he was President. We were accompanied on this tour by a typical retinue including Charlie Ross, Dad's Press Secretary, Stanley Woodward and William Hassett, Matt Connelly, Clark Clifford and Brazil's Ambassador to the United States, Carlos Martins, and Senhora Martins.

The first lap of our journey ended in Trinidad that afternoon. The weather was scorching hot and the tropical rain bucketed down at intervals. Fortunately, as the plane set down, the rain stopped long enough to permit us to land. We spent the night at the house of the Commandant, which was in the middle of the jungle. The house was set high up, on a second-story level, because it is always so damp in Trinidad. The vivid green of the foliage seemed to press against the screens (there were no windows) like a wall. When I went to my room I found some enormous, unidentifiable crawling thing

177

just outside my screen, so I didn't sleep a wink all night. I detest bugs, spiders, and insects of any kind. They always seem to give me the creeps.

It didn't matter much whether I slept or not, as we took off from Trinidad at the unearthly hour of 3 A.M. The rain was descending in sheets by then and I feel very dim at three o'clock in the morning. One hilarious thing lightened our departure. All our diplomats and staff were dressed in formal clothes—striped trousers and morning coats—in order to be properly garbed for the reception to be tendered us at Galiao, across the bay from Rio de Janeiro, since they would have no opportunity to dress on the plane nor time after we landed. It was funny enough to see them in this dignified attire in the wee hours of the morning with the rain streaming down. But just before the take-off, while the motors were being revved and we were all in the plane with our seat belts fastened, we missed Charlie Ross. He wasn't there and it developed that nobody had remembered to wake him! Mr. Hassett got off the plane and sprinted through the jungle in his striped pants in the teeming downpour to retrieve the missing passenger. Needless to say, when he got back to the plane with Charlie Ross, his pants were slightly the worse for wear. He had got wet to his knees and the creases had definitely disappeared.

From Trinidad we flew across the jungles and the Amazon to Belem, Brazil, to refuel. We all received jungle kits and machetes, just in case we crashed in the jungle. I didn't find this particularly cheerful, and didn't think I would have strength to use a machete if I ran across some of the insects I suspected were in the jungle! We were flying at 19,000 feet and the Amazon is certainly the biggest river in the world. At our speed, it took twenty minutes to cross it, but I was reliably informed that it was two hundred miles wide at one place. It was a beautiful flight, although we were so high the jungles beneath us were only a vague green blur. We flew into the dawn and this was the first time I realized the sun comes up in the sky long before its light reaches the earth. We flew in brilliant sunlight while the earth below was still wrapped in darkness.

As we crossed the Amazon, the dawn began to make itself felt on the earth and we could see the reflection of clouds and our plane in the water below. We watched ourselves fly over the Amazon in this mirror. It was very exciting and made more of an impression on me than crossing the equator, which I had never done before, but

178

which didn't seem to be fraught with any particular drama in an airplane.

We arrived at Galiao at 2:45 P.M. and were met by Secretary Marshall and Mrs. Marshall, Ambassador and Mrs. Pawley, and several Brazilian officials. There was a color guard and a band that played the Brazilian national anthem and *The Star-Spangled Banner*, and then our party moved down to the wharf where a boat was waiting to take us across the bay. The city of Rio, bulwarked by mountains, with its magnificent skyline and busy waterfront, loomed before us. Rio has one of the most beautiful situations in the world and the whole city sparkled like one of the jewels for which it is famous.

When we arrived at Rio the red carpet seemed to be about a mile long. President Dutra was waiting and came to greet Dad, and a twenty-one-gun salute was fired. I put my hands over my ears and said ouch, but I hadn't heard anything yet! So many salutes were fired in the following weeks that Admiral Leahy finally got a roll of absorbent cotton and presented it to me to enable me to stuff my ears. Twenty-one guns make a lot of noise: the recoil sets up a terrific vibration and I am hypersensitive to sound. Twenty-one-gun salutes were part of my problem as the daughter of the President!

We were driven to the Embassy in a parade. The streets were lined with thousands upon thousands of people, all cheering and throwing confetti and paper. The paper sifted down like snow and fell all around us during the entire line of march. I never saw such a tumultuous welcome.

At last we reached the Embassy and as soon as we could freshen up, we set out for Cotete, the Presidential Palace of Brazil, to pay our official call. It was all gold and crystal and looked like the palace in a fairy tale. President Dutra was very charming and made us feel genuinely at home. That night we dined at the Embassy with Ambassador and Mrs. Pawley and Secretary and Mrs. Marshall. I sat by Secretary Marshall, which was enough to make my evening. "I had such a good time," I wrote in my diary. "He is such a wonderful man."

The next morning we were up early and off to Petropolis to attend the closing hours of the Monetary Conference. The route was mountainous and we drove through fog and rain most of the way. But the Hotel Quitandinha made up for everything. It is so fabulous that no description could be adequate and I will forgo the effort. Dad addressed the conference that afternoon and made a good speech, which was received with loud applause. Then we went back to Rio.

The USS *Missouri* was lying in the harbor—oh, my ship—and we got on a little cruiser and went out to board her. It was the second of September and the second anniversary of the signing of the Japanese Armistice aboard the *Missouri*. When we arrived, we received what seemed to me to be an unusually noisy twenty-one-gun salute. When President Dutra arrived, he received another one. Dad made a little speech for the occasion, and a Brazilian gentleman responded. After that we embarked on the cruiser and left. As we departed the usual twenty-one-gun salvo was fired. President Dutra got on his cruiser and left. Twenty-one more guns were fired. This made eighty-four guns in a very short space, and in spite of Admiral Leahy's cotton my ears were gone!

We told Secretary and Mrs. Marshall good-by at the wharf. They were returning to Washington with Hank Meyers on the *Sacred Cow* that night. I then made a mad dash to the Embassy to get dressed for a party at the Guinles'. It was a cocktail party, and they are held appropriately late in Rio. The Guinles lived in the most fabulous apartment I have ever seen. Senhor and Senhora Guinle and their two sons and their wives all lived in the same building. The rooms were enormous and floored throughout with beautiful marble, which gave directly onto grassy lawns. The rooms were filled with flowers and crystal chandeliers and handsome people.

Around eleven o'clock, we began to think about dinner. Stanley Woodward, Matt Connelly, Clark Clifford, Charlie Ross, Anita Pawley (Ambassador Pawley's niece), and I set out for the Casablanca where we dined and danced until after one o'clock. Oh, those Rio night clubs! There was a marvelous zither player there and I fell in love with the zither. Mother and Dad had been dining officially somewhere and nobody had thought to tell them where I was going. When I got in around two, they were pacing the floor, wondering where I had got to in that fantastic city. They were afraid I wouldn't be able to speak Portuguese if I got lost!

The next night one of the most fabulous evenings of the trip transpired. President Dutra's two daughters and their husbands took me to the opera. We sat in the Presidential Box and received a great welcome. In fact, the Latin Americans applaud at the slightest provocation and the whole opera was enlivened by storms of applause and bravos, or by hisses when they didn't happen to like it! The opera was *Tosca* with Gigli, and he had to sing one of his arias, *E Lucevan e Stellè*, three times to satisfy the audience. Even the musicians in the orchestra cheered him. The Brazilians have the pleasant custom of serving coffee, wine, and sweets between acts and this lends an added sociable note. I had a wonderful time and I never saw more warmhearted or generous people than the Dutra family. They were constantly wracking their brains to think of ways of pleasing or interesting us and making us happy.

The next day, which was Thursday, September 4, I had to pack. We moved from the Embassy to the Laranjeirao Palace, and what a palace it was! Admiral Leahy, who said he couldn't pronounce it, dubbed it the Laryngitis Palace. The rooms were so enormous it wore you out to walk across them. My bathroom was bigger than the kitchen at home. Everything in it was marble, including a huge, old-fashioned bathtub. I had to climb up on something to get in the tub. The faucets were all pure gold and the spigots in the tub were cast in the shape of dolphins. The water ran out of the fishes' mouths, both hot and cold. Mostly cold. I never could find the heater. You could swim in that bathtub, but of course I don't swim.

The dining room was magnificently paneled in mahogany with insets of red brocade, but there were so many enormous windows that there wasn't much wall space. All the furnishings, rugs, and pictures in the palace were museum pieces. There was an ornate Steinway piano in the drawing room, with golden pictures against a background of blue. It was unique and badly needed tuning. All the floors were marble or inlaid wood, and the ceilings and windows seemed astronomically high. The windows were all hung with elaborate curtains of heavy satin. It was really sumptuous.

That night we went to dinner at the Cotete Palace, the Brazilian White House. It was a small dinner party and the table was most exotic. It was decorated with 1,500 orchids in about 150 varieties— in fact, all the known varieties—and resembled a swarm of butterflies. The Cotete is in the ornate French tradition, with everything in massive keeping. It was lovely to look at, but I don't know how it would be to live in.

The incredible surprise of the evening was Mrs. Dutra's gift to me of an aquamarine and diamond bracelet. For once I was speechless. My father could scarcely believe this. He is always teasing me about the way I chatter. I can usually find words, but when I saw that bracelet I couldn't. Mrs. Dutra also gave Mother a gold bracelet set with the largest aquamarine anybody ever saw. It weighed down her wrist and was absolutely stunning.

After dinner there was a concert. A pianist, a singer, and a guitarist made up the ensemble. There always seemed to be music in Rio.

The next day was probably the most exciting day of the trip and I will let my diary take over.

Friday, September 5
Ambassador and Mrs. Pawley came for lunch. We all then went to a joint session of Congress which Dad addressed. He made a good speech. The Congress building was all marble, though not as large as ours. We paid a brief visit to the Supreme Court Justices in the Palace of Justice. They were dressed almost like Quakers in long robes.

Tonight was *the* night. We went to Itamarati Palace, which is the Foreign Office, to a huge State Dinner. The table again was lined with orchids of all kinds. Two enormous Venetian glass chandeliers lighted the room and there were four panels of tropical fruit in greenery pouring from cornucopias from the ceiling to the floor. My dinner partner was the Argentine Foreign Minister and he spoke no English. We had to get along with my bad Spanish. After dinner we went outside to a scene which I shall never forget.

In the garden there was a long reflecting pool, surrounded by candles made in short fat glasses with tallow and wicks like votive lights. There were hundreds of these and four white swans swimming in the pool. We sat at one end under a red canopy with easy chairs and oriental rugs on the floor. At the other end of the pool there was a stage and the background was all arches—huge with blue curtains, outlined in red. The chandeliers were made of candles, burning to make the open air look like a salon. Here the Ballet from the Theatre Municipale danced, accompanied by the orchestra from the theatre, concealed at the right of the stage. The entire picture was framed by giant royal palms in two rows from end to end of the pool and stage. At the end, as a surprise, Gigli sang two beautiful arias.

We then went inside and upstairs—we were constantly going up and down stairs—and had champagne. We are floating in the stuff now. We came back downstairs and went home. I had a bath in the marble tub and nearly drowned. I forgot the water came out of the fishes' mouths and it sprayed me but good.

One amusing incident took place at dinner. The Colombian Ambassador, who spoke *some* English, sat on my left and the Argentine Foreign Minister, who spoke no English, on my right. The Colombian Ambassador tried to translate the Argentine's conversation for me. Although I have studied Spanish, I don't speak it fluently, but I do understand it up to a point. At one moment in the evening, the Argentine Foreign Minister paid me a very flowery compliment (I suppose he was taken with the fact that I was a blonde!). I looked at the Colombian Ambassador and waited. He hesitated, smiled, but finally he did translate it for me. The dinner that evening came in ten courses and was as remarkable as everything else. Pheasant was served as one course. These came in roasted but wearing their own feathers which had been painstakingly put back exactly as they were originally, on enormous silver platters.

The next day was Saturday and we went to the Embassy to a morning affair for Americans living in Rio. We all stood in line and greeted them and Dad made a short speech. It was a very emotional occasion and one caught a glimpse of the wistfulness of foreign-service families who leave the United States for two or three years at a time and never see home.

After that we went for a drive all around Rio and wound up on the mountainside, where we got stuck in the mud, but finally made it to the home of Senhor and Senhora Fontes for luncheon. They had a fine modern house with a natural lake and pagodas around it and a beautiful vista. Mother and Dad sat downstairs with the big shots, but I was assigned to a table upstairs where the young people and the lesser brass sat. We had a riotous time in English, Spanish and Portuguese and the mixture of languages seemed to add to the fun. Our raucous laughter drifted downstairs where everything was more proper.

"What in the world were you doing up there?" Mother asked me later. "I never heard such screams of laughter."

"That's what comes of sitting below the salt," I told her. "You're envious." I think everybody at the Number One table was envious.

≥ That night we went to dinner at our Embassy. The table was loaded with orchids and roses in wild profusion, but the *pièce de résistance* to me was the glass of ice water at my plate. I hadn't had anything but carbonated stuff (and I don't mean champagne) since

I had left the American Embassy. There's no wine like water, when you're thirsty. After dinner there was a state reception and Dad gave President Dutra the Medal of Merit. Only three other persons had ever been granted this distinction—Alemán, President of Mexico, the Prince of Iraq, and Churchill.

Sunday, September 7, was Brazil's Independence Day. I had been up half the night packing and I had to arise at 6:30 A.M. Mother, Mrs. Pawley, and I and the rest of the party left ahead of Dad for the reviewing stand to watch the parade. Brazilians love a parade and this one went on for four and a half hours. I discovered a Brazilian custom that I *don't* like (almost the only one), and that is that they stand to review a parade, no matter how long it goes on. Four and a half hours can get to seem like four and a half years after the first two hours. The real notables—Mother, Dad, President Dutra, and the Archbishop of Brazil had armchairs, but the rest of us had to stand up.

We had one camp stool at the back of the reviewing stand and when I thought my aching feet couldn't take it another minute, Matt Connelly tapped me on the shoulder and said I could sit down on the campstool for just two minutes. He held a stop watch on me and then somebody else had the campstool for two minutes and so on, in rotation. That saved our lives and our sense of humor.

In spite of my complaining, the parade was colorful and exciting. The Dragoons wore uniforms that dated back to the time of Napoleon. The Cavalry of Brazil's West Point were in gorgeous blue and red uniforms and the Marines wore red coats, white breeches, and black boots and hats. There were bands, bands, bands, all the time. There was one wonderful thing about the music. In a Brazilian parade there is always one band kept opposite the reviewing stand, so there is continuous music all the time, no matter what is going by. I think this is a custom that we could emulate, instead of having the bands only march in the parade.

That night we boarded the *Missouri* to return home, taking with us many happy memories and affectionate emotions toward Brazil and her people. Senhora Novelli, President Dutra's daughter, gave me a charm from Baia, where charm bracelets originated and a pair of amethyst-and-diamond earrings. She took the earrings off her own ears and put them on mine when she discovered that my birthday was in February. I have never known such generous people.

We departed in a roar of gunnery. When we got on the launch to put out, a salvo was fired. All the shore batteries were firing salutes, but, thank goodness, in deference to Brazil's Independence Day custom, the *Missouri* did not have to respond. We put to sea but watched the city as long as it was visible on the horizon. Rio presents a magnificent sight from the harbor. When it disappeared we settled down, or you might say we collapsed, to relax and rest. It had been a wonderful week but you *do* get tired. Our quarters aboard the *Missouri* were comfortable and Captain Robert Dennison was most solicitous.

We left Rio on Sunday, September 7, and by Tuesday I had rested up enough to get back in action. Stanley Woodward and I took on Dr. Graham and Admiral Foskett at deck tennis and trounced them soundly. That night I got my first glimpse of the Southern Cross blazing in the sky, after a spectacular red and gold sunset. The clouds were banked low on the horizon and the sun went down behind them, bathing the sea in an unearthly saffron glow. I was so interested in the brilliant stars over the tropic waters that Dad began to give me astronomy lessons. I had one every evening, using the *Missouri's* navigation charts as textbook and the sky as laboratory.

The days fled by in gales of laughter and happy camaraderie. The meals were high points. We had printed menus and place cards at every meal and the ship published a digest of the news twice a day, so we had our own private newspaper. It made one of the best news sheets anyone has ever put out. We had a movie every night, deck tennis every day, and there were lots of other gala goings-on. Since it is fairly unusual for a girl to enjoy a trip on a battleship, I append herewith my private log of part of the journey.

Wednesday, September 10, 1947

Got up at 10:30 and had lunch down in the general mess . . . horrible name for a good meal . . . with all the men. We are soon to cross the equator and I'm a pollywog—which means, never crossed the line on a ship. All the pollywogs have to be initiated. So far all I've had to do is wear a raincoat and so'wester and boots but I haven't kept them on. It all seems so ridiculous. But the grown men have to act like boys now and then, I suppose. I haven't seen anything like it since I was in Junior High School and even then we weren't so silly.

The ship's doctor was transferred in a breeches buoy today to the escorting destroyers which will take him to a merchant ship where a seaman is ill. It was quite exciting as both ships kept moving and it was done quite fast. I wouldn't ride in one of those tiny chairs over all that deep ocean for anything.

Davy Jones came aboard with his pirate crew at 1800 hours. He came with subpoenas for all of us to appear tomorrow in King Neptune's Court to answer charges for coming into his domain. At 8:00 A.M. no less, ouch!

We played shuffleboard today and Mr. Ross and I lost but good.

Thursday, September 11, 1947

Today King Neptune came on board and at 8:00 we all had to go and greet him. I had to lead the pollywog Ensigns in *Anchors Aweigh*. The rest of the party got the royal dirty works ending up in a tank of oily water and running down between two rows of seamen with heavy ropes beating on them. I didn't much like this horseplay.

The Captain came to dinner.

Sunday, September 14

We all went to church on the fantail and sang hymns. It was a short service. We are in a somewhat heavy sea now and we have been sprayed all morning on deck.

We played deck tennis today. Mr. Woodward and I against Admiral Foskett and General Graham. The deck was so wet I sat down hard once. Mr. Woodward sat down hard and hit his head at the same time. It *is* possible.

We went to Captain Dennison's quarters for dinner tonight—all of us. It was delicious. I got a real sunburn today. During the day all the photographers took their pictures to be sent over the wires. Otherwise they have left us strictly alone on board ship. We are all very grateful for this.

(When photographers were allowed aboard the *Missouri*, they came with this understanding, and they lived up to it. White House photographers cooperated with such arrangements whenever they were made and never went back on their word or published pictures of us which might have been deleterious. They took one hilarious shot of me in mid-air, aboard the *Missouri*. I was reaching for the ball and the picture looked as if Mr. Woodward had kicked me up off the floor. It got in the papers but I didn't mind, it was so funny. The White House corps were always kind and considerate.)

186

Monday, September 15

What a terrible day. First I had to get up early. Then the huge 16 inch guns were fired. Five salvos. The first and last with 3 guns at once. My ears and my nerves were gone. It is a frightening feeling when the deck shakes and you feel it all over, not just in your ears. They also launched the planes by catapult and landed them again, which is the most interesting part. The ship swerves and makes a slick in its wake, then the plane lands on the slick and guns the motors to catch up almost to the *Missouri* and hooks on a rope sled which the ship tows along. Then the big crane swings over, hooks on the plane and swings it back aboard. One pilot had kind of rough going due to a change in the wind, but he made it.

Tuesday, September 16, 1947

Another awful day. They fired the 40 MM guns using drones as targets. The first 4 drones nosedived into the drink but they shot at the 5th and brought it down. Tonight I had dinner in the Wardroom with 4 Ensigns. Draybent, Cole, Kelly and Blanding. We listened to records, then saw *Song of Scheherazade*.

Saturday, September 20, 1947

We arrived in Washington at 8. Mother and I have been frantically unpacking and packing again. Jane came for lunch. We inspected Dad's new office rug and draperies. They are blue.

Mother and I took off from the National Airport at 3 P.M. for home. Drucie was at the airport to see us off. We flew through fog and rain and arrived in Independence at 5 o'clock. Home at last.

Sunday, September 21, 1947

We all had family dinner together. My own bed feels so good!

I'm glad I had the chance to enjoy my own bed for a few nights, because in the months ahead, I found myself sleeping in a different one every night. In October my long-awaited concert tour materialized and I became a veteran of the one-night stand.

187

15: A wandering minstrel I

The music-loving public—bless their hearts—come to hear music, but I don't believe many of them realize what exertion is required before the musician walks on the stage to offer up his art. Why should they? They pay their money and they take their seats. If they beat their hands together at the end, the artist is repaid beyond words. Lots of people, in other kinds of work, struggle as hard to succeed and never hear that wonderful sound of applause.

I had certain advantages as a novice, but nothing can remove the problems of packing and traveling, catching trains and planes, singing in strange halls with strange pianos and strange acoustics (and I do mean strange!), sleeping in strange beds, meeting strangers and going to parties when you feel ready to fall apart. I have known young musicians, at the outset of their careers, to drive an automobile all night to the next engagement, catch forty winks, rehearse all afternoon, give the concert, go to a late party where they make themselves personable, get in the car and drive the rest of the night to the next engagement. Sometimes the hall will be half empty after all that! They need applause and I hope they get it.

I had a vacation of about two weeks in Independence after I got back from South America. On the fifteenth of October Mother left for Washington, Vietta and I packed my concert dresses, the last thing to go into the luggage. Mrs. Shaw, Vietta, and I left that afternoon for my first concert engagement in Pittsburgh. We arrived the next morning and I scurried to the hotel to get ready for a broadcast at 9 A.M. This was followed by a press conference. That afternoon I rehearsed at the Syria Mosque, where the concert was to be given. It was an enormous old building with a great auditorium lacking all intimacy, but the acoustics were fair.

On October 17, the day of the concert, Mother and several loyal friends flew in from Washington. I don't know whether anybody realizes how difficult it was for my mother to get away from her strenuous duties in the White House and join me. The details of her tenure there have never been known, because she did not choose to exploit them, but she worked from morning until night. In addition she was always being required to divide what little time was left between my father and me and her own mother, no one of whom seemed able to navigate without her. The sight of her staunch person always gave me the courage I needed.

Mr. and Mrs. John Snyder, Jane Lingo, Mrs. Fred Vinson and Mrs. Mesta, Marvin Coles, Marvin Braverman, and Frank Handy also put in an appearance. I felt cherished to have three beaus and six good friends aboard and only hoped that I wouldn't catch a familiar eye from the stage. I have heard people say that they select some one person in an audience to sing to, but I sing to all of them. Nothing is more disconcerting to me than to glimpse a familiar face, except to hear the sound of a familiar laugh. That really throws me off.

I had a steak and baked potato around five o'clock that afternoon. This is my usual fare before a concert. Afterward, I always hope for a good hamburger and a chocolate malted milk, but usually I have to go to a party and settle for Lobster Newburg! I took a short rest and went to the hall about an hour ahead, warmed up and got dressed. I wore the pink and gold lamé Indian dress that Madame Pola had made for me. Aunt Mary and the Wallaces called me just before the concert to wish me luck.

This was my concert debut! I suddenly realized and felt lightheaded.

I began to sing at 8:40 P.M. I wasn't exactly nervous, but I kept getting through each song, until I came to the end of it. I mean by this that I was aware that I set the end of the song as a goal, and then took up the next number. I realize that this was not ideal, for determination seemed to be mixed with lyricism, but maybe that's my nature. I couldn't tell whether I was singing well or badly.

Afterward there was a reception for about four hundred people, which seemed to go on forever. Everybody was complimentary, but I've never been so tired in my whole life, and I've been tired! I felt absolutely drained. I called up Daddy after the concert, and he seemed to be satisfied. I can't say that I was.

The next morning I left for Independence with Mrs. Shaw and Pete. My chief interest was in the newspapers. As was to be expected, the critics took me apart, but hinted that I just might have a future. Right along with the tremendous appeal of applause for anybody in my business is the disturbing prospect of the critics' reaction—often a melancholy vista.

My next engagement was in Fort Worth, Texas, and on November 1. I was accompanied on this trip by Vietta, Mr. Lib Knowland, my flutist; Mrs. Shaw, my accompanist; Mrs. Strickler, my teacher; and Mr. Dorsey, my bodyguard! Lib Knowland was accompanied by Edna, his wife, which made seven in all and a fairly unwieldy entourage. Lib was an old friend of mine. He had been flutist for the Kansas City Symphony Orchestra when I met him. Edna was a darling. They added a note of gaiety to the tour.

We arrived in Fort Worth on Sunday morning and were met by Mr. Amon Carter, publisher of the *Fort Worth Star-Telegram*, and a battery of reporters and photographers. I was presented with a bouquet and then went to the Fort Worth Club where Vietta and I stayed.

I gave the concert the next night and I felt personally that it was much better than the one I had given in Pittsburgh. Every experience eases the way a little for the next engagement.

I left for Amarillo that night and almost missed the train. Amon Carter, Jr., had invited me to a cocktail party and a dinner at the Country Club and we stayed so late that I practically had to run and jump on the last car. My entourage was frantic.

I gave the Amarillo concert on Friday, November 7. May Peterson Thompson, who formerly sang at the Metropolitan was there and reviewed my performance favorably. We were all invited to her apartment and she gave a whole lesson on the program I had chosen for Amarillo.

The next day was freezing, but I was up at dawn to drive to Oklahoma City. We were met by a police escort outside the city but barely made my broadcast engagement and the luncheon that was being given for me. I had a rehearsal with the concert master of the Oklahoma City Symphony at five o'clock that afternoon and then went to a tea at Mrs. Mesta's. All Mother's bridge club had come down for the concert, including Aunt Beuf and Aunt Natalie. This was a complete surprise and I was so happy to see them.

I sang a matinee engagement with the Oklahoma City Symphony on Sunday, November 9. The audience seemed unusually enthusiastic. I sang two encores with Mrs. Shaw and Lib Knowland, and received twenty-one curtain calls. For a while there, I thought somebody had organized a claque!

We arrived at Little Rock at the witching hour of 4:45 A.M. This is not my time of day. (It's all right with me if you *stay* up to 4:45 but it's not so good if you have to *get* up.). It was pouring rain and everything looked so dismal and dreary.

The next day was Armistice Day and I went to a luncheon with nine hundred members of the Masonic Lodge. You can hardly fail to have a good time when you're out with nine hundred men! Edna Knowland, Lib's wife, had cooked fried chicken and peas and potatoes in the tiny kitchenette off their room in the hotel and this varied the monotony of restaurant fare. It was such fun, and you have no idea how you can pine for home cooking on the road.

The next day I gave the concert. Everybody said it was the best yet. I hoped so. I hoped I was improving.

It was difficult for me to come to any objective conclusion about how the concerts were going. For one thing, I was always in a dead run in the daylight hours, and after the concerts I was so tired. People were unfailingly kind and crowded around to offer gracious compliments, but it was impossible for me to tell whether this was a tribute to my father's daughter or my musicianship.

Concertizing is a lonely business. When you are out there on the stage with people waiting for you to entertain them, you are incredibly alone. There is nobody to share the responsibility. After the last reception guest has departed and you are by yourself, your doubts and qualms may creep out to haunt you in the dead of night. I tried not to let them.

I was often discouraged in the pursuit of my musical career, and the first tour is a grueling experience. It was easy enough for me to remember that I could have been safely at home, enjoying myself, spared the rigors of travel and exposure to the frank estimates of the press, but that was not what I wanted. I wanted to be on the stage. I wanted to sing and to make a contribution with whatever little gifts I had. All I could do was to keep trying.

In all honesty, I sometimes wished secretly that I could give the whole thing up or that I had never left home. I wondered why I had been so dead-set on being a concert singer. There were moments —usually around one of those dawn's-early-light debarkations from a Pullman car in rain or snow—when I felt inadequate. There were moments when I felt that my management, well-intentioned and hard-working as it was, lacked professional experience. There were moments when I wished I could start over and do everything differently.

There was no use brooding over such matters. I was commited to a line of action and the important thing was to get the job done to the best of my ability. This I endeavored to do in the face of all discouragement. It is only just to add that there were moments when I was warmed and heartened by the responsiveness of audiences, and this is a satisfaction that transcends everything else. I didn't know exactly where I was going, but I knew I was on my way, and hope balanced off discouragement.

After Little Rock came Memphis and Shreveport. I sang on Sunday afternoon, November 16, in Shreveport. The concert went off fine and we had a very enjoyable dinner at the home of Mr. and Mrs. Ed Neild (Mr. Neild is the designer of Dad's library), but we were stricken at tragic news we received there. Lib and Edna Knowland, who had been with me on all of the tour, were driving to Tulsa to join me and had an automobile wreck. Edna, who had just been gallantly cooking fried chicken in a little pantry for hungry troupers, was killed. Lib was injured and hospitalized. This put a pall on my spirits. But the show had to go on. People say lightly, "The show must go on," but unless you've tried it when you are miserable, you don't know what it means.

After Shreveport we forged on to Tulsa. The concert seemed to go all right but I continued to be bothered by the acoustics of the hall. At Tulsa, my party split up and went in several directions. Mrs. Gossard accompanied me as far as Cincinnati. I was on the train all day and I didn't mind a bit, because I was so tired my bones were wilted. When I pulled in on November 21, Washington looked like paradise.

Everything was normal in Washington. I was up and at the family board for breakfast to give a play-by-play report of my travels. Mother and I went on a shopping tour and I bought a new outfit which I sorely needed. The road can do your garments in.

That night Dad had a stag dinner for all the staff and newspapermen who had accompanied us to Brazil. Mother and I ate in the upstairs living room, but the music of the Marine Band wafted up to us. At eight o'clock we heard a bugle sound mess call, just as it had on the USS *Missouri*. We felt very nostalgic. Afterward Dad showed a movie appropriately entitled *The Road to Rio*, with Bing Crosby, Bob Hope, and Dorothy Lamour and we slipped downstairs to see it. The thought of a movie running and me not there was too much!

On Monday I sat in on Mrs. Helm's weekly press conference in the Red Room and held forth with the press girls on my impressions of my tour. Dad had invited the Cabinet for lunch, so Mother and I ate upstairs again. Mother who was constantly planning elaborate lunches and dinners was often found eating off a tray in some nook or cranny. Lots of meals in the White House are for men only, but Mother planned and organized them and saw to the smallest detail.

On November 26 I had conferences with Patrick Hayes, the local manager for my Baltimore and Washington concert engagements, scheduled for December. I made a recording with Jack Adams of CBS for his broadcast. All this time I was having fittings on additional clothes. Madame Pola had come down and brought my new concert dress—gorgeous white brocaded satin. I always loved that dress.

On Thanksgiving Mother and I went to the Baptist Church with Daddy for the 10:00 A.M. services. The next morning I hit the road again.

I sang at Des Moines, Iowa, on December 2, but I spent a few days in Independence before going there. Ray Mitchell, the concert manager at Milwaukee, had sent me a lovely new song he had written just for me and I practiced that, thinking that I might sing it when my Kansas City concerts came up. Before I left for Des Moines, Mother's bridge club gave a luncheon for me at the University Club in Kansas

194

City and presented me with a charm for my bracelet—a solid gold piano in miniature.

When I got to Des Moines the city was covered with snow and ice. The next night I sang to a half-empty house. Fifteen hundred people who had bought tickets were prevented from attending the concert by the blizzard. I sang much better than usual. Wouldn't you know?

I sang in Denver on Sunday evening, December 7 (Pearl Harbor Day—what a long road I had traveled since that day), and I felt cheered. It was getting a little easier. The Denver critics gave me good notices. I didn't know whether I was improving or the critics were slipping!

I left the next day for Milwaukee. I was delighted to find when I got there that Frank Handy had come over from Ypsilanti, Michigan, to make himself useful. It was wonderful to have a friend around. I sang Ray Mitchell's new song that night, *The Waltz of the Birds,* for the first time anywhere and the people loved it. I had a big house—more than 3,000 people. After the concert we attended a reception at the Museum of Art. Then Frank and I came back to the hotel and talked for hours.

When I left Milwaukee on the morning of December 10, the city looked like a Christmas card. A regular snowstorm was catapulting down and I began to get the Christmas spirit with a vengeance. I was headed for Independence, and scheduled to sing in Kansas City on December 15. As soon as I got home Aunt Nat and I rushed out and I did all my Christmas shopping. I couldn't wait!

The next morning I went back to the grind. I rehearsed in the afternoon and gave a press conference for all the high-school papers. The children were so sweet and excited and scared and I felt so old when I looked into the serious faces turned up to mine. They had brought me a poinsettia which they presented with a speech. I treasured that tribute they had pooled their money to buy. The next day I rehearsed all day long in the Little Theatre.

I tried out the hall on Monday and spent a lot of time with the lights. I was especially anxious to have this concert go off well because I was a local girl trying to make good. I sang with all my heart that night and the audience was kind. They gave me tremendous applause, and as soon as it was over about half of them rushed back-

195

stage, and it was a mob scene. I knew most of them by their first names.

The next day I collected Grandmother Wallace and we entrained for the East. For the first time, we were planning to spend Christmas in the White House. I dropped Grandmums and assorted knobby bundles in Silver Springs, Maryland, and went on to Baltimore without going home.

I sang in Baltimore on Friday, December 19. Madame Pola had sent me a new concert dress made of pink and peach lamé. It looked just like ice cream and of course anything that looks like ice cream is for me! I had a wonderful audience in Baltimore, including my mother, who shelved her responsibilities for a few hours and rushed over to hear me. After it was over, we drove back to Washington. I gave her all my news and she briefed me on the Christmas plans.

The clan was beginning to gather. Aunt Mary Truman came the next morning, and I was so glad to see her I didn't do a thing all day but enjoy her company.

On Sunday, December 21, I rehearsed for my first Washington concert, to be given in Constitution Hall. I practiced in the East Room and had a final fitting on my wonderful new white satin brocade gown with the spreading skirt. Then I went over to Constitution Hall to try the acoustics. I kept thinking of all the great musicians who had performed there and what I had to live up to, but I couldn't let myself brood on that!

I sang there on Monday night, December 22. There were 3,800 people. Every seat was filled. Flowers poured in. The Cabinet sent me a great basket of red roses, which I placed on the piano, and I received eleven bouquets over the footlights. I gave the best concert of the tour that night and I was happy it went well, because so many of my friends were in the audience and most of my relatives were in Dad's box. I was so excited, I don't think I closed an eye all night and I had to get up early and do a broadcast for Drucie Snyder on WBC, a local station, where Drucie was now a working girl.

My first tour was over and I drew a breath of relief and let Christmas set in.

I had spent every Christmas of my life to date in the house on Delaware Street in Independence, but I'm glad I had the experience of that Washington Christmas. The White House was beautifully decorated, with a huge Christmas tree in the East Room, against the

French doors. It was an evergreen tree, trimmed entirely in silver and white, with fragile silver baubles and tinsel and icicles. Of course there was also a decorated tree on the lawn, lighted with myriad glimmering lights. The switch was thrown by the President with due ceremony.

We had our family Christmas tree in our quarters in the second-floor lounge. We always have our presents after breakfast on Christmas morning, but I usually sneak one or two to open when I get in from midnight services. All the family came for Christmas that year —Fred and Chris and the children from Denver; Uncle George and Aunt Beuf, Aunt Natalie and Uncle Frank and Uncle Vivian and Aunt Louella from Independence; Aunt Mary from Grandview. The only missing face was Mamma Truman's, and how we missed her sweet face.

Several of my beaus were in town and I had a whirl. I went to the Mayflower with Bobby Stewart and to the Chevy Chase Club with Frank Handy and to the Princeton Triangle show with a party which included Chris and Fred and Jane Lingo and John Montgomery. On Christmas Eve I went to the Earle Theatre to a Salvation Army show for underprivileged children, and led them in singing *Silent Night*. Dad gave his Christmas greeting to the nation that evening and lighted the Christmas tree on the lawn.

Annette and Irv Wright and Alex Radford and I went to the Washington Cathedral at midnight for the Christmas Eve service. It was utterly beautiful—I believe it was the most beautiful service I ever attended. The great Cathedral was lighted by thousands of candles and all the members of the processional bore lighted tapers aloft. The organ rolled out the triumphant music and the choirboys sang like angels. The weather was bitter cold—real Christmas weather —and I was so happy to be at home.

On Christmas morning we had the tree with appropriate squeals of delight. I had such a stack of presents that I was embarrassed, but not too embarrassed to enjoy every one. We had a late-day dinner in the State Dining Room with all the children at the table. The centerpiece was made of wonderful holly boughs and Mother had concealed a tiny and silly present, attached to a red satin ribbon, under the boughs for each person. The ribbons led to each place at the table and we all pulled them out at the same time with appropriate commotion like a Jack Horner pie. I had got a fine powder

197

puff. It had required over an hour to open my presents, opening them steadily one after another, but nobody had given me a powder puff. They had given me nightgowns, slips, scarves, Paris perfume, gold pencils, a blue fitted overnight case for my travels, and pound upon pound of chocolates.

I took colored pictures of the family and the table and the tree and everything else all afternoon, as I had become a regular shutterbug. As twilight came down on the city, it began to snow in great powdery flakes, which seemed to put a fitting seal upon a perfect Christmas Day.

Christmas week was crowded with engagements. Marvin Braverman took me to a cocktail party and to see *Caesar and Cleopatra*, with Claude Rains and Vivien Leigh, and then on to Jane Lingo's dance. I didn't sit down one minute and never danced more than three bars with one partner. (This isn't as much fun as it sounds.)

On New Year's Eve I attended Dad's press conference and heard him make a good speech about the New Year and its prospects. Jane Watson and her brother Dick came for dinner and at ten o'clock my own dance began. The White House was decorated with dozens of red poinsettias, which matched the scarlet coats of the Marine Band. It was a gala affair with all the traditional observances of New Year's Eve. At midnight we had supper in the State Dining Room, whose dignified sobriety had been transformed with big red balloons tied to the chandeliers and the walls. Champagne corks popped, whistles whistled, and we donned our paper hats and wished each other the best of all possible worlds in 1948.

As I trudged up to bed, memories of the year 1947 whirled through my head like a child's kaleidoscope. It had been wonderful and terrifying and happy and sad and rewarding and bewildering. I had inched forward a little in my life work and I had lost Mamma Truman. I wondered briefly about 1948—election year—but I had no way of forecasting what would happen, any more than you did.

16: Flutterby

Way back at the beginning of this book I mentioned the speech idiosyncrasy I had as a little child, where I got words turned around. During the first half of 1948, it seemed to me that this inversion of my tongue finally made sense. I was more than a butterfly. I was a flutterby. I lived it up.

Early in January Mrs. Earle Stewart (Louise) invited Drucie and me to spend a week end with her at River House in New York. We got in the afternoon of the ninth of January, and after the amenities I got dressed in my new black lace and we set out for the Persian Room of the Plaza, with Dick Watson, Sherman Fairchild, Jacques Frey, Orin Lehman, and Louise. We renewed acquaintance with Hildegarde, who was holding forth there in fine form. This time she gave me a whole bouquet instead of one rose.

The next afternoon Drucie and I went to see Maurice Evans in *Man and Superman*. He invited us to have tea with him in his dressing room between the second and third acts and we stayed so long that the curtain went up and we were unable to return to our seats without crossing the stage. Maurice took this calmly and told us we could watch the last act from the wings. Drucie and I tried to take it calmly but we were bursting with excitement, and the boards under our feet turned into large pink clouds. That night Jane Lingo came to dinner with a crowd. She had been at the same matinee and had seen us go backstage and she had observed that we didn't return. She was *green* with jealousy.

That night we went to see the D'Oyly Carte company in *Trial by Jury* and *The Pirates of Penzance* and the performances left nothing to be desired. I was in seventh heaven with my beloved Gilbert and Sullivan. We wound up at the St. Regis for supper, with Bobby Stewart and a crowd of friends. Bobby ordered champagne and ginger ale and kept pouring champagne in my glass and ginger ale in Jane's. Such a charming mistake!

When I got back to Washington, my old friend Joe Crowe was waiting to discuss my income tax with me. We spent a morning on this painful subject, with which I had had no experience as I had never before been gainfully employed. I cannot understand figures, but Joe was finally able to get it through my head that a lot of my bank account was going for taxes in the routine manner. I knew without thinking about it that it was worth it, just to live in America.

That night Mother and Dad entertained at a Treasury Reception for 2,000 people. I don't know whether my morning wrestle with Internal Revenue had any effect on what happened or not, but Drucie and I suddenly became incorrigible. I guess we had been proper about as long as we could stand it, for that night we did absolutely everything we weren't supposed to do. We gamboled down the State staircase right behind the Cabinet—a serious breach of protocol. We hid behind the ferns in the Blue Room and made faces between the fronds at all the aides who were standing in front of Mother and Dad. They had trouble keeping their faces straight and they were *furious*. We sauntered around and spoke to whomever we pleased and ignored all the people we were supposed to greet.

I had on my ice-cream-pink lamé and I just switched around all over the place; Drucie was no help. She incited me! It was a childish exhibition but the aides got even with us. They ganged up and not one of them asked us to dance all evening.

Then I went to the Army and Navy Reception and saw General Eisenhower (it was about this time he announced he wouldn't run for President) and my hero, General Marshall. That made my day.

On Thursday, January 22, 1948, I had my first television broadcast. I was on the air for fifteen minutes with Ruth Crane, a news interviewer, and it was fascinating. Burke Crotty, WMAL-TV's Washington director, said I made a good showing and that I was a "natural" for a newscaster or a woman's-interest program. I didn't think anything more about it, due possibly to the fact that Mother and I went to the Navy Relief Ball at the Mayflower that night and I danced with Robert Taylor. Imagine!

On February 2 I had lunch at the Capitol with Mrs. Le Fevre and pinned a medal on a little boy named Joseph Fisher, who had saved a child's life. I bought the first ticket for the Lighthouse Campaign for theatre supplies for the blind and had my picture made over and over. That afternoon, Mother gave a tea at the White House for the unveiling of my portrait in the State Dining Room. The members of the Cabinet were there, and a great many other people, and I shook hands until I was limp.

That year Mother and I were invited to attend the Mardi Gras celebration in New Orleans where I was destined to christen a towboat. On the fifth of February, we set out on the train, hoping for a rest. It was not forthcoming. Everywhere the train stopped we had to get off and greet reporters and photographers. We got off at Atlanta at 9:00 A.M., came back and took a nap; we got off at Montgomery, Alabama, a few hours later, came back and took a nap; we got off at Mobile, where we were presented with a basket of home-grown camellias, pink for me, white for Mother, and came back and took a nap. At Biloxi we got off and went to the Biloxi Hotel. Biloxi was so changed we couldn't find many familiar landmarks. But we saw our old friends the Luxichs whose house we had rented so long ago. It was so warm that I went wading in the surf. The next day we had lunch at Pass Christian and drove to New Orleans with Mr. Rudolph Hecht. We got there in time to see one of the carnival parades from our hotel window. (They have one every night during carnival week.) Mayor DeLesseps Morrison and Mrs. Morrison called on us, and also Mr. Bull, who owned the shipyard which had made the boat I had come to christen, with Mrs. Bull.

The next morning we embarked on a small craft that took us up the Mississippi to a shipyard where I christened the towboat. It came in two sections and I had to christen each section with a different bottle. We came back into New Orleans then and the Bulls gave me a necklace, with a detachable diamond sunburst, which can be used as a pin.

I still wear this sunburst, and whenever I look at it I remember that exciting week. (The sponsors of ships usually are given some sort of memento of the occasion.) As the daughter of the President, I was the recipient of numerous beautiful gifts, which were tendered to me personally. People often express curiosity about gifts that are made to the President or to members of his family, so you may be interested in the background on this matter. In the natural course of events, hundreds of gifts poured into the White House while I lived there. Gifts from heads of states to the President of the United States were considered by him to belong to all the people. Most of these things will eventually be on display in my father's library. Gifts made to my mother and me were largely personal and became our property. Protocol decreed this.

The astonishing assortment of unsolicited presents which poured into the White House were acknowledged and remanded to the gift shelf on the third floor of the White House. Here they remained for one year. Mrs. Roosevelt had instituted this custom during President Roosevelt's administration and we continued it. This year of grace served as a protection, since people have been known to send the President a gift and follow it up with a bill!

I received a few lavish presents—silver, china, and jewelry—which I continue to cherish. With all the things that poured in, it would have been easy to become spoiled. I tried to remember that many of these presents were an expression of gratitude to the government of the United States and that I was merely a convenient and likely symbol. Although I was happy to own such tributes, the smallest offering from the family or old friends, which has been chosen just for me, always meant more to me. I was sometimes embarrassed by the riches thrust upon me which I had done nothing to deserve.

After the christening ceremony, we had lunch at International House and I reviewed the Children's Carnival Parade. Then we went on a tour of New Orleans landmarks and houses, went down Royal Street and bought some perfume, and then went to dinner at Antoine's as the guests of Mr. and Mrs. Schroeder. We had Oysters Rockefeller, a specialty of the house, and Café Diablo at the end. It came in a great silver bowl and was all on fire with brandy. Wow!

After that we set out for the Mystic Ball, which I opened on the arm of a dashing masked cavalier. He gave me a silver cigarette box, but I never saw his face. I didn't know whether to be glad or sorry about the last. The ball was gorgeous and after I had danced there, I went to the Comus ball, which I also opened. At the Comus all the costumes were after the fashion of birds, and some of them were fabulous. I received so many favors everywhere I went that I had no place to pack them and crawled on the train carrying them in my bare hands.

I got back to Washington in time to leave for New York for the week end, which is practically a record, even for a flutterby. I had a date for lunch aboard the SS *America* and I didn't want to miss it. Considerable stir was raised at this time when Walter Winchell reported that I was engaged to Frank Handy. There was nothing to it, although Frank had been one of my nicest and most faithful beaus. I didn't pay much attention to it as I was going to see the D'Oyly Carte company that night in *Patience*, with John and Barbara Eisenhower, and Frank was a sensible and understanding man. When I become engaged, my father and mother will announce it— not Walter Winchell.

On Valentine's Day I went to an austerity dinner at the French Embassy. I had been dieting all day (as was my custom when I was invited to that Embassy where the cuisine was in keeping with the grand tradition of France). That night we had shrimp, cold meat, rice, and salad. When I took only one piece of meat, Mr. Van Kleffens, who is now president of the UN, said to me, "Miss Truman, I think you had better help yourself more generously." He was right. I was ravenous and I nearly starved. Helle Bonnet said that as long as France was in straitened circumstances, she felt that the Embassy should reflect the home country's problems. I thought this was a good object lesson and that I ought to go hungry for once myself to see how it felt.

My twenty-fourth birthday now hove into view. Jane Lingo gave a supper party for me and Mrs. Peter Rathvon gave a birthday lunch for me at the Mayflower, with a pink and white cake and all the trimmings. Jeanette MacDonald was there and it was at this party that I met Jim Davidson, her manager, who eventually became my manager. Flowers, gifts, and telegrams poured in and my thank-you notes poured out.

Mother and Dad and I went to the Jackson and Jefferson Day dinners. I remember them as being composed largely of smoke and oratory. Oratory I can bear up under and I've proved it, but a roomful of smoke gets me down. Dad left for Key West and Mother and I settled down to a tiny oasis of peace and quiet. Dad came back and on March 17 I made the following note in my diary:

Wednesday, March 17, 1948
Dad made his speech to Congress asking for Selective Service. He made one of the best speeches he's ever made. He sounded mad. Things have gone far enough in Europe and we need an Army to back up what we say, he said. And most particularly to say *no*. And be able to mean it. I watched the speech on television.

Mother and Dad have gone to New York. Dad makes a speech to the Irish there tonight. Mother went to see some plays. I don't feel like New York. [I *must* have been sick!]

&ed; It was this month that I received a proposal of marriage. Spring was in the air and we were driving home from a pleasant dinner in Chevy Chase, when my companion popped the question. I had a premonition that he was going to ask me and I didn't want him to, because, as much as I liked him, he wasn't *the one*. I had some kind of romantic idea about *the one*, who would come along and sweep me off my feet—some enchanted evening, as they say in the song.

I guess the main trouble was that this nice and eligible and faithful swain just hadn't swept me off my feet. He was inclined to let me do anything I wanted to and I think (at the advanced age of thirty-two) that the kind of man who will sweep me off my feet is the one who will tell me what to do in no uncertain terms and see that I do it.

Anyway, he took no for an answer.

I felt a little melancholy when I got home—a bittersweet emotion —I was at once sad and happy . . . happy that someone had liked me enough to ask me to share his life, sad that I wasn't ready to do it. I still wonder what route my life would have taken if I had said yes. But there's no use wondering about such things. As my friend Shakespeare said, "There is a destiny that shapes our ends, rough-hew them as we may."

This was a delicious spring. I remember wandering around the White House grounds one Sunday late in March, taking snapshots with my camera of the magnolias and wisteria and the blossoming fruit trees. I took a picture of Dad, standing in front of the White

204

House. I thought to myself, "I wonder where we'll be this time next year," and I felt a twinge, as sharp as rheumatism.

The first week in April we made a little expedition to Williamsburg, aboard the yacht *Williamsburg*. So accustomed had we become to rapid transit that it was quite a shock to discover that we traveled only forty miles overnight. This was occasioned by the fact that we ran into a fog which slowed us to a crawl. Dad waked everybody up at 6:30 A.M. (how did such an early riser as that man ever have a daughter like me?) and told us that we were still a hundred miles out of Williamsburg and would have to transfer to cars. The whole purpose of taking the *Williamsburg* had been to avoid driving, but we dutifully got ourselves up and off and into a motorcade. It was chilly and rainy, and what that does to my hair!

Mr. and Mrs. John D. Rockefeller III met us and we drove to William and Mary College, those beautiful old Christopher Wren buildings set around a lovely quadrangle and shaded with old trees. We had to sit outside in the drizzle for speeches and the awarding of degrees. Lord Alexander and Prime Minister Mackenzie King of Canada both spoke and so did Dad. It rained hard on Dad's speech, which was mercifully short. After the exercises we had a delicious lunch at the Williamsburg Inn, where the food seems to be the epitome of good American cooking.

The sun made the supreme effort and came out for a few minutes afterward and I went sightseeing with Captain Dennison, Colonel Landry, the Air Aide, and General Graham. Williamsburg had changed a lot since the last time I was there. That was when I met Drucie. Of course, Drucie and I had been entranced with Williamsburg and the thing that had entranced us most was the carriages which you could hire and drive around in, in the approved eighteenth-century manner. Drucie and I were wild to ride in a carriage and began to nag our parents about it.

They said they would be happy to have us go and would go with us if we cared to pay for it and give them a little treat. Drucie and I had about a dollar between us, but we marched up to hire a carriage. We were chagrined to discover that they cost five dollars per hour, so we decided to foot it and let our parents do likewise. I told this story to Mr. Rockefeller and he said that I could have a carriage ride on him. But I have never had time to collect it.

We boarded the *Williamsburg*, which had finally put in, about six that evening and started back home. I was audibly hoping that there would be no fog to deter us, but while I was champing at the bit about this, I thought of the English colonists who had crossed an unknown ocean and arrived on that wild shore in 1607. What spirit that must have required! After I remembered those hardy souls I didn't say anything else about the inconvenience of the weather.

On the sixth of April, Prince Charles, Prince Regent of Belgium, arrived for a visit. I invited Jane and Drucie to tea and we were all aflutter because we had heard that he was a bachelor. He arrived punctiliously at four forty-five in the afternoon and Dad met him. An honor guard, composed of detachments from all the armed services, was drawn up in front of the White House to present arms and the Marine Band played the Belgian national anthem and Our Song. Drucie and Jane and I had scuttled down to the hall to hear the music and see the Prince arrive. We had to turn around and sprint for the Red Room, where we belonged, when the party turned by the front door to come in.

Drucie and Jane and I were presented to His Royal Highness and he was as charming as advance reports had indicated. He was one of my favorites of all the visitors who came to the White House. He seemed such a good, kind man, and reminiscent of the stories of his father, King Albert, one of the heroes of World War I. His only purpose seemed to be to do the best he could by his nephew, Prince Baudouin, who subsequently became King.

Prince Charles spent the night in the White House and there was an especially splendid stag dinner given for him by my father that evening. When I went to Europe in 1951 I was entertained by his mother, the Dowager Queen Elizabeth, widow of King Albert, at her palace in Brussels. Prince Charles brought us a dozen antique Brussels plates, lavishly decorated with orange and gold and bearing a picture of a different Belgian church or city in the center of each. They are exquisite and we treasure them. He gave me, personally, a beautiful silver cigarette box with his crest on it, which I still keep on my coffee table.

The following evening, Prince Charles entertained at the Belgian Embassy at a dinner in honor of Mother and Dad, and I was invited. It was a small party, and small parties always seem best. I sat between two handsome Belgians who had me speaking French before the evening was over.

On April 12, we celebrated Dad's anniversary in the White House. The newspaper editors gave a dinner in honor of Mother and Dad, and I went to a dinner dance at the French Embassy and danced my feet off.

The next day, Mother had four separate groups of women to the White House and we were shaking hands from morning until night. My mother never seemed to rest. There was something going on all the time. One afternoon the Annapolis Choir sang for us in the East Room and a few days later the West Point Choir sang. When these choral societies went on tour, they usually favored us with a rendition of the program and I always enjoyed them.

On April 19, Mother had a luncheon and I shook hands with about fifty people. At two-thirty she had a delegation in and I shook hands with thirty people. All I had to do was shake hands but Mother had to ride herd on all the details and shake hands too. At two-thirty-five, when we had shaken the last hand, the three of us left for the opening game of the baseball season. Dad threw out the ball, but I am sorry to report that the New York Yankees mopped up the diamond with the Washington Senators—12 to 4. Sometimes the Washington Senators reminded me of their namesakes in the Capitol.

Mother left early to do more handshaking, although she loves baseball, and Dad and I decided to have a hot dog. This seems like a simple matter, but nobody looks very attractive or dignified eating a hot dog with mustard and we never knew when the TV cameras were going to swing on us. Dad watched the cameras while I ate my hot dog, and then I watched them, so as to be able to warn him to stop chewing if the TV lens swung our way. This was a hilarious business and lightened the dullness of that particular ball game.

On April 21, I did a publicity stunt for Government Bonds. I was photographed investing my concert tour profits, buying bonds from Secretary Snyder. There was never any fakery about such stunts. I really had to *buy* the bonds. I had been thinking fondly of another fur piece, but it was a good thing I put my money in government securities. I sent them to Uncle Frank in Independence to stow in the safety deposit box. As time went by, I forgot all about them— not that I'm rich enough to lose track of any portion of my pittance —but they just slipped my mind. The other day, Uncle Frank reminded me that I still had them, and it was like pennies from heaven.

207

Anything else I'd have bought would certainly have been worn out by now, but these bonds have been drawing interest.

On May 4 Mother had a reception for 3,000 government girls. That was a handshaking to end handshakings. I fell by the way, but my mother was in there pitching, until the end. If you can imagine 3,000 girls drinking tea in one place, you can get some idea of the chatter that went on, but it was nice. They were all dressed up and looked pretty.

Mother and Dad and I went to a benefit for the National Symphony Orchestra where we saw the *première* of *The Search* at the opening of the new Fifteenth Street Cinema. I pushed a button that made the curtains pull back for the first time. I wore my new canary yellow faille with gold accessories and felt very stylish. Mrs. Mesta gave a big party afterward.

Mr. and Mrs. Tom Clark gave a dinner for my father on his birthday, May 8. Robert Merrill was there, and for the first and only time in my life at a formal function of this sort, I sang. Mr. Merrill and I sang a duet. I just did it on the spur of the moment. I gave my father my portrait that year and it is one of his favorite birthday presents. When I interviewed Mother and Dad on Ed Murrow's *Person to Person* TV show recently, I had to keep steering him away from dragging that portrait into the range of the camera.

On May 13, Mother had that unique thing for her—a free day—when her calendar was perfectly clear. This was like manna from heaven. We had lunch with Jane and Mrs. Lingo and Mrs. Davis, Annette's mother, and afterward I drove Mother around in the convertible. She loved that because she could window-shop and act natural, which isn't very easy in an official limousine. My mother had very few days off in all her years in the White House. In fact, I can't remember another one.

The next evening I went to the Young Democrats dinner and Dad made a corker of a speech. He spoke from notes—off the cuff—and this is really the only way for him to speak. I was thrilled, and glad I was a Young Democrat.

That morning I had been scorekeeper for the golf tournament staged by the Juvenile Delinquency Branch of the Department of Justice, and the Attorney General's office. Bing Crosby, Byron Nelson, Gene Sayers, and Del Webb were in my foursome. It poured down rain and there was some of the worst golf played that it has ever been my privilege to witness.

Attorney General Tom Clark, whose concern over juvenile delinquency inspired the *Washington Post* to dedicate its second annual National Celebrities Tournament to the problem, teed off. He held his club like a baseball bat, gave it a roundhouse swing, and the ball went approximately twenty yards and landed in a detachment of soldiers who all ran, terrified. When Bing got up to tee off, he did a little ballet step before he addressed himself to the ball. He also teased me constantly by trying to persuade me to give him a low score. I was wearing a white flannel coat which got wetter and heavier as the downpour increased and weighed me down. I went nine holes with Barbara Ann Scott, the figure-skating champion, and then gave the whole thing up. I had been keeping score and carrying an umbrella at the same time. I gave my umbrella to Bing and retired to the Columbia Club House.

Edgar Bergen and Charlie McCarthy were there. Charlie was got up in white tie and tails for the tournament, as he said he was an *indoor* sport. He started a brash flirtation with me and I gave him as good as he sent.

Mr. Thomas Watson of IBM and the Boy Scouts of America invited me to New York to take part in the Scoutorama Program at Madison Square Garden on May 22. I stayed with Louise Stewart at River House and made a speech and sang *God Bless America* to the convocation. The Scouts seemed to like it. At least they made a terrific noise, but maybe they were just working off pent-up energy. I made a recording with Tex and Jinx McCrary for their radio show and then rushed back to Louise's apartment to change into evening clothes and attend an official dinner at the Waldorf with Dick Watson, given by Mr. and Mrs. Pouch. After that I returned to Madison Square Garden and did my Scout routine again for the evening performance. Tom and Olive Watson and Dick and I wound up for supper at the St. Regis Roof, that beautiful pink and crystal Viennese salon which seems to be made for waltzing. We waltzed.

Grandmother Wallace had been seriously ill for several weeks, and on May 28 I went to Independence. She was slightly improved when I arrived, but not really well. I immediately fell to work polishing the silver. You know how a house deteriorates when the family is away. I looked around speculatively at the kitchen walls and made up my mind to paint the kitchen and pantry. Washington and New York fell away and I decided to plant a garden. I am not noted as an agriculturist but it looked simple and Grandmother wasn't equal to bossing it this year. I went to town and bought a bunch of seeds and planted them and promptly a covey of fat robins flew down and ate them up. I was furious, but nothing daunted I went and bought some more seeds and enlisted the aid of Menefee, the yardman, who got them deep enough in the ground to be safe from the birds.

Time demonstrated this was one of the worst gardens ever produced by anybody. Part of the problem was that I didn't know enough about horticulture even to buy seeds. I wanted some zinnias, but I bought the giant variety, which ran to treelike foliage and no flowers. The nasturtiums came up with holes already in the leaves. I don't know how the bugs managed to get at them before they came up, but I reared the only nasturtiums I ever saw that came out of the ground already perforated.

Right after I got home I wrote in my diary:

June 1, 1948
Grandmums is off on another tangent about my so-called career. She opposes it. I must go on with it—not that I care particularly!

I felt that I had come to a crossroads as far as my music was concerned—that I had to set out on a different course or give it up. It was too late to give it up. I had not been altogether satisfied with my showing on the concert stage and I had been given a lot of bludgeoning advice by critics and well-wishers. The whole thing had got in my hair and I didn't know what to do about it. I think these problems accounted for my depressed outlook and also my zeal at housekeeping, which was much more marked than usual. I even played cards that month, and I don't much like cards.

I suppose my whole flutterby season had been tinctured with these reservations about my career—that I was racing madly around and indulging myself in every pleasure that offered to keep my mind off more pressing matters. Now I was in the house on Delaware Street and I had plenty of time to think. All the glitter and glamour were far away. It was hot and dry. Grandmother was ailing. I was plain Mary Margaret. It was a good thing I had time to think for a few days, because I didn't have time again that year.

17: Whistle stop

On January 4, 1948, the Gallup Poll came out in favor of my father as the most likely candidate to succeed in the forthcoming elections. However, the poll had been known to err, especially so far in advance, and nobody in my family counts his political chickens before they hatch. In a free country the voter has a right to change his mind any minute.

If my father hadn't wanted to be Vice-president and had not wanted to live in the White House, it is reasonable to wonder why he decided to run again in 1948. He did not consult me on this matter, any more than he consulted me in 1952 when he decided *not* to run. He didn't think it was my department. I think he decided to run because he felt that it was his duty. He hadn't finished the job.

I do not feel equipped to discuss my father's problems as President, but he had a great many and some of them were concerned with his own party. Almost everybody must remember the difficulties he met with what he frankly termed the "Do-Nothing Eightieth Congress." There were a lot of defeatists in the Democratic ranks, as there are apt to be in any large group of people. The Democrats were quarreling among themselves and many of them were not in love with my father's policies. Some of these policies were an inheritance from the Roosevelt administration, and my father was simply struggling to carry them out.

As spring faded into summer, there were those who did not think that the Democrats would nominate Dad for President. They wanted a sure winner, and the politicians and the Gallup and most other polls were, by now, dubious. My father knew this, but it seemed to him that the people were still with him, and his first consideration has always been the people.

My emotions on this subject were concerned with what my father felt his duty to be. I wanted what he wanted. My mother and I abided by his decisions.

When he decided to take a nonpolitical hop-skip-and-jump across the country, we packed our clothes and said good-by to Independence. This and the campaign tour which followed were at once grueling and inspiring experiences and I would not take anything for my memories of them. They outshine all the glamour that I have been so willing to describe here, for during those trips, I came to appreciate the caliber of people who combine to make this nation. I shook hands with them from daylight to daylight!

My journal gives a fairly superficial coverage of the first trip, but since it covers many main events, I append it here:

Sunday, June 6, 1948

We met Dad at 7 A.M. and got on his train and had breakfast. We met the train in Omaha. Our first stop was Grand Island, Nebraska, and we had a wonderful turnout. The delegation gave Dad a pair of beautiful silver spurs and a peace pipe. They gave Mother and me corsages. We stopped at Kearney then, and went to the Baptist church. All people there looked like a cross-section of the real USA. Our next stop was North Platte, Nebraska, where we had a nice crowd.

At 5:45 we arrived in Cheyenne, Wyoming. A reception was given for us at the Governor's Mansion. Governor Hunt and Mrs. Hunt gave Dad a Stetson hat and jade cuff links and Mother jade earrings and me a lovely jade pin. We left about 7 P.M. and had dinner on train. All the aides came for dinner and we had a gay time. Then we stopped in Laramie, Wyoming.

Monday, June 7, 1948

We got up and went out on the platform at Pocatello, Idaho, at 7:30 in the morning. Horrible hour but a good crowd anyway. I had breakfast and went back to sleep. At 1:30 we arrived in Ketchum, Idaho and drove to Sun Valley. We stayed at the Averill Harrimans' cottage there and went up the long ski lift to 9,000 feet at the top of Baldy Mountain. More fun. Needless to say, I also came *down* in ski lift. I brought a snowball down with me. Lots of snow in those hills! We had dinner and saw a movie of Sun Valley in wintertime, and Mother and I went to watch an ice-skating exhibition. Sun Valley is modeled on a Swiss village and is very appealing. The Idaho delegation called on Dad and seemed quite friendly and all for him.

Tuesday, June 8, 1948

One day wasn't long enough in Sun Valley. We drove 4 hours to Idaho Falls with several stops on the way. Dad made a speech in Idaho Falls and then we got back on the train and had lunch and headed for Butte, Montana. We arrived there about 8 P.M. and had a grand parade and reception. Dad made a wonderful speech in Butte. The school band, which is one of the best I've ever heard, played and went through their fancy drill routines.

Wednesday, June 9, 1948

Governor and Mrs. Walgren met us at Spokane. We all drove to Grand Coulee Dam after Dad made an unexpected visit and short speech to the Communications Convention. Grand Coulee is tremendous. At this time of flood, a million acres of water, a foot deep, was going over it every 24 hours. That's what you might call a lot of water over the dam!

Spokane gave us a rousing welcome this morning and a huge crowd was out. We stayed on the train and went through Everett, the Walgrens' hometown where we had dinner and then the train crept down to Olympia, four hours late. Senator Magnuson, "Maggie," met us in Spokane. We got off in Olympia and went to the Executive Mansion.

Thursday, June 10, 1948

We left Olympia at 8:30 and drove about 2 or 3 hours to Bremerton. Dad made a speech and the big turn-out cheered. There are people out to see him at every crossroads.

Senator Maggie introduced Mother and me all day. We got on the Governor's yacht, the *Olympus*, and went to Pier 91 at Seattle. Had lunch aboard and a magnificent view of the Olympic Mountains. They are breathtaking to see. They are the most mountainous-looking mountains I have ever seen in my life, even including Switzerland. We arrived in Seattle and drove to the Stadium for Dad's speech. It was filled to capacity. About 10,000 came. But then the surprise! Downtown Seattle gave us a reception such as I've never seen. Ticker tape, confetti, and thousands of cheering, yelling people. I was in an open car and had more fun and got my mouth full of confetti. Dad dedicated a new Veteran's Center in Seattle. Then we drove to Tacoma which took hours, due to many stops. In Tacoma we had another big crowd and another good speech. In each city we drove through there were streets lined with crowds and my arm is paralyzed from waving and my mouth stretched in a perpetual smile.

We got back to Olympia at 7 and a reception at the Capitol where we met all the officials.

Friday, June 11, 1948
Last night after a short rest and a good dinner at the Mansion I went to see and hear the Governor's pet project—his organ and organist at the Rotunda at the Capitol, next door to the mansion. It was beautiful and I sang a few songs down low, because of my cold. It was like singing in a tiled kitchen, because the Capitol is all marble.

We got up fairly early and Mother, Rose Conway, and I drove to Oregon, outside of Portland to catch the train. The train had to go over a big detour the day before due to floods. We drove through water on the road and saw great devastation everywhere. Dad flew over it but couldn't see much because of rain and mist. He made a speech at Portland which we heard on the radio while riding down the road.

We have been going out on the back platform all day at various stops and there has been a stream of officials through the car each time.

Saturday, June 12, 1948
We picked up Lieutenant-Governor and Mrs. Knight in Sacramento. Then I had to pack frantically as plans changed and I learned that the dinner is not to be formal. We were met at Berkeley and paraded to the campus of the University of California where we ate a picnic lunch. We then went to the platform and watched the Academic procession. Daddy gave a fine speech on Foreign Policy and told how the Russians have stopped the UN at every turn and haven't cooperated at all. We changed clothes at the President's house and had dinner there.

After dinner we drove to the Fairmount Hotel in San Francisco to spend the night.

Sunday, June 13, 1948
Mother and I slept very late. It felt so good. Dad had a breakfast with the ILO and saw customers every ten minutes. We had another luncheon and the same thing all afternoon except when we went to Golden Gate Park. The Elks put on a Flag Day ceremony before about 50,000 people. It was beautifully done.

Mother, Rose, General Vaughan and I went on a tour of Chinatown with Mr. Albert Chow and his family. It was fascinating. We ate a Chinese dinner and oh my, shrimps sour and sweet, duck and so many wonderful dishes.

The train left about 10 for Los Angeles. I saw San Francisco from the Top of the Mark with Mother.

We arrived in Los Angeles June 14th about 10:14.

Monday, June 14, 1948

Rode in a parade to the Ambassador. There was a huge crowd, well over a million, and they cheered and screamed and yelled for Dad. There was a luncheon given by the Los Angeles Press Club and it was extremely nice. Dad made a terrific speech, off the cuff, naturally. He is always better that way. People came and went all day. You can't imagine how I tore around seeing all the disappointed women who couldn't see Dad. It is kind of fun to get them in a good humor and watch them go away happy. Mother is busy doing the same thing only more so. Mother and I went to see Aunt Jessie MacDermott in San Marino, came back for a big reception. We left for east 7 P.M. Phew!

Tuesday, June 15, 1948

We are still on the way home. We stopped in Albuquerque to give a speech for Mr. Anderson and stayed about 45 minutes. Acting Governor Montoya got on the train and rode with us until after dinner. This is very barren land but the rocks are beautiful. I was made an honorary colonel in the New Mexico National Guard here.

8✊ I have never forgotten that trip and the impression the people made on me or the impression my father made on the people. As one reporter said, he leaned over the rail of the observation car and talked as if he were leaning over the fence and discussing the political situation with his neighbor. It was a two-way conversation. At one town when my father was discussing the Eightieth Congress in his usual strong terms, somebody in the crowd shouted, "Lay it on, Harry! Give 'em hell!"

My father stopped and looked at the man and said, "I will! I intend to!"

People were lined up fifty deep on the sidewalks in the cities, and all along the route they were on the roofs of barns and filling stations. Lots of them had brought their children and they held them up to see Dad. There was something immensely touching and encouraging about the personal way they took him to their hearts.

Mother and I came in for a lot of applause as part of the family group. It never occurred to us that we provided any political capital. We had just come along to look after Dad. (I kept worrying because I never had time anywhere we stopped to get him a Father's Day present.)

I never discuss politics and I didn't on this trip, although the reporters badgered me about it. I told them all I planned to vote for

Dad in November. In fact, I avoided giving interviews, for I did not want attention focussed on me. Occasionally I got caught when some Pi Beta Phi sister, turned reporter, would board the train, ride to the next town, seek me out, and give me the grip! Then I would have to give an interview—of sorts. But Dad was certainly the star of the show. He was relaxed and happy, and spoke his mind.

I got home to tragic news. My friend and partner on many happy occasions, Bobby Stewart, was killed in a plane crash in Mt. Carmel, Pennsylvania, on June 17. The plane, which was also carrying Earl Carroll, hit a transformer. It seemed such a senseless accident and waste of young life. Bobby was six feet three, a naval officer, who had undergone some of the worst shelling in World War II. Louise Stewart, Bobby's mother, was shattered, and Drucie and I arranged the flowers. It was a blistering day and we nearly expired with the heat. It was miserable to think that Bobby wouldn't be on the telephone or demolishing a plate of ice cream or teasing us any more. It's always hard to believe that somebody your own age can be dead.

I didn't feel much like festivity after that. The weather was very hot and I was very tired. In fact, I note one unique entry in my diary to the effect that I came home from Sunday lunch at the Mayflower with Marvin Braverman and went upstairs to find that Dad was taking a nap. I went into Mother's room and she was taking a nap. I went into my own room and took a nap myself. This seems to be the only time in our history in the White House when all three Trumans took a nap simultaneously.

We had to get ready then for the Democratic National Convention in Philadelphia on July 14. Uncle Vivian and Aunt Luella and Aunt Mary joined us in Philadelphia and we had family reunions when we could find each other. The weather was stifling and everybody was tired, hot, and uncomfortable. There was the usual carrying-on that goes with a convention. Somebody had brought a floral arrangement to the platform that had live pigeons in it. The poor things flew blindly around the hall.

Whatever the sentiments of members of the Democratic party had been at the beginning of the year, it became apparent at the Convention that my father was the leading contender for the nomination. Though I think my mother would have welcomed retirement from

216

the political arena, she acquiesced because she knew how profoundly my father wished to finish the job he had started. Dad was quickly nominated with 947½ votes to 263 for Senator Russell. My diary had the following to say:

Wednesday, July 14, 1948
We left for the Convention in Philadelphia at 6 P.M. Half of Alabama and all of Mississippi walked out on us. Senator McGrath gave me a gold badge which says Assistant to the President. We waited in his office, backstage, until it got too hot with so many people and then we moved outdoors behind the platform. I was on a television show at 1 A.M. Dad was nominated about 10 and when Governor Donnelly made the nominating speech it touched off a demonstration lasting 55 minutes. Dad made a terrific speech in which he said he would call back the Eightieth Congress. Senator Barkley was nominated for Vice-president.

Thursday, July 15, 1948
We got home at 5:30 this morning. We've been up 23 hours. We found General Pershing had died. The end of an era, I guess. Dad served under him in World War I. Aunt Mary came home with us and I took her for a ride this afternoon. Uncle Vivian and Aunt Luella came in later today from Philadelphia.

General Pershing's body lay in state in the Rotunda of the Capitol and Dad went there to pay his respects. The police on duty didn't recognize Dad and wouldn't let his driver park. "Just move over," the policeman said. "General Marshall's car is going to be parked here."

Dad leaned over and looked at General Marshall and grinned and General Marshall's face registered his horror. The policeman nearly fainted.

ƺ➣ As soon as I got back to Missouri I shucked out of my city clothes and donned my blue jeans and old torn shirt and started in to paint the kitchen and pantry. I painted all the china closets apple green and gave everything several coats. It was a much bigger job than I had anticipated and seemed to go on all summer. I watered my garden, which looked very measly. Grandmother Wallace had had another bad attack and we were all worried about her.

I commented in my diary:

Tuesday, July 27, 1948
Dad made a grand speech to his Special Session of the 80th Do-Nothing
Congress. He laid it on the line and they are not very happy about that
or any part of it. If they do anything it is because Dad asked for it, and
if they don't do anything they are remiss. It poured rain again tonight.

Saturday, July 31, 1948
Mother, Beuf, Daw and I drove to the Fairfax Airport to meet Dad who
flew in from New York and Washington. He had just dedicated the new
International Airport, Idlewild, in New York. There was a good crowd
at Fairfax and here at home. The Secret Service lost one of Dad's suitcases and that is the end. Of all people's suitcases to lose, if they can't
even keep track of his! He came out from Kansas City with a motorcycle escort which was a little noisy and threw drivers into a tizzy. We
had a Truman family reunion dinner that night. Twenty-eight of us sat
down to the groaning board.

The next week Drucie Snyder flew out to visit me and we had
a little round of parties. I gave a luncheon for Drucie so she could
meet my old friends. We took her to all the local soda emporiums,
including famous Blue Springs, and she agreed she had never had
such a chocolate soda. We drove her all around Crackerneck Road
to show her where Jesse James used to hide out and jump down on
moving trains to rob everybody. Drucie was duly impressed.

Aunt Natalie had a family picnic for Drucie with the usual incredibly delicious food. After two helpings of everything and especially chocolate icebox cake, somebody present remarked that Drucie
and I both were as fat as pigs, and we ought to watch our calories.

Drucie and I were incensed. We hadn't noticed we were fat. We
were challenged to weigh on the bathroom scale. To our utter horror,
we found that I weighed 149 pounds and she weighed 160. We
immediately went on a stringent diet, which was pretty easy at the
moment as we had just finished dinner. Business at the Blue Springs,
Missouri, drugstore declined. Drucie left and almost missed the train.
I told her she was too fat to run. We almost had to pitch her on
after it was moving.

I watered my garden, gave Grandmother a permanent wave and
went to a card party with Bob Kirby. I can't play bridge, but nobody
caught on because I held such terrible cards that *nobody* could play
them. I really despise cards. I painted the kitchen—second coat—had

218

my hair cut off short and everybody complained. I bought some clothes and saw Mother and Grandmums off to Denver. I stayed with the aunts in Independence while Mother was away and it was very difficult to diet. On September 4 I left for Washington.

Thomas E. Dewey had been nominated for President by the Republican party and Dad was about to hit the road.

18: We, the people

Dad inaugurated his 1948 campaign in Michigan on September 6, Labor Day. When I arrived in Washington from Independence on September 4, he met me in Silver Springs, Maryland. (He often met me in Silver Springs.) It was a foregone conclusion that I would be going campaigning with him. He didn't ask me or tell me—it was just an accepted fact. Like the Three Musketeers, the Trumans had always been one for all and all for one. We didn't have to talk about it.

I knew that this race transcended political or personal aspiration and was concerned with principles and policies and responsibilities to the public about which my father had passionate convictions. Perhaps any man who becomes President of the United States is so imbued and so moved that he lives beyond self. My father had always been responsible, honest, earnest, and willing to knock himself out, but now he was on fire with what he believed, and driven to tell the people what he thought, in person as far as possible. It was as if he had to talk to the whole population, one at a time. When anybody said anything to him in the middle of a speech and he heard it, he took time to answer back. He didn't address voters; he talked to people, as one of them—which he was. I don't think he thought much about winning or losing. He just had to tell everybody what he had learned and what he thought we ought to do.

"I don't want you to vote for me," Dad said, over and over. "I want you to get out on election day and vote for yourselves—for your own interests, your own part of the country—your own friends."

I gave up any thought of a concert tour and shelved everything I had brewing. I knew my father liked to have me around, but it wasn't until we got to Detroit that I realized he considered me as an integral part of his program. He didn't tell *me*. He introduced me to the audience as his best campaigner and a real asset to him. As you can imagine, this was a heady thing for me. I suppose he based this on the fact that people had occasionally asked for me on our first whistle-stop trip. (A certain amount of interest in me had been generated by the publicity attendant on my singing career.) Also, while people like to look at the President, they also want to see what his women-folks are like and what they have on. I wish I could claim his accolade, but Dad was his own best campaigner.

I had been around on other campaigns, and I told Dad he would have to stop calling me "Baby." I'll never forget some politicians who came to the house in Independence once. I was about eighteen years old at the time, and when I came in, one man looked at me in such amazement that I said, "What's the matter? You seem so surprised."

"I'm surprised all right," he said. "Your father has been telling me about his baby for an hour. I expected you to be about two years old!"

You simply couldn't have this sort of thing in a national election, I pointed out. However, it didn't do a bit of good.

On Sunday, before we started, I got up for breakfast with Dad on the South Portico. Mother was in Denver, where she had gone to become honorary godmother to my new cousin and namesake, Margaret Wallace. My Uncle Fred and Aunt Christine are Catholic, and Mother had received a special dispensation from the Archbishop to serve. I was mistress of the mansion in her stead again, and hastened to have the piano officially tuned.

After breakfast Dad and I went out the front door and took a walk. The Secret Service men and ushers had standing bets on which floor and which door of the White House Dad would go out. It added interest to life! We wound up at the garage and I got out the convertible and we drove out to Mt. Vernon, followed by the usual retinue. He told me how to go, although I already knew. He drove back. We gathered up our luggage and left for the station, from which we departed for Detroit at 3:30 P.M. I acted as hostess in the absence of Mother, and invited all the gang on the train to dinner with us.

The next day was a day to be remembered. Running true to form, I had to get up at 6:15 A.M. We were due to arrive in Grand Rapids around 7:00, and as it was, we pulled in early. I swallowed breakfast and got ready for the handshaking. Dad gave his first speech of the day at 9:15. Although it had been pouring down rain, the crowd was enthusiastic. I was presented with a great bouquet of red roses, which I placed on the War Memorial.

We clambered back on the train and pushed on to Lansing. We didn't get off there, but it seemed to me that half the population of Michigan got on. Among these was Frank Handy, the announcement of whose nonexistent engagement to me had been so widely publicized that, for the first time in history, the White House had to call a press conference to deny a matrimonial rumor. Frank was in high spirits and announced that he was going to ride the train into Detroit with me. I had to stop and argue with him. He wouldn't understand what impetus this would give to the gossip mill. But it would have, and I made him get off, though it would have been fun to have him.

I gave interviews and received red roses at every stop, introduced people, and tried to make myself useful. We grabbed a hectic lunch before the train pulled into Detroit, and it was a good thing, because we didn't have time after we got there.

We drove in a cavalcade to Cadillac Square, where Dad spoke to about 200,000 people who gave him a tremendous ovation. This speech was broadcast over a nationwide hookup, and when it was over we drove to Hamtramck, a city within the confines of greater Detroit, where the entire population is Polish. We had a tumultuous reception here and they gave me beautiful flowers everywhere I turned. Dad spoke at Hamtramck, and then we drove to Pontiac. People were crowded along the roadside the entire route, a distance of some twenty miles, and we smiled and waved and bowed and greeted for twenty miles. When we got into the city limits, the crowd thickened to a mass and the park was overflowing. The meeting in the park looked like the typical campaign picnic you read about in history or see in plays—a real all-American occasion.

The train caught up with us at Pontiac and we got back into the air conditioning gratefully. Flint was our fifth stop, and this small town gave us one of the nicest and most enthusiastic welcomes of the whole day. I thought Dad's speech here was unusually good, and the people seemed to love it.

After we got back on the train we had a fairly calm dinner with Mr. Oscar Chapman and Mr. Jack Redding, two of the hardest-working and best campaigners we had, and pushed on to our sixth stop of the day, Toledo, Ohio. There was another huge crowd to welcome us, although it was past midnight. They gave me a marvelous bouquet of orchids and roses and Dad made his sixth speech. The last one was as fervid as the first one. You might think six speeches between morning and midnight would wear a man down, but he was as fresh as a daisy. The day had been a success, and good for our cause. If a crowd had collected anywhere along the route back to Washington, I believe he would have risen at 3 A.M. and marched out in pajamas and robe to give them the word.

The next week end, New York was on the agenda. Dad spoke at the Academy of Arts and Sciences and I slipped off to my own apartment and went out on the town. I went to dinner with Asa Phillips, and Giles Stedman and we made a foray on the Village Barn in Greenwich Village. I wore a scarf over my head and a pair of glasses and nobody recognized me. I was able to dance in peace and didn't shake a single hand all evening. I struggled up the next morning in time to get to Dad's hotel and have breakfast with him. The rule holds if you are in the same town!

On Friday, September 17, Dad and I hit the road again. General Marshall came down to the train to see us off and complimented me on my outfit. That was enough to make my day. Mr. Alben Barkley, Dad's running mate, also saw us off and gave me one of his well-known kisses.

That day we stopped at Baltimore, Harrisburg, Altoona, Pittsburgh, and Crestline, Ohio. This tour was highly organized and we all got "poop sheets" which outlined every minute of the day, gave synopses of where we were to go and what we were to do when we got there, who would board the train where, who they were, and why they were there.

Our party consisted of Dad, Matt Connelly, Charlie Ross, Clark Clifford, Dr. Wallace Graham, Jonathan Daniels, William Bray, Jack Romagna, Rose Conway, Myrtle Bergheim, Alma Eichinger, Louis Mild, Dewey Long (can't think where he got that first name!), Harry Charnley, John Boardley, Betty Douglas, Eva Hesters, India

224

Edwards, and me. This list included all the clerical help, assistants, and assistants to assistants. In addition, there were 36 newspaper correspondents, 8 radio correspondents, 5 photographers, officials of the American Express, Pennsylvania Railroad, and Western Union, and a detail of Western Union men who took care of the press, who got on and off at various towns. The press car was fitted out with tables and typewriters like a newspaper city room, and there was one whole car devoted to the mimeographing of releases.

One of the most important and valuable members of the party was Dr. Graham, who watched over the health of the family all the time, but in this instance I think he really kept us all alive. He went with us every foot of the way and it was a great comfort to have him. His infectious enthusiasm never failed to spur the crowds, and Dr. Graham is a man you instinctively trust.

As official hostess for my father, I checked the menus and shuffled guest lists for breakfast, luncheon, and dinner when there was time to sit down to a meal. We made so many stops every day that sometimes we had to snatch sandwiches between appearances. Dad's car had a special acoustical box built on the rear platform. A plastic bill had been extended out about ten inches from the top over the observation end, with blue velvet curtains that could be pulled over the doors and windows while Dad was speaking, to keep the sound from bouncing off the metal sides of the car. The train was inspected and checked for operating efficiency at stated intervals, and by and large we did pretty well at keeping to our schedule. The entire track from the Eastern seaboard to California was heavily guarded to avoid accidents or other troubles.

I usually kept a big bouquet of red roses in the lounge. I always had red roses to spare, because they were presented to me so often by well-wishers. (In fact, I sometimes wished people would hand me a bunch of petunias, just to change the mixture!)

The President's car, the "Ferdinand Magellan," was a regulation Pullman that had been made over into a lounge, four bedrooms and one bath, dining room, and galley. It was neat, not gaudy. The National Association of Railroads had converted the car and sold it to the government for one dollar, for the use of the President, during Mr. Roosevelt's administration. It was covered with armor plate, had three-inch bulletproof glass in the windows, and weighed 265,000 pounds.

Our special train had seventeen cars. The press car was fitted up somewhat like a city room. The most interesting car, I think, was the communications car, which was operated by the Army Signal Corps. This car had a radio teletype which made it possible for Dad to keep in constant touch with Washington throughout the tour. News was received in code, decoded and telephoned back to the "Ferdinand Magellan." Messages could also be sent from the communications car. It required a couple of Diesel engines on the communications car to generate electricity for the teletype machines. My father was also able to talk on the long-distance telephone in a matter of minutes. Telephone lines were kept open in all the towns we passed through to the White House and the State Department.

A pilot train—a locomotive and a couple of cars—preceded our train as a security measure, so we wouldn't be inadvertently blown up or wrecked. It never occurred to any of us that we might be, but the railroad officials who were handling the train went to the most elaborate precautions to make our long journey safe and satisfactory.

Everybody on the train paid regular railroad fare plus Pullman fare, as they would have on any other train. Everybody had to have a ticket. The railroads may have lost money, because of the special nature of the train's routing. But there was no free-loading.

Dad made one of his best speeches at Pittsburgh, which had a good many memories for me. When we pulled into the yards I thought about the last time I had been there, to inaugurate my concert tour. It occurred to me that everything you do in your life somehow paves the way for something else. If I was any real use to Dad in his campaign, maybe it was because I had had experience with a whistle-stopper of my own.

In Pittsburgh our train drew up alongside the Freedom Train, which had on display the famous documents of American liberty. Dr. Graham, Clark Clifford, and I went through part of it and it was absolutely fascinating. Such a wonderful idea.

On Saturday, September 16, I got up accidentally at 5:45 A.M. We were at Rock Island, Illinois, and everybody else was still asleep. I felt as if insult had been added to injury when I discovered that I had forgotten to set my watch back an hour for Central Standard Time. We stopped at Davenport, Iowa, Iowa City, Oxford, and Grinnell before breakfast. In every town the people were packed solidly along the railroad tracks. They all seemed friendly. When I waved good-by at Oxford, I think all of the 5,000 greeters returned my wave. A sea of hands went up. When I got to Iowa City, sixty of my Pi Beta Phi sisters had got themselves to the train at 7:21 A.M. I was overcome with this tribute.

Senator Gillette, the Democratic nominee for Governor, boarded the train outside Des Moines to have breakfast with us and we finally sat down to our bacon and eggs. The platform was packed with people and they were standing all through the yards. We pulled into Des Moines a little after ten. Mother got on there. I have *never* been so glad to see anybody in my life.

As soon as we had said hello we all piled off the train and got into cars and drove to Dexter, Iowa, where Dad was scheduled to attend a plowing contest and give his major speech of the day. The plowing contest was held on the farm of Mr. and Mrs. R. K. Weesmer, who were our hosts. It was hot and dry and that good Iowa soil rolled up in clouds of dust as the plowshares bit into it. You could scarcely breathe. But there were 85,000 people gathered in that small town to hear Dad speak. Who wanted to breathe!

Dad made a rousing speech and then we all repaired to a big tent for a hearty farm lunch. After that, we got in an open car and drove the forty miles back to Des Moines in the broiling sun. I was wearing a blue and black tie-silk dress and it was practically plastered to my person. We got back to the train and that afternoon we made platform appearances at Melcher, Chariton, and Trenton.

Mother and Dad and I had dinner together, with no guests. We had to catch up with each other's news. We arrived in Kansas City around nine-thirty and set out immediately for Independence. I had to get to Independence so I could register. I was particular about registering, as I had a vote I wanted to cast on November 2.

Sunday at home was a real boon. Mother and I went to church and Vietta cooked one of her famous dinners with everything I like best. Mother packed (thank goodness I had never unpacked), and Dad had a sore throat, which surprised nobody but him. At eight-thirty that evening we set out again for points west.

Our first stop on Monday morning was Denver, Colorado. We rode in open cars in a parade where thousands were gathered along the line of march. Dad spoke extemporaneously in the House of Representatives of the Colorado legislature, and made his major address from the steps of Colorado's gold-domed State House. That afternoon we stopped at Colorado Springs, Pueblo, Canon City, and Salida, Colorado. By now we were on the Denver and Rio Grande Railroad, which travels through some of the most picturesque country in the United States. It picks its way through the high snow-crowned mountains and down the fabulous Royal Gorge, whose scenic splendor we enjoyed just before we sat down to dinner with the Colorado delegation who had got on the train in Denver. Mr. Harry Karr, the division passenger agent for the Pennsylvania, who was on the train from start to finish, deplored the fact that the President went through the Gorge. He was a nervous wreck. "Why, it's only thirty feet wide some places," he said. "Let one boulder roll down and we'd be shooting the rapids in here."

The opening gun the next day—Tuesday, September 21—was at Glenwood Springs, but I didn't make it. I slept right through. I finally pulled myself together and got up in time for an appearance at Grand Junction, Colorado. We got there at 9:05, and for some reason everybody on the train got off except Mother, Dad, and me. Dad immediately began to dictate letters to Rose, and Mother and I fell to writing our ubiquitous thank-you notes. (There is no new way to say, "Thank you for the orchid!") When Dad had got his pressing mail out of the way he went to work on his Salt Lake City speech. In a little while, the staff came back and the train moved on to the next stop—Price, Utah. After that came Helper, Utah, Springville, Provo, and American Fork. We appeared and reappeared and at 5 P.M. got into Salt Lake City.

Dad spoke in the Mormon Tabernacle in Salt Lake City to an enthusiastic crowd estimated at 15,000. I was fascinated with the Tabernacle, which was designed by Brigham Young. He is said to have sliced a hard-boiled egg in half and put toothpicks in it to describe to the architect the sort of building he wanted, which could be filled and emptied in a minimum space of time. All the doors of the Tabernacle open out all around it, so a crowd can disperse in a few seconds. The most exciting thing to me, however, was the great organ, which I had often heard on radio, and the acoustics of the place, which beggar description. Needless to say, I am always interested in "halls."

After the speech we got on the train again and I managed to stay up until we got to Ogden, which we achieved at 11 P.M. I didn't know anything else until Sparks, Nevada, the next morning. From Sparks we drove to Reno. At Reno, Dad got so excited that he referred to the opposition as Republican "mothbags"! He had intended to say "mossbacks." Several members of the press corps thought this was pretty funny and considerable publicity was given to the fact that the President had blown up in his lines. I thought "mothbags" was an interesting switch!

We rejoined the train and after numerous stops during the day, arrived at Oakland, California, at 7:00 P.M. We drove from Oakland to San Francisco with a motorcycle escort and Dad spoke on the steps of the City Hall to thousands. We then drove back to Oakland and he spoke in one of the parks to more thousands. This was followed by a reception, at which Mother and I shook hands with what seemed like thousands. We didn't get out of Oakland until 3:00 A.M.

From San Francisco to Los Angeles, the tracks seemed to be lined with people. We stopped at Tracy, Modesto, Merced, Fresno (where 15,000 people met us), Tulare, Bakersfield (Governor Warren's home town, where again we had a huge crowd), Mojave, Burbank, and Los Angeles.

In Los Angeles Mother and I attended a reception for ladies at the Biltmore, and then later to Gilmore Stadium to hear Dad speak. He made one of his best speeches—"threw the book at Dewey," as one reporter said. Dewey was scheduled to speak in Los Angeles the following evening. When the Democratic committee set out to obtain the Hollywood Bowl for Dad's address, they discovered that the opponent's contingent had rented it for two nights, the night Dad spoke and the night Dewey spoke, on the pretext of testing the lighting!

In Los Angeles we got into a Donnybrook about the car Dad was to ride in during the parade. Usually we rode in open-top convertibles —new ones—and some of the press corps insinuated that the big crowds we drew were the result of the average American's desire to see a new automobile! Although the war had been over three years, new cars were still difficult to obtain.

Most of these streamlined cars were without running boards. When we got to Los Angeles, the Secret Service refused to permit Dad to ride through the metropolis in a car that had no place for the security officers to stand and guard the President. Immediately a search was instituted for an open-top car with a running board. This took quite a bit of doing, but finally they came up with an old 1934 Lincoln. This anachronism belonged to Cecil B. De Mille, who is said to have voted for Dewey.

San Diego was next on the agenda. We got in there at 7:00 A.M. and I was feeling very sorry for myself until I heard about the people who had stayed up all night to be sure of a seat in the stadium when Dad spoke. The San Diego parade was sensational and there were 30,000 people jammed into the stadium, although it was early in the morning. After San Diego we started back east (we'd gone about as far west as we could go and still be in the United States!) and struck out across the American desert. We paused briefly at Colton, California, Yuma, and Phoenix, Arizona.

The next morning was Saturday and I waked up in Lordsburg, New Mexico, where we had stopped. We paused at Deming, New Mexico, and got into El Paso at 11:00 A.M. We got off there and stayed half an hour. Dad spoke in the Union Station to a mob of people. Mr. Beauford Jester, Governor of Texas, Congressman Reagan, and Speaker Rayburn boarded the train there and rode with us through Texas. I was glad to see "Uncle Sam" Rayburn, whom I had known since childhood. He is one of the great Americans, and it is always a privilege to be with him. The Texas delegation dined with us that evening and we had more fun. The day was a real "stopper." We stopped at Sierra Blanca, Valentine, Marfa, and Alpine.

Sunday morning I got up at 5:45 A.M. without a word of complaint. For the first time in my life I didn't mind. We arrived at Uvalde, Texas, at 6:00 A.M. and former Vice-president John Nance Garner had invited us to his house for breakfast. We had a real Texas repast: fried chicken and rice, ham and eggs, bacon, fruit, and coffee. This was the biggest breakfast I ever ate in my life, but everything is bigger in Texas. Dad was so happy to see Mr. Garner. They sat around after breakfast cracking jokes, yarning, and kidding each other. It was a wonderful break in the monotony of traveling.

However, we had a schedule to keep and pushed on to San Antonio. It was in San Antonio that Dad made one of the finest speeches of his life on the subject of world peace. But it is lost to posterity. Through some slip-up in the coverage, nobody took it down. It seems such a pity. We fell exhausted into bed and got in forty winks because the train stayed in the yards until nearly five o'clock in the

230

morning. I don't know whether you have ever slept on a train for ten nights running or not, but it gets so that the wheels are in your head and the bumps and grinds are part of slumber. It was a thrill to sleep lying still, and you get to be grateful for small favors.

The next day we stopped at New Braunfels, San Marcos, Austin, Temple, Waco, and got off at Fort Worth and drove in a motorcade to Dallas. I rode with Amon Carter, Jr. Dad spoke to a mass meeting of 15,000 enthusiastic Texans at the Rebel Stadium in Dallas. Then we got back on the train and headed for Bonham, Speaker Rayburn's home town. This meeting was held outdoors and it was bitter cold. I nearly froze to death.

When the speech was over, we met the Rayburn clan and most of the inhabitants of that part of Texas. They came in droves and kept coming. I never saw such a receiving line. After several hours of it Governor Jester boomed, "Sam, why did you leave the front door open?" and got up and shut it. As soon as the front door was closed and locked, the people started coming in the back door and through the kitchen.

The next day we established a beachhead in Oklahoma. It was the most crowded day of the whole trip. We stopped at intervals of thirty minutes all day long, beginning at Marietta. At Ardmore we rode in a parade and Dad made a speech. We got to Oklahoma City an hour late, but Dad made a fine speech there. Mother and I attended a reception given for us and then went with India Edwards back to the Skirvin Hotel, where Mrs. Mesta had arranged a supper for us.

I was supposed to get up and out on that back platform at Shawnee the next morning, but I couldn't make it. When we got to Seminole, I was there, though. Governor Turner and ex-Governor Kerr (then running for the Senate) boarded our train and rode through Oklahoma with us. After Tulsa came Claremore, Vinita, then Neosho, Missouri, and Springfield.

The last day of September was a real mess, due to insufficient escort service and a shortage of police. Governor Green of Illinois was a Republican, and I guess he didn't believe advance reports about the size of our welcoming committees. We made seven stops that day and we were all worn to a frazzle. We got into Kentucky two and a half hours late, which puts a crimp in a prearranged program. We made Louisville just in time to go on the air in the Armory, which was jammed with 8,000 people inside and 10,000 people outside

231

trying to get in. We were all worried about Dewey's speech that day, since he said he would make definitive statements and we expected the worst. But as usual, he didn't say anything very important. After the Armory speech we got back on the train and went to bed.

I had to get up early again the next morning (when didn't I?) to greet the citizens of Shelbyville, Kentucky, where my Truman grandparents were married. Life was just one stop after another the next day. The pauses came every half hour and Dad was getting hoarse again. That night he spoke at the Auditorium in Charleston, West Virginia. There wasn't an empty seat in the house and it was estimated that 5,000 people stood patiently outside. We had dinner in the Executive Mansion and gave ourselves the week end off.

On Monday I packed my scattered garments and got off the train, joining Drucie, Mr. and Mrs. Snyder. (They were riding in Mr. Dan Schaefer's private car and it was so antique it had a real fireplace in the sitting room, but it was a rough-rider.) Drucie and I had been invited to attend the Veiled Prophet Ball in St. Louis, and out of the one-night stand I jumped into the middle of glamour.

The Veiled Prophet Ball is the outstanding social event of the St. Louis season. It comprises a coronation ceremony, where the Queen of Love and Beauty is crowned by the mysterious monarch, the Veiled Prophet of Khorassan, whose identity is never made known. The Queen is considered the first lady of the debutantes for the season and must promise not to marry during her reign—one year—when she relinquishes her crown, sceptre, and prerogatives to a new queen. The entertainment is unusually lavish and beautiful in setting and costumes and St. Louisans look forward to it from one year to the next.

We got into St. Louis on the afternoon of October 5 and were met by photographers and reporters. Drucie and I were scheduled to do a dual TV show after the ball and as soon as we had repaired the ravages of travel somewhat (it would have taken me several weeks really to repair mine!) we went into rehearsal. My date for the ball was John Morrison of St. Louis, and Drucie went with Bob Lashly. The boys came by that evening and took us to a cocktail party, along with Mr. and Mrs. Snyder, and to the Veiled Prophet parade. The floats in the parade, manned by the Merry Krewe of Khorassan, were all done up in a Mother Goose–rhyme theme and were very elaborate. We got back to the Park-Plaza Hotel in time for a late

232

dinner and heard Carl Brisson sing. Then we stopped around the corner to the Plaza where a dance band was holding forth, and for some reason we didn't get in until three o'clock in the morning!

Drucie, who is a tall, beautiful girl with a queenly bearing and well-chiseled features, had a marvelous, sophisticated dress for the ball, of gray faille taffeta, made with a décolleté neckline and tiny little straps. The skirt was draped across the hipline and wound up in an enormous pouf of bustle behind. She had a gray maline stole, fastened with a circle of diamonds, and silver slippers. The dress set off her fine coloring. I had a white slipper-satin dress with thirty yards of skirt and a close-fitting bodice which was decorated with pink chiffon hollyhocks in a spray from neckline to waist. I had white satin slippers and my gloves were spangled with sequins. We thought we looked pretty fancy. John and Bob arrived at seven-thirty and we swept off to the ball.

The coronation and ball were held in the Keil Auditorium which had been transformed into a royal court for the occasion. The boxes were draped in silver lamé and the entire floor covered with white sateen. A green pavilion had been erected over the throne and the rest of the room was done in peach satin. The Veiled Prophet, whose face you never see, and the Queen and her Maids came from a smaller pavilion at the back of the auditorium, emerging to form the processional from behind white silk curtains. There was a guard of Bengal Lancers in brilliant military dress, and the gowns were exquisite. The Queen and her ladies all wore magnificent trains in a brilliant spectrum of white, chartreuse, green, red, and pink. The Queen was Helen Dozier Conant, a beautiful girl, who did justice to the occasion. It was all gorgeous.

After the coronation, Drucie and I did our TV show. Drucie interviewed me and we talked about the pageant and introduced the Queen and her court. It was just too bad that this happened before the days of color television!

After that we adjourned to the Gold Room of the Jefferson Hotel for the Queen's Supper. The whole room was done in gold, with splashes of purple, the royal colors of the Veiled Prophet. The scene was lighted entirely by gold candles flickering in gold branched candelabra, and the tables were covered with gold cloth and centered with masses of yellow chrysanthemums and yellow rose buds. What a beautiful sight!

We stayed there until 3:30 A.M. and then dropped Mr. and Mrs. Snyder. Since we hated to waste the rest of such a good night, Drucie, John, Bob, and I pushed on to the University Club where we danced until dawn. I got back on the train at seven o'clock in the morning. We managed to get up in time for dinner that night. As I say, this was different from the plowing contest, but it too was a portion of America.

I went home for the week end, but bright and early Monday morning, October 11, I was back in harness. We got into Cincinnati at 7 A.M., a cold, dreary, drizzly day. We got off and went to the Netherlands-Plaza Hotel for breakfast and Dad made his speech. We got off again at Dayton, Ohio, where Governor Cox was our host. He had been a candidate for the Presidency in 1920, with Mr. Roosevelt as running mate. Governor Cox asked us to lunch and Secretary of Commerce Sawyer was there, along with Governor Lausche of Ohio. We got off once more in Akron and Dad spoke in the Armory, which was filled and running over. People always came down to see us get off and get on, and when we pulled out of the stations, the little boys ran alongside the train as long as they could keep up. This seemed to be a characteristic of little boys from Seattle to San Antonio and from New York to San Diego. I was always afraid one of them would get hurt. Another characteristic of little boys, and big ones too, was that they all called me by my first name. "Good-by, Margaret," they would call as we faded into the distance.

The next day was Columbus Day, presumably a holiday, but I could hardly tell the difference. Our first stop was at Richmond, Indiana. Once more I forgot to set my watch at the change of time and wasted a whole hour getting up too early. This was one way to get me up—just move back and forth across the time line! We stopped at practically every crossroad all day, but Bill Bray and I managed to get in a few hands of gin rummy. He won.

As little as I like card games, I played a lot of gin rummy on that jaunt. Although the reviewing of it sounds and seems climactic and exciting, the atmosphere of the train was often boredom, especially after the first few days. Campaigning settled into a sort of routine. Dad was introduced, received a token of the town or the country we were moving through—peaches, walnuts, ten-gallon hats—spoke his earnest words and introduced Mother and me to the crowd. My mother, who has no taste for putting herself on public view, bore up graciously. I, who make no secret of being a ham, enjoyed parting the blue velvet curtains and appearing on the platform—at least if dawn had broken! Even I wearied, however, and the sight of the rear platform of a railroad car still makes me feel tired.

The stops were the great breaks in the monotony of endless miles. When you travel day in and day out for weeks you exhaust all your resources for amusement and the world begins to seem like endless reaches of railroad track. I used to sit by the window and take idle snapshots of the country going by—telephone poles whizzing past, flat plains, deserts, untenanted country roads. I don't know *why* I did it. These blurs are the most undistinguished snapshots of my camera career. I just didn't have anything else to do.

Most of the people on the train were very busy. Dad was always working on his next speech. Mother and I were along for the ride, and our job was to render the situation normal. We weren't charged with any responsibility but that and the greeting of the people, when we were invited to appear on the platform. Of course Mother looked after everybody—not only our own party but any member of the press corps who needed an aspirin or a button sewed on—but I couldn't find anything to do between stops. Needless to say, we both endeavored to lend my father moral support—not that he really needed it. He didn't require cheering up, but he liked to have us *there*.

Springfield, Illinois, was the high spot of the day. Dad placed a wreath there on Lincoln's tomb and we attended a dinner at the St. Nicholas Hotel. Then there was a great torchlight parade to the Armory, where we were greeted by a packed house of enthusiastic listeners. What is there about torchlight? Stirs you up.

Since I'm always talking about getting up in the small hours of the morning, I ought to include the fact that I did sleep until noon on some days. On October 13 our first stop was at 12:50 P.M. I made it to the rear platform in the nick of time. Everybody slept but Dad. He's an early riser to end early risers and he got up and worked. We got off at Superior, Wisconsin, piled into cars and drove to Duluth and back and then headed for St. Paul, where Dad made one of the best speeches he ever made. He got better and better as time went on, and he could sense the response of the people to his plain talk.

By morning we were in Madison, Wisconsin, where we debarked and went out to the campus of the University of Wisconsin. Dad

235

spoke in their assembly hall. The students raised a cheer and we had an enormous crowd there. From Madison we went to Milwaukee and Dad spoke in the ball park to 12,000 people on the atomic bomb and its implications. He had an engrossing subject and you could hear a pin drop in the ball park when he was talking.

We arrived in Indiana on the morrow and the Indiana delegation got on the train. The crowds had been growing in size and scope every day and in Indianapolis that night we had one of the biggest turnouts. There were more than 100,000 people to hear Dad speak. He wowed them.

On Saturday, October 16, we hove into Washington, after a multiple number of stops. We got here at 4 P.M. and tore up to the White House to put on a new face for the tea we were having at five. (No rest for the weary!) We had 150 important campaigners to tea and wrung their hands because we appreciated what they were doing. I finished the day washing my hair, not a minute too soon. What weeks of train travel can do to your looks! I had a strong inclination to burn all my clothes, because I certainly never wanted to see any of them again, but it occurred to me that the campaign wasn't over, so prudence got the better of whim.

Washington was just a one-night stand that time. I might not have got up at all that Sunday, but the word came that the Missouri University football team, which had just walloped Navy off the gridiron on Saturday, was coming by, so I could not resist rising to the occasion. We shook hands and I could scarcely forbear to groan. They were handsome boys with tremendous shoulders, and their lightest handclasp was a bone crusher. Still, they *had* beat Navy.

On the morning of October 18, we forsook the train and flew in the *Independence* to Miami, Florida. We landed at ten-fifteen in the morning and paraded through Miami and Miami Beach to the Roney Plaza Hotel. Mother and I received an aggregation of twenty orchids and more roses than we could count. It was lovely and warm in Miami and I hated to leave all that sun and surf after Dad's speech at the American Legion Convention Hall, but North Carolina was waiting.

We flew to Raleigh and got to our suite in time for dinner with Mr. and Mrs. Jonathan Daniels. Dad spoke from the Capitol steps the next day and at the unveiling of a statue to Jackson, Johnson, and Polk, Presidents North Carolinians claim, at the State Fair

Grounds. It was cold, damp, and drizzling, and in Raleigh I saw my favorite sign of the campaign: "North Carolina may be cloudy but it sho' ain't Dewey!" We took off from Raleigh at four-thirty that afternoon and arrived in Washington an hour later.

I was now so accustomed to this endurance test that I did not fall apart as might be expected but put on my evening clothes and went to the opening concert of the Philadelphia Symphony Orchestra. Eugene Ormandy was conducting. I went with Mr. and Mrs. Curt Schiffeler and Admiral and Mrs. Nimitz and had supper with the Schiffelers at the Raleigh Hotel afterward. Eugene was there and he was very gallant to me.

The next night Dad made his radio speech on the Taft-Hartley bill, with Tallulah Bankhead introducing him from New York. It was a good show. We all trouped downstairs to hear it and had considerable trouble getting there. The White House had a feeble elevator at that time, and to get it to descend you had to take the button off, stick a pencil in the hole, and give it a twist. This elevator seemed to me to be not only a disgrace but dangerous. Mother had been standing up all afternoon shaking hands with the Colonial Dames who had come to tea in droves. I hated for her to have to walk.

We stayed in Washington the whole week end and left on Monday for Chicago, stopping everywhere. We got off only once—at Gary, Indiana—and stayed an hour. Dad spoke and we clambered back on, arriving in Chicago at 2 P.M. What a night that was in Chicago! The parade was miles long and the people were jammed along the line of march to the curb and overflowing everywhere into the street, so that the police had to drive them back before we could proceed. There was entertainment and a dazzling fireworks display before the speech. Dad spoke in the stadium, which holds 25,000 people. There were about 30,000 in it and 10,000 more trying to get in. The noise was deafening and reminiscent. Dad had been nominated for Vice-president in the same hall with the same sort of mob scene. I remembered it all too well.

There was one thing about whistle-stop campaigning: I lost plenty of weight. I not only didn't have time to eat, but when you get on and off a train as many times as I did the next day, you get way ahead on your exercise. It seemed to me that I was climbing on and off all day long. The big meeting and major speech of the day took place in Cleveland at the local stadium that night. Enthusiasm was frenetic.

237

You could almost see it build, from day to day, like a cyclone whirling up. It was a fascinating thing to watch.

After Cleveland we didn't stop until we got to Massachusetts. We started getting off the train early in the morning and had dismounted and reembarked five times (with presentation of flowers to Mother and me on each occasion) before we got to Boston. Dad spoke and we stayed overnight there. There was a fabulous reception for us, and Mother and I received old-fashioned flowers, made into nosegays with paper lace.

At Providence we turned south and came back to New York, arriving at four in the afternoon. Dad made five speeches before we could get to the hotel. He spoke to the garment workers in Union Square, to a crowd in Sarah Delano Roosevelt Park in the Italian district, at the Democratic Club, and one more place I can't remember. That evening we went to a dinner in honor of Senator Wagner and then on to Madison Square Garden, which was mobbed. Dad and Tallulah Bankhead both made grand speeches. The next morning we set out for Yonkers, where we made two stops, gave interviews, got roses. Then we stopped in the Bronx for lunch in the Plaza Concourse Hotel and Dad spoke again. Afterward we went to Harlem, where we had one of the nicest and most dignified meetings of the entire campaign. The Negro ministers of Harlem presented Dad with the Roosevelt Award, inaugurated by the Negro Presbyterian Church, and he was never more proud of anything.

In addition to all the people gathered in parks, stadia, halls, and pavilions, the streets and roads in and around New York were crowded from stem to stern. I wonder how many million faces I looked into that day. It was a tremendous experience. There were people there whose bloodlines ran back to every country in the world and now they were all Americans, with the right of choice in a free election. You can't help getting excited when you think about that.

One of the things that interested me most about the campaign was the apparent inability of the press corps to sense the growing enthusiasm of the public for my father's cause. It seemed to me that it rolled up like a tumbleweed on the prairies we traversed as the days went by. It was true that in some of the early stages the response of the public had been more polite, and out of deference to my father's office, than partisan. There was more hand clapping than cheering. In big stadia in big cities, there had been empty seats. It

238

was reasonable to believe that some of the onlookers came to see what a President looked like, rather than to back him up.

But just as I can sense the sudden blessed concentration of an audience when I am singing, it was possible to feel that growing climate of conviction. Even I—and I was biased from the start—could note the change. But the press corps—those noses for news—remained virtually unmoved. A few of them always were for us, but I doubt there was a single conversion on the entire tour. They were there, but most of the newsmen seemed convinced that Dewey was going to win. Even when they were astute enough to observe my father's advancing popularity with his audiences, they could not reverse themselves. One reporter recognized the symptoms but said he felt that the people of the United States were in the mood to give Harry Truman anything in the world he wanted except the Presidency.

We were coming to the end of our hegira. That night we entrained for St. Louis, where Dad spoke at the Kiel Auditorium, the same place I had lately been waltzing at the Veiled Prophet Ball. It was quite different that night. It was packed with 17,000 (15,000 outside) yelling partisans and Dad made an off-the-cuff speech that was a real triumph. Drucie, Bob Lashly, Jack Morrison, and I went to the Park-Plaza and had a sandwich for old time's sake and I ran to get on the train before it pulled out.

The next day was Sunday, Hallowe'en, and I was in the house on Delaware Street. Home! I couldn't believe it. I went to church, went to a movie, and washed my hair. What bliss. No matter what happens, you *have* to wash your hair now and then.

The tumult and the shouting died and Dad made ready for his last speech. He was as cool as a cucumber. It never occurred to him that he could lose. I had no qualms about it either. I had seen too much. But an awful lot of other people didn't think he had a chance. It was reliably reported that the newspapers were 8 to 1 in favor of Dewey. Many of the reporters who had traveled on our train had been condescending. Contempt was lying around in hunks. But the *people* came to listen. What they heard came straight from my father's heart. Sometimes it was almost poetry and sometimes it was nearly slang, but it was always honest and vigorous and his own idea.

Physically it was gruelling, even for me, and my parents were almost forty years older. But there is no length to which the spirit cannot drag the body. If you have real conviction you don't get tired.

239

19: Who could ask for anything more?

We had traveled 30,000 miles and Dad had made 351 speeches. Nobody knows how many million people we had been in contact with. We had had a lot of fun, and so, we thought, had the people. They seemed to have taken an interest in us as human beings and we had reciprocated. Once in Barstow, California, a lady had called up to Dad, who was standing on the rear platform of the train, "President Truman, you sound as if you had a cold!"

"That's because I ride around in the wind with my mouth open," Dad called back.

He had introduced Mother as "The Boss." (Mother finally put a stop to this in Lima, Ohio, but he continued to call me "Baby" to the bitter end.) He had told everybody, from coast to coast, that it had taken me four years to get a degree and he had got one in thirty minutes! But mixed in with the jokes and the wisecracks had been his sincere concern over the facts.

Still the polls and the press and even the gamblers didn't give Dad a chance. Fifty leading political writers predicted that Dewey would be victorious. A St. Louis betting commissioner was reported to have said that Dewey was a 15-to-1 favorite. The Gallup Poll and Elmo

Roper both predicted defeat for Truman. When Dad announced in the Biltmore Hotel near the end of the campaign that he would sweep the country, the reporters all laughed as if it were a big joke. Well, they had to laugh out of the other side of their mouths.

When he made the final speech of the tour in St. Louis, Dad said, "We have told the people the truth, and the people are with us. The tide is rolling. All over the country I have seen it in the people's faces. The *people* are going to win this election!"

We pulled into Independence on November 1. That night we went to a dinner given for Dad by the Shrine in Kansas City and Dad broadcast his last speech from the house.

I wrote in my diary:

November 1, 1948
The campaign is all over. Now we wait until tomorrow is done to see how the voters decide. We can take whatever comes, but I wonder if the country can.

The next day was unusually tense. Though I was convinced that my father could not lose, there was very little one could read or hear that was encouraging. The day dragged on forever. I wrote:

Tuesday, November 2, 1948
We voted at 10 o'clock. I was #103. It looks like a big vote. Later: What a night. I haven't been to bed at all. I've been running up and down the stairs all night answering the phone on the direct-line telephone talking to Bill Boyle who gave me the returns. We are ahead, but at about 1:30 A.M. we hit a slump—then gradually came up again. Dad has slipped away to Excelsior Springs and the reporters are going crazy trying to find him. They have offered me anything if I'll just tell them in which direction he went.

It is impossible to describe one's emotions at such a time. Every obvious card seemed stacked against us and everywhere you heard about the Dewey landslide, but when the first returns began to come in they revealed an early trend toward my father. It seemed to me that commentators were all Republicans that night! They kept urging the people to wait for the deferred Dewey landslide. As the night wore on and Dad's lead became more marked, they began to try to explain the landslide that seemed to be coming from the opposite direction. There were some pretty funny explanations.

There were also some real die-hards. Dad said he waked up at

242

4 A.M. in the hotel at Excelsior Springs and turned on the radio. H. V. Kaltenborn was saying that although the President had a two-million-vote lead, the election would have to be decided by the House of Representatives. That Dad couldn't possibly be elected by a majority vote! The final figures showed that he had polled 24,104,836 votes to Dewey's 21,969,500, carried twenty-eight states and the thirteen largest cities of the country. The Democrats had a majority in both houses. Who could ask for anything more?

Dad got up, only slightly earlier than usual, and along with his jubilant Secret Service men who were loyal to him went to the penthouse at the Muehlebach in Kansas City. Needless to say, the campaigners had gone wild and were engaging in snake dances all over the place. I stayed up all night long in Independence, wearing my best black dress and a pair of ballet shoes to take the load off my feet. I went out on the porch when the excitement was running high and the press reported subsequently that I had appeared on the gallery in "my robe and slippers." A fine way to talk about my basic black.

The next day, November 3, was really hysterical. I wrote:

Wednesday, November 3, 1948
We have won. I still can't believe it is all over and over so well. Dewey conceded about 10 o'clock this morning. I am so tired. I am packing frantically and the phone is ringing madly. There was no celebration planned in Independence and they suddenly got one together and the entire square around the Courthouse was jampacked with 20,000 friends and relatives and neighbors. We've known most of them for years. It was really very touching. I heard the news that Dewey had conceded while up town when all the bells in the town went crazy and I thought that somebody had short-circuited them.

We left home at eight o'clock the next morning—Dad, Mother, Grandmother Wallace, Vietta, and I. The Snyders joined us in St. Louis. Nobody had had any sleep for what seemed like aeons, but there was no chance to get any. Joyous committeemen boarded the train at every junction and their beaming faces were wonderful to see.

There was some fascinating reading matter to be had that day. In St. Louis somebody presented Dad with a copy of the *Chicago Tribune* with its famous banner: DEWEY DEFEATS TRUMAN. "That's one for the books!" Dad ejaculated. *Life* magazine printed a picture of Dewey with the caption: "The next President of the United

States." The Kiplinger newsletter predicted that Dewey would be in office until 1957. Commentators, editorial writers, and pollsters began to eat raw crow and try to explain "Wot hoppened!" A correspondent of the *Berkshire Evening Eagle*, L. S. Briggs, sent in a poem that seemed to sum up matters:

> O section, cross-section and sample,
> O postcard and phone call and bell!
> O Crossley, Roper and Gallup,
> O George!
> O Elmo!
> O Hell!

But the *people* (who won the election) went around congratulating each other. A tremendous spirit of camaraderie developed. Strangers jubilated together on the street. The people seemed to have renewed faith that they were in the saddle and had a personal representative in the White House.

When we arrived in Washington on November 5 there was a tremendous ovation. Over three-quarters of a million people lined Pennsylvania Avenue from the railroad station to the White House . . . so many people and all apparently so happy. We rode in an open car with Vice-president Barkley and his daughter, Mrs. Max Truitt, and everybody greeted my father affectionately with shouts of "Hiya, Harry," and the bands played *I'm Just Wild about Harry*, which got to be a regular theme song. What a thrill it was to come back to Washington with what amounted to a triumphal entry. I was so proud of my father.

&❧ We were back in the White House politically, but at this juncture, it looked as if we weren't going to be there long in person. For months Dad had been complaining to the Commission of Grounds and Buildings about the condition of the weary old structure. The Commission had been checking it and reporting, but now Dad was convinced the floors were so fragile that life there was actually becoming dangerous. On Saturday the sixth of November, the Commission came to the conclusion we would have to move into Blair House while the White House was bolstered up.

Mother had come down with a cold (and no wonder), but Maurice

Evans was in Baltimore playing in *Man and Superman* and this was too close at hand for Drucie and me not to react. We drove over there and saw *Man and Superman* again. That night I went to the Shoreham with Admiral Giles Stedman. Drucie was there with Marvin Braverman and there was a gala crowd of people in the room, most of them friends of mine. We had a hilarious evening, reviewing the election and laughing about the sick look on the faces of the poll takers and the crow-eating department in the newspapers and the wrong-guessers who were paying off bets pushing the more successful wagerers around the streets in wheelbarrows, and other horseplay. When you win against such odds you've got to be permitted a little gloating.

The next morning I talked over the long-distance telephone with Ted Malone, a radio commentator I had known in Kansas City years before. Both ends of the conversation were recorded and that afternoon I heard it broadcast over his radio program in New York. Such fun—this modern age! Dad left for Key West by plane that morning and Mother and I were scheduled to follow him by train.

I had tea with Mrs. Mesta on Monday and Marvin Coles took me to the Statler for dinner and we danced and danced. I had the satisfaction of seeing two prognosticators of Dad's downfall there and they turned paler than they already were when they saw me. One of them had the nerve to come all the way across the room and tell me that she had always been for us. It always amazed me that people thought I could be so stupid.

Tuesday, November 9, was a real wild day. To begin with, a hurricane was rumored to be blowing up and heading for the Florida coast. We were also heading for the coast of Florida—I had been frantically shopping for beach shoes and other sporty items—and the thought of meeting head on with a hurricane did not charm me. My mail was piled halfway to the ceiling and I dived into it in the morning and dictated until I was hoarse and signed letters until I had writer's cramp. Marvin Braverman took me to the Shoreham for dinner that evening, and who should be there but Drucie with Marvin Coles. Those Marvins certainly got around.

We were living in chaos at home, as the house was about to fall in. Everything there was in an uproar. If you can imagine moving out the contents of the entire White House, you will get a rough idea.

To complicate matters, an Indian prince, who was a diplomatic guest, was esconced at Blair House with his retinue. We couldn't very well move in until he chose to terminate his visit.

The next day, while the Prince was out for lunch, Mother and I hotfooted it over there to look around and get a few things straightened out about our moving, since it now looked as if the renovation of the White House might be a major project, requiring many months. As a matter of fact, the need to repair it became dramatically evident a few days before the campaign started when Dad went upstairs and found that my Steinway piano had fallen through the floor. A large hole had opened up in the second floor and the piano was sitting there tipsily, with one leg in the hole. When the engineers went into the matter they discovered that the whole building needed to be braced and it's a thousand wonders it didn't fall down around our ears. The traditional fall social affairs at the White House had to be canceled in view of the condition of the building, and Mother and I left for Key West.

❧ The Little White House at Key West is actually part of a Naval Station, and when Mother and I went to Key West, we stayed aboard the *Williamsburg* and joined Dad in the daytime. This trip to the Key was in the nature of a rest for him after his strenuous campaign. About the only public thing he did there was to dedicate Truman Avenue, a street in Key West named in his honor. There is also a Margaret Street in Key West which crosses Truman Avenue, so I saw my name in street signs!

The beach at Key West was quite a walk and since I am no lover of walking *or* swimming, I went only in the mornings. We made one jaunt in the *Williamsburg* to Fort Jefferson in the Dry Tortugas. The fort was built in 1830 and used until 1869 as a Federal Naval Base. A detachment of American Marines was stationed at Fort Jefferson as late as 1904, but the fort is now deserted and fallen into picturesque ruins.

On the eighteenth of November we set out in the *Williamsburg* to the Republic of Cuba—Mother and I and several members of Dad's staff. We landed at Havana and were met by Ambassador and Mrs. Butler and the Cuban Foreign Minister and his wife. We were driven around town and saw Morro Castle, Hotel Nacional, where the most important battle of the Revolution was fought, and shopped on the

Prado, where the stores are excellent. We had luncheon aboard the *Williamsburg*, took a siesta, and then dressed to pay our official call on Señora Prio at the Presidential Palace. The Palace was all marble and gold and crystal, similar to the palaces in Rio, and we were served champagne, although it was early afternoon. We went on to tea at the American Embassy, which was quite handsomely decorated and landscaped. The garden was gorgeous. On the way back to Key West we ran into the tail of the hurricane which had been threatening for days, and had a rough passage.

We stayed in and around Key West for a couple of weeks and flew back to Washington on the twenty-first of November to be home in time for Thanksgiving, which we spent at Blair House. The following Saturday, we took the train for Philadelphia to see the Army-Navy game. It was a dismal football game, which ended in a 21-to-21 tie. We had to sit on the Navy side that year, but we had our Army banners with us, which made us uniquely unpopular with surrounding seat mates. The midshipmen almost took them away from us when we insisted on flaunting them around.

On November 29 I came to New York to make a few phone calls and stand for a few fittings, with Madame Pola, of my Inauguration clothes and to attend the Opening Night of the Metropolitan Opera. I wore my white satin Dior gown with the pink flowers across the front, a white fox stole, and a pair of long white gloves from Paris. I was the guest of Jane Watson for the week end and we dined at the Watsons' before the opera. I was on television between the second and third acts of *Otello*, which was also televised in its entirety.

The first-night assemblage was quite brilliant, but with the usual antics carried on by people who came to be seen rather than to listen to the music. Such bores! One lady made a great outcry about losing her diamond bracelet. The crush in Sherry's and the Opera Bar between acts was terrific, but I don't think anybody stood on his head opening night that year. Jarmila Novotna was in our box and Tom Watson, Jr., was with us.

&❧ On December 3 Dad and I went to the Father-Daughter Dinner given by the Washington Press Club. Grandmother Wallace was quite ill at the time and Uncle Fred had come on to be with her. I was worried about her, but I couldn't give in to it. One of the problems of public life is that the show must go on, no matter who is sick at home. I don't believe most people think about this.

Dad and I were introduced as the "Traveling Trumans" and performed an act. We played a duet together—*The Jenny Lind Polka*, which Dad had taught me when I was about six. When we sat down to play, I announced that I was a union member, but that I had obtained a special dispensation to play with somebody who was non-union! We played the duet very slowly and deliberately—the way we did when I was six—and it brought down the house.

Drucie and Mr. Snyder also did an act entitled *Fireside Finance*. Drucie was a radio commentator, interviewing the Secretary of the Treasury. They discussed the public debt.

"Why do we have it, anyway?" Drucie asked.

"Because we know that all we owe we owe to our country," Mr. Snyder said.

All the girls were pinned with orchids and we had a fine time.

The next day we all went down to Norfolk and boarded my beloved ship, the *Missouri*, for a presentation ceremony. The state of Missouri had presented the battleship with a massive silver service, bearing the Missouri state seal on one side and the Navy seal on the opposite side of each piece. Drucie and I walked around this magnificent gift, admiring it, and automatically we picked up a silver plate and looked on the bottom to see whether it was sterling! Photographers got some excellent photographs of this rude but feminine gesture. When we boarded the *Missouri*, the twenty-one-gun salute was fired practically on top of us and when we disembarked the same thing happened. My ears ached.

On December 8 we were back in Washington and went to a tea given by the Democratic women where the handshaking went on forever. On the tenth of December Madame Chiang came to tea with Mrs. Marshall. She was very charming but very shrewd. She talked to Dad for a long time, seeking aid for her cause. This indeed was the principal topic of the tea-table talk.

Washington was already preparing for the Inauguration when we left it for Christmas in Independence. A medal with a bas-relief of Dad on one side and a feminine figure symbolizing Liberty, surrounded by forty-eight stars, with thirteen of them representing the original colonies in larger scale, had been struck off by the United States Mint for sale during the ceremonies. C. P. Jennewein, a New

York sculptor, designed this medal, which is quite beautiful. A marvelous silk flag, bearing the President's seal surrounded by stars, was in the making. People were planning floats and stunts for the parade and the air was full of excitement.

Christmas was quiet that year, due partially to the frail health of Grandmother Wallace. It was a family time, though, and I always liked that. I saw Aunt Mary and Uncle Vivian and Aunt Luella and all the Wallace clan. I had some time for brooding, and in my diary for the last day of the year I brooded as follows:

December 31, 1948

This has been quite a year and it has all been Dad's. I haven't accomplished a thing in 1948, but I've learned a great deal. Perhaps I'll be set to go on in 1949. It has been an exciting year. There will never be another quite like it, but then I suppose each year has its own special characteristics. This one will always be unique because it showed the world that we are a free nation, corny as it may sound, the will or the welfare (however this is translated) of the people is the supreme law in this land. (Missouri's motto is "Salus populi suprema lex esto.")

20: Happy days are here again

My father has a happy nature, but I don't remember a time when he was so actively happy as he was the first month of 1949. He had received an unusual vote of confidence.

On January 5, he delivered his State of the Union message to Congress, in which his genuine concern for the people was emphasized. He asked for legislation in the fields of social welfare, social security, education, medical care, economic controls, low-rent housing, and civil rights. He asked for a repeal of the Taft-Hartley Act and a rise in the minimum wage. Mother and I were there to join in the applause. I wrote:

Wednesday, January 5, 1949
This was a wonderful day. Dad made his speech, the State of the Union message to Congress—the 81st Congress—and we hope a better one in every way than the 80th. They were enthusiastic and it looked so wonderful to see those many Democrats and those few Republicans.

Mother and I went to luncheon in the Senate Dining Room afterward with Mrs. Fred Vinson, Mrs. Anderson, Rosemary McMahon, and Mrs. Mesta. We had a grand time greeting old friends who came

251

back in this election, who had been missing for two years, and others I had met on the campaign tour who were elected to the Eighty-first Congress.

The next day, Mother and I went to New York for fittings on our dresses. Mother had a pearl gray satin and silver lamé with a silver thread design in the shape of a feather—a beautiful Ducharne fabric—for the inaugural reception at the National Gallery. It was made on princess lines, floor length, with a little train. The deep V-neck was outlined with cutouts of the feather motif. This dress is now in the Smithsonian. For the ball, she had a black panne velvet trimmed with Alençon lace, and for the Inauguration ceremony, a two-piece gray and black costume in Rajah silk with a straight skirt and a peplum jacket, with which she wore a hat of moonstone straw cloth trimmed with pink roses. She also had a short, dark blue satin brocade with a design in periwinkle blue, trimmed with black Chantilly lace. With this she wore a pretty hat, which was decked with cornflowers and hyacinths.

I had a royal blue faille taffeta in a black and gold plaid design, with a full skirt, tight bodice, high neckline, and leg-o'-mutton sleeves—very quaint. I also had a black afternoon dress with a lace top and the skirt trimmed with bands of bronze taffeta, and—wonderful surprise—a new ball gown. I hadn't planned to have a new one but expected to press into service one of my old concert dresses for the Inauguration Ball. But Madame Pola had it all ready. It was "Margaret Pink" tulle with pink and gold brocade on one shoulder and the bodice. It had four full skirts with manifold yards of tulle and a tulle bow on one shoulder. For the Inauguration ceremony, I had a gabardine suit in fireman red with a hat to match. Mother had a lovely hat for her pearl gray dress made of flat ostrich feathers in mauve, with curled ostrich plumes, shading from gray through mauve to pink.

Dad had striped trousers, a morning coat, and a high silk topper which looked elegant on him. He hates to get dressed up, but he took a lively interest in our fancy new wardrobes.

Washington was also furbishing itself. The Eightieth Congress, acting on the theory that the next President would be the first Republican in sixteen years, had voted quite a large appropriation for the Inauguration. We Democrats inherited it! The streets were decorated and floats for the parade were spectacular.

252

On January 15, I took time out from being the President's daughter to be a career woman and to sign a contract with Mr. James A. Davidson, who managed my musical career for a number of years. Then I had to have the final fittings on my clothes and run out to buy a pair of slippers to go with the ball dress. Madame Bonnet had brought me another dress from Paris—a luscious Christian Dior in mauve pink satin with an off-the-shoulder line and a great wide skirt. This dress was about an inch too small for me, and I didn't have time to lose weight. I had it altered but it almost squeezed the breath out of me. However, I was determined to wear it.

The avalanche of relatives and friends began to arrive, and after that there was no chance to do anything. Missouri sent the largest delegation to the Inauguration in history, more than two thousand people. People poured in from all over the world, and my schedule reached a new high in activity:

Tuesday, January 18, 1949

The Infantile Paralysis Drive opened today. I was the Mistress of Ceremonies for a 15-minute show with Senator Margaret Chase Smith, Miss Betty Smith, the author, Shirley Temple and John Agar. Tonight the Truman-Barkley Club dinner was held at the Mayflower. Georgie Jessel was M.C. The Purdue University Glee Club sang and it was charming, but the smoke was horrible. I wore my orange satin ballerina-length dress with the coat of brown tulle, bronze gloves, bronze shoes and a pouch purse.

Wednesday, January 19, 1949

I managed to catch a little sleep this morning. Shawsie and Coleman Branton came for lunch and went with me on the round of teas. First we went to the Lingo reception at the Colonial Dames Club for just our family and a few friends. Next was the University Tea at George Washington University, where I cut the cake, then on to the Shoreham for the reception honoring Governor and Mrs. Forrest Smith of Missouri. I got back and hurtled through the bathtub and put on my mauve pink satin gown from Paris and set out with Mother and Dad for the Elector's Dinner. Then on to the Gala, which lasted three and a half hours. Entertainment was all by stars: Dorothy Maynor, Tagliavini, and many others. I loved it, but my dress was plain too little for me and practically cut me in two. Oof!

Thursday, January 20, 1949

Today is the big day. Weather is wonderful. Up at 8 and breakfast with everybody at 9. We all left for St. John's Church for a short prayer

253

service at 10. Then back to the house and the Congressional Committee Escort for Dad arrived. We left for the Capitol at 11:25 and that was the last time we were on schedule all day. Mother and I waited in Senator Barkley's office with Mrs. Max Truitt, his daughter and official hostess, until 12 or after, then went out onto the platform. Senator Barkley and Dad were sworn in and Dad made his speech. I found it very moving. The Marine Band played.

From there we went to Les Biffle's office for a quick lunch and I was starved. We then started the parade at 1:50 instead of 1. The Senate had had an argument over precedence on the platform before the swearing-in by Chief Justice Vinson and Justice Reed and delayed the whole day.

We rode in an open car, Mother, Mrs. Truitt and I. I had on my scarlet suit and hat. We got off at the reviewing stand in front of the White House and watched the parade.

The parade was a lot of fun. Drucie and I sat together and we got up and made an elaborate pretense of salaaming and bowing when the George Washington University float went by.

Mother and I had to leave before the end to get dressed for the reception at the National Gallery. I watched the parade from my window while I was dressing. I also watched it on the television set and I knew what was coming around the corner by the Treasury, then I would dash to the window to watch it go by. We arrived at the National Art Gallery at six instead of five. Dad and Vice-president Barkley made two speeches apiece to the thousands we couldn't shake hands with. Then we shook hands with about a thousand VIPs. I got the family off in a corner for some tea and cakes to keep them going.

We all had a late dinner at Blair House and by the end of dinner it was time to start dressing for the ball. I wore the Margaret-pink tulle and brocade job. The ball had about 10,000 people in a space for 5,000, and more fighting to get in. I took a group of my friends back to Blair House about 1:30 and we drank hot chocolate and ate sandwiches until 3:30. I have a slight cold. My feet hurt! But it has been a perfect Inauguration Day, the first one with good weather since 1928 and no untoward incidents. Nobody at all got hurt.

Friday, January 21, 1949
The head of the Truman-Barkley Club of Minnesota came this morning to give me a candid camera. It is very beautiful and I love it. I had a treatment for my cold. I *have* to stay up. This afternoon we went to the Snyder Reception for all of us and we shook hands with about 1200 people. Then we got into our glad rags and went to the Shoreham for a reception for Vice-president Barkley and Mrs. Truitt. I got to bed about 1 o'clock. Early for me!

254

We really did have fun that week. At the Lingos' reception, Dad stayed more than an hour, because he was enjoying himself so much. The guest list was confined to our family and a few close friends, which gave us a chance to relax. When we left the club, Dad was practically mobbed by a crowd of several hundred teen-age girls, mostly from the Holton Arms School nearby, who gave him a rousing cheer. Of course, he *loved* it.

At the reception for Governor and Mrs. Smith of Missouri, Dad, completely unintimidated, introduced Mother as "my boss" and me as "her boss." This was news to me! Inauguration Day for Dad began with a breakfast with all his old buddies from World War I—the members of Battery D of the 129th Field Artillery. Lots of "remember the time" and plenty of jokes.

The streets were full of celebrating sounds, and after the Inauguration ceremony was over the parade set in and lasted for hours. West Point cadets, Annapolis midshipmen, Missouri mules, barelegged girl drum majors. When a band played *I'm Just Wild about Harry*, Dad, standing on the reviewing stand, did a little jig to the music. All seventeen of our relatives were on the reviewing stand and my fourteen-year-old cousin, David Wallace, really lived it up.

The Inaugural Ball was brilliant. It was held at the National Guard Armory and I had my own box, with Jane Lingo, Drucie, Mary Ogden, Marvin Braverman, and Marvin Coles. All the White House aides were my beaus for the dance. Xavier Cugat, Benny Goodman, and Guy Lombardo played, and you can scarcely beat that. The floor was jammed with people—mostly celebrated—in beautiful clothes, diamonds, pearls, and furs. In fact, it was so jammed you couldn't move a foot. I never saw such mass dancing. The aides were got up in full-dress splendor and were blazing in gold braid, gold lace, epaulets, and decorations. It was like being in a musical comedy, and of course there was a glittering array of entertainers to provide professional amusement.

Everybody looked wonderful, and I have rarely seen so many magnificent gowns, so many diamonds and jewels, so many healthy, happy-looking people. But the happiest of all was my father, in impeccable white tie (that man has a real flair for wearing clothes and I love to see him dressed up), whose face was shining like a new moon, for this had been his day of days. It's wonderful to be happy and know it.

255

As soon as Inauguration was over, we all went back to work. Relatives and friends folded their tents and departed. Dad went back to the office and between the massive requirements of getting on with his program, he signed 10,000 answers to letters of congratulation. Did you ever try signing 10,000 letters? Mother began to try to figure out how to carry on the stringent demands of protocol entertaining in the limited space of Blair House. On January 30 we received the last word about the unfortunate condition of the White House. The ceiling had sagged six inches in the East Room, where those enormous chandeliers had twinkled above so many important heads. It's a thousand wonders one of them hadn't crashed down on a diplomatic reception with death in its wake and no accounting for how many international incidents! At any rate, the entire inside of the building had to be removed, to the bare shell of the outer walls, and completely rebuilt. It was scheduled to take a year at the minimum.

I began to pack once more and to think about my neglected career. On the last day of January, I left for New York. Reathel Odum, Mother's personal secretary, went with me as friend and companion. Reathel is a small, pretty girl, with clear-cut features, soft dark hair and eyes, and a sweet, engaging smile. She had been my father's secretary before she was my mother's and used to baby-sit with me when I was a little girl in Washington and she was a very young government girl. We moved into my apartment, where we lived like any two girls, marketing, cooking our own dinners, taking care of our clothes, and running around to plays, concerts, and parties.

I went back to my music. I worked with a professional opera singer that year, who had offered to coach me on the fine points of a singing career. I studied and practiced very hard—almost too hard. I had a regular schedule for work and practice, and along with the various duties that continued to come as a result of my father's position, I often felt exhausted and beat.

On February 17 I celebrated my twenty-fifth birthday. Mother came up for the event. Louise Stewart was sailing for Europe on the SS *America* that day and there was a birthday luncheon for me aboard with Commodore John W. Anderson, the captain, as host. The ship's confectioner, William Soiter, had made me a fine birthday cake. We had a quiet little celebration afterward in my apartment, which was overflowing with flowers, telegrams, and gifts, and Mother took Reathel and me to see *Where's Charley?* with that irresistible Ray Bolger. What a dancer!

About this time, the Artists' League of America was making up a composite beauty, and I got in the list of glamorous ladies, which included Rita Hayworth, Madame Chiang, Linda Darnell, Jane Russell, and I don't know how many more—by an ear! The Artists' League announced that they had chosen my ears because they were exact replicas of those found on Greek sculpture! The only time I ever thought of my ears was when they were registering a twenty-one-gun salute.

I was also elected Woman of the Year by the Hasty Pudding Club of Harvard University. They congratulated me for sticking to my music through thick and thin and asked me to help them start off their second hundred years by singing a song in their annual show. They said I could sing anything I liked except a Yale song. Unfortunately, I had to decline this engagement.

I went to Washington on March 4, as I had been invited to christen a new airliner for Pan-American Airways. When I unpacked, I discovered that the hat I had planned to wear wasn't in the luggage and was therefore in my apartment in New York. This was always happening to me while I led a double life, between Washington and New York. Sometimes I felt like a schizophrenic!

Mother and I had to rush out and buy me a spring hat, which I loathe—not just the spring hat I bought, but all spring hats. I am sure the millinery industry will take exception to this ungracious remark. I was once photographed going into a church with a handkerchief over my head and they sent me anguished and piteous telegrams, declaring that I was ruining their business. It was one of my great responsibilities not to ruin anybody's business, but do I *have* to like spring hats? They won't stay on my head and I'm always dragging them off and sitting on them by mistake. Between not liking this hat and worrying about whether the bottle would break tomorrow, I was in a fret. The fact was I was so tired I couldn't navigate and didn't have enough sense to lie down.

Drucie, Jane, and I went to the Washington Airport the next afternoon. The ceremonies were held from a platform built in a huge hangar and there were many, many speeches. Vice-president Barkley made a funny one, which was nice. After the oratory, Mr. Juan

Trippe and Captain Flower of Pan-American and I went up on a smaller, higher platform and I struck the bottle against a small plate near the nose of the plane. It broke, but good! It went all over the plane and also all over me, including my flowery hat. I christened the plane the *America* and asked God to bless her.

I went back to New York to the grind of work and practice. I had more professional photographs made for my projected tour. Dad left for Florida on the *Independence* and I wanted to go along, but there was my music—demanding, demanding. Drucie came up for a short visit and told me she was in love. I was thrilled for her. We went out on the town and saw *The ANTA Album*. Drucie went home. One of Drucie's beaus took me to the Plaza and confessed that he was in love with her. It was very embarrassing, as he wasn't the one *she* was in love with.

I was feeling increasingly weary and on March 13 I came down with a heavy cold and had to go to bed. Even with pampering, the cold didn't seem to mend, so ten days later I went to Washington to consult Dr. Graham. While I was there, Mr. and Mrs. Winston Churchill were visiting Washington, and Mother and Dad gave an official dinner for them. I reported it in my diary as follows:

Thursday, March 24, 1949
Mr. and Mrs. Churchill are coming to dinner and there are hundreds of people standing outside waiting for him. Some have been there since I came in about 5:30. Later: We had a very nice dinner. I sat between Secretary Acheson and Captain Christopher Soames, the Churchills' son-in-law (Mary's husband). The ladies had coffee in the drawing room afterwards. We had dinner in the dining room of Lee House. All went well except the stuffed cucumbers with the fish course were awful and Mother had told them to be careful and consult Vietta but they didn't. They were absolutely like stone. The party broke up about 10:30. I hope everybody didn't have to go home and take bicarbonate of soda!

Mr. Churchill had brought a beautifully bound copy of his little book on painting to my mother. She asked him to inscribe it. I found the pen and ink for him and he sat down with the book. About 15 minutes later he was still writing and I simply couldn't wait to see what the inscription would turn out to be. When he finally gave it back to me and asked me to please take it over to my mother I managed to get to Mother without reading it but when she opened it and I looked at it all it said was "For Mrs. Harry S. Truman from Winston S. Churchill" and the date.

I went back to New York and started getting together some spring clothes. I ordered a light print and a white fitted coat, and a dark blue Princess dress with a brilliant red Rodier woolen coat.

April began auspiciously.

Monday, April 4, 1949
The signing of the Atlantic Pact.

Tuesday, April 5, 1949
Worked this morning as usual but half an hour early so that I could go to lunch in the Sert Room at the Waldorf with Mrs. Dean Acheson and Mrs. Warren Austin. We then drove to Flushing Meadows and the opening of the UN General Assembly. With Secretary Acheson and Ambassador Senator Austin. The opening was most impressive. I saw dozens of friends from all over the world. I dashed back to tea at the Thomas Murrays'. So many of them, 8 or 9 children, all but one grown and so nice and so much fun. Then a quick change of clothes and back to the Waldorf to a reception for the Heads of the Delegations given by the Austins. Phew. Funny little sidelight. As I pulled away from the Murrays' I was peeking out of my car window to see who was getting into the car pulling away from the Russian Embassy and saw Gromyko peering out of his car window to see who was in my car. Very funny . . . to me anyway.

Tuesday, April 12, 1949
Tonight there was a total eclipse of the moon at 10:28. Four years ago (is it possible?) today, Dad took the oath of office as President in the Cabinet Room at 7:08 in the evening. I'll never forget when he phoned Mother she cried and I felt as though someone had slapped me hard. Nothing has been the same since but it has been an interesting experience thus far and what a school for the study of human nature!

I went home for Easter and went to church, first to the Episcopal Church with Mother, next to the Baptist Church with Dad. I seem to do everything at least twice. I also went to the opening ball game and came back to New York.

The cold I had contracted in March was still with me and I often felt it was going to be permanent. The last of April it got worse and I finally got on the train and went home, arriving with a high fever. Dr. Graham diagnosed it as bronchial pneumonia and ordered me to bed. At the time it suited me fine, as I didn't feel like standing up. After a few days' rest, I got up and looked at myself and was tired of the way I looked. I cut my hair off until it was almost a shingle, and I'm sure Dad could have murdered me. He always takes an interest in my hair-do. I dragged out to a dinner Mrs. Mesta was giving for Mother and Dad and came home and went to bed again, feeling worse and worse. Dr. Graham came and painted my throat with gentian violet—ugh. I had a laryngeal spasm, which seemed to cut off my breathing. I thought I was going to die, but I lived.

I went to Washington around the middle of May, as President Dutra of Brazil was making an official visit and I wanted to see him again. We were entertaining at intimate dinners in the crowded quarters of Blair House, but gave the large dinners at Carlton Hotel. Once at Blair House such a torrential rainstorm fell during a small dinner that the Marine Band had to be ordered to play louder and louder, to shut out the sound of water, dripping through the eaves. It wasn't much like the marble palaces of Rio and I often wondered what President Dutra thought of our rather primitive official setting. Whatever he thought, he was always kind and complimentary.

President Dutra called on us at Blair House and we gave him a large dinner at the Carlton Hotel. There was a huge horseshoe table, banked with iris and white flowers, which looked quite chaste and beautiful. There's no use trying to impress Brazilians with *exotic* flowers. Orchids grow on trees there.

The next day, Secretary and Mrs. Acheson gave a dinner for the Dutras at the Larz Anderson House, which is available to the Secretary of State for diplomatic entertaining. The following day the Brazilian Ambassador gave a magnificent dinner for the honored guests at the Brazilian Embassy. The reception was held under a striped tent and the rooms were all decorated with red roses and hundreds of candles. My dinner partner was Senhor Nabuco, the Brazilian Ambassador. He kindly spirited Mother out of the receiving line early. Only an Ambassador would think of such a courtesy.

If Mother's job had always been a heavy burden, it was profoundly increased by our move to Blair House. Although we all loved Blair House and I personally preferred to live there, because it seemed more like a home, it was too small and poorly equipped to carry the load of entertaining required of the President's family. When we had official small dinners, we usually had cocktails in Blair House, adjourned to Lee House for dinner, and while we were dining, the ushers and other help would strip Blair House of carpets, move all the furniture and polish the floor for dancing, before we got up from the table. The next morning before sunup, they would have to charge in and put Blair House back together.

Diplomatic guests were often quartered in Lee House, while we occupied Blair House. Since the houses were side by side, we sometimes heard restless diplomats pacing up and down in the Lee House garden in the middle of the night. It would have been interesting to know what vast international problems kept them from slumber. Molotov was a guest at Lee House. I'll never forget it, largely because of one of his food preferences. For breakfast he required cold tea and salad!

I stayed in New York several more weeks, practicing hours every day. Frank Handy was in and out and we went to lunch or dancing. I was still denying rumors that I was engaged to him, but the newest one was that I was engaged to Blevins Davis of Independence, which was just as erroneous as all the others.

Reporters had also got into a twit when I went to see the Philadelphia Symphony Orchestra off in May on the SS *Parthia* for their month's tour of England and Scotland. It was true that Eugene Ormandy, the conductor, was also sailing, and it was true that Eugene, who had conducted for me at the Hollywood Bowl, was a great friend of mine. In fact, I actually went to see Eugene off, but he was just a friend. I had learned to brush off romantic rumors, but they nagged poor Eugene about it.

The engagement of my friend Jane Watson to Jack Irwin had been announced and she had asked me to be one of eight bridesmaids. I gave a small dinner and dancing party at Blair House for Jane and Jack in May. It was at this party that Tom Watson was holding forth about the terrible habits of souvenir-takers. Tom said making off with souvenirs was just the same as stealing. We had quite an argument about this, and before dinner was over we managed to slip a silver teaspoon with the White House crest on it into Tom's pocket. He was really beside himself when he found it some time later.

The wedding took place on June 2 at the Brick Presbyterian Church in New York. The bridesmaids' dresses were pale blue organdy, embroidered with big white polka dots, and we had flower wreaths to wear on our heads and bouquets of white carnation and stock. Mother came up for the wedding, and when she was going into the church she ran into Lawrence Tibbett, who sang the wedding music.

261

Lawrence hailed her and stopped to chat. "I just saw Margaret," he said. "She's in the wings!"

Mother was shocked to have the sacred halls of a church referred to as "wings," but she had about got accustomed now to the theatrical lingo of my friends.

There was a large reception at the Pierre Hotel, and I made the horrendous mistake of leaving the precincts before Jane had tossed her bridal bouquet. The connotations never occurred to me. I was taking Mother to see *South Pacific*—my eighth time, but she hadn't seen it—and it got so late I had to run. However, the papers made a big point of my ducking out before the tossing ceremony. Jane said she had planned to throw it right at me, as the rest of her attendants were married. There was considerable editorial speculation about my avoiding even the symbols of approaching matrimony. You can't win!

I spent the Fourth of July week end in Washington. We left on July 2 for a cruise on the *Williamsburg*, and I append the log:

Saturday, July 2, 1949
Got up for breakfast and to run errands for Dad. Jane and Drucie came by and we went to the *Williamsburg* for the week-end cruise. We immediately got into shorts and out into the sun. Secretary Snyder took off for Paris at noon and flew over the ship and dipped his wings to us and we waved scarves and shirts. We took a sunbath. Then went to Blackiston Island and went swimming. Then we went down to the mouth of St. Mary's River.

Sunday, July 3, 1949
We had breakfast with Dad and Admiral Dennison. We left Patuxent and headed into Chesapeake Bay. We passed a three-masted schooner this morning. So pretty. We had lunch and took a sunbath. This afternoon we had a huge and very funny reception for the men who boarded the *Williamsburg*. Clark Clifford, Oscar Ewing, Mon Wallgren, George Allen, Stu Symington and Clint Anderson. We put silly signs on their doors. We had a Hawaiian band (mess boys), and a red carpet, some old piece left over from somewhere. We gave ruffles and flourishes on drum and bugles. Showered them with confetti and had the ship decked in signal flags, an official welcome. Pinned a sign on George Allen saying "sucker." We all laughed ourselves silly.

On July 6 I was back in New York at my practice. Mother was in

Independence that month and I would go down to spend the week ends with Dad in Washington. One week end we went to Sandy Springs, Maryland, to dine with the Achesons, and to see some of the beautiful handmade furniture that Mr. Acheson makes as a hobby. The President rarely goes out to dine, but Dad loved to eat dinner with his intimate friends in their own homes, and I think he did this more than most other Presidents. It came natural to him to visit.

The French Line gave a dinner aboard the *Ile de France* on her maiden voyage and Jane Lingo called me up about some extra men. Everybody seemed to look on me as a magician in this respect. I couldn't *command* men, but I did fix it up and we had fun. See diary:

July 29, 1949

Jane got in this afternoon. George Williams and Bill Zimmerman came up from Washington and came by for us. The French Ambassador and Helle Bonnet picked up the whole party and we had a police escort to the *Ile de France*. There was a magnificent dinner on board, but the air conditioning broke down and we nearly smothered. We took a tour of the ship and it is beautiful. We danced on the deck after dinner. There was a floor show and the ship was lighted up from stem to stern. It was a lovely evening.

Mrs. Mesta invited me to be her guest at her house in Newport, Rhode Island, that summer and for the first time I saw beautiful old Newport, rising in shadowy grandeur above the rocky shore. New York had been so hot and dirty. Newport was so cool and clean. I am prepared to admit that I lead a pretty pampered life all the time, but it was nothing compared to Newport. I had a lovely room, done in apple green and pale beige, looking right out over the Atlantic Ocean. Charlotte and Bull Reese were there and Mr. Tyson and Bull took me to a little street carnival in town and we rode the Ferris wheel. Let's look at the record:

Saturday, July 30, 1949

Went wading in the ocean and got some sun. We went to lunch at Mr. Frederick Prince's home—Marble House. It is huge and magnificent and all marble inside. Looks like a palace in Rio. He is an old dear. Also saw the Vanderbilt estate, The Breakers, which is so ornate you don't believe it when you see it. We had tea with the Bruguieres and they

263

have an all-blue-flowers garden. It is exquisite. Perle had a small and beautiful dinner at Mid-Cliffe and then we all went dancing at Bailey's Beach Club. It is so cool tonight I need a blanket.

Sunday, July 31, 1949

Had my breakfast in bed *again* and we saw Betty's home—Beachmound. Betty is ill in Westport and couldn't come up. We had lunch at the Clambake Club. After lunch we called on the Stuart Duncans who have an English manor house. I have seen so many homes I am house-happy. We drove back to Providence and I caught a 10 o'clock train back to New York. I had a chance to study some music on the way down. Mother got into Washington this morning.

Mother came up to New York shortly afterward to see Mrs. Mesta off as envoy to Luxembourg. On August 16 the United States Lines gave a luncheon for Mrs. Mesta aboard the *America*. It was one of the nicest large luncheons I ever attended. (There were about eighty people.) We stayed aboard until they blew "All ashore that's going ashore," and then stood on the pier to watch her sail down the river. I made up my mind that the next time I went aboard that vessel I was going to sail with her!

The next day Mother and I pulled out for Independence. Home, as ever, looked good, and Vietta tried to outdo herself. Never saw such food. She seemed to be trying to build me up. Oh, happy summertime in sweet, somnolent Independence, home of the automobile ride, the chocolate ice-cream soda, the Canasta game on the back porch, the aunts, uncles, and cousins. It nearly killed me to take that midnight rattler back to New York on August 29, but duty called me. I was about to raise my voice again.

21: Purple Pin

When my concert entourage went out on the road, we were referred to as "The Purple Pins." This was because my manager, Jim Davidson, kept track of his artists by sticking those little colored pins in a map of the United States. Our pins were purple.

On my way back to New York from Independence that August of 1949, I thought quite a lot about my music. I was thinking about it when Reathel Odum got on in Salem, Illinois, to join me, and I was still thinking about it the next morning when Dad met me in Washington and handed me a bandbox full of my winter hats. (I didn't get off the train in Washington but Dad toted my hats down to me.) In the two years that had elapsed since I had been out on the road, I had worked very hard on my voice. I had a new manager, a new coach, and a new accompanist. I wondered if I was the same old me. I hoped that I had improved with the effort I had applied, and profited by all the professional advice I had received, but you never can tell until you get up there on the stage. I think now that one can work too hard and take too much advice. A certain amount of counsel is fine, but you have to be yourself, in the last analysis. Too much can confuse you and rob you of confidence.

As soon as I got back to New York, I began to work with Herman Allison, who is still my accompanist. I went to Madame Pola's for fittings. I had more professional photographs made. I went over plans for a radio show to take place on December 20 with Dr. Frank Black and Robert Shaw; ran scales, practiced; sang all the songs I had chosen for the program over and over. I did nothing but work. Near the end of September I gave my whole program for Jim Davidson at Town Hall, to see how it rounded out. Jim seemed satisfied.

The tour began on October 2, and I sang all over the map. The night before the first concert, I found myself very calm. That *really* worried me! I wore a white brocade dress and it seemed to me that the program went very well. During that tour I sang at Atlanta, Georgia, to an enormous house, 5,500 people, a good audience. It was very hot there and I can recall standing on the stage with the perspiration running down my back. It tickled and I remember thinking that I couldn't laugh. I sang at Rocky Mount, North Carolina, and at Raleigh, North Carolina, and Lucy and Jonathan Daniels asked me to their home for Sunday dinner. I can't tell you how wonderful it was to have a home-cooked meal. We talked and talked. Jonathan was then in the middle of his biography of my father.

A critic from one of the St. Louis newspapers flew out and cased one of my concerts, just like a football scout, because I was due to sing in St. Louis. I sang there with Vladimir Golschmann conducting the orchestra. I wrote in my diary:

> *October 29, 1949*
> Tonight finally came and went. It went off very well and Golschmann was most complimentary. Vice-president Barkley was there. He brought Mrs. Hadley with him and they look awfully close to being engaged to me!

I suppose it was human nature to gossip about somebody else's engagement when so many had gossiped about mine. But in this case, my instinct turned out to be correct.

I sang in Columbus, Ohio, and there was a big fire in town with screaming sirens and all the other noise. Just before I left for the concert, my hotel caught fire! But by that time nothing fazed me.

I sang in Battle Creek, Michigan. Frank Handy came over and took me to lunch and this reopened all the speculation about him as my future husband. Poor Frank, he couldn't tip his hat to me without having the papers insist we were bound for the altar. It's amazing our friendship survived.

Well, I wasn't engaged, but Drucie was. She called me and told me that she and Johnny Horton had made up their minds. John was Major John Ernest Horton, one of the White House aides. (Drucie's real name is Edith Cook Snyder, and when the engagement was announced some people didn't know who *Edith* was!) I wished Dru a world of happiness and climbed on the train and shuffled off to Buffalo, where I was due to warble on the morrow.

This tour wound up late in November. On the whole the critics had been kind. I felt that the criticism was fair, even good. I still had my Washington concert at Constitution Hall and some radio dates. I didn't get home for Thanksgiving—I was still touring—but I arrived on November 26. The next day I sang at Constitution Hall.

I determined to have a quiet day. I ran some scales in the morning and had my steak and potato at one o'clock. I put on my make-up at 2:30 and ran scales for another hour and set out for the Hall at 3:45. I went on at 4:20 in the afternoon. The house was completely sold out and it was a grand audience. I sang three encores. After the concert the Washington newspaperwomen, sometimes called the "news hens," gave a reception for me at the Raleigh Hotel. I had a wonderful time and felt that I was back at home after years of being away.

The Purple Pins disbanded for a space then and I went to Key West with the family where I stayed until December 7. I spent a few days in Washington and then took the train to New York to get ready for my radio engagement with Dr. Frank Black on December 20. On Sunday, December 18, Reathel and I went to St. James to church and then had lunch. That afternoon I began to feel terrible. It must have been something I ate, but I, Dr. Truman, diagnosed it as nerves.

Oh, brother! At 5 A.M. on December 19 I waked up with ptomaine poisoning of a virulent nature. I finally crawled out of bed at 10:30 A.M. but I could hardly stand up, I felt so awful. I ran what passed for some scales and set out weakly for Carnegie Hall and the rehearsal with Dr. Black and the Robert Shaw Male Chorus. Everyone couldn't have been more considerate, but why is it that every time I have a big engagement, I come down with something or

267

somebody gets sick or somebody dies or some terrible crisis hangs over me? I've never been able to figure it out.

Jim Davidson bought me a plate of soup at the New York Athletic Club and then I went back to Carnegie Hall for a press conference and the photographers. This was very wearing, and as soon as I could I dragged home to the apartment and went to bed. I saw that I was probably going to live, but I certainly felt like death warmed over.

The day of the broadcast, December 20, I stayed in bed as long as I could. A hairdresser came in (Miss Jule) to try to repair the ravages of illness on my coiffure. At 3:30 P.M. I went to Carnegie Hall for a dress rehearsal, which was important because it was recorded. Then home to bed. I finally got up and put on my gold brocade dress, and Jim Davidson came for me at 7:30. The broadcast was said to have gone well, but I felt disappointed in my part of it. I thought I could have been much better and might have been if I hadn't been playing ptomaine as a dual engagement. After that I *had* to go to a supper party that Jim gave for me at the Mirilton. I talked to Mother and Dad, trying to sound bright and gay. Then I packed. When I shuffle off this mortal coil, I'll bet I have to pack first!

Dad and I went to Independence on December 23. Mother had gone ahead of us. All I wanted to do was lie down and not pack and not practice and not talk. And maybe not even think. Everybody let me do it. Blevins Davis gave a dinner party for us, but I eschewed social life as far as possible and sat around with Grandmother. I eschewed public life too, and all I did in that respect was to unveil an equestrian statue of Andrew Jackson on the lawn of the Courthouse of Jackson County. I didn't even sing my customary solo at Trinity.

On New Year's Eve I took the train for Washington. The train seems a melancholy place to spend New Year's Eve, but I welcomed it. It's so quiet in a Pullman. Anyhow, as a veteran Purple Pin, I felt absolutely at home there. I had packed my Christmas presents in a cardboard box (the thought of packing one more thing numbed me), which looked so messy that as I was leaving the house, my maternal parent yanked me back in and packed them in a suitcase. I disposed this suitcase and several others around my compartment and went to bed and did not know when 1950 arrived.

268

My next concert was scheduled for Syracuse, New York, on January 9. I unpacked so I could repack! When I got to Syracuse, it was buried under a blizzard. The snow continued to fall out of the sky like feathers, and many people who had bought seats couldn't get to the hall. As a result, I sang better than usual!

Drucie had invited me to be her maid of honor, and as her wedding was a prominent Washington social event, parties were flying thick and fast. I went to Washington to give a dinner for her and John at Blair House. The members of the wedding party were invited to dinner and a large group came in later for dancing. Drucie was my dearest friend and it stands to reason that I might have felt a little wistful to see her join the growing ranks of my wedded girl friends, but I didn't. I had discovered that when my friends married, I had two friends instead of one. I never experienced the yearning at weddings that I understand is *de rigueur* for single girls. In fact, I think many other people have been more anxious to see me married than I have been to *be* married.

At the wedding rehearsal, we had a big practice session for the ceremony of the train. Drucie was to wear a white dress, buttoned down the front, with a standing collar and long sleeves and a long train, made of magnificent heavy white silk her father had brought her from the Orient. We took a white sheet to the rehearsal and I practiced arranging it at the strategic moments in the service. When I had got it letter-perfect, as I supposed, we adjourned to the Wardman Park Hotel for the bridal dinner.

Drucie was married on January 26, a beautiful mild day in mid-winter, in the National Cathedral. She was a popular girl and her father and mother were equally popular. The Cathedral was packed. I don't know whether you are familiar with the National Cathedral in Washington, but it is a huge building and it seemed a mile from the door to the altar, over the circuitous route the bridal procession took. In fact, I'm convinced that it *was* a mile. Only Craig Stephens, the best man, and I went all the way to the altar with Drucie and John. I had a sea-green chiffon dress over turquoise taffeta with a hat and slippers to match, and between trying not to trip over the hem of my bouffant gown, carrying my bouquet, hanging on to the ring Drucie was to give John, and worrying about the train, I thought that walk would never end. After the ceremony, when Dru turned around and I had to rearrange the train, I found

269

it quite different from a sheet! It was so long and heavy that I practically had to heave it up with both hands and hurl it to get it out of her way as she started back down the aisle. She was so entranced I was afraid she would trip herself.

The wedding reception was held at the Chevy Chase Club and was the biggest wedding reception I ever saw. The bridal attendants stayed upstairs as much as possible, but in spite of that we shook hands with 2,500 people. When the happy couple finally set off on their honeymoon, I went home. After my prolonged walk and standing to shake hands, I was in the mood to put my feet up. About ten o'clock the telephone rang.

"Hi," said Drucie.

"Where in the world are *you?*" I demanded.

"We're at the Shoreham," Drucie said.

"What are you doing *there?*" I asked her.

"Playing Canasta!" said Drucie, and began to giggle.

Nothing changes Drucie.

ᘛ On February 1 I signed an RCA Victor contract to appear exclusively with National Broadcasting Company. Jim Davidson took me to the RCA Victor offices for lunch with the president, Mr. Folsom, and Mr. Chotzinoff and several others. We ate fifty-two floors up in a beautiful dining room that had a disappearing television set. It was behind an oil painting, which slid aside to disclose the screen. There was the usual press and photography at lunch and they took what seemed a million pictures of me signing the contract and autographing the big "His Master's Voice" Victor dog.

Shortly thereafter I became a Purple Pin again. I resumed my concert tour, and on my birthday I was far from home. I was singing in Miami on February 17 with the Miami Symphony Orchestra, staying in the guest house of the University of Miami. Somebody realized it was my birthday and gave me a delightful tea. Dad sent me an enormous icebox cake by air mail. It was packed in dry ice and arrived with every rosebud in perfect condition.

The Purple Pins crept across the map. In Beaumont, Texas, I was standing on the stage giving it my all and just as I hit a high note, all the lights in the auditorium went out! This was pretty disconcerting, but it was finally established that I hadn't short-circuited the system with my voice—just a power failure.

In Corpus Christi, Texas, I discovered the world's best hamburgers—at Wimpy's. I always hunt up a hamburger and a chocolate malted milk after a concert, and I became quite a connoisseur of American hamburgers. Nobody has ever equaled Wimpy's.

In Austin, Texas, a huge, ugly bug landed on the platform at my feet just as I was about to open my mouth and sing. (I hear it was a praying mantis.) I couldn't sing until Herman Allison, my accompanist, came and took it away. The audience was convulsed and so was I. (Herman was less convulsed!) But in Austin I had my biggest and nicest audience of any tour—6,500 people full of enthusiasm, consideration, and the milk of human kindness.

In San Antonio I met one of the favorite conductors of my career, Max Reiter, of the San Antonio Symphony Orchestra. He conducted when I sang at Waco, Texas, and became a good friend of mine. In fact, I loved Texas. It was very kind to me.

ᘔ᠍ This portion of my tour wound up around the first of April and I went to Key West to join the family. It was on this occasion that Drew Pearson published an item in his column to the effect that my father was wroth with the late hours I was keeping and had a summons ordering me home broadcast over a loudspeaker, during a dance I was attending with a young lieutenant j.g. This was a ridiculous and false story. My father was involved in a poker game at the time and was far more interested in the pot than in where I was. In fact, he didn't even know I was still out. Nobody broadcast anything over a loudspeaker and when my escort, Dennis Moore, and I came in about 1:30 A.M. Admiral Dennison was pacing the floor in high dudgeon and laced into the young man about staying out so late. When he had finished berating him he turned both barrels on me.

"Now see here, Admiral Dennison," I said. "You can't talk to me like that." Of course I would never have spoken to Admiral Dennison in such a smarty-pants way if we hadn't been such devoted friends. He was like a member of the family—an uncle—so he felt free to boss me and I felt free to talk back. It was all in the spirit of good clean fun.

271

He said I was keeping his personnel out too late.

"But I'm not in the Navy, so don't yell at me!"

"I want to see you both at early church services in the morning," he barked. "Do you understand?"

"Okay! Okay!" I said, bristling.

The next morning I got up at 5:30 A.M. and was in my seat for the Sunrise Easter Services before the sun rose. About thirty minutes after the services started, I saw Admiral Dennison sneak in and rather sheepishly get to his seat.

I never let him forget it.

We left Key West on Monday, April 10, the day after Easter, and I cite this as an example of what could transpire in twenty-four hours while I was the President's daughter. We were airborne at Key West at 10:04 A.M. and landed in Washington at 1:55 and had lunch. Mother and I caught the Congressional to New York to attend a dinner Louise Stewart was giving in honor of Mrs. Mesta at the Pavillon. After dinner, with four escorts (count 'em) I adjourned to the Stork Club and danced until 2:30 A.M. The next morning I was back in Washington. Señor Gabriel Gonzalez Videla, the President of Chile, and Señora Videla and their daughter Sylvia were due for a visit!

The Videlas arrived on April 12, at 3 P.M. on the nose, thanks to Colonel Francis "Frenchy" Williams of the *Independence*, who landed them exactly on time. There was a big reception at the airport, with the inevitable twenty-one-gun salute and many speeches.

The President and his family were so nice. I have found most Latin Americans attractive, but President Videla was a consummate charmer and his wife and daughter were equally endearing. They came to Blair House for a family gathering where the President enchanted the President and I sang. President Videla spoke little English, but this seemed to have no effect on the flow of his witty conversation, and we all managed to understand him somehow, and he understood us.

We entertained for them at the Carlton Hotel with a large dinner. The rooms were massed with pink hydrangeas and there was a big horseshoe table with a fountain in the center that flowed red wine. The table was decked out in pink roses, bluebells, and baby's-breath. The next evening Secretary and Mrs. Acheson entertained with a beautiful dinner at the Larz Anderson House for the Videlas.

272

Mr. Jessup, our roving Ambassador, was my dinner partner—a fascinating man. After the dinner there was a brilliant reception and ball at the Brazilian Embassy. I danced the samba with President Videla and he was the most marvelous dancer. He adored to dance and said American ladies were excellent partners. In fact, he loved dancing so much that he did not wish the ball to be over. The Brazilian Ambassador had decreed that the music would stop at 2:00 A.M., but the President refused to stop and it went on until 3:30. He then left the building, since he was the ranking personage and nobody could go home until he did. But he came back and it was rumored that dancing continued until 6:00 A.M.

I had left before then. That night I was wearing a dress of black lace, posed over white silk and trimmed with velvet bows. It was the first dress I had ever had which had absolutely no top. This made me feel very soigné until I looked down after a fast rumba and observed that my strapless bodice was slipping. I was horror-struck. I beckoned one of the aides and told him to stand in front of me with his back to me, while I located a brooch I was wearing and anchored my topless wonder. I managed to secure it somewhat, but my poise slipped slightly with the neckline and I couldn't help feeling nervous in the speed and intricacy of the samba!

The Videlas stayed in Washington only seventy-two hours but exhibited such amiability, vitality, and good will that there has scarcely been a more exciting official visit. When President Videla got to New York and satisfied all his official obligations, he entertained at a private party at the Plaza, to which he invited me. He asked only personal friends and danced to his heart's content, and we all had a wonderful time. That night I was dancing with Mr. Stanley Woodward when Mr. C. Ulric Bay, our Ambassador to Norway, danced by with his wife.

"Psst," he said to Mr. Woodward. "I'm AWOL from Norway—unofficial visit. Don't tell the Boss you saw me!" Then he danced gaily off.

I knew that he was referring to my father and I just grinned. In a minute he danced past again and noticed me, did a double-take, and clapped his hand to his brow.

"My God," he said. "I didn't see *you!*"

"I won't tell if you won't," I told him.

I was working and practicing and selecting songs for the fall season's tour, but the first week in May I went to Washington, since we were scheduled for another tour. Dad had decided to clear up some misconceptions about foreign policy by talking to folks. Before we left, the Prime Minister of Pakistan, Liakat Ali Khan, and the Begum visited us and they gave me a beautiful gold-threaded sari, which I had made into a concert dress, and a magnificent necklace of gold, enamel, and pearls with dangling earrings to match. I have worn these on many occasions and they make an effective set for a concert appearance. I am very proud of them.

Mother, Dad, and I and the usual staff left by train on May 7 for the Grand Coulee Dam, with several stops in between. In fact, I never saw so much water over so many dams in such a short space of time. We went to three dams in about a week where we spudded them in or dedicated them. Dad had his sixty-sixth birthday aboard this train, and eighteen cakes were given him en route.

When we got back, we were all sick except Dad. Mother, Grandmother Wallace, and I were all in bed simultaneously and Doctor Graham galloped from room to room as if it were a hospital. I recovered first and had to take over some of Mother's hostess duties. Mother had planned a luncheon honoring Mrs. Mesta, aboard the *Williamsburg*, and I was sent out to pinch-hit.

It was at this luncheon that Madame Morgenstierne, the wife of the Ambassador from Norway, complimented the meat course.

"What is this delicious dish?" she asked.

I said it was chicken.

"But nonsense, my dear," she said. "It is the most divine *veal* I ever tasted."

I said to myself, you don't argue with the Ambassador's wife.

That night Mother was asking me how it went and I told her that Madame Morgenstierne had complimented the veal.

"Veal!" cried Mother. "I ordered *chicken!* Don't tell me you had *veal.*"

"I thought I recognized chicken when I tasted it," I said.

Finally we all recovered, and over the long Decoration Day week end we scattered in all directions. Grandmother Wallace flew to Independence. Mother went on the train. Dad took the *Williamsburg* up the river and I went to New York on the noon balloon. Sylvia and Leonard Lyons were giving a big party for Mrs. Mesta. Ed Sullivan had invited me to lunch at Sardi's on June 12, and there I found I was to appear on his *Toast of the Town* in the fall, my first national TV appearance.

On the nineteenth of June I went to Independence. It was such a relief to be able to do my laundry in a Bendix and drive my own car! I caught up with my old friends, and Shawsie and I listened to music on the wonderful new record player her uncle, Alonzo Gentry, had designed and built. Trouble was brewing on the other side of the world, but in common with most people I had no inkling that it was so serious.

On June 24, Dad flew home. He got in at 2:00 P.M., looking grave. Although he did not discuss it with me, I gathered that there was something in the wind about Korea. He was waiting for a call from Secretary Acheson, but he was usually waiting for a call from somebody, and that day Chris and Freddy and the children arrived from Colorado Springs with the usual pandemonium, so I didn't think much about it.

My diary for the next few days had this to say:

Sunday, June 25, 1950
The call came from Secretary Acheson about 12:45. I had just gotten back from church with Mother. Dad took it and a few minutes later he went to pack and told me to call Kansas City and get Eben Ayers to call all the people who came out with him to say that he would arrive at the airport between 2:00 and 2:15. Which he did. He took off with Colonel Williams in a cloud of dust. Everything is extremely tense. Northern or Communist Korea is marching in on Southern Korea and we are going to fight.

Monday, June 26, 1950
Last night Dad said we would resist the aggression of Northern Korea. Tonight he sent the 7th Fleet to guard Formosa and he is going to send planes and troops.

July 3, 1950
Mr. Herbert Hoover wrote Dad a wonderful letter, offering his services in Korea.

July 4, 1950
Dad called me at 8:30 A.M. for breakfast. I went back to sleep. He called me at 9:30 A.M., and I got myself dressed in 15 minutes! I drove Dad down to Leesburg to General Marshall's house. Dad and General Marshall had a conference and I was shown the garden. I drove and Dad bossed. He has such a strong sense of direction that he is always right,

275

but in common with the rest of the family he lets you pass a corner and then says: "You should have turned there!"

I went back to New York and began to work on my career. I was doing research at the New York Public Library for my first RCA Victor Album of Early American Songs, with the Robert Shaw Male Chorus.

Leonard Warren had recommended a singing teacher to me, Mr. Sidney Dietch, and on July 18 I saw him for the first time. He is still my singing teacher. Our troops landed in Korea that day and I went back to the library and worked on my ballads and folk songs.

In my diary I wrote:

Thursday, July 20, 1950
I had my first voice lesson with Mr. Dietch today. I'll never be too enthusiastic about anything in voice again but I think he is the answer to my problems vocally. Only time can tell.

Tonight Greta Kempton had me to dinner at her apartment. Then we went to see *The Happy Time*. Afterwards we met Leonard Lyons at Sardi's and Claude Dauphin, the wonderful French actor of *The Happy Time*. Mrs. Lasker and Frank Loesser, the famous song writer, were there, also. I saw Ray Bolger. We all went on to the Stork and went upstairs and Mr. Loesser played the score of his new show, *Guys and Dolls*. The music and lyrics are marvelous. Also Ray Bolger taught me the two-step on the sidewalk in front of Sardi's.

The discouragement about my singing reflected in this entry sprang from a sharp disillusionment I had suffered from an adviser. My confidence had been so rudely shattered that it took me many months to retrieve it, and the recovery had been slow and painful. I suppose all musicians, at some moment in their careers, must have similar experiences. In my case, it has served finally to whet my determination.

That July I went down to Southampton to spend a week end with Rita and Tom Murray, Jr., at their home there. Ann and Henry Ford II had a buffet luncheon and Tom and Rita gave a beautiful dinner dance which looked like all those pictures you see of social life in fashionable magazines. The garden was illuminated and hung with lanterns and we danced there, under the lighted trees. I danced with Gary Cooper, who dances the way he talks—yup and nope —and with Van Johnson, who dances the way he looks.

I also christened a Capitol Airliner—not with champagne but with rose petals yet! Anyway you didn't have to *break* them! There were also pigeons who were supposed to fly out, but they didn't. I hope it wasn't a mechanical failure! Shawsie came to visit me and we made like tourists. We went to the UN Building and to the Algonquin and we took Jeanette MacDonald to lunch at the Ritz Garden. After lunch we were due to catch the Washington train and there was some sort of terrible traffic tie-up in Seventh Avenue. (There usually is.) We finally had to get out of the car and run for the train. So help me, I ran right through one of those carts they use to haul dresses in the garment district! We caught the train but didn't stop panting until we got to Philadelphia. I gave a luncheon for Shawsie aboard the *Williamsburg*. She went back to Kansas City and I went back to New York.

I flew to Independence in August to attend a dinner given for Dad at the Muehlebach, where he received the Order of Constantine. General Walker had been killed in Korea and General Ridgway had succeeded him. Louis Johnson had not resigned yet! I went to Washington to talk to the paraplegics at Halloran Hospital. When I talked to them, I was ashamed of myself for ever having complained about anything.

On September 1 Dad made his excellent foreign policy speech over radio and television. I was in Washington. Mother had had to go home to Independence due to the illness of my grandmother. Along with the heavy schedule my mother experienced as the President's wife was the constant worry about Grandmums, whose health had failed steadily. Dad and I took the *Williamsburg* up the river for the long Labor Day week end and we missed her so much.

In October I resumed my Purple Pin existence. I went on tour again. I appeared in Ed Sullivan's *Toast of the Town* during this interval and came down with the flu and had to cancel a concert at New London, Connecticut. (It took me five years to get back to New London. I sang there in the spring of 1955.) Dad went to Honolulu for a conference on the Pacific problem. He came back looking disheartened.

On November 4, Evelyn Spencer Horton was born. Drucie and John's daughter was my first godchild. I was singing in Erie, Pennsylvania, that night with the Erie Symphony Orchestra.

The tour ground on and I began actually to feel like a purple

277

pin—at least I felt black and blue. On December 3 I made a guest appearance on Tallulah Bankhead's *Big Show* over NBC. Most people will remember Tallulah's great radio show which lasted an hour and a half and cheered many Sunday evenings. Douglas Fairbanks, Jr., was also appearing when I did, and during a break in the rehearsal at noon he took me to lunch. He was so charming and such a genuine person, and he was a tremendous help to me on this occasion, which I found fairly confusing. I had been on radio many times, but I was unaccustomed to the hustle and bustle and the enormous number of people involved in *The Big Show*. Fred Allen, Mindy Carson, Joan Davis, Phil Silvers, Meredith Wilson, and Douglas were all on the show the night I was.

I was standing in the wings, shivering, when Mr. Fairbanks noticed my nervousness.

He came over and took my hand and held it and said, "Now, now, calm down!"

He was so attractive that I said, "I don't know whether this is a way to make a girl calm down or not!"

ॐ The next thing on the agenda was my Washington concert, which wound up the tour. In many ways, it was an ill-fated concert. It took place on December 5 at Constitution Hall and I was so tired that I didn't make sense. When I went out on the stage, I realized that something was terribly wrong. There was a mood of unrest and misery in the audience. This can be a disconcerting thing to a performer. I did not discover what it was until the concert was over. I wrote in my diary:

Tuesday, December 5, 1950
I gave my Washington Concert tonight. I was so tired that I had awful nerves. The most shocking thing occurred today and was kept from me. Charlie Ross dropped dead. I can't believe it. Poor Miss Florence and poor Dad. Charlie was a tower of strength and trust for Dad. We'll never see his like again.

I hold no brief for my performance on that occasion. I don't know how I sang. The spirit of an audience has a marked effect on a singer, and the atmosphere was charged that night not only with grief but with mystery. I think I should have been told that my friend had died.

278

Several critics were extremely frank about this concert. One learns to laugh off the harsh words of those who sit in judgment. A performer who cannot learn to laugh them off is lost. But occasionally circumstances conspire to swamp the sturdiest spirit who happens not to be performing. Almost everybody must remember that my father wrote an angry letter, which was rather tastelessly made public and became the subject of controversy. I suppose that some people will remember that letter in preference to my father's many important accomplishments.

I am unable to comment on the letter, since I never saw it. Among the scribbled notes in my father's diary the following extract appeared:

December 9, 1950
Margie held a concert here in D.C. on December 5th. It was a good one. She was well accompanied by a young pianist named Allison, whose father is a Baptist preacher in Augusta, Georgia. Young Allison played two pieces after the intermission, one of which was the great A Flat Chopin Waltz, Opus 42. He did it as well as it could be done and I've heard Paderewski, Moritz Rosenthal and Josef Lhevinne play it.

A frustrated critic on the Washington Post wrote a lousy review. The only thing, General Marshall said, he didn't criticize was the varnish on the piano. He put my baby as low as he could and he made the young accompanist look like a dub.

It upset me and I wrote him what I thought of him. I told him he was lower than Mr. X and that was intended to be an insult worse than the reflection on his ancestry. I would never reflect on a man's mother, because mothers are not to be attacked, although mine was.

I've been accused of putting my baby, who is the apple of my eye, in a bad position. I don't think that is so. She doesn't either—thank the Almighty.

I *didn't* think so, either. An opinion on my singing didn't matter to me one way or another, but I appreciated my father's insistence on being a human being first, and the Devil take the hindmost. I was glad that chivalry was not dead.

22: *Innocents abroad*

The year 1951 built to a rising crescendo. I started it off by trying out the new waffle iron I had got for Christmas when my uncle Fred came to town. The waffles all stuck and batter managed to get all over the apartment. My godchild, Evelyn Spencer Horton, the daughter of Drucie and John, was christened and I raced down to Washington to stand as sponsor for little Lyn. I went to a performance of *Fledermaus* at the Metropolitan and sat in Mr. Rudolph Bing's box with Bob Odell. Bob brought me home at a reasonable hour and I bade him farewell, went in the bedroom and put on a new face and went to the ANTA Ball with another fellow. Somebody took my picture at the ball and it got in the papers. Bob Odell called me the next morning and said, "Well, I see you had a late date!" I couldn't get away with anything.

On January 21 I did my second TV show with Ed Sullivan. I wore an old-fashioned costume, played the spinet, sang two songs, and danced the steps that Ray Bolger had taught me on the sidewalk in front of Sardi's. The set was a replica of an old mansion, which gave the act a little drama. At least they let me move around this time and I felt more natural.

Newsweek decided to run a feature story on me and *Time* also decided to do a piece. Unfortunately, they seemed to decide on this simultaneously. On January 26 the photographer from *News-*

week arrived and took pictures for an hour. The photographer from *Time* had chosen the same day for sittings. As the *Newsweek* photographer lingered on, I began to be nervous that the *Time* photographer would arrive and they would meet each other in the hall! I managed to avoid this but *Time* arrived on *Newsweek's* heels. Mr. Chaliapin, the artist who draws portrait covers for *Time*, also came and sketched me.

Bill Sullivan took me to Carnegie Hall to hear Toscanini conduct Verdi's *Requiem*. This was one of the most moving musical experiences I ever had. Toscanini's rendition was magnificent and the music soared and mounted until it seemed to push back the very walls of the old building. Afterward we went to a party given by Sylvia and Leonard Lyons at their home on Central Park West. The guest list of this party was like a roster of the best entertainers in America. I append it for that reason. Present were Fred and Portland Allen, Jack Benny, Danny Kaye, Robert Merrill, Jose Ferrer, Louis Calhern, Lynn and Frank Loesser, Abe and Carin Burrows, and Lilli Palmer and Rex Harrison.

It is reasonable to ask what happened at a party in which so many luminaries were gathered in front of one fireplace. Well, it was like any other party in which good friends who know each other will meet, with one remarkable difference. All the guests *performed* on the spur of the moment, and I felt as if I had a front-row seat at all the plays and musicals and shows on Broadway and on the air waves rolled into one. To obtain a foothold in a conversation among such wits offers quite a problem. I was content to applaud.

A new production of *Richard II* had opened in town and John McClain, the drama critic of the *New York Journal-American*, invited me to go with him to see the show. In the middle of the first act, John drifted off into slumber and slept soundly until the lights came up. Due to my passion for Shakespeare, I wasn't as charitable toward John's weariness as I might have been.

"How do you like it?" I asked him.

"Oh, great!" John said heartily.

"How do you mean great?" I asked.

"Fine production, fine production," John said.

"How can you tell?" I asked.

"I can tell," John said.

"I hope you are going to give them a good notice," I said, miffed.

"Naturally," said my sleepy friend.

He did, too. If he hadn't I'd have clobbered him.

He got even with me, though. He told Leonard Lyons that although he was a bachelor, when he took me out my Secret Service men made him feel like an erring husband.

One of the events of that winter was a luncheon given by RCA on the occasion of the launching of a Treasury of Victor Records, which covered a time span from 1907 to 1951. Among the celebrated artists I met that day were Fritz Kreisler, Frieda Hempel, Frances Alda, Giovanni Martinelli, and Rotier. I was sitting with Mr. Alfred P. Sloan and I confessed to Mr. Sloan my long-time worship of Martinelli.

"Every time I see Giovanni Martinelli, I want to throw my arms around him and hug him," I said.

Later on, Martinelli was called on to present awards to artists who had been recording for RCA Victor thirty years or more. Mr. Sloan introduced him. When he got up on the platform, he craved permission to tell a little story about Martinelli. Before he began I knew that he was going to repeat what I had just told him. I was in an absolute agony of embarrassment. I really wanted to murder him. He told the story, omitting my name, but my blushes must have given me away. When people praise me for always trying to say the right thing, I remember occasions like this. To some extent, anybody in my position has to do it in self-defense. It is almost unbearable to have your friendly enthusiasm broadcast from the stage of the Metropolitan.

⮑ But such irritations are soon forgotten, and certainly they were that year, for at long last I was making tentative plans to go to Europe. I had wanted to go since I could remember—I think since I first knew that one of my maternal great-grandmothers derived from Rounds, England . . . such a lovely name. I had earned enough money concertizing to pay my way, and I proposed to go to Europe like any other girl on a holiday. Annette Wright and Reathel Odum wanted to go, and we made up a congenial threesome.

It soon became apparent that I couldn't go exactly like any other girl. For one thing, two Secret Service men would have to go with me. For another thing, the matter of security entered into it. If I went to Europe it would immediately be taken as a sign that no war was expected during the summer of 1951, and the influx of American travel there would immediately be greater. The cold war had set in in earnest, aggravated by the Korean situation, and there had been considerable tension. Reasonably, my father would not permit me to go gallivanting off if there was any threat of danger, and who would be in better position to know? One must think of this sort of thing. Even the President cannot prophesy surprise attacks. Witness Pearl Harbor.

Reathel and Annette and I had planned to stay in hotels and be tourists but the Chief of Protocol recommended that we stay at embassies and legations, for security reasons and because such residence would be less harrying and more convenient to the representatives of our government in foreign places.

I wanted to go to Europe to look and learn and I hoped for as much freedom of action as possible, but it became obvious that, for better or worse, the trip (which was essentially a private one) would be looked on as an instrument of international good will. I had an opportunity to be useful. While I may have had some brief pang at the loss of opportunity to be footloose and fancy-free, I welcomed any opportunity to be useful, and of course, I appreciated the opportunities which would accrue to a semiofficial position.

There were a few snide references to this trip in the public prints which insinuated that my entourage and I were traveling at government expense and playing the red carpet to a fare-thee-well. I would like to correct this misapprehension. I earned my trip to Europe with one-night stands.

&❧ The official announcement of my departure was made on May 17, but prior to that I had been taking every medical shot known to man and trying to get enough clothes together for six weeks in six countries that could still be packed in three suitcases. Since quite a few evening clothes had to be included, this was the neatest trick of the year. Nobody can say I hadn't had experience with packing. I made it. I had my passport and I was absolutely bursting with excitement. I was so thrilled I was about to fly off in small pieces, and went through bon-voyage parties in a happy daze.

Reathel, Annette, and I sailed on the SS *America* on May 26. Mother came to New York to see us off. She looked as cute as a button in a dark faille suit with big buttons and a white, rough-straw sailor hat, which I always liked better on her than the flowery ones. She was as excited as I was. At the press conference aboard, somebody asked her if she wasn't going to join me later on the Continent. "Certainly not," Mother said. "I want her to have a good time!"

How can I go off and leave this darling woman, even for six weeks? I asked myself, but Mother was gay as a cricket, charming everybody, and she *wanted* me to go on my own. The cabin was banked with red roses and I had a great big sheaf of five dozen to hold, from Alexander de Manziarly, an official of the European Travel Commission. I had on a navy blue outfit with shoes to match and a pistachio green coal scuttle in the way of a hat. When the boat whistle sounded "All ashore that's going ashore!" there was the usual flurry of handshaking and kissing, and Mother started for the gangplank. I went with her. I was so accustomed to seeing people off at sailing parties, I almost got off the ship. I couldn't believe I was actually going. As the tugs towed the *America* into the middle of the river I looked back at the waving multitude on the pier and tried to pick out Mother. As the stretch of water widened between me and my native land, I had one pang of homesickness, but this was soon lost in the fascination of a great ocean liner.

Diana Churchill Sandys, the daughter of Sir Winston and Mrs. Churchill, was also aboard. She had been in New York visiting her sister, Sarah Churchill, who was then appearing on Broadway in a play called *Gramercy Ghost*. I had helped Diana to get passage on the ship, as all Europe-bound steamers were booked heavily that summer and reservations were hard to come by. I looked up Diana and we all went to lunch.

We were seated at the captain's table—Diana, Reathel, Annette, and I. It was a nice table and we had a lot of fun. The balmy leisure of shipboard set in, where, caught between destinations, nothing one leaves behind or nothing that lies ahead has to be coped with. We went to church on Sunday and explored the ship from stem to stern. We played deck tennis and went to the movies. We lay in our deck chairs with our neglected books in our hands, sunning ourselves. Captain John W. Anderson, the captain of the *America*, invited us to cocktails in his quarters before the Captain's Gala Dinner. We ate like starved things, everything from Beluga caviar to hamburgers. Oh, it was grand! Only one untoward thing happened. Reathel felt seasick and immediately swallowed the prescribed Dramamine. Nobody had told her it was a sedative. She slept a whole day and was absolutely furious.

The crossing was so delightful that I almost hated to see land, but on June 1 we sighted Ireland—with an old gnarled castle high on the side of a hill, a crumbling church spire swathed in ivy, and the incredible green of that island, lapped by its blue sea. It was like a fantasy.

The next day we put in at Le Havre and a battery of French reporters and photographers came aboard. They were pretty much like reporters and photographers in America—slightly more voluble. Some were delightful. Others were not. It was a gray day at Le Havre and when we crossed the English Channel, England was shrouded in her immemorial mists.

We landed at Southampton at 5 P.M. and were met by a delegation consisting of Mrs. Penfield, Mr. Mallory Browne, Mr. John Kelly, Mr. Curle, the American Consul, and the Mayor of Southampton. The Mayor was a lady; nevertheless she was referred to and addressed as *Mr.* Mayor. She made me a warm little speech of welcome and gave me a bouquet of red and yellow roses. This was followed by a press conference, a newsreel interview, a radio broadcast, and a tour of Southampton's magnificent new pier.

After that we caught the boat train. My first experience of English trains made me love them for life. The car was all mahogany inside and fitted out with armchairs. Between each two chairs was a table, laid for dinner. Dinner was served right there and you didn't have to get up and adjourn to a diner or *wagon-lit*. The train had a funny, puffing little engine, much smaller than our engines but thoroughly efficient and somehow reminiscent of the British character, which I came to love.

I sat with my face pressed to the window, looking out on the enchanting countryside. It was so beautiful and green and alive with flowers and so *neat*. Every little house had its private garden, brilliant with spring flowers and emerald lawn, which looked as if every blade of grass had been individually trimmed with manicure scissors.

Finally we pulled into old gray Waterloo Station where we were welcomed by Ambassador and Mrs. Walter S. Gifford and Mr. Penfield. The photographers swarmed, but the Ambassador got us away and to the Embassy, a beautiful residence at 14 Prince's Gate (I shall never get over being enthralled by English addresses), and I pinched myself and tried to realize that I was actually in London—in Shakespeare's London and Thackeray's London and Dickens' London, in beautiful and battered and courageous London, which had stood like a Colossus, stemming the Nazi tide, such a few short years ago. I was awash with sentiment and I couldn't believe I was really there.

ε❧ For the next six weeks I lived in a fairy tale. It was a fairy tale then and it is a fairy tale now. I wished every day to be every girl in the world so that all I saw and did and experienced could happen to every romantic creature alive.

At ten-thirty the next morning, which was Sunday, Mrs. Gifford took Annette and me to Matins at Westminster Abbey. The atmosphere of this old church, where so much of the drama of England has transpired, closed round me, and all the history I had studied seemed to come alive for the first time. How could I listen to the service, when the Poet's Corner was just over there, and the stone effigies of knights and their ladies, with their little marble dogs crouched at the foot, bearing their ancient dates were hard by? I'm afraid my eyes kept straying from the prayer book. I did join in the hymns.

After church, Mr. and Mrs. Gifford and I set out for Chartwell, where we had been invited to luncheon by Mr. and Mrs. Winston Churchill. We were a small party (Mrs. Churchill was in the hospital recovering from an operation) and the informality and warmth of welcome made me feel completely at home. Mary Soames, Mr. Churchill's youngest daughter, and her husband, Captain Christopher Soames, were there, and Mrs. Churchill's sister.

Mr. Churchill was informally got up in a striped overall-type costume that had a short, zippered jacket and what appeared to be a ten-gallon American cowboy's hat. It looked like a Stetson and I dare say he had received it at some American function. Anyway, it became him. He was in rare form, full of twinkling jokes and teasing remarks. What an extraordinary and wonderful person he is.

After luncheon he gave me a tour of Chartwell—not all of it, of course, as it is actually a five-hundred-acre farm. He led me around the manifold gardens and fishponds and the swimming pool, which he is reputed to have built himself. (He fancies his own bricklaying and often lays brick in his off-hours.) He was very proud of the landscaping and plantings and pointed out his favorite shrubs to me with his walking stick. Needless to say, I admired them heartily. Mr. Churchill gave me one of his own paintings to take back to my father as a present.

Late in the afternoon, we raced back to town and went to Lambeth Palace, where we were received by the Archbishop of Canterbury, who gave us tea. The Archbishop, Dr. Geoffrey Fisher, couldn't have been more charming and had a demoniac twinkle in his eye. We were soon all laughing. Mr. Humphrey Fisher, one of the Archbishop's sons, dropped in, and he and the Archbishop gave me a tour of Lambeth Palace, which was built in 1100 A.D. During this tour the bell in the church tower began to peal. In fact, all the bells in London rang out, as they do on Sunday at 5 P.M. I was beside myself, engulfed in history, and if I were a bell, I'd have been ringing!

After tea, we rushed back to the Embassy to dress for dinner. We dined at the Embassy and then went to Festival Hall (the Festival of Britain was in progress in 1951) to hear a concert by the London Symphony Orchestra. It was a beautiful concert and I was much impressed by the modern hall.

On Monday morning, June 4, we set out bright and early for the Tower of London. Mr. and Mrs. John Foster Dulles had arrived in London and Mrs. Dulles went along with Reathel, Annette, and me, and accompanied by Commander Hudgins. We were met by Colonel H. Carkett-James, the Governor of the Tower, and an honor guard of Irish and Coldstream Guards, on duty at the Tower, and of course, by the wonderful Beefeaters, in their Tudor dress.

We were shown all the armor and weapons and medals and decorations and the Crown Jewels. These were fabulous. (Later, when I met Princess Margaret, she asked me whether I had looked at the Crown Jewels. She said she hadn't seen them in a long time.) The jewels were in a new burglarproof, shatterproof glass case, especially lighted, and were valued at $140,000,000. There were 6,000 diamonds in one crown.

After the sightseeing tour, we repaired to the Royal Pavilion at the Festival of Britain, where we were greeted by Lord Ismay, chairman of the Festival, and several others, and had lunch in the Pavilion. Then we toured the exhibits of the Festival for an hour.

"There's something I want to ask you," said Lord Ismay.

"Yes?" I said, expecting some probing question.

"How can you walk in those *heels?*" he said.

The streets of the Festival were jammed, but most of the exhibits were so technical that I didn't make much headway with them. Annette and I finally slipped off and made an incognito survey of Piccadilly Circus and Bond Street. We hadn't seen them and we couldn't bear it another minute.

That night Mr. and Mrs. Gifford entertained with a dinner party at the Embassy for me. Her Royal Highness Princess Elizabeth and her Royal Highness Princess Margaret came to dinner. Among the guests were Mr. Anthony Eden, Mr. and Mrs. Douglas Fairbanks, Jr., Captain Mark Bonham-Carter, and Mr. William Wallace.

I wore a silver lamé crinoline gown, with a shallow neckline and puffed sleeves. There had been great speculation in the newspapers as to whether or not I would bend the knee to English royalty and in every press conference from the moment I had decided to go to Europe, one of the questions had been: "Will you curtsy?" I had parried this by saying that I hoped I would always do the proper thing.

I met the Princesses at the top of the stairs at the Prince's Gate residence with Ambassador and Mrs. Gifford. It seemed to me that the correct thing was to do in England what the English did. I curtsied. The newspapers reported this as a deep and skillful curtsy, but I don't know. I don't think Americans really *can* curtsy. They just bob! Anyway, I made it down and up. Princess Elizabeth wore a marvelous green taffeta gown and Princess Margaret was dressed in white satin.

Princess Elizabeth, who is now Queen of England, is an endearing person and, in addition, she has always struck me as unusually intelligent and absolutely aware of what the score is all the time. Princess Margaret is pretty and vivacious and has a gay, charming laugh. They are both so much more beautiful than their photographs indicate, with lovely eyes and fresh, beautiful, English complexions.

One must always address royal ladies as "Ma'am." This bothered me very much as it sounds bucolic to me, and I had to keep reminding myself to say it. After dinner we had a new Danny Kaye

289

movie and I was delighted to find that the Princesses enjoyed the movies as much as I do, and that they are especially fond of American films and most especially of Danny Kaye. He is a great favorite of theirs.

I also delighted in the company of Mr. Anthony Eden (this was before he was knighted), who had long been one of my heroes, and of Mr. and Mrs. Fairbanks, whom I cherish as friends.

On Tuesday, June 5, I had been invited to luncheon at Westminster Palace, at the home of the Speaker of the House of Commons, by the Speaker, Colonel Clifton Brown, and Mrs. Brown. We were early and Mrs. Gifford and I set out for a tour of the Houses of Parliament. While we were standing on one of the terraces, the royal yacht of King Haakon of Norway brought the monarch in state up the Thames River to Westminster Pier, where a pavilion had been erected, and he was greeted by Queen Elizabeth and the two Princesses. There was something so exciting about this. It harked back to the olden days. It was the sort of thing that could happen only in London.

I also witnessed the opening of a session of the House of Commons, with Speaker Brown leading the processional into the chamber, wearing knee breeches, a black robe, and a long, curled, silver wig, with the golden mace borne before him. We sat in the Peeresses' Gallery to listen to the Commons debate. The Government and the Opposition sit facing each other and there is something about the Commons that reminds you of a cockpit. Members of the Loyal Opposition seem to choose to sit around in positions of ennui! As a matter of fact, the debate wasn't very exciting that day.

That evening I attended my first English theatre. We went at seven-thirty to see *The Waters of the Moon*, which displayed the remarkable talents of three great actresses: Dame Sybil Thorndyke, Edith Evans, and Wendy Hiller. The early curtain time and the bustle and confusion of English playhouses enchanted me, right along with everything else. The English treat their theatres with great informality. There is always a bar in the building. Many people smoke during the performance. Refreshments are served to you in your seats between acts. We had coffee and cake without moving out of our seats, and I found this very comfortable. The play was mild, but the battle for the center of the stage by the three great ladies of the theatre was an interesting tournament to watch.

The next day I had to get my hair done—that was all there was to it. Even this rite was reported in the newspapers. Mrs. Gifford, Mrs. Dulles, Annette and Reathel and I had luncheon in a restaurant and went to the matinee of *Antony and Cleopatra* at the St. James's Theatre, with Laurence Olivier and Vivien Leigh. That evening Mr. and Mrs. Douglas Fairbanks took me to the same theatre to see the Oliviers in *Caesar and Cleopatra*. I went backstage to meet them and they both kissed me. It seemed that I had announced somewhere that the two shows in London that were a must for me were their shows. This had boomed business. After the theatre, Douglas and Mary Fairbanks gave a party for me at Les Ambassadeurs.

The next day, Thursday, June 7, was one of the most exciting days of my life. The first thing on the agenda was Trooping the Color, the magnificent medieval ceremony, in honor of King George's birthday. I went with Mr. and Mrs. Gifford and we had seats in the diplomats' area, at the Parade Ground near Whitehall Palace.

King George, in whose honor this fete was given, was too ill to appear, and for the first time, Princess Elizabeth took the salute in his stead. Queen Elizabeth, dressed in that ethereal blue which reflects her eyes, and Princess Margaret, wearing lemon yellow, arrived in an open carriage. Between them was a newcomer to the ceremony, Prince Charlie, who was then only thirty months old. What a picture they made!

Trooping the Color is indescribable and I try to describe it only because I wish to share the memory. The bands marched and countermarched. The mounted Household Cavalry Band, in gold tunics and black hats, followed the intricate line of march. The Mounted Guardsmen wore armor which glinted in the sun. There were detachments in red tunics with white sheepskin saddles and white plumed helmets and detachments in blue tunics with black sheepskin saddles and red-plumed helmets. There were brilliantly dressed Horse Guards. The whole exhibition went off like clockwork. They marched in slow time and quick time and all around the Parade Ground like a great quadrille.

Three cheers went up when Princess Elizabeth trotted up from

Buckingham Palace on her big chestnut horse named Winston. She was riding sidesaddle and wore a long blue riding skirt and a short red jacket, gleaming with gold braid, and the blue ribbon of the Order of the Garter. On her head she wore a tricorne, with a cockade of white osprey feathers. With her clattered the high officers of the Grenadier Guards, in scarlet coats with high black bearskin shakos, and the King's splendid plumed-and-armored Cavalry. The massed hundreds of redcoats stood motionless, as if they had stopped breathing, as Princess Elizabeth rode into the parade field. She gave the salute and smiled at her family and King Haakon of Norway, who sat in a gallery.

Princess Elizabeth wheeled her horse and gave the salute again as the band played *God Save the King*. She then inspected the troops to the tune of the triumphal march from Verdi's *Aïda*. I was choking with excitement.

After that we attended a session at the House of Lords. I saw the Lord Chancellor march in the procession that opened the session, in a brilliant red robe and wearing his curled silver wig. I had met him in his chambers before and he had permitted me to examine his wig and a big leather pouch (in which the Lord Chancellor immemorially carries the King's Speech on opening day) and the golden mace, which always goes before and symbolizes the Government's power. The House of Lords was old and beautiful, with huge magnificent thrones for the King and Queen to sit on, but the session was rather poorly attended that day. Afterward, we had tea with Lady Jowett.

8 As if this weren't enough to render me speechless in one day, I was invited to dinner that evening at Buckingham Palace, by Queen Elizabeth. This dinner was followed by a ball at the Embassy in my honor, and my feet had long since ceased to touch the earth.

I had saved my best gown for this occasion. It was a gray tulle with an off-shoulder neckline and a voluminous skirt of many layers. When we got to Buckingham Palace, I yearned to be a tourist and gape, but there was no time and that was no place. It was beautiful, with very high ceilings and splendid traditional Palace décor.

The other guests included King Haakon of Norway, Princess Elizabeth and the Duke of Edinburgh, Princess Margaret, the Duke and Duchess of Gloucester, the Duchess of Kent, and many peers and peeresses, as well as a group of young people. When we went into the reception room, we were arranged in a circle, as we arrange guests at the White House. There were two mirrored doors facing Mr. and Mrs. Gifford, and I expected Queen Elizabeth to come through those doors and greet Mr. and Mrs. Gifford first. However, she came through a door beside me and greeted me first. Of course, I curtsied, since I felt this to be protocol. She smiled and shook hands with me, inquiring how I was enjoying my visit to London. I was really flabbergasted. She was so natural and sincere.

Queen Elizabeth was the prototype of the queen in the fairy tale. She was so beautiful. Her hair was black as a raven's wing and her eyes were the color of delphinium and her complexion was like porcelain. Her gown was mauve-pink, hoop-skirted, and sprinkled with sequins. She wore a diamond tiara on her dark hair, and a necklace of great round diamonds, diamond bracelets, and dangling diamond earrings to match.

King George, whose illness was already grave but rarely mentioned for state reasons, was unable to attend the dinner. The Duke of Gloucester acted as host. The table was superb and I was stricken with a yearning to bear off one of the hand-written menus, but I simply hadn't the courage. Souvenir hunter that I am, I felt I had to draw the line somewhere. I later confessed this desire to Mrs. Gifford, who eventually told Queen Elizabeth. When I returned to England in 1952, the Queen sent me not only the menu for that dinner, but the little folder which contained a list of the musical selections we had heard that evening. This is the sort of thoughtfulness which endears her to the world, for her genuine kindness and consideration is visited on all who come in contact with her. I wanted to sweep her a curtsy to the floor and say, "Ma'am, you are a darling!"

After dinner, Queen Elizabeth asked Mrs. Gifford to bring me over so that we could have a real visit. We sat and chatted and after a few minutes King Haakon came over and joined us. That elegant old monarch joined genially in our conversation and time ran on. We had a *long* visit.

I saw that Mrs. Gifford was beginning to look more and more nervous. Finally she approached Queen Elizabeth and spoke to her in a low voice.

The Queen smiled. "You will simply have to interrupt," she said to Mrs. Gifford.

Mrs. Gifford turned to King Haakon. "Your Majesty," she said, "I hope you will forgive me, but we are giving a ball for this young lady this evening and she must be at Prince's Gate to meet her guests, among them Princess Elizabeth and Princess Margaret."

"Nonsense," said King Haakon.

Mrs. Gifford looked anguished.

"I say nonsense," said the King. "You saw me having a flirtation with the daughter of the President of the United States, and you have come to break it up!"

Could anybody resist a man like that?

I also had a conversation with Princess Elizabeth that evening in which I discovered her delicious sense of humor. We were talking about the curtsy and how much publicity had accrued to it and I said that Americans were rather untutored in the curtsy. Princess Elizabeth said that occasionally the British found it difficult. She and the Duke of Edinburgh had attended some function, where the ladies were sweeping the floor. One lady got off on the wrong foot when she made her curtsy. As a result, when she moved away from the royal presence, she had to use the same foot she had started with, so that her feet were all mixed up and she was practically hopping around like a chicken.

Just before we left the Palace, Princess Elizabeth said to me, "If you will excuse me, I don't believe I will attend the ball this evening."

I remembered her sitting so straight and dignified on her horse during the long pageant of Trooping the Color in the morning, taking her sick father's salute, and my heart went out to her.

"Ma'am," I said, "I think you've already had a busy day."

She smiled at me like an angel.

The ball was a beautiful ball. At midnight, I suddenly had a feeling that my tulle dress might turn to rags and my slippers disappear and a pumpkin drawn by mice might turn up in front of 14 Prince's Gate! Nothing like that happened, of course. There were about two hundred and fifty people dancing, and so many lords and ladies I had great trouble keeping them straight, and we danced until 3:30 A.M. and so to bed, as Samuel Pepys said, but who could sleep!

On Friday we drove down to Stratford to see the birthplace of

294

my beloved Shakespeare. The local authorities had wanted to break out with pomp and ceremony, but I begged them to let me be a *tourist* just this once. As it was, we had a fabulous time. I went through Anne Hathaway's cottage and had dinner at the Shakespeare Memorial Theatre restaurant as guest of the Executive Council of the theatre. I stopped at the City Hall, where we had refreshments with the Mayor and Mayoress of Stratford, and we drove around the beautiful little town on the banks of the river Avon.

After dinner we saw the production of *Richard II*, with Michael Redgrave, and it was superb. Mr. Redgrave was marvelous and the setting, which followed the Elizabethan style as far as possible, was so interesting.

During the first interval, Mr. Anthony Quayle, the director of the theatre, presented me with a perfect replica of the old Globe Theatre. It had been made especially for me by John Craig, a member of the Royal Air Force and grandson of Ellen Terry, and a year's research had gone into it. I was so touched by this that I almost broke down. The little theatre is a marvel of perfection in miniature scale and I treasure this wonderful, wonderful gift, so typical of the thoughtfulness of the English. There is not another model like it in the world, and when I subsequently made an effort to present it to the Shakespeare Memorial Theatre in Stratford as a permanent ornament to their lobby, they would have none of it. I keep it with me all the time, and ever so often I take it out and look at it and the whole lovely day at Stratford rises in my mind's eye.

Michael Redgrave invited us backstage to have coffee with him and we had a most pleasant half hour. Then we drove back to London, past the forbidding battlements of Blenheim Castle. I continued to feel unreal.

The next afternoon, Ambassador and Mrs. Gifford and Annette and I went to a garden party at Cliveden, the home of Lady Astor. The party was for charity and Queen Elizabeth was there. The Queen, instead of entering into the exhausting routine of shaking hands, at certain intervals would move among the guests so that they could all get a glimpse of her. While the promenade saves physical wear and tear, I think I would rather shake hands!

While the Queen was walking about on the lower terrace, allowing everyone to look at her, I heard somebody calling me in a

295

rather peremptory fashion. I didn't believe it, but then I heard it again. Finally, Jakie Astor, Lady Astor's son, came and stood at my elbow.

"Will you come down on the lawn?" he asked.

"Were you calling me?" I asked.

"That was Mother," he said. "Will you come down on the lawn?"

"But the Queen is promenading now!" I said. "Why?"

"Because Mother wants you to," he said simply.

I went, but I felt embarrassed. However, you do not refuse Lady Astor much that she wants. The Queen spoke to me and we were photographed together.

ೆ Cliveden was magnificent and the gardens were so enormous and complex that I run out of adjectives. They looked like a Constable painting. Suddenly, on walking around a screen, I thought I heard familiar voices. And I did! I ran smack into Robert Sherwood and his wife Madeline, and Roy Leifflen. Old Home Week!

That night I had one of the few free evenings I had in Europe and it was wonderful. Bruce Mitchell, Ronnie Egan, and Roy Leifflen took Reathel, Annette, and me out on the town. Knowing my passion for Gilbert and Sullivan, the boys had arranged for us to see *Iolanthe*. The show was so marvelous I still can't talk about it. After the performance we went backstage to renew acquaintance with Martyn Green. Then we had dinner and went dancing at the Savoy. Protocol departed and Americans let their hair down. It was sheer delight.

The next day was Sunday and Ambassador and Mrs. Gifford and I were invited to Chequers to luncheon, as the guests of Prime Minister and Mrs. Attlee. Mrs. Attlee had sent me a warmhearted note in her own handwriting, and I looked forward to seeing the Prime Minister again, for I remembered him affectionately from his Washington visit. Chequers, which is the country home of the Prime Ministers of England, was old and fascinating, full of the great relics of England's past—Cromwell's sword, Queen Elizabeth's ring, which she dispatched to James VI of Scotland, to signify that he was to ascend the English throne as James I. There was a portrait of Queen Elizabeth I there and one of Anne Boleyn, looking doe-eyed and beautiful. After this excursion into history, we played some languid tennis and drove back to town.

That evening I dined with Diana Churchill Sandys and her husband Duncan, in their house on Vincent Square. It was a happy, informal party and I had my first taste of Devonshire cream, which *no* adjective will describe.

On our last day in England, Annette, and I took Mrs. Gifford to lunch at the Coq d'Or and made a pilgrimage to see the little statue of Peter Pan in Kensington Gardens. One of the butlers at 14 Prince's Gate was very anxious to have me see this statue, and I didn't want to disappoint him. There is something so touching, and somehow typical, about the English people's devotion to this figment of James Barrie's imagination. It is a sweet little statue to a dear little boy who never lived, although his address in the story was Kensington Gardens. But in the reasonable, rational, serious, solid Britons there seems to be that streak of fantasy which would worship Peter Pan, and this makes me love them.

After that we took the boat train to Harwich and embarked for Holland. Annette and I stayed up to see the ship well launched in the North Sea and then collapsed.

We arrived at the Hook of Holland the next morning by the dawn's early light. We were met by Ambassador and Mrs. Chapin and Mr. Wallace Erwin and drove to The Hague for breakfast at the Embassy. Immediately after breakfast, we got in cars and drove to Amsterdam, where we were greeted by Burgomaster and Madame D'Ailly, who served coffee and cakes. We then went to the Rijks Museum and subsequently had luncheon in the Excelsior Restaurant of the Hôtel de l'Europe. I believe this was the best meal I had in Europe, if not the best meal I ever had in my life. We then boarded a small boat for a sightseeing trip through the canals, and returned to The Hague in time to get dressed for a white-tie buffet dinner and dance at the Embassy. Prince Bernhard attended this party, along with several government officials and young diplomats.

The next morning we set out on a sightseeing tour of The Hague, and at eleven o'clock I left for Soestiijk Palace, forty miles away, to lunch with Queen Juliana. Reathal and Annette went along and also Mr. Adams and Mr. Erwin, and the girls had lunch at a hotel and went sightseeing.

Queen Juliana and Prince Bernhard greeted me warmly at the portal of the Palace and we had a really informal family lunch with Princess Beatrix, then thirteen, the heiress to the throne in attendance and no one else. I was flattered by this. Queen Juliana is a down-to-earth, friendly person and if you put her down at 219 North Delaware Street, Independence, Missouri, she would delight everybody just as she does in the most sophisticated setting. Prince Bernhard, wearing his dapper white carnation, was gay and lively. I had a good time. I collected my tourists and we drove back via Gouda, where we saw the magnificent Cathedral. I had a choice of Gouda or Doorn, the home of Kaiser Wilhelm, but I chose Gouda.

At Moerdijk we were met by a car and drove to Antwerp, where we were greeted by city officials, then on to Brussels. We arrived at the Embassy in Brussels at 4 P.M. on June 14 and that evening attended a formal dinner given by Foreign Minister and Madame Van Zeeland at their home. The next morning I went sightseeing in Brussels and at 11:30 A.M. I was received by the Prince Royal, Prince Baudouin, at the Royal Palace. We had a thirty-minute chat, mostly in English. His English was much better than my French! After that I rushed back to the Embassy for a press conference and at 1 P.M. I went to the home of Queen Elizabeth, the Queen Mother of Belgium and widow of King Albert, to a luncheon. I wore a navy blue silk suit and a velvet hat with a pink faille lining to this affair, which was quite formal. There were about a dozen people there, and the Queen engaged me in conversation for a long time. Fortunately we had music in common. The Queen still practiced the violin about two hours a day, which made for an *entente cordiale*. She was a lively and entertaining conversationalist. She also showed me around the Palace, and I regret to state that the thought of walking through one more palace bowed me down. My feet were killing me!

From Brussels we went to Luxembourg, where Mrs. Mesta had arranged a full week end. We got there Saturday afternoon about four o'clock and never stopped. As soon as I could put on a new face, we set out for the Royal Palace, where I was received by Her Royal Highness the Grand Duchess Charlotte, in a private audience. We dined that night at the Legation and went on to a ball at Château de Beggen, attended by many of our soldiers in the Occupation Army in Germany.

Sunday morning I was scheduled to place a wreath on the Luxembourg Monument du Souvenir at 12 noon. At 12:30 P.M. I placed a wreath on the grave of General Patton in the Military Cemetery in Hamm. (That was my day for placing wreaths.) We then drove to Vianden, where we had lunch at the Hôtel Heintz, and set out for a tour of the Château de Vianden, one of the most historic castles in the Duchy of Luxembourg.

I was greeted at the château by the Burgomaster of Vianden, Mr. Victor Abens, who made me a speech, to which I responded in my halting French. This surprised everybody, including me. I guess I just got carried away. I was shown through the castle by Mr. Folmar Mico, the guardian of the château. The castle was built before the thirteenth century and is considered the seat of the Nassau-Orange dynasty, and is one of the most famous châteaux in Europe. During the war, the underground, which was busy offering resistance to the Germans, hid out in it. Mr. Abens was a resistance hero.

The Grand Duchy of Luxembourg looks like the beautiful set of a beautiful operetta and I expected to see Nelson Eddy and Jeanette MacDonald prance out of a grove any minute and start singing *I'll See You Again*. The people were exceptionally kind and sweet, and when we drove away, the children had entwined our car with garlands of flowers and they gave me a little present.

That night Mrs. Mesta entertained for me with a reception for the Legation staff at the residence, and Foreign Minister and Madame Bech gave a dinner for me at the Hôtel Brasseur.

The next morning I said farewell to Luxembourg, which seemed especially dear because the people were all so nice, and set out for Paris by car.

At Reims, Reathel, Annette, and I had to go to the powder room. We realized that we had no money and got the giggles. We borrowed 500 francs from the driver and went into a café.

"Ask the man where the ladies' room is," I nudged Reathel.

"How do you say ladies' room in French?" Reathel asked.

We brooded on this for a while and came up with a literal translation. After a certain amount of confusion, we were finally directed and found that we had gone to considerable trouble for nothing. Ladies and gentlemen patronized the same room!

That was Monday, June 18. We got to Paris late in the afternoon.

My first view of Paris was obscured by a fine mist. It was raining and her monuments and towers rose out of the gray chiffon atmosphere like exquisite architectural ghosts. Paris is beautiful, even in the rain. We went to the Embassy, were greeted by Ambassador and Mrs. Bruce, and unpacked and changed clothes.

At 9 P.M. we went to a ball given for us by Mr. and Mrs. Kenyon Bolton of our Embassy at their home, *Jif sur Yvette*, just outside of Paris. This was a real gala. The next day I saw the Jacques Griffe collection and succumbed to a few purchases. My wardrobe, under the stress of social life and constant packing, was the worse for wear. Mrs. Bruce and I lunched at Maxim's and went to see Notre Dame and that brilliant little jewel, St. Chapelle, which bowled me over.

That night President and Madame Vincent Auriol entertained for me with a dinner at the Elysée Palace. The Vice-premier, René Pleven (he subsequently became Premier), was present, also General and Mrs. Eisenhower, Ambassador and Mrs. Bruce, and Charles Munch, the conductor of the Boston Symphony Orchestra. I wore my gold sari dress. After dinner we went to the Comédie Française to see a new production of Sophocles' *Antigone*. At the theatre, we were met by M. Pierre Aimé Touchard, administrator of the National Theatre.

Our entrance was very dramatic. President Auriol conducted me up the long flight of red-carpeted stairs to the box, and we were preceded by two gentlemen in eighteenth-century dress, satin knee breeches, damask coats, and powdered wigs, bearing aloft branched candelabra with burning candles. A guard of honor was drawn up at intervals on both sides of the stairway, wearing brilliant uniforms with epaulets, shining gold helmets with plumes, and gold breastplates. I remembered that musical in which Jeanette MacDonald had powdered her nose, using a breastplate for a mirror, and I could scarcely resist doing the same thing as I looked at the soldiery, standing at stiff attention with their swords raised in a salute! I too pined to powder my nose in a breastplate! It seemed like the only opportunity I might ever have. Besides, I'm sure my nose *needed* powdering.

The next day, Paulette came to the Embassy with her new fall collection of hats. I selected three. To clear up any misapprehensions, I would like to state at this point that all the clothes and millinery I purchased from French couturiers were paid for by me out of my own pocket, just as the mink scarf I bought after my first singing engagement was paid for by me. I bought several evening dresses to wear on the concert stage on this trip. We then dashed to the old Astoria Hotel, then Army headquarters, for lunch with General and Mrs. Eisenhower. The General was the only gentleman present among a large collection of ladies. When he was twitted about it, he announced that he had planned it that way on purpose—he was no fool! We had a lot of fun. After lunch, General Biddle came in to explain NATO's setup and SHAPE to us, and this was very interesting and instructive.

I then had to rush to meet Madame Helle Bonnet at Christian Dior's, where I saw his collection. I ordered two beautiful evening dresses for my concert tours and Helle and I went to have tea at a sidewalk café, which I had been yearning to do. I didn't get much time to sit around at cafés.

That Wednesday evening was my only free night in Paris. I had been cherishing the thought of it. Roy Leifflen, Bruce Mitchell, and Ronnie Egan, who had flown over from London, called for Reathel, Annette, and me at the Embassy in the late afternoon and took us to the Eiffel Tower, where actually I got my first view of Paris, though I had been there three days. The top of the Eiffel Tower is the place to see Paris for the first time. We were there just at sunset and it was a thrilling sight.

From there we went to the famous Tour d'Argent restaurant where I had smoked salmon, steak, chocolate soufflé, and coffee and tasted the pressed duck to please M. Claude Terrail, the proprietor. It was fine, if you like pressed duck. At one point they turned out all the lights in the restaurant so we could see Notre Dame illuminated, and that was very thoughtful of M. Terrail. It was a lovely sight.

We had had a lot of plans for that evening, but they were ruined by the press, who followed us so persistently that we had no peace. I was so furious at Art Buchwald, who I thought had started the whole thing, that I wouldn't even speak to him. Reporters hounded us everywhere we went, marched in behind us at the Lido, and when we got to Montmartre they seemed to have picked up recruits. So we gave the whole thing up. Mr. Buchwald later wrote in his column that I had spent a pretty dull evening in Paris for a President's daughter—or anybody's daughter, for that matter. I couldn't agree with him more.

Sunday I went to church at the American Cathedral and then to shop in the Flea Market. I went to the races at Longchamps that afternoon and to the opera that night, where I heard *Traviata*. At seven-fifty Monday evening we entrained for Rome, at the Gare de Lyon, on Rapido Seven. I love Italian trains!

We arrived in Rome on Tuesday afternoon, June 26, and were met by Ambassador Dunn and Mrs. Dunn, Minister Thompson and Mrs. Thompson, Mr. Looram, and several Italian officials. That evening Ambassador and Mrs. Dunn entertained with an official dinner at Villa Taverna. The next morning I put on my sightseeing shoes and embarked on a tour of the Coliseum and the Forum. "How can I react to anything else?" I asked myself, but I did. I defy anybody not to react to these marvelous ruins, where the layers of civilization mount one on top of the other, and you can see the living past exposed. I had lunch that day with Count and Countess Sforza at Villa Madama.

On Thursday, the twenty-eighth of June, I had a private audience with Pope Pius XII. Bishop O'Connor had called at Villa Taverna to give me the invitation the day I arrived. At 8:30 A.M. I drove to the North American Catholic College where I conferred with Bishop O'Connor on Vatican protocol. I wore a high-necked black dress with wrist-length sleeves and a skirt that touched the floor and a black lace veil. I wore a little make-up, since I scare myself when I don't have lipstick on. (When the photographs of this occasion were published, I looked so solemn and funereal that Dad took to calling me the Mother Superior.)

I felt that this was a solemn occasion, however, as I was escorted to the Court of St. Damascus where the Palatine Guards in their bedizening orange and purple medieval uniforms snapped to attention. We climbed the red-carpeted stair to the Consistorial Hall and passed through nine other regal halls to arrive at the Papal Antechamber.

The Pope received me in the Vatican Library. If a man can be said to be beautiful, I would say he was a beautiful old man. His fine, intelligent face was thinned down until the handsome bone structure dominated it and his very spirit seemed to shine through with a special luminosity. He talked to me for about twenty minutes in the most easy and gracious manner, seeming to be genuinely interested in me as a human being. He asked me to convey his cordial greetings to my father and mother and asked me lots of questions about America, about which he seemed to have an intimate knowledge. His manner was gentle and gay, not forbidding, and he spoke exquisite English in the most affable manner. At the conclusion of the audience, he gave me a silver medal.

There was a great hue and cry when I emerged from the audience, with the press demanding to know whether or not I had kissed the Pope's ring. My answer to these rude questions was that I hoped I had conducted myself with politeness. Actually, the Pope had put me at my ease by shaking hands with me.

I found him a most attractive and inspiring person and I can understand the enthusiasm of Italians for him, as they congregate by the thousands in St. Peter's Square for his blessing and shout his name, which literally means Papa, in affectionate frenzy. I have thought of him often and my meeting with him was one of the highlights of my fabulous journey.

At six o'clock on the evening of July 3, we embarked on the maiden voyage of the SS *Constitution* for New York. We spent the Fourth of July at sea, half asleep. Our crossing was pleasant but uneventful. Secretary Snyder boarded the *Constitution* in New York bringing the personal greetings of my father, and Mother came next. I was so glad to see her, and what stories I had to tell her. The reporters came next, largely to see whether or not I had managed to get engaged. The burden of the interview was what I thought of European men! I could write a book!

I was happy to be home, but I could never forget the hospitality that had been shown me. Surely no girl had ever had a more marvelous experience. On the eleventh of July, the Honorable Melvin Price, Representative from Illinois, read into the *Congressional Record* an editorial from a St. Louis newspaper entitled "Good-Will Saleswoman," which seemed to indicate that I hadn't let anybody down. I was glad.

Still, I sometimes thought about the bicycle I never rode through the English countryside; the little place in the Pigalle I never got to see because the news hawks were hounding me, and my inability to strike off down some hill road in Italy with a good companion, and the ability to be just struck dumb by some beautiful sight, without the necessity of saying the right thing. But you can't have everything, and I had the most.

In November of that year, we were overjoyed to have a short visit from Princess Elizabeth and the Duke of Edinburgh. My father,

303

who certainly thought of the Princess and her handsome consort in the frame of their diplomatic reference, was also unable to keep from thinking of them as people. He was much taken with the Princess from the moment at the airport when she finished her little speech and gave him a wistful smile from her tired eyes. (She had just completed a long official tour of the Dominion of Canada.)

Dad had forgot his prepared address and welcomed her off the cuff, so to speak, when he is always at his best.

"I hope you will like the United States as much as my daughter Margaret likes England," he said.

The Princess said that free men everywhere looked to the United States, and my father, overcome, responded, "Thank you, dear."

My mother marshaled the household forces for the dinner we gave for them, bemoaning the limitations of Blair House and the fact that the Monroe gold plate lacked soup spoons, salad forks and fish forks and knives. The menu had to be planned to get around these deficiencies. Besides the honor guests and ourselves, the dinner guests included Chief Justice Fred Vinson and Mrs. Vinson, the British Ambassador Sir Oliver Franks and Lady Franks, the Canadian Ambassador Hume Wrong and Mrs. Wrong, Senator H. Alexander Smith and Mrs. Smith, Senator Brien McMahon and Mrs. McMahon, Senator Theodore Francis Green, and Acting Secretary of State James E. Webb and Mrs. Webb.

My father keynoted the dinner by saying, "When I was a little boy, I heard about a fairy princess—and there she is!" The Princess wore a magnificent brocaded gown, the blue ribbon of the Order of the Garter, a diamond coronet, and a diamond necklace. I must say I knew what Dad meant. She looked like the heroine of every fairy tale. And the Duke of Edinburgh, who is one of the handsomest men in the twentieth century, was a perfect prototype of the fairy-tale hero. He virtually stopped traffic when he appeared on the streets in Washington.

They were in Washington only forty-eight hours, but in that time they had to squeeze in four receptions, two dinners, one luncheon, three public functions, and a sightseeing tour. At the reception at the British Embassy, they shook hands with more than 1,500 people. This is more exhausting than receiving curtsies or hand kisses, but the Princess bore it with good grace. I watched her standing there with her chin up and her fine eyes looking straight at everybody, and she was already every inch a queen. My heart went out to her, for I had some faint idea of what her public life was destined to be like. And she had no hope of retiring to private pursuits at the end of four or eight years! She would be standing in receiving lines as long as she lived.

Everybody was in the usual protocol tizzy during this visit. The State Department issued a ruling that handshaking and "How do you do" would be sufficient to greet the royal guests. But some ladies (who could) swept the floor with deep curtsies, and some bobbed. Charlie Brown, the ancient Negro messenger at the British Embassy, curtsied to both Princess Elizabeth *and* the Duke of Edinburgh!

23: Farewell, a long farewell

Most people involved in politics dread an election year no matter what happens. In 1952, everybody stopped asking me whether I was going to get married and started asking me whether Dad was going to run for President again. I didn't know. Other people asked me whether I wasn't trying to persuade him to do so. I wasn't. If I had been it wouldn't have done any good. My mother and I never interfered in my father's affairs or tried to influence him in such important matters. He made all his own decisions. Most men do.

People get curious notions about a President's family. Because a President's decisions may go down in history, they seem to feel that historic circumstances surround the making of these decisions— that the President gathers his brood around him and they all discuss it in hushed voices. I don't believe the president of a big corporation consults his wife or child when he makes some major move in policy. Perhaps the closeness of our family circle has given rise to this impression where we are concerned. When it comes to a President, security matters are often involved, so that it is even less likely he will bring his problems home.

I suppose many people will feel that I do have fascinating memories or anecdotes about such things that I am withholding, but this simply isn't true. When General MacArthur was recalled from the Far East in 1951 this matter came up in every press conference or wherever a reporter could get my ear, not only in America but in Europe. I happened to be singing a concert in Dallas, Texas, the night my father decided to bring General MacArthur home, but if I had been in Washington, I would probably have read the news in the paper, just as I did in Dallas.

My father made such decisions alone—on his knees, I imagine.

I started election year appropriately—on a train. Dad put off a conference and came out to Silver Springs to meet me. He was extremely busy. Prime Minister Winston Churchill was due to arrive for a visit, and he was hard at work on secret papers, but I rarely came into Washington that my father didn't find time to meet me.

The Prime Minister arrived on January 5 and came to luncheon, accompanied by his entourage—Mr. Anthony Eden, Lord Ismay (who had deplored my high-heeled slippers), and Lord Cherwell. I was permitted to greet them and have a little chat with each one. The value of my trip to Europe was really borne in on me then, because I could speak to them as friends and remember them in their own settings. I can't tell you how exciting this was to me. I always found Mr. Eden one of the most attractive men I ever met in diplomatic circles, and it does not surprise me that so many ladies were mad about him. He has the kindest eyes I ever saw.

Dad accompanied Prime Minister Churchill down the river on the *Williamsburg*. They returned on January 16, and I invited Sarah Churchill Beauchamp and Tony Beauchamp, her husband, to stay at Blair House while her father was in town.

The Prime Minister addressed a joint session of Congress on January 17 and Mother, Sarah and Tony, and Mr. and Mrs. Gifford and I had seats in the gallery to hear his magnificent speech, delivered in that thrilling voice which has inspired people wherever it has been heard around the world.

After the speech we all set out for the British Embassy to lunch, and I had the inestimable privilege of sitting on Mr. Churchill's right! It had never occurred to me that I would ever sit on the right hand of the Lion of Britain. We even discussed politics, and the Prime Minister said, in so many words, that he hoped my father would be a candidate for President of the United States again. I didn't say anything to that. How could I? I didn't *know* whether he was going to run or not.

General Marshall, my other great favorite, was the honor guest at this luncheon and General Marshall and Mr. Churchill got to talking about the civil war in Teheran and Africa. The conversation was so fascinating that nobody got up from lunch until four o'clock in the afternoon.

We had to fly then, for Mother was giving a tea for wounded veterans at Blair House at four-thirty and Sarah and I went along to help her. When the tea had been cleared away, Mother and Dad entertained at cocktails for the Prime Minister and his party. Then we all rushed off to dress for the state dinner Mr. and Mrs. Acheson were tendering Mr. Churchill that evening at the Larz Anderson House.

It was a beautiful dinner—all white roses and sparkling crystal and burnished silver. The table positively gleamed. Mr. Acheson injected a light note by making a very amusing toast to Prime Minister Churchill, who responded with such beautiful words that I felt the tears start in my eyes. After dinner there was a reception for about 250 people, and then dancing.

When the Prime Minister bade me good night, he thanked me for having Sarah and Tony down and then he kissed my hand. My hand, by now, had been often kissed, but I don't think I ever got such a thrill out of a hand kiss. When a man like that kisses your hand, it makes you feel humble and proud and as if your hand were a museum piece! We came back to Blair House and brought Christopher Soames, Mary Churchill's husband, with us for a visit and sat around talking about England until all hours. The next day we all went with Dad to his office and told the Prime Minister good-by. He was in fine form, and seemed to have enjoyed his visit.

I went back to New York to the routine. William Pahlmann, the interior designer, was doing a feature for *Life* magazine and asked me to participate. The idea was that Mr. Pahlmann studied my personality and decided what sort of furniture, fabrics, and ornaments became me best. He chose Early American things for me and I was photographed in a setting that he created on the spot. I thought this would be fun and it was, except that Secretary Robert Patterson had died that morning, and I was so upset that I was on the verge of tears throughout the sitting. The dress that they had chosen for me had a plunging neckline, and although it was beautiful I felt called upon to resist it as usual, in the interests of dignity. I wore my own dress and Mr. Pahlmann let me.

One funny thing did happen that day. The sitting took place in the large barnlike studio of Arnold Newman on West 66th Street, a good place for studios since there was a lot of room, but a rather evil-looking neighborhood. My Secret Service detachment were right on my heels and since I liked them to be as unobtrusive as possible, I asked them to go up the stairs and wait for me, a flight above the studio. They were always amiable, but they didn't propose to let me out of sight in that elderly building.

When the sitting was over, I came out to the elevator and Mary Hamman, the Home Furnishings editor of *Life*, came with me to say good-by. As I stepped into the elevator two burly figures whizzed past her, got in the self-service elevator, and we shot down. Miss Hamman immediately jumped to the conclusion that I had been kidnapped and almost had a heart attack. She felt she would receive the blame and was leaping to give the alarm when somebody reminded her that I always had two Secret Service agents at my heels!

The Pahlmann article was eventually printed and I looked Early American!

Drucie Horton did a television show in New York with Faye Emerson and I gave a dinner at the Carlyle for Drucie and John. John was too nervous to go to the studio with Drucie performing, so I stayed with him in the apartment and monitored the show there. Drucie did fine and we toasted her success at the dinner party.

I went to Washington for my birthday on February 17 and Mother and I celebrated together. We went over and toured the reconditioned White House, which was still pretty much of a shambles. Dad went there every Sunday, just like any other householder, to note the progress or the lack of it and then to prod the people in charge, again like any householder. The repairs went on interminably, and sometimes it seemed to me that the contractors must have thought the Democrats had had the White House long enough!

I noted in my diary for February 17 that Dad was trying to come to a decision about running again. He told Mother that he really didn't want to run, but that his decision devolved on whether or not a good man could be found to be the candidate for the Democratic party. My mother felt that my father deserved a few years of leisure and she wanted to go home. She never said anything about it anywhere and people who tried to discuss it with her came up against a blank wall. My mother had never ceased to think of 219 North Delaware Street as home and the White House as a place she was visiting, with more responsibility and hard work than satisfaction. As devoted as my father is to my mother, his loyalty to the American people and his own party had to come first. But he set out to try to find a man to be candidate. This is all I ever knew about his brooding on a possible third term.

I went off on my spring concert tour shortly thereafter and it was May before I got back to Washington.

I was singing in Portland, Maine, when the attempt was made on my father's life by the three Puerto Rican assassins. It was considered wisdom to keep this news from me, and Reathel spent a difficult day intercepting phone calls and keeping the papers out of my reach.

Finally Mother called to give me the word.

"There's been a shooting here," she said. "Now don't get excited!"

"What?" I cried, getting excited.

"One of the guards was killed," Mother said sadly. "Your father and I had intended to leave the house together a few minutes later."

"Are you *all right?*" I demanded.

"We're all right," Mother said. "Now don't worry."

It was impossible not to worry. A guard had given his life. Suppose the gunmen had arrived twenty minutes later! But we had considered this eventuality before in my family. In spite of all the careful protection provided for the President, there are times when he must stand alone and be exposed to the whims and hatreds of unbalanced persons.

"Anybody who wants to commit suicide can attempt to assassinate the President of the United States," Dad said. "With our present efficient system of protection, it is unlikely that a murderer of the President can escape."

Dad is a complete fatalist in such matters. He was never afraid and I don't think he ever gave such things much thought. He was always more careless of his own safety than the people who were provided to protect him liked him to be. He flew with the same abandon, in all sorts of stormy weather, putting his faith in the pilot and the Lord.

It never occurred to me that anybody would shoot at him or Mother or me. Even after it happened, it was impossible to dwell on. If you let yourself get afraid of such things you can become neurotic.

I guess I didn't sing very well that night.

I was singing in Allentown, Pennsylvania, on April 30, and the next day Reathel and I drove to Washington and I saw the new White House for the first time. It was spick and span and very beautiful—like a decorator's dream. But also like a decorator's dream, it looked even more impersonal than it had before. The impress of personality and years of living which had given it a rough-and-ready patina had vanished, and now the second floor looked a bit like an elegant department-store window.

Mother and Dad gave the first party in the new setting that afternoon—a diplomatic reception. Unfortunately, the cooling system broke down. The White House is no different from any other house when it comes to things like that.

More than 1,500 people came to the party and Mother and Dad shook hands with all of them. At the end of the reception they were both worn to a nub. We had started a campaign to keep Dad from going back to his office to work on reception days, as going back to a desk after such a workout was almost more than a human being could stand. But he went back that day. The steel strike was in progress and he was preparing a paper.

I was busy showing people through the new White House during the reception. One of the callers was Francis B. Sayre, the grandson of Woodrow Wilson.

"Is that tiny bedroom just off the Rose Room still there?" he asked me.

"Sure," I said. "Why?"

"I was born there," said Mr. Sayre.

Dad had a luncheon next day for President Samoza of Nicaragua and Señora Samoza, and Lillian, the daughter of the President and Señora Samoza, and my old school friend, came for a little visit at three. At four, Mother and I attended a garden party at the home of Mrs. Robert Lowe Bacon for St. John's Orphanage and stood in line for what seemed hours, but was only one hour, as at five we had to be at the Larz Anderson House for a garden party given by the White House aides. Dad joined us there. Back in line we went and more handshaking ensued. Between noon and sunset, Mother and I had done four different things in four different places. That would finish off a lady wrestler, but we got ourselves together and made the curtain at a production of *The Constant Wife*. Dad was supposed to go with us, but the steel strike kept him chained to the desk until the third act, when he finally was able to put in an appearance.

He had finished the paper he proposed to read in the Cabinet Room on May 3 when the representatives of labor and the steel manufacturers met. He let me read it, which I felt was an honor. It was strong stuff and pulled no punches.

"Sometimes you have to talk to them like a Dutch uncle," Dad said. That was what he did.

On May 15 Mother gave a luncheon for Señora Videla, the wife of the President of Chile, which I simply had to attend. Drucie was also giving a lunch in my honor at the Shoreham that day which I simply had to attend. I had to leave Mother's lunch at the coffee and race over to the Shoreham to make Drucie's.

On May 31 Mother and Dad gave a dinner for Mrs. Mesta in the State Dining Room, in which all the new gold plate, the gold-and-mirror plateau for the center of the table, and the green-and-gold china were broken out. The flowers were red roses and white snapdragons and the big gold chairs were used around the table. It was quite a do—very lush—and Mrs. Mesta loved it. I must say the State Dining Room seemed much less gloomy after its face lifting.

General Eisenhower called on us the next day. He took a look around the new diggings, but I don't know whether it occurred to him then that he would one day, not long off, be living there!

I was charmed by the new White House, but actually my mind wasn't on it very much. It was now settled that Drucie and I would sail on the maiden voyage of the USS *United States* on July 3 for Europe. We had our passports and our plans. It had been a long time since Dru and I had gallivanted off together. Our itinerary included England, Ireland, Scotland, Wales, Switzerland, France,

Austria, Germany, Denmark, Sweden, Finland, and Norway. One of the highlights for me at least, was the Salzburg Festival. Everybody seemed actually glad I was going. John Horton had promised to baby-sit with Lyn, the baby, and Drucie and I were in a real swivet of delight.

This was an unofficial trip, or as unofficial as I could manage. One Washington editorial writer, after the Swedish incident which occurred during this tour implied in a rather snide manner that perhaps I should have waited until my father got out of the White House to go to Europe. This man had a right to his own opinion, of course, but I also had a right to tour Europe as long as I was in position to pay for it. Besides, for all I knew at that time, my father might have been in the White House for four more years!

Of all ships the old *Missouri* was bound to be my favorite, but when I saw the SS *United States*, that lean greyhound of the seas, in her berth in New York, I'll admit I was torn. How beautiful she was and is—trim as an arrow, simple and swift. She was built to Navy specifications and was the culmination of a long dream on the part of William Francis Gibbs, the naval architect, who drew the first designs for her in 1945, and actually had tears in his eyes when she crossed the invisible line at Bishop's Rock to establish her record and become Queen of the Seas.

Drucie and I had beautiful accommodations. I think every one of the 1,600-odd passengers on the first crossing had a party, for there were more than 8,000 visitors to the ship and the noise of popping champagne corks was deafening. Mother and Mr. Snyder and John Horton came to see Drucie and me off. We pulled away at noon with the bands all playing, the air filled with confetti and streamers and the bon-voyage shouts of thousands on the pier, and sailed down the river accompanied by a flotilla of tugs and small craft, all blowing their whistles madly.

One of the delights of this voyage was the friendship of Commodore Harry T. Manning, the captain of the *United States*, and a man after my own heart. Commodore Manning, who scarcely went to bed or closed an eye throughout our crossing of three days, ten hours, and forty minutes and was under the most intense nervous strain all the time, never failed to have time for Drucie and me. He joined us for dinner on the first night out and the next day, July 4, he let me take the wheel and steer the vessel and blow her

314

whistle to celebrate American Independence! When photographers were taking our pictures on the bridge Drucie's skirt blew up. "Get in the wheelhouse!" Commodore Manning barked, and wouldn't let photographing proceed until all was in order. On the Glorious Fourth, Drucie and I went to three cocktail parties and missed him at dinner and we were fit to be tied. We were crossing the Grand Banks and the fog had closed in, so he had to return to the bridge before we arrived.

The next day I had a press conference and also broadcast a radio show by telephone, ship-to-shore, from the ship in conjunction with Pegeen and Ed Fitzgerald. Aunt Mary Truman was driving down a country road in Missouri in her car when this happened and she heard my voice describing life on the new liner out of the blue! We had dinner at the captain's table that night, with the Commodore as host. He stayed with us until two o'clock in the morning, returning to the bridge only at intervals. He danced with us and was so gallant that Drucie and I, in a fit of hero worship, went to our stateroom and wrote him a sonnet (or what passed for a sonnet)! When we had finished this paean of praise we had great trouble getting up our nerve to present it to him. We finally did, and the Commodore gave us each an autograph in which he said, "An historic crossing with historic companions!"

The night before we crossed the line, the ship was wild with excitement. There were hundreds of parties going on and I don't think anybody went to bed except me. I went to my room at 2:45, but after I went to bed I couldn't sleep, so I might as well have stayed up. Commodore Manning had invited Drucie and me to come to the bridge at 5:45 A.M. on July 7 to view the end of our race across the Atlantic from that eminent vantage. Unless you are acquainted with ship lore you cannot realize what a special invitation this was.

Bruce Mitchell, whom I had met on my first crossing on the *America*, and William Pahlmann, who had designed the décor for me in *Life*, were also making this maiden voyage. They offered to take Drucie and me up to the bridge. They arrived at 5:30 still in their evening clothes as they had not been to bed, and we made our way up. When we got to the door and started in, Commodore Manning bellowed, "Who is that? You can't come in here!" We all fell back and Drucie and I started to quake. However, the Com-

315

modore drew Drucie and me inside and sent Mr. Mitchell and Mr. Pahlmann to the deck just below, which was still a pretty good vantage.

Drucie and I were so terrified that we moved over to a corner and sat down on a cot and didn't say a word. The ship was racing through a heavy gale, blowing rain and sea water up over the bow and into the windows of the wheelhouse. There was only one mile of visibility when the radar, the fathometer, and the radio went out. We were making 36 knots an hour and the Scully Isles, all rocks, were only a few hundred yards off our course. Only Commodore Manning could have done it! He turned his huge vessel out of harm's way without ever lowering the speed. We passed Bishop's Rock at exactly 6:16 A.M. and the Blue Riband was ours! There was no question about its being ours. The *United States* had cut more than ten hours off the *Queen Mary's* record. Just a long week end to Europe by ship!

The moment of crossing the line was almost too deep for words. I will never forget it. I was aware of the privilege that had been extended to us, for Commodore Manning guards his bridge jealously, and I still can't quite believe that I was actually there.

It was the roughest sea and the wildest weather I have ever seen. The Commodore made certain that the British newspapermen who were on the bridge saw Bishop's Rock by radar, which fortuitously began to work again, because it was impossible to see it through the storm. Mr. Gibbs, the designer of the ship, was very kind to Drucie and me too. He had a wonderful dry sense of humor and he was deeply moved by the gallantry his creation displayed.

After Commodore Manning got rid of the press and photographers (and it was no problem for the Commodore to get rid of people—his was the voice of command!) he relaxed and let happiness flow over him. He gave us a cup of coffee, and it was then we found out that in the midst of his great tension before we passed the Rock, he had called our stateroom to tell us to be sure and wear sweaters, since it was apt to be chilly on the bridge. Can you imagine a man taking such thought of two flibbertigibbet girls at such a time!

Though the weather continued foul, we were given a rousing welcome at Le Havre. There were five fireboats shooting out their powerful streams of water, tootling of whistles, and a British air-

316

craft carrier wailed its siren and gave us three cheers. Not in a hundred years had America boasted a liner that was Queen of the Seas. We anchored in Le Havre for the night and the noise went on all night long. I would have liked to sleep. The trip across the Atlantic had consumed ninety hours, but I don't think I had slept more than fifteen of them.

Drucie and I had been problem children throughout the voyage. The clock system of the entire *United States* is controlled from one place. Drucie and I did something to our clock which wrecked the whole system—I'm sure this came of a suppressed desire on my part!—and for a while nobody had the time of day. Then we wanted to get our porthole open. We took this up with the Commodore, who issued instructions that it was to be opened in our behalf. Nothing happened, but since he is a bear for detail, he asked us if it had been. We sheepishly said no, so he raised the roof and people came running and opened the porthole.

We used to take turns hanging our heads out at night. It was full moonlight on this voyage and the sensation was remarkable— to be shooting along through the silent sea at 36 knots an hour with the moon turning the ocean to molten silver. We had no cheer for boat drill, which always seems to take place very early in the morning. We didn't show for boat drill and this became a *cause célèbre*. Everybody is *supposed* to go to boat drill. But why do they have it at the crack of dawn?

Our arrival at Southampton was a triumphal entry. What a thrill it was to be present on this occasion and see the demonstration accorded the *United States* by that old sea dog, England. From below the Isle of Wight, as we steamed through waters that have entertained most of the historic vessels of the Western world, we were met by a flotilla of English ships—large and small, old and new— channel steamers, ferryboats, motorboats, rowboats, yachts, tugboats, small pleasure craft, practically anything that would float, loaded to their gunwales with cheering people. Along the Solent, in the Hampshire countryside, on every beach and pier, people were massed, shouting "Welcome! Welcome!" and waving wildly. Anybody who believes the English are reserved should have seen them that day. They love ships—not only their own, but good ships of other countries.

As we approached our berth, big excursion vessels packed with

317

crowds came alongside; naval vessels and sailing craft joined the escort. Their whistles piped and tootled and shrilled and the *United States* thundered responses in her deep bass bellow, like a conversation. As the tugs came alongside to warp us into the pier, Vampire jet planes began to zoom and hurtle up and down the Channel. The pier was jam-packed with thousands of people and every building around the wharf was crowned with gesticulating humanity. A little naval sloop suddenly set off a series of flares that spelled out "United States," and over an amplified microphone a voice shouted, "Commodore Manning, we welcome you!" The *United States* replied with three sharp blasts of the whistle. A salute was fired, and for once I didn't mind it. As our nose touched the pier, four bells sounded. It was just six o'clock. The Southampton Police Band struck up *Anchors Aweigh*, and then played *God Save the Queen* and *The Star-Spangled Banner*. Our ship's orchestra, lined up on the deck, responded in kind. It was almost too wonderful to be borne.

Aboard, we were a shambles of emotion. Many were weeping. James Black, a man from Flushing, New York, who had been born in Scotland and was on the way to revisit his birthplace, got out his bagpipe in a transport and played *The Road to the Isles*. When the gangplank went down Mayor Edwin Burrow of Southampton, Admiral of the Port, wearing his gold chain of office, came aboard and greeted us and escorted us to shore, where we were met by a party from the Embassy.

England was in the full tide of summer. Ambassador and Mrs. Gifford met me at Waterloo Station and off we went to Prince's Gate. I felt as if I were coming home. That week I visited Scotland Yard and went over Westminster Abbey with a fine-toothed comb. I had luncheon at Buckingham Palace with Queen Elizabeth and her consort, the Duke of Edinburgh, and Princess Margaret. Her Majesty was as beautiful as ever, but graver with new responsibilities and the sorrow attendant upon the loss of a beloved father.

I went to a garden party at the Palace and had tea in the royal tent with the Queen. I went down to Stratford and dined with Colonel Flower, chairman of the Shakespeare Memorial Theatre, and witnessed a great production of *Coriolanus*. Ambassador and Mrs. Gifford took me to the theatre, where I saw *The Young Elizabeth*. Duncan and Diana Churchill Sandys gave a cocktail party for me. Martyn Green called and invited me down to the Shepperton Studios, outside of London, where he and Maurice Evans were embroiled in making *Mr. Gilbert and Mr. Sullivan*. I was wild with joy, and after a fantastic amount of rearranging, including regrets to a garden party at 10 Downing Street, Drucie and I set off in fine fettle, and for a happy day, including lunch at the studio, I saw Martyn and Maurice bring Gilbert and Sullivan to life.

Ambassador and Mrs. Gifford entertained with an enormous cocktail party for Drucie and me. It was at this party that I lost my petticoat. Queen Elizabeth and Princess Margaret were just leaving, and with Mrs. Gifford I was going down the stairs ahead of them to say good-by at the door. Halfway down, I felt something slither around my waist. I clapped my hand to my hip and sure enough, my petticoat was unmoored.

"Mrs. Gifford," I whispered frantically, "I can't go to the door!"

"You *have* to," said Mrs. Gifford. "What in the world is the matter?"

"I'm losing my petticoat!" I croaked. "I'll have to disappear."

"Petticoat or not, you will have to be at the door when the Queen departs," Mrs. Gifford said firmly. "You *can't* disappear. Can you hold on to it?"

"How can I curtsy with my petticoat coming off?" I demanded. "Oh, what shall I do?"

"Maybe I could anchor it," Mrs. Gifford said.

Suddenly reason came back to me.

"All right," I said, looking in all directions. No one was coming and I let it fall in a circle of ruffles around my feet. I then stepped out of it, leaned over, and picked it up.

During this frenetic interchange, we had been moving sedately down the stairs. As we passed the coatroom, I flung the petticoat with main strength and awkwardness through the door, where it landed in front of the butler, Epps.

"I say, ma'am," he burbled. "You can't leave *that* here!"

"Where else can I leave it?" I asked out of the corner of my mouth. "Just put it anywhere out of sight," and I walked on with my head in the air. I took the stricken expression off my face and when the royal family came I was able to make the amenities with a straight face, but you could probably see through me!

After everybody had gone, Mrs. Gifford and I collapsed. Mrs.

Gifford told me subsequently that she was actually glad it happened. When Mrs. Eisenhower lost her petticoat, in much the same manner, Mrs. Gifford knew exactly what to do!

During that visit in London, I had lunch at Hatfield Hall with Lady Salisbury, who showed me the treasures of the house, including a letter from the first Queen Elizabeth to Essex, written in the crabbed hand of a very old woman. Bruce Mitchell gave a party for me and I sat between Noel Coward and Douglas Fairbanks. I went to a ball at the Dorchester. It was a charity ball. I believe the Duchess of Kent was in attendance. I remember that I wore a lavender satin gown by Dior and danced with Douglas Fairbanks. There were many elegant gowns that night, and English women always look especially stunning in their evening clothes.

Shortly after I sailed on the *United States*, it was announced in the newspapers that some of my maternal grandfather's relatives were waiting to greet me in Ireland, including the news that Grandfather Wallace had been born there. I got a characteristic letter from my mother about this matter, while I was in London:

The White House,
July 4, 1952
(It seems like Sunday
with Dad at home)

Dear Marg—

I guess you are having some nice cool breezes on the broad Atlantic at this point, but so are we. You haven't a thing on us as to *weather*. Louise Stewart came down with me but went to lunch when we reached Philadelphia and when she came back, I was sound asleep. She didn't come into our room until we stopped in Baltimore.

Fred Vinson and Dad and I are going to the baseball game this afternoon. Double header! I haven't seen one in years. "Mama" Vinson said she wouldn't sit on a hard seat that long.

The thing about your grandfather Wallace being born in Ireland is popping up again and I want it settled, once and for all. You will probably have an excellent opportunity to do it in Dublin at a press conference. His name was David Willock Wallace and he was born in *Independence, Mo.* His father was Benjamin Franklin Wallace and *he* was born in Green County, Ky. The original Wallace family did come from Ireland in *1684*. There has never been a "Robert" (as quoted in the papers) in the entire family history. The current story is that I am

320

the daughter of "Robert" and that he still lives somewhere in Ireland. I'm sick and tired of it.

The house is spotless. Julia is very ill of a cold or virus pneumonia, but Wilma is on deck today. (It was her holiday to work anyway.)

Pennington got here with your "goods and chattels" about 8:30 last night.

Uncle Frank reported grandmother much better (Dr. Graham agreeing) so I shall not go before Sunday evening and maybe not then. Everything is under control here.

I hope you can read this. I am hurrying as I have to dress for lunch and the ball game.

I hope you ended up with a cheerful table.

Lots of love to both of you.

Mother

P.S. Please remember me to Ambassador and Mrs. Gifford and tell them I think they are wonderful to take you on *again!* (I can hear what you are saying at this point.)

She enclosed a clipping about her alleged relatives in Tipperary, on which she had scribbled, "This is *too* ridiculous!"

I went to Dublin on the Irish Mail, but my alleged relatives did not put in appearance. I was met by Ambassador Francis Matthews and Sean Nunan, the Secretary of Irish External Affairs. Ambassador and Mrs. Matthews gave a beautiful party for Drucie and me, and Mr. Frank Aiken, Foreign Affairs Minister for Ireland and Mrs. Aiken, gave a dinner party for me. The menu was in Gaelic and there were several kinds of potatoes! We made a round of calls and went sightseeing and went down to Killarney. The high spot of Ireland for me was a night at the theatre, where I saw the wonderful Abbey Players.

I wrote a letter to Mother and Dad while I was in Dublin which I quote:

Ireland is really beautiful, but the sun rarely shines. It is so cold that I have to wear a sweater under my wool suit. The Matthews gave a beautiful dinner for us last night. Mr. De Valera came. Mr. Matthews says it is the first invitation he has accepted since they arrived eight months ago. Mr. De Valera is almost totally blind so he rarely goes out.

Bishop O'Connor is here on a visit and he came also. He is the Bishop who took me to see the Pope last year. The Papal Nuncio here is an American—Archbishop O'Hara from Georgia. He asked to be remem-

321

bered to you, as did Bishop O'Connor. It's so funny to hear that Georgia accent coming from those red robes! He is very nice.

We have seen the Book of Kells and Trinity College. Dublin is not large but I guess you would say it has charm. The inhabitants are trying to turn back the clock and speak Gaelic, so it always seems as if Dru and I had wandered on a stage set and we must always try to remember our lines. They (the Irish) are all actors!

༄ We motored to Edinburgh in a little car that had absolutely no springs, and stayed at the Caledonian Hotel. The Stars and Stripes were flying from the flagpole to welcome us when we arrived. Mr. Charles Derry, the American Consul General of Scotland, took us in tow and we were shown the sights. Edinburgh is a beautiful city with one of the most delightful High Streets I ever saw. It looks like a medieval dream.

In London I had expressed a wish to see Holyrood Palace and Queen Elizabeth had forwarded cards to us for a special tour. Mr. David Ruthven conducted us all over the Holyrood, which is the oldest building in Scotland. I also visited the Castle in Edinburgh and we dined with Dr. Glenn of Washington. Drucie and I even managed a movie, and stood in line, unnoticed, waiting for seats, and had a shopping spree, looking for Scottish tweeds.

I wrote to the Wallace uncles and aunts from Edinburgh and since the letter contains some highlights of the trip I append a portion of it:

We are sitting in the midst of a lot of history at the moment. I have found Edinburgh a beautiful city in a dark and sombre way. Nearly all the stones in all the buildings are black with smoke, wind and age. We went to Holyrood Palace this morning and had a fascinating guide. We saw the royal apartments and got stuck in the "lift." Scary! I can look right out my window and see Edinburgh Castle. It is forbidding to say the least. I'm glad I saw it. There isn't too much left to see here now. Just museums. Holyrood was exciting. I half-expected Mary to come around the corner!

I did two things in the last two days—one for Beuf and one for Aunt Nat. I took a side trip in a car to Dryburgh Abbey, where Sir Walter Scott is buried—for Beuf. There is nothing there but ruins, but he and his wife, his son and daughter-in-law and his son-in-law, Lockhart, are buried with him. Field Marshal Haig is also there. His family are the traditional lords of the manor in that area.

For Aunt Nat, I went to the cradle of her church—John Knox's St. Giles. I saw his house and the pulpit which overhangs the street, where he preached against Mary Queen of Scots and the Roman Church.

We have had a good trip in the car. We stayed in Wales at Llandudno (pronounced Klan-did-no) the first night out of Ireland, and York the next night. There, to me, is the most beautiful cathedral I have ever seen. It has the loveliest windows and such grace in its huge arches. I like it best of all I've seen—here or in Ireland, England or France. It has a quality all its own and still looks like a church, not a national monument like Westminster Abbey, which I like too, for its history. We drove to Linlithgow and Bo'ness. It has just gotten dark here and it is 11:20 P.M.! We have done most of our sight-seeing on the road after six o'clock in the evening.

In Ireland we saw St. Patrick's Episcopal Church, where Jonathan Swift and his Stella are buried. And saw in Christ Church, the tomb of Strongbow. I seem to be on a tour of churches.

We leave tomorrow night for London, change to the Golden Arrow for Dover and Calais and then Paris. I used to think they put the whole train on the Channel boat but one must, alas, alight and embark and debark and re-alight or something.

I feel completely cut off here and everything fell apart last week. I almost came home.

(When I look at this last line, I wonder what happened. I can't remember! Could it have been an omen?)

In Paris, Ambassador James Dunn met us, along with Madame Bonnet. I went to the Dior showing, with the usual results! I had lunch with President and Mrs. Auriol at Rambouillet and went to Coq Hardy to dine one day. I presented a Missouri State Flag to the American Cathedral.

It was in Paris on July 26 at 6:30 A.M. that I received a telephone message from the United Press, that Governor Adlai Stevenson had been nominated as candidate for President of the United States on the third ballot at the Democratic National Convention in Chicago. My father had long since announced that he would not run again, and this made it official. I had been following newspaper reports of the convention with keen interest. Mother and Dad had flown there and I had a momentary pang that I wasn't on deck. The news smote me with mixed emotions. The days were now literally numbered until we would be private citizens again, and there was joy and sorrow mixed in my feeling. I was glad about Governor Stevenson. I knew what confidence my father had in him.

From Paris we went to Switzerland, first to Geneva and then to Bern. I went up the Grindelwald in the chair lift and was much impressed with the Alpine world. From Bern, accompanied by Ambassador Patterson, I made a trip to the Principality of Lichtenstein. Drucie and I spent the night at the castle of Vaduz, as guests of Prince Henry and the Princess of Lichtenstein, who gave us a small family dinner party. We also dined with the President and Madame Kobelt.

Salzburg was all I had hoped. I heard the Mozart *Marriage of Figaro,* and was the guest of the Austrian Chancellor, Dr. Leopold Figl, at a performance of Verdi's *Otello.* Chancellor Figl also gave me a reception where I met many of the musicians.

From Salzburg, we went to Germany, where the Army took over. We toured the Nieubiberg Airbase and went into Munich for luncheon, drove to Garmisch for dinner and an ice show and boarded a train for Heidelberg. We toured Heidelberg and vicinity all day and I looked around furtively for the Student Prince!

We were greeted in Berlin by Major General Lemuel Matthewson, the U.S. Commander in Berlin, and by Cecil B. Lyon, Director HICOQ in Berlin. We arrived on the private train of High Commissioner Walter J. Donnelly. I was received at the West Berlin City Hall by Acting Mayor Walther Schreiber, and Mrs. Schreiber gave a tea for me. Sam Rieber, Deputy High Commissioner, nearly had a nervous breakdown before he got us out of Berlin, but it wasn't in Berlin I had trouble.

From Germany we went to Denmark. We arrived in Copenhagen by motor after a horrendous drive and were cordially greeted by Madame Ambassador Eugenie Anderson and Mr. Anderson. In Denmark I had the inestimable privilege of visiting Elsinore with a copy of *Hamlet* in my hand and following the line of action through the dark and gloomy castle.

From Denmark we went to Stockholm. We were met by Ambassador Butterworth, who had arranged a pleasant program. But in Sweden the situation began to deteriorate. To begin with, it was here the rumor started that I was in love with Governor Adlai Stevenson. Of all my rumored engagements, this struck me as the most farfetched. I knew and liked Governor Stevenson, but we

324

had, as far as I could remember, never gone anywhere together or been entirely in one another's company. I denied this report with my usual vehemence, for I thought it might be very embarrassing to Governor Stevenson. As for myself, I knew somebody would say that I would do anything to stay in the White House, even get married.

I was conducted on a tour of Drottningsholm Castle and went to a private performance of *Il Geloso Schernito* by Pergolesi in the Drottningsholm Castle Theatre, which is an exact copy of Marie Antoinette's. It was a command performance by Prince Wilhelm, who sat on a throne and had me sit beside him on another one.

I was also taken on a tour of the City Hall and it was here the incident occurred which received such worldwide publicity. My Secret Service agents were accused of "roughing up" newsmen and photographers who wanted to take a picture of me. There was not a word of truth in the Swedish newspaper reports about this matter. I feel the incident was fomented for some reason that I have never been able to understand. Most of my press in Sweden had been quite flattering, but two or three of the papers now turned on me and printed the most cruel and tiresome witticisms, such as "Miss Truman is in no danger of her life here—she does not plan to sing!" or "The King of Sweden arrived today. *He* needs no armed bodyguard."

While I think the less said about this matter, even at this late date, the better, I would like to state that Hans Melin, the Swedish police officer who had been assigned to assist the three FBI agents assigned to me, denied categorically the entire story, and stated for the record that my guards were unarmed, but that he himself *was* armed.

At the end of the report, Officer Melin said, "Finally it should be stated that the officers from the FBI are not only what the newspapers call 'bodyguards' but also handle baggage, meals, hotel accommodations and other tasks connected with the journey. During their stay in Sweden they have in no way and at no time resorted to any police measures against either Swedish or foreign citizens. Whenever such measures have seemed warranted, I myself have taken them."

In view of the controversy stirred up by this incident in the United States, I would personally like to add that my guards were guiltless and that I believe the incident was deliberately planned by unsympathetic persons. I would also like to say in my own behalf that I did not choose to have Secret Service agents protect me. They are assigned to guard the members of the President's family.

There was one funny photograph made of me in Sweden. I have got on my determined smile, but for some reason I look as if I were gritting my teeth!

It was a relief to get on the *Aallotar* and sail for Finland. Needless to say, the Swedish incident dogged me on the rest of my tour in Europe, but the Finnish people were very kind and considerate. We left Finland on the Swedish ship *Bore* (what a perfect name) for Stockholm again. We got in a fearful storm on the Baltic and were four hours late in arriving. We missed the Oslo train, but I am grateful to say we set out for Oslo by motor. I was not sorry to see the last of the Venice of the North. My dear friends the late Ambassador and Mrs. C. Ulric Bay met us in Oslo.

We happened to be in Norway during the two-day celebration of King Haakon's eightieth birthday. Since King Haakon had flirted with me at the age of seventy-nine in Buckingham Palace, I took a personal interest. I had luncheon at Skaugam, with her Royal Highness Crown Princess Martha, and Ambassador and Mrs. Bay gave a beautiful white-tie supper dance at the Embassy in my honor, which was attended by the Norwegian Princesses.

The next day we entrained for France, boarded the *United States*, and turned our faces toward home. Our first act on board ship was to have a *hamburger!* Mother, Secretary Snyder, and John Horton met us in New York, accompanied by Roy Leifflen and Bob Odell. The press was on hand. They asked me about Sweden. They asked me if I hadn't urged Dad not to run again. They asked me if I were really engaged to *anybody*.

The rest of that year was as frenzied as the first. I got off the boat and went straight to Los Angeles, where I did a TV show with Jimmy Durante on September 2. Dad had now taken the stump for Governor Stevenson and we were off on a whistle-stop trek again. Dad set off the charge that opened up Tiber Dam. We went to Hungry Horse. We went to Tacoma, Seattle, Montana. We went to San Francisco, Colorado, and back to Missouri to register. We went to Buffalo, New York, where the opposition had hired children to break up the meeting by yelling us down. We finally got back to New York and there were 20,000 people jammed in Grand Central station to meet us. Dad made a ringing speech in the station. Dad then set out for New England and Mother and I switched. She joined Dad and I returned to the White House. It had been so long since I had slept in my own room, I scarcely recognized it.

Maurice Evans came to town in *Dial M for Murder*. Of course Drucie and I were right there. The cast came to the White House for tea afterward, and I showed them over the building. John Williams, one of the actors, was British, and when I was giving my guided tour I said, "Now this is the room in which you will see the beams scorched by the blaze when the British set fire to the White House."

"Oh, I say," John Williams said, in that inimitable English accent. "I *am* sorry!"

I had a few hours of leisure, which I improved by cataloguing Dad's medals. Then we started out whistle-stopping again. We went to Minnesota, Iowa, Illinois, and Michigan. In Detroit Dad made a speech which was received with acclaim.

It was in Ohio that Mike Di Salle introduced Dad from the platform one day and said he would like the people to meet Margaret Truman's father! I was sitting there half asleep, but this statement electrified me. Dad really did laugh. "I'm a back number already," he said.

Mother met the train in St. Louis. What a relief to see her. We finally got home to vote.

For the next few days, I refer you to my journal:

Tuesday, November 4, 1952
We voted this morning. We spent the day on the train in unutterable suspense. And we got clobbered. Ike won by 3,000,000. Oh well, let *them* worry for a change.

Wednesday, November 5, 1952
We arrived in Washington this noon. I think everyone feels worse than we do. We did all we could and I feel like a little girl out of school. Rid of that awful responsibility. I can speak my mind for the first time really in my life, as just a private citizen.

Monday, December 1, 1952
Grandmother has had another partial stroke. She doesn't answer or eat.

Mrs. Eisenhower came to talk over housekeeping details with Mother today.

Thursday, December 4, 1952

I came down to Washington for the big Cabinet dinner tonight. Governor Stevenson is staying here. He and I went down together. He read me a letter which was sent to him to give me. I must say I liked the reading better than the content. He is most charming and lots of fun but is so smart he scares me somewhat. Grandmother still in a coma.

Grandmother Wallace died on December 5 at 12:37 P.M. I was on the train en route to New York. When I got off at Pennsylvania Station, I was handed a message which read: "Fernlake's mother died today at 12:37. She requests that her daughter be told." *Fernlake* had been the code name for Mother during the war. I don't know why they used it that day except that my mother's sense of privacy was always at work.

I never left the station. I got on a train headed for Washington and went home to do what I could for my mother.

The next day Vietta and I went to the Hines Funeral Home to put on Grandmum's favorite earrings. She looked the way she had when I was a little girl—not a trace of her long illness. It was very hard for me to take—giving her up. She had called me her Sugar Lump and she had been a part of my life every day I could remember.

In the last forty-eight hours, I had witnessed the end of two eras. The Cabinet had ended a government era with the dinner I had attended, and Grandmum's death ended an era in my own life. On the eighth of December we took Grandmother back to Independence, and then came back to Washington. Christmas was rather sad that year. All the relatives came but it was impossible not to feel gloomy. Just before Christmas we had a welcome visit from Premier Menzies of Australia, who came to the White House with his daughter for tea. We had Christmas dinner in the State Dining Room for the last time.

I began the year 1953 rehearsing a TV show with Milton Berle in New York. I came back to Washington for a dinner given by the Harry S. Truman Library, Inc. I went with Dad, who couldn't stay, because he was dining with Prime Minister Churchill at the British Embassy. My dinner partners were General Marshall and

Sam Rayburn, and I represented the family on this occasion. General Marshall had to go with Dad, but Uncle Sam Rayburn took over. To say I had a good time was an understatement. I stayed to hear them raise over $500,000 for the library. I was interested to observe who turned up at this dinner after we were out of office. I was delighted with some who came and amused by some who failed to show!

Prime Minister Churchill came to the White House for a conference with Dad in the study that day, and I was, as ever, enchanted to see him. Secretary Acheson, Mr. Harriman, Mr. Lovett and Mr. Makin, the new British Ambassador, and Secretary Snyder attended the conference. In my diary, after the name of Mr. Averell Harriman I put in parentheses "Governor of New York?" My political prophesying had improved.

From that day on the twilight of our term gathered in at the White House. Packing accelerated.

We had actually been packing for three months. I had been hauling my treasures piecemeal to New York, one at a time, arriving loaded down from each trip to Washington. I had brought my silver boxes and photographs and many of the gifts that had been made to me, to furnish my apartment. Now my collection of demitasse cups and the Meissen tea service Mrs. Mesta had given me and my Dresden figures went into barrels, and my books and records and musical scores and pictures into boxes. I separated the sheep from the goats in my wardrobe. My piano was crated and dispatched to Independence. I packed up my trunk of souvenirs.

Mother supervised the packing of the family effects and all my father's documents and books and mementos were crated and sent to Independence, to be incorporated eventually in the Truman Library Collection. It was a mammoth job, but when moving day rolled around, we were already moved.

When I dressed that last morning in the pink bedroom, it was already stripped of personality and looked pleasant but untenanted. I settled my hat, put on my coat and took up my gloves, and ran down the stairs for the last time as a daughter of the White House. I might have gone through all the public rooms, sentimentally remembering so much that had transpired in them—the faces of the people I had met, the waltzes I had waltzed, the words that had been said to me—but there wasn't time. The car was waiting, and in an hour or so the new incumbent would take the oath.

"Come on," Mother said to me, and we went out into the January cold.

We didn't talk much. I know that Mother was already thinking of the peace and familiarity of 219 North Delaware Street, without the burden of responsibility she had endured for so many years. I was thinking about New York and all I had to do next week.

Inauguration Day (but not for us) was January 20. There was one happy surprise. Dad, in secret, had brought Major John Eisenhower home from Korea to attend his father's Inauguration, and that thought seemed to add to everybody's pleasure. I was standing a little forlorn in the crowd after the ceremony, and General Marshall came up behind me and kissed me.

Secretary and Mrs. Dean Acheson gave a luncheon for Mother and Dad that day. On the way to lunch I turned around and said to my father, "Hello, *Mr.* Truman!" He roared. It was the first time in twenty-eight years of my life that I had been able to address him without some title. He was Judge Truman when I was born.

We went to the Matt Connellys' for cocktails and then it was time to go to the train. President Eisenhower had provided the Presidential private car for my father to go home in. Henry Nicholson, my father's Secret Service man, was with him to the last minute and went to the train, loyal to the end. When we got to the station we were staggered to find that it was packed with a mob of people carrying banners and shouting cheers. There were more than 5,000 people jammed in the Washington Terminal and we had great difficulty getting through the crowd to board the train.

Mother and Dad held an impromptu reception in the car. I was trying to get people through the crowd who wanted to get in— the Snyders and the Achesons and various others—and I'm convinced some people went through the car to shake hands with Dad and Mother three or four times. So many ladies took it in their heads to kiss Dad good-by that his face was smeared with lipstick.

Reathel Odum, forever faithful, and some of the newspaper corps rode to Independence in the car with Mother and Dad. I didn't go, as I had to get back to New York to take up my neglected career. When the train pulled out a great shout went up and many of the women present started to cry. Mrs. Fred Vinson was standing beside me, crying as if her heart would break.

"Oh, Margaret," she sobbed, "I can't bear to see you leave!"

"I haven't left," I said. "I'm standing right here by you!"

"Oh," said Mommy Vinson, surprised. "That's so!" and began to cry again.

ᢓᴗ Roy Leifflen, Warren Baker, and John Horton had brought me to the train. Drucie was sick with a feverish cold so I went home with John and we watched the Inauguration Ball on television, with our feet up. I must say, it was kind of a relief not to be in that jam.

"They don't do it a bit better than we did," Drucie sniffled, blowing her nose.

"No," I said. "I don't believe they do."

"We don't have to smile at *anybody*," Drucie said. "Let's make faces at each other."

"Ain't it the truth," I said inelegantly and made a face at her.

The Republicans were still dancing, long after I was sound asleep. I had sworn that when we got out of office, I was going to stay in bed for a week. I was right. The next day I had a sore throat and was horizontal for quite a while, but that hadn't been what I had in mind.

Before I left Washington I drove by the White House. It already looked remote.

"Farewell, a long farewell," I thought, and turned my face toward the future.

24: Person to person

It had been widely prophesied that when my father got out of the White House, my so-called career would fold and the public would lose interest in plain Margaret Truman. Since I had done everything I could think of not to trade on my father's position and to stand on my own feet from the beginning, I felt more optimistic than the gossipers. I do not believe that hard work goes astray, and I knew that I had worked. I was willing to go on working.

I continued my singing lessons with Mr. Dietch. I continued to fulfill the bookings that my manager, Jim Davidson, arranged for me. I continued to appear on television and on the radio as NBC directed. I served at benefits and made public appearances that seemed judicious and I found that my calendar was just as crowded as it had been when my father was President.

My happy social life also continued. Sylvia and Leonard Lyons had long since taken me under their wings and introduced me to a group of charming people whose work and interest in life was the theatre. I found them stimulating and their talk was like nectar to me. Leonard occasionally took me on his nightly rounds as a Broadway columnist and I met entertainers of every ilk from musicians of hot jazz to Shakespearean actors. Oh, the tables down at Sardi's!

The routine of my life changed very little. Mr. Dorsey ceased to trail me, and I no longer required a chaperone. I lived alone in my apartment, made breakfast and sometimes dinner, did my personal laundry in the bathroom, ran scales, was coached in languages, rehearsed and performed. My Washington beaus got up to New York now and then and I found that I had many friends in New York. I got down to Washington occasionally to see the Hortons, check on my godchild, Lyn, and admire Drucie's new dishwasher. I honestly didn't think much about past grandeur. I was too busy with the present.

The first date I had after I became a private citizen was with Jack LeVien.

"What would you like to do tonight?" Jack asked me.

"I'd like to walk down Broadway and go to a *regular* movie," I said.

Jack is in the movie business, and probably hadn't done such a thing in years. But part of the pleasure of a movie is the audience. Sitting there in the anonymous dark, you laugh or cry or suffer suspense in unison. You miss that at command performances.

We tried it, but I guess people hadn't exactly forgotten what I looked like. A good many of them came up and asked me for an autograph, so I was unable to feel very wild and free. Anyway, you don't depart the habits of several years in a few days.

In March of 1953, Mother and Dad and I were invited by Mr. and Mrs. Ed Pauley to pay a visit to Coconut Island in Hawaii, which they own in conjunction with three or four other people. We set out for the Pacific Coast in a private car provided by Mr. Averell Harriman. There was the usual turnout of reporters and photographers at our departure, just like the old days. On this occasion I permitted myself one extreme luxury. I refused to pose on that back platform! I just walked straight into the car and sat down.

We sailed on the SS *President Cleveland*, one of the President liners, and for a solid month we didn't do a thing. The trip had been planned as a rest for my parents after their arduous labors, and I was perfectly willing to do nothing. At that point the most desirable thing in life was to look at a calendar and not see a single appointment on it.

There was really nothing to do on Coconut Island, a fairly primitive place and sparsely populated aside from the people who manage the estate. We lived in a very pleasant guesthouse, with a great lanai, and I would have enjoyed myself except that I have little feeling for the Tropics, where everything seems to creep and crawl. The bane of my existence there were the little frogs which came in veritable clouds when dusk fell. The lanai was a big room with one whole side open to the elements, and a half-dozen frogs got in every night. Dad would let one get practically into my lap and then he would say, "There's a friend of yours," in a soft voice. I would scream bloody murder, which seemed to give everybody else a lot of pleasure.

My war with frogs arrived at such a pitch that Mother and the Pauley children connived to put a big old iron frog named George from the lawn into my quarters. I went into my bathroom one night and there sat George, much larger than life. I let out a howl and fled and wouldn't go back until they had got it out. Mother went around chuckling for days. I was somewhat relieved to get back to New York in May, where at least there were no frogs underfoot.

I worked all that summer. NBC had given me a sabbatical on my contract to make the trip to Hawaii, and I stayed in New York to make up the time. I did all sorts of shows and appreciated the experience. I had now had the opportunity to do interviews, guest appearances, straight drama, variety, singing, dancing, and comedy with such people as Milton Berle, Martha Raye, Tallulah Bankhead, Ed Sullivan, and Jimmy Durante, and appeared on various panel shows such as *What's My Line?*

I particularly enjoyed the shows where I was permitted to read lines, sing and dance, even clown. A good many people have expressed the opinion that it was beneath my dignity to clown, but it now seemed to me that my dignity was my own affair. This may have been a nice way of saying that I'm not good at it, but I refuse to be convinced of this. I like clowning. I like to watch it and I like to do it. I think it's marvelous to be able to make people laugh.

Mother and Dad had settled into 219 North Delaware Street in Independence, if you can call it settled. They had to put a lock on the front gate, controlled from inside the house like a buzzer in a brownstone, to keep casual strangers from walking in. The old house became a tourist mecca and cars from every state in the Union still drive around it. Sometimes you will see a whole family drawn up in front of the fence for a snapshot, using the house as the backdrop. The mail continued to pour in and Mother and Dad continued to try to answer it. No provision is made by the United States government for this exigency when a President becomes a private citizen, but other private citizens expect to have their letters answered.

Mother and Dad came to New York in the fall of 1953 when Dad made a speech before the American Jewish Congress. While we were attending this dinner, we received the information that a group of FBI men were dining in the same hotel, and went over to pay them a visit. Everybody recognized Dad, but when I got to the door a guard barred my way until somebody told him my name. Ah, fame! "That just goes to show you how much good it does you to appear on television!" I said.

I gave a dinner party for my parents at the Hotel Carlyle while they were in New York. I made the mistake of ordering roast beef. I instructed the captain to bring my father a well-done piece of meat. But a well-done piece of meat in New York is not the same as it is in Independence, Missouri. We had to send this piece of meat back to the kitchen twice to get it properly browned. I felt that it was practically worn out before he got around to eating it.

I made a concert tour after that and got home for Christmas. Dad met me at the station in Kansas City and took me out the back way. Dad was already engaged in classifying documents for his memoirs. Mother had been doing things to the house. Grandmother's room on the first floor had been transformed into a pretty Victorian guest suite. My room had a new mauve pink carpet to match the ceiling and soft blue woodwork to go with the flowered wallpaper. The kitchen was all done up in green. Mother had hung the White House portraits and incorporated many of the gifts and mementos we had received in Washington into the décor. We had our usual family Christmas.

I went back early in January to New York to embark on my concert chores. The big excitement of that spring was my proposed first appearance on the legitimate stage. I played the role of the schoolteacher in *Autumn Crocus*, the Dodie Smith play selected for me by the late Constance Collier, with whom I coached for two and a half years, and who was one of the great influences in my life. Morton (Tec) Da Costa directed the production.

336

Some of the happiest moments of my life were spent in the rehearsal of this play. I love rehearsals, when a whole imaginary world begins to take shape before your very eyes and you find yourself turning into the character you are playing. From the first readings on the bare stage to the final dress rehearsal the progress of the play is thrilling. Then you discover how one little bit of business may expose a whole facet of the author's character; how an inflection in the voice can change the entire meaning of a scene. I love the camaraderie of the cast when they are all working together to produce a finished entity—the bull sessions that follow, the lukewarm coffee in the paper cups, the dried-out sandwiches, the enthusiasm, excitement, and even the temperaments involved.

The play was to tour the summer straw-hat circuit and we opened at the Pocono Playhouse in Mount Hope, Pennsylvania, on June 28, 1954. You may remember that this was the same day on which my father was stricken with a very sudden and critical illness and had to undergo major surgery. He waked up in the night in severe pain from what he judged to be indigestion, but it turned out to be a gall bladder attack. Fortunately, they got him to the hospital in time.

This crisis followed a fairly well-established pattern in my entertainment career, but when Mother called me, I didn't think of that. I thought only of canceling my debut in a stage role and getting home. Mother and Dad both firmly opposed this. Dad was going to be all right. I must not alter my plans. I was at last persuaded, and set about trying to control my frantic worry.

Just before the curtain I was called to the telephone and a telegram, purporting to be signed by my mother, was read to me. The message said that my father was very low and that I was to come at once. I was frantic, but since I had been in constant touch with the family by telephone, there was something not quite right about this telegram.

I immediately called home, and Mother had not sent me a telegram. Everything was as well as could be expected there. Dad was improving. I then set out to check the local telegraph office. No such telegram had been received. I came to the conclusion that some fiendish ill-wisher had concocted this grim joke just to upset me. I went out on the stage determined to show whoever it was.

The play seemed to go well. I got five curtain calls and *Variety*

337

gave us a good notice. My father made a remarkable recovery and I finished the nine weeks' tour without further difficulties. I loved being an actress, and if I have the driving ambition I am often credited with, it is to be an actress on the legitimate stage.

In the fall I did more concerts, and during the latter part of November, I flew to California to appear on Jimmy Durante's NBC-TV Texaco Star Theatre on November 27 and to fill a radio commitment. It is always a joy to work with Jimmy, who treats me like a human being on and off the set. He has been one of my devoted advocates and has encouraged me and spurred me to new efforts. On this show we did songs, patter and shuffle, and comic repartee. Anyway, *we* had a good time.

From California I went directly to Independence for the Christmas holidays, returning to New York to attend the inauguration of Mr. Averell Harriman as Governor of New York in Albany. I had worked in his campaign, and you will recall that I had once prophesied that he would become Governor of New York. When I was making public appearances in an effort to get votes for Mr. Harriman, the old rumor that I was going in for a political career came up again.

I expect to work for the Democratic party whenever I see fit, but I never expect to run for office. I have no ambition to be a Congresswoman or even a committee woman. Aside from the pitfalls and agonies of these careers, which I am in position to know, I do not feel especially equipped for such jobs. I feel that my role is to lend a hand, not enter the arena.

Along with the rumors about my political career were rumors about political matchmaking. The fact that I had been seen in the company of Adlai Stevenson during the campaign and the inaugural ceremonies revived that gossip. The fact that Governor Robert Meyner of New Jersey was known to have taken me to dinner induced the Cassandras of the press to predict our engagement. I am not engaged to either of these gentlemen. They are my friends. I am apt to go to dinner with them again, but that doesn't mean that the gossipmongers can get their hopes up. One of the things about this sort of romantic publicity which I don't believe I have mentioned is its effect on my other beaus. Every time my nonexistent engagement to somebody new is announced in the papers, one of my long-standing and earnest suitors calls up in a frenzy. One man I

338

enjoyed knowing stopped calling entirely. The press does me no favor to announce that I am engaged again, and I thought they might get tired of it after I became a private citizen. I made it plain when I moved to the White House that I would never marry while my father was President, but nobody believed me. As I have stated earlier, when my engagement is announced, my parents will announce it in the accepted manner.

Just after Easter, I set out on my spring concert tour. Shortly thereafter I was invited to appear on CBS-TV *Person to Person*, substituting for Ed Murrow, and interviewing my own family. NBC graciously permitted me to fill this engagement.

Person to Person is a fascinating show, whoever happens to be appearing, and I could not keep from thinking how amazing the modern world is. I sat in a New York studio, talking to my parents at 219 North Delaware Street, Independence, and I could *see* them. They couldn't see me, which may have been just as well. Needless to say, I had come down with an attack of laryngitis a week before and had been spending days in bed trying to get my voice in shape.

Because the *Person to Person* show seems typical of laconic Truman three-way telephone conversations which we still indulge in, I append it here. This script was taken down by tape recorder and presented to me on a record.

MISS TRUMAN: Good evening! I'm Margaret Truman. The name of the program is *Person to Person*. It's all live and there is no film.

It's not possible for Edward R. Murrow to be here tonight. He is in London following up the British election results. He asked me to help escort you through a home in Independence, Missouri, that I know very well—I was born there. And our guests tonight will be two persons of whom I'm very fond—my mother and father, Mr. and Mrs. Harry S. Truman. We'll be ready in twenty seconds.

Harry S. Truman is a former President of the United States. He spent almost twenty years in Washington as Senator, Vice-president, and President. He loves politics and people, particularly Democrats.

Since the Trumans left Washington, I have been living in New York, but our family home is where it always has been, in Independence, Missouri. It's a rather rambling, Victorian-type house. It was built eighty-nine years ago,

339

shortly after Abraham Lincoln died. It has twelve rooms and stands on the corner of North Delaware Street and Truman Road, about a half acre in all.

It's exactly nine and a half miles from here to my father's present office in the Federal Reserve Bank Building in Kansas City. As he drives himself to work each morning down Truman Road—it will always be Fifteenth Street to me—he passes Truman Car Wash, Truman Road Grill, Truman Pharmacy, Truman Palmistry, and Truman Road Hamburger Shop. And when he makes the thirty-minute trip home each night, he can still note Harry's Tavern, Harry's Café, and Harry's Used Furniture.

We love Missouri.

When my father was a Senator we used to spend about six months a year in Independence. Or Mother did. Dad was frequently out speechmaking.

Later when my father was at the White House Mother always came home for the summer.

Now this has been the only home for my parents for the past two years and three months; that is, when Dad isn't out gallivanting around and talking to people.

We have never had cameras in the house before. But I hope they are working tonight.

Good evening, Mrs. Truman!

MRS. TRUMAN: Good evening, Margaret.

MISS TRUMAN: Good evening, Mr. Truman.

MR. TRUMAN: Good evening, Margaret.

MISS TRUMAN: Oh, Dad. Ed Murrow suggested that I lay down some ground rules. Here they are. I ask the questions. Some he suggested and some are my own. Other friends of mine have asked me to ask you and Mother to show us around the house and I am allowed to make fair comment. Agreed?

MR. TRUMAN: It's all right with me.

MISS TRUMAN: Mother?

MRS. TRUMAN: Absolutely.

MISS TRUMAN: Say, is it cool on the back porch tonight?

MRS. TRUMAN: A little cool after a real hard storm.

MISS TRUMAN: Well, I heard about that. Say, Mother, I guess we will be able to dispense with the usual phone call tonight.

MRS. TRUMAN: I hope so.

MISS TRUMAN: What's new at home?

340

MRS. TRUMAN: Not too much new at home. What's new with you?

MISS TRUMAN: Nothing, not a thing. How are all the aunts and uncles?

MRS. TRUMAN: Oh, fine, fine. They are all listening and watching.

MISS TRUMAN: They'd better be. Dad?

MR. TRUMAN: Yes.

MISS TRUMAN: So many people ask, "How are your parents making out from their switch to Pennsylvania Avenue and Washington to North Delaware Street in Independence?"

MR. TRUMAN: Well, I think we are doing very well. I always like the home town better than any other place I know of. I didn't have anything particular against Washington but I think that Independence is a much better city.

MISS TRUMAN: He is likely prejudiced. Mother?

MRS. TRUMAN: Yes.

MISS TRUMAN: Please tell everyone why you went back to Missouri instead of staying in Washington.

MRS. TRUMAN: There was never any question about staying in Washington. Never any question of not coming home. Is that reason enough?

MISS TRUMAN: That's reason enough. I'll buy that. Mother, have you and Dad had dinner yet?

MRS. TRUMAN: Oh, yes. Oh, we had to have dinner and get ready for this.

MISS TRUMAN: I guess so. Where is Vietta?

MRS. TRUMAN: Oh, she's in the kitchen.

MISS TRUMAN: Oh, Vietta knew me before I knew her. I was three years old when she came to work with us. She raised me too. Hi, Petey.

VIETTA: Hi, Margie.

MISS TRUMAN: How are you?

VIETTA: Fine.

MISS TRUMAN: I must tell everyone that Vietta stayed eight years at the White House as sort of master of bread and rolls, and when I had my first concert Dad insisted she go with me. Now she is the big wheel in the Independence kitchen. Anything you want to add?

VIETTA: No, you said it all.

MISS TRUMAN: I guess so. Say, I haven't had a chance to talk to you since the big party celebrating Dad's seventy-first birthday and groundbreaking for the new library. How many people were there?

VIETTA: Between 200 and 250. I had plenty of help.

341

MISS TRUMAN: You got that in. Someone asked me the other day did you like living at the White House?

VIETTA: I most certainly did.

MISS TRUMAN: What did you like most?

VIETTA: I liked to gather around and meet all the big people, all the Congressmen.

MISS TRUMAN: Oh, that's a good line. I know you must have something cooking in the oven. You always do. What is it tonight?

VIETTA: Well, tonight one of your favorites. Brownies.

MISS TRUMAN: Ah. Hey, are those for me?

VIETTA: Yes.

MISS TRUMAN: All right, I have got you dead to rights. Don't forget. Bye-bye.

VIETTA: Bye-bye, honey.

MISS TRUMAN: I want to go back and talk to Mother and Dad. Mother?

MRS. TRUMAN: Yes.

MISS TRUMAN: Are we still getting a lot of sightseers and visitors?

MRS. TRUMAN: Oh, loads of them, yes.

MISS TRUMAN: All the time?

MRS. TRUMAN: All the time. Every day. We had a funny experience the other night. Dad and I went over to see your cousin across the street and there were so many out here in front of the house we couldn't come home. We had to spend most of the evening on the front porch all by ourselves because our cousins weren't at home.

MISS TRUMAN: Fine.

MRS. TRUMAN: Isn't that ridiculous?

MISS TRUMAN: Yes. What about the time someone picked your tulips? You remember?

MRS. TRUMAN: Oh. Well, yes, some woman came in the back yard and started picking all my beautiful white tulips and one of the men on the place went down there and asked her just what she thought she was doing and she said she didn't think Mrs. Truman cared if she took some of her tulips. She took all she wanted.

MISS TRUMAN: Fine thing, after all the work you did.

MRS. TRUMAN: Yes, isn't it?

MISS TRUMAN: Dad, we know you're not the greatest believer in the accuracy of poll takers, but on your morning walk around town, do you ever take a poll of how people feel toward you?

MR. TRUMAN: Whenever I meet them I can tell very well that they are

342

happy to see me. There are a great many of them who don't know me as well as those home folks do, that are somewhat awed by the fact that I once lived in the White House, but it doesn't bother me because that never occurs to me, and I can see how I'd feel if I were meeting a President and I still lived here in Independence as a private citizen.

MISS TRUMAN: Everyone who stopped at the house in recent years knows we have a big iron fence around the property with a gate that opens only when we push a button in the house. Incidentally, Ed Murrow's television men tell me the gate needs an oiling.

MRS. TRUMAN: I am afraid he was telling the truth.

MISS TRUMAN: Dad, why don't you explain why you have that fence out there?

MR. TRUMAN: Well, the fence had to be put up to offset the American propensities for collecting souvenirs and tearing the house down. I was told that when Herbert Hoover went to Washington as President, they took the doorknobs off his house and almost tore the house down, and that was done before they placed the guards there to prevent it. The Secret Service decided that the fence would save our property from being destroyed. It is an old story that Americans like to collect souvenirs. When I was in the First World War it was said that the British fought for the control of the seas; the French for the freedom of France; and the Americans fought for souvenirs and they are still fighting for them.

MISS TRUMAN: Mother, we were talking about tulips a minute ago. How does your garden grow?

MRS. TRUMAN: Oh, we have had some wonderful rains and the garden is all in bloom, especially Mrs. Lasker's Peace roses. They're gorgeous.

MISS TRUMAN: That sounds nice. Daddy?

MR. TRUMAN: Yes.

MISS TRUMAN: Brace yourself.

MR. TRUMAN: For what?

MISS TRUMAN: I am frequently asked what kind of work—manual work, that is—you do around the house.

MR. TRUMAN: I do an immense amount of it from a rocking chair.

MISS TRUMAN: How many times have you mowed the lawn in the past few years?

MR. TRUMAN: As I remember, I think about once.

MISS TRUMAN: Uh, uh. That right, Mother?

MRS. TRUMAN: I don't remember the once.

MISS TRUMAN: Well, that's what I thought. Dad, you used to tell reporters that the White House was a jail. Do you feel free now?

MR. TRUMAN: Well, substantially so; practically as free as I expect we ever will be. For some reason or other I don't suppose we will ever be as free as we would have been if we hadn't lived in the White House.

MISS TRUMAN: I think that sounds logical. Mother, for years we had Secret Service men around us, at least Dad and I did. Do you miss Washington?

MRS. TRUMAN: Oh, yes, I miss Washington. I miss Washington a lot. I loved it there but I am completely happy at home. Of course, the Secret Service men didn't bother me as much as you and Dad.

MISS TRUMAN: I remember you lost them.

MRS. TRUMAN: Yes, I did, early in the day.

MISS TRUMAN: That's what I thought. Mother, would you and Dad show us to the living room, please?

MRS. TRUMAN: Yes, we'd love to.

MISS TRUMAN: All right. This is our side porch. It leads on down to our dining room. We usually have our meals here. No kibitzing, Mother. No kibitzing. No kibitzing. Those stairs are the way up to the upstairs bedrooms. Come on, Mommy, are you having my trouble?

MRS. TRUMAN: No, I'm having mike cord trouble.

MISS TRUMAN: Well, first off let's show everyone the portrait of Dad that you like so much.

MRS. TRUMAN: Yes. Here it is.

MISS TRUMAN: As we know, that's yours, right?

MRS. TRUMAN: Strictly mine. No library, no museum ever gets it.

MISS TRUMAN: All right, Dad, while we are at it, let's show the painting of your daughter and get it over with.

MR. TRUMAN: Right over here.

MISS TRUMAN: Someone asked me recently, Daddy, did your father ever say that your house in Missouri creaks and groans like the White House. Answer, please!

MR. TRUMAN: Yes, it did creak and groan just like the White House. It doesn't groan so much now.

MISS TRUMAN: Remember the night, speaking of ghosts, that you heard a knock on your bedroom door in the White House?

MR. TRUMAN: Yes, I heard the knock and got up and answered it about

344

three o'clock in the morning. There wasn't anybody there. I think it must have been Lincoln's ghost walking up and down the hall.

MISS TRUMAN: It happened two or three times, didn't it?

MR. TRUMAN: Yes, several times.

MISS TRUMAN: Mother, do you think Dad could tell about the time we had Annette and Jane as guests in the Lincoln Room?

MRS. TRUMAN: Yes, if he will tell it straight.

MISS TRUMAN: He could try.

MR. TRUMAN: Did I ever tell anything any other way but straight? I made arrangements for one of our tall doormen to put on a tall hat, act the part of Lincoln, come up and pay you a visit. My nerve failed me and I didn't do it. I was afraid it might scare you.

MISS TRUMAN: Dad, I just won a small bet. Before Ed Murrow left he said that I couldn't steer you away from politics this long. I win, but you'll get your chance. I have a lot of things that he wants me to ask you so in a moment we will come back, so don't go away.

MISS TRUMAN: This is Margaret Truman again. Ninety seconds ago I left my parents in the living room of our house in Independence and I see they are still there. Mr. and Mrs. Truman, I'm back.

MRS. TRUMAN: You told us to stay here.

MISS TRUMAN: Dad, do you have anything left up your political sleeve?

MR. TRUMAN: No, nothing in particular.

MISS TRUMAN: I want Mother to answer this one. Have you made sure that Daddy takes things easy since Dad left Washington?

MRS. TRUMAN: That's a laugh—between the piles of mail and the many, many visitors, it's a little difficult.

MISS TRUMAN: Yes, so I hear.

MRS. TRUMAN: I'm doing my best.

MISS TRUMAN: So many people want to know what you do to relax inasmuch as you don't fish, hunt, or play golf.

MR. TRUMAN: Well, my only relaxation is to work, and I never have known anybody to be injured by too much hard work. It is the lack of it that kills people.

MISS TRUMAN: Well, now I think I will ask you to show us the way to the music room.

MR. TRUMAN: All right, we'll try. Here is another picture that is right interesting.

MISS TRUMAN: No fair. No fair. Go on right by that. Right on by that.

MR. TRUMAN: You can't sell *it* either.

MISS TRUMAN: Dad, how is the book coming?

MR. TRUMAN: Coming along all right. I think we will meet the deadline on the fifteenth day of June, and the book will probably be published about the fifteenth of September, I hope.

MISS TRUMAN: I know you once had the stories of your years in Washington up to 1,000,000 words. How long is it now?

MR. TRUMAN: We have had to cut down to about 500,000. That is a very hard job, but I think we are going to succeed in doing it.

MISS TRUMAN: That still sounds like a lot of words. Mother, how is the proofreading going?

MRS. TRUMAN: It is still pretty strenuous.

MISS TRUMAN: Everyone in the Truman family knows that when Mother gets to proofreading on anything Dad is working on, that means it is on the way to completion. Back in the other room we saw the paintings, one of me and one of Dad. Dad, let's look at Mother's. I think that's awfully good.

MR. TRUMAN: That is a wonderful picture of your mother.

MISS TRUMAN: That's my favorite. Let's see some non-Truman paintings. You two sit and I will introduce them.

Over Dad's shoulder is a present to Dad from Sir Winston Churchill painted by his own hand at Marrakech. I brought this home from London when Sir Winston asked me to bring it to my father. Now, over the piano is an original given to us by Grandma Moses. Dad, now it's your turn to explain things. Could we have the history of the piano, please?

MR. TRUMAN: Well, this piano is the one that was purchased for you when you were a very little girl. You had your first lesson on it and it's been your piano ever since. It gets a right good workout when you're at home.

MISS TRUMAN: I think I was seven or eight. Do you remember the first thing you taught me on that piano?

MR. TRUMAN: Yes, I think it was a little waltz I taught you. I think I can still play it.

MISS TRUMAN: Mother, is the piano tuned?

MRS. TRUMAN: Well, fairly so.

MISS TRUMAN: Dad, when you did that television tour through the White House you showed everyone you could still play. Let's prove you still haven't lost your touch.

346

MR. TRUMAN: Let's try and see what happens. Then you can tell whether the piano is in tune or not. This is your waltz.
[*Mr. Truman played the piano.*]

MISS TRUMAN: Isn't that Paderewski's *Minuet?*

MR. TRUMAN: Yes, that's part of it.

MISS TRUMAN: Good hearing you play!

MR. TRUMAN: Not nearly all of it.

MISS TRUMAN: I enjoyed that. If you want to go back to your chair, I have another question to ask.

MR. TRUMAN: Fire away.

MISS TRUMAN: Ed Murrow wanted me to ask you, just how much influence and help was Mother when you were in the White House?

MR. TRUMAN: She was a wonderful influence and help. A President is in a bad way if he doesn't have a First Lady that knows her job and is a full support to him. She's the greatest help a President can have. Mine was.

MRS. TRUMAN: Thank you.

MISS TRUMAN: Mother, let me switch from Washington to Kansas City. How is your baseball team doing?

MRS. TRUMAN: We are doing pretty well. We are going to have a great team before the season is gone.

MISS TRUMAN: You're the sports fan of the family. Have you seen anything good on TV lately?

MRS. TRUMAN: A few good things, yes. But I haven't been able to find a wrestling match—none at all.

MISS TRUMAN: Dad, how is the new library coming?

MR. TRUMAN: It's coming along all right. They have the ground graded and they are digging the foundation now. They have the signal to proceed to finish in about a year and two months.

MISS TRUMAN: That's good. Are you going to travel toward the den now and show us some of that?

MR. TRUMAN: Yes, I think so. I have a picture of the library out here I want to show you.

MISS TRUMAN: Mother?

MRS. TRUMAN: Yes.

MISS TRUMAN: You've been cleaning up again. What happened to Dad's work table?

MRS. TRUMAN: We had to have some room in here today.

MISS TRUMAN: That's a good excuse. Mother always cleans up. Where's the picture, Daddy?

347

MR. TRUMAN: Here it is.

MISS TRUMAN: That's the picture of the library. That's something I haven't seen.

MR. TRUMAN: Quite a picture.

MISS TRUMAN: Have they made much progress since the groundbreaking two weeks ago?

MRS. TRUMAN: Oh, yes, a lot of progress. And he goes by most every morning on the way to the office to see just what they are doing.

MISS TRUMAN: Are you going to go easy on the Truman Library builders?

MR. TRUMAN: What's that?

MISS TRUMAN: Are you going to go easy on the Truman Library builders?

MR. TRUMAN: I'm going to watch them put it up and I'll see that they do it right, just as I always do whenever I had anything in charge like that.

MISS TRUMAN: Sidewalk superintendent! How much have you stored in Kansas City ready for the library?

MR. TRUMAN: There is an old big vault full of books, papers, and pictures and things of that kind that will go into the library when it's up. There is a tremendous collection of Bibles in the vault that will be very interesting when they are put out for the people to see.

MISS TRUMAN: How much is it all going to cost, and how much cash has the committee raised so far?

MR. TRUMAN: It is estimated that the library itself will cost $1,700,000 and we have collected $1,200,000, and I think the rest of it is in sight. We will have the money all collected by the time that the library is ready to use.

MISS TRUMAN: Good! Dad, to get serious, I suppose someday the scholars will go through your personal papers and draw up a summary of your administration. What do you hope you will be remembered for?

MR. TRUMAN: I hope to be remembered as the people's President. I have always said that there are a great many important organizations with lots of money who maintain lobbyists in Washington. I'd say 15 million people in the United States are represented by the lobbyists in the city of Washington. The other 150 million have only one man who is elected at large to represent them—that is, the President of the United States. When he goes back on them they are in a bad way.

MISS TRUMAN: What do you think has been the most important development in the country or world since you left Washington?

MR. TRUMAN: I think we are approaching a peace settlement and, I hope, the end of the cold war. The signing of the treaty is a step in that direction.

MISS TRUMAN: A moment ago I saw the icon you received from Queen Helen of Rumania. Do you recall the circumstances surrounding that gift?

MR. TRUMAN: The government of the United States, at my direction, sent 200,000 tons of wheat to the starving Moravians and the Queen of Rumania presented me with this icon, which came out of the mosque of St. Sophia—Constantinople, it was then.

MISS TRUMAN: You know a lot of people have said to me, "Your father sure loves a fight." True or false?

MR. TRUMAN: Well, I never promoted a fight, but I never ran from one if it was necessary to meet things head on.

MISS TRUMAN: Mommy, do you want to say a few words about politics specifically or in general?

MRS. TRUMAN: No, not in either category, thank you.

MISS TRUMAN: Well, that's definite. Dad?

MR. TRUMAN: You know your mother never talks about such things.

MISS TRUMAN: Ed wanted you to talk about the campaign in '48. He wanted to know what made you so sure you would win.

MR. TRUMAN: Well, I have been through a similar experience on two or three occasions and I had come to the conclusion that when the people know the facts and they know that you are telling the truth and stand for the things that are for their best interests they will vote for you, and I was very well assured if I could see enough people and talk to enough people I could be elected, and that is what I did and this is the way it came out.

MISS TRUMAN: Well, tell me, what is the toughest decision you had to make?

MR. TRUMAN: To go into Korea to save the United Nations Republic of South Korea.

MISS TRUMAN: Dad, what advice do you have for young people who want to go into politics?

MR. TRUMAN: Well, the best thing they can do is to study history, particularly the history of their country, their city, their county, and their state, to read all the history they possibly can and study about what makes men act and the

349

biographies of the people whose histories are important to a person who wants to go into politics—and the fundamental thing is that a politician must be fundamentally honest, intellectually or otherwise. Unless he is—he won't make it.

MISS TRUMAN: There goes the clock. Mother, what advice do you have on raising children?

MRS. TRUMAN: Oh, absolutely none. Do you think I have had any luck?

MISS TRUMAN: Let's make it specific. What advice do you have for me?

MRS. TRUMAN: That's a loaded question.

MISS TRUMAN: I don't know, but I think I have had about the best.

MR. TRUMAN: I have found the best way to give advice to young children is to find out what they want and then advise them to do it.

MISS TRUMAN: Oh, I see. Well, we are coming along here pretty well on our timing and everything, so I think perhaps you'd better say we have had a good time visiting.

MRS. TRUMAN: Wonderful.

MISS TRUMAN: Yes.

MR. TRUMAN: It has been wonderful.

MISS TRUMAN: It's good seeing you. At least I can see you.

MRS. TRUMAN: Lots of fun. Wish I could have seen you at the same time.

MR. TRUMAN: If we could have seen you it would have been perfect.

MISS TRUMAN: Well, I have to go now, so I guess I will have to say good-by. Thanks for the party. Have a nice time.

MRS. TRUMAN: When will we talk to you again?

MISS TRUMAN: Well, I might talk to you later again tonight.

MRS. TRUMAN: Good. That will be wonderful.

MISS TRUMAN: Next week Mr. Murrow will be here to visit with W. C. Handy, composer of the *St. Louis Blues*, and that talented actress and writer, Cornelia Otis Skinner. It's almost as much fun to work on this show as it is to be at home watching, and most of the credit goes here.

And now, as Ed Murrow would say, from *Person to Person*, good night and good luck.

I wish I could have been in both places at once. As far as I can ascertain there had been much housecleaning and furbishing of 219 North Delaware before the broadcast. Heaven forbid a spot of dust should show up in front of a nationwide audience! There was also a little grumbling on the part of Mother and Vietta about the complexity of wires and equipment that took over the house. Cameramen are apt to smoke, and Mother was horrified to come into the dining room and find a great overflowing ashtray of dead cigarettes and ashes on the floor in plain view!

As soon as the show was over Vietta wrapped up the brownies she was making and mailed them to me, so they shouldn't be a total loss. They were right up to standard.

This show gave me a deep sense of satisfaction, since it seemed to me that I had finally established myself as a separate entity. When I introduced my father and mother to the television audience I felt that I had at least managed to keep abreast and to make some contribution to their lives as I had always yearned to do. The show was well received by the press, and the next week, when Ed Murrow returned to *Person to Person*, he announced waggishly that he was substituting for Margaret Truman. Letters poured in and people stopped me in the street to say that I had passed muster.

I had been out of the White House two years and I felt that at last I was on my own way.

25: Footnote to history

When you embark on autobiography you take courage by the forelock. The re-creation of a past, no matter how short or immediate, makes curious demands upon the recollector. I realize that some effrontery is involved when a woman (not especially profound, nor even wishing to be profound), who has arrived at a minor celebrity through circumstance and who is only a shade past the three-decade mark, undertakes to write her "life." I would not be human if I did not hope that my "life" is still before me.

It stands to reason that if I were a great woman who had fought her way singlehanded to success, or a historic figure, the public could be expected to take an interest in my days. Since I am neither of these so far, but what people usually refer to as "a nice, normal girl—like your sister or the girl next door," but blessed beyond average fortune, my instinct in undertaking autobiography was to share what befell me personally. I entered into it as if I were writing a long letter home.

I know that much that is trivial and frivolous has found its way into these pages. Triviality and frivolity are part of most lives. They have been part of mine. Much that was grave and important in the world I lived in will not be found here. It has not been my intention or even my province to deal in such matters, which can be more ably dealt with by others.

353

I am aware that there has scarcely been a more dramatic, earth-shaking, and often terrifying time to be alive than the second quarter of the twentieth century. I was thirteen years old when Adolf Hitler marched on Austria, but I was a woman before he finally gave up the ghost, and I was aware of the terror and misery he visited on a large part of the earth's surface. I knew that Benito Mussolini wreaked havoc and spilled blood in which his own was eventually mingled. I knew, as anybody sensible knew even in the safe confines of the United States, that horror was in progress across the sea—invasions of property and privacy, warping of souls, banishment of pride, battering of honor, deprivation, destruction, and death. I knew that human beings were robbed of all they held dear, that families were divided against each other, that masses of people slaved and sickened in unspeakable prison camps, were exterminated like flies or reduced to levels that make the imagination stagger. I knew that orphaned children grew up like wild animals, that refugees trudged the bombed roads in their torn shoes and hid in caves like beasts. I knew that men crawled through stinking jungles and died of wounds and disease; that death rained from the skies and people's lives were cut off in the middle of a sentence. I knew that civilization tottered, and that even here at home, we lived with "the nettle of danger."

I knew it the way your sister or the girl next door knew it. Like her, I was serving food in a USO canteen, talking to depressed soldiers who had it all before them and couldn't imagine it any more than I could. I was singing songs to take their minds off the present and the future. I was appearing at bond rallies, because there were people who thought that might help our cause. I was rolling bandages and giving blood at the Red Cross. I was writing letters to the boys I knew in military service. I was going to church and praying that freedom would prevail. I was doing whatever I could. Although I stood on the periphery of grave affairs, often within earshot of great decisions, I am no more equipped to write "the purple testament of bleeding war" than any other sheltered American girl of my generation.

I was moved at what I heard and read, and saddened, and often bewildered. Sometimes I was frightened. I had opinions, but they had no better foundation than anyone else's opinions. I suppose they were pretty callow. At any rate, they had no effect on world events and would be valueless here. I couldn't write about the wars, because I wasn't there and I don't know how. What I have tried to do is to write about myself and what happened to me. I am sure that criticism will be leveled at the blithe nature of this chronicle which transpired in such a dark and gloomy time, but that's the way it was. Maybe most women are like that—like those doughty females who got in their carriages with a picnic lunch and headed the horses toward the battlefield when Washington, D.C., was in hearing distance of the guns of the Civil War. I don't presume that the description of a ball gown, or the memory of a party or the sound of music, will make much of an impression on history— although it has always seemed to me that a woman's dress or a love letter could conjure up the climate of a period more readily than all those textbooks I read at George Washington University—that was not my intention. I have chosen the title of this book advisedly. It is the lovely French word for memory, and this is my memory book.

I have had no thought of writing history. The best I could hope to write would be a footnote to history. As the only child of the President of a great world power in a cataclysmic time, I will certainly be expected to make some comment on this man who will belong to history—to evoke him in special ways, available only to a daughter who is, as he has often stated publicly, the apple of his eye. I find this very difficult. I love my father and I admire him and respect him. I cannot treat him with the lightness and the jocular humor which distinguishes most tales of fathers and makes a good story.

For one thing, though my father loves a joke, he is a serious man. He has always been serious, hard-working, honest, and forthright, not given to the outrageous or whimsical individualities that go with a "character." He does not run roughshod over anybody or go in for dynamics or domineering or wild antics. He studies the merits of the case and tries to act accordingly. He is stubborn and determined when he feels he is right, but he makes up his mind only after long and solitary consideration. This may make better statesmanship than it makes copy.

As a matter of fact, I do not want to poke fun at my father even in the most affectionate manner, or make him out a character, because he isn't. When I have been asked to do this on radio and television shows, I have refused. If I cannot engage in comedy without holding up the members of my family to ridicule, then I will not engage in comedy. Such jokes are a broken crutch, and while my father has the gift of laughing at himself, I do not wish or intend to make him do it on my account.

I know a little about this sort of thing. When Leonard Lyons took Mother and Mrs. Mesta and me to see *Call Me Madam*, in which Ethel Merman impersonated Mrs. Mesta and I was the butt of what few jokes this musical had, I laughed. Mrs. Mesta was a good sport. We all said it was a lot of fun. But down deep, I didn't enjoy it. I thought it was vulgar to ridicule people who were helpless to protect themselves, even in a spirit of high good humor.

No more do I intend to articulate moments of deep emotion that have taken place in my family circle. I do not consider these public property, nor do I feel called on to exploit them. My father, my mother, and I all have a strong sense of privacy. Each of us respects the privacy of others. We have lived public lives and we have given to the public the full measure of our obligation to them, but in our family we have maintained that strong core of privacy which makes for the best family relationship. There have been moments in all our lives which can never belong to anybody but us.

Perhaps this is best exemplified by what happened last Christmas at home. My father came in the living room one day and my mother was making a small fire on the hearth out of what appeared to be letters or documents. As the flames licked up the handwriting, my father said, "What are you doing, Bess?"

"I'm burning your letters to me," Mother said.

"Bess!" said my father. "You oughtn't to do that."

"Why not?" my mother said. "I've read them several times."

"But think of history!" my father said.

"I *have*," said Mother.

&> I do not know what history will make of these remarks or whether, in the twenty-first century, for instance, people will understand or care about the sort of affections and loyalties and trust and confidence I have enjoyed. I hope they will, since there is little in life that surpasses these things, as far as I know. What can I say about my father that will make you see him whole—except that

356

he cares. He cares about everything, and nothing is too much trouble. His philosophies are singularly basic—the greatest good for the greatest number; the end can never justify the means; do as you would be done by; do the best you can; don't give up; don't be afraid; the friends thou hast and their adoption tried, grapple them to thy soul with hoops of steel; the quality of mercy is not strained. Most of them derive from the Bible or Shakespeare, his favorite books, and from the experience of living. He was born kind.

What can I say of my mother except that she is courageous, proud, modest, and dedicated. Her sense of duty is unique and her sense of fun is also unique. Her standards are lofty, but she is satisfied to set an example by living them and makes no effort to impose them on others. She has a respect for the fitness of things and an insistence on comporting oneself with dignity which may seem old-fashioned in a period which tends toward blowzy informality, but which have stood the test of time.

The listing of these virtues will embarrass my father and mother, and I do not mean to leave the impression that they are plaster saints. They get huffy. They get mad. They get their feelings hurt. They get bored. They are both stubborn as mules. They sometimes think I'm crazy. They disagree. One of them thinks a girl shouldn't stay out so late at night. One of them thinks a girl should get up at 7 A.M. no matter what time she got in at night. One disapproves of the other's language. Both disapprove of my lifelong tendency to speak slang. One likes to dance; the other one doesn't. One likes bridge; the other likes poker. One thinks publicity is not quite nice. The other one knows publicity is a necessity at certain times, and insists on it. One enjoys sitting on a bank with a fishing pole; the other turns pale with ennui if he has to go fishing. One leans toward the conservative in dress. The other will wear a shirt with hibiscus printed on it if not prevented. One takes to flying like an eagle; the other detests flying, but will steel herself to do it if necessity demands. Both think a fool and his money are soon parted, and that sometimes their daughter is foolish. One thinks the other is always trying to spoil me, and she couldn't be more right! One can't go to bed until I get home at night, not because she doesn't trust me implicitly, but because she wants to hear all about it! One goes soundly to sleep at the drop of a hat, even on election night, and can't understand why anybody else wants to stay up. One thinks it is a sound idea to hear a woman out and then make up your own mind about the matter under discussion. The other knows a man hasn't got the sense he was born with when it comes to taking care of himself and is always ready with the aspirin, the needle and thread, and the advice on wet feet and not sitting in a draft and other instructions. One thinks there is more than one way to skin a cat, so when he was being nagged to mow the lawn in Independence, Missouri, the other day, he decided to do it at 11 A.M. Sunday morning when everybody was passing the house on the way to church! One likes his meat cooked until it is dark brown and the other one thinks that ruins meat. One is an Episcopalian and the other is a Baptist, and it's always going to be that way. They both have a strong sense of tradition and family and have exhibited an abiding respect for each other's in-laws. They both like watermelon, each other, and me.

It has been insinuated that I am tied to an apron string or that I am Daddy's girl and therefore not a free agent. I submit that I have had more freedom than most young women my age when it comes to family dictum. When I decided on a stage career, my family not only reared no stumbling blocks, they cooperated in every way possible. When I decided to take an apartment in New York and leave the parental roof, they not only did not object, they helped me find an apartment. I have never had the impetus to run wild or needed to rebel. There hasn't been any reason for it.

If I have tried to live up to the high standards my father and mother have established, by precept and example, it is because I *chose* these standards. I am devoted to them and I want to please them, but this was not the motivating factor. I am convinced that this is the best way for me to live.

I have never had a major quarrel with my father. We have disagreed, as people must invariably disagree, but though we are both high-tempered, we have never lashed out at each other or inflicted wounding scars. For one thing, I have always been amenable to guidance, and I have every reason to know that my father is a wiser and more experienced thinker than I am. If he can be charged with the destinies of a nation, who am I to resist his conclusions about my affairs? If he hasn't been able to change my mind about a few things, I have still had enough sense to accept his advice. My father is a peaceable man and does not enjoy quarreling, as some men do.

My mother and I have occasionally bickered like sisters or any other two women living under the same roof. I have criticized her Spanish accent or her lack of enthusiasm about one thing or another. When Mother and Dad got back to Independence, Missouri, after my father had retired from the Presidency and found the station and the platforms and the railroad yards full of a cheering multitude of people, who could no longer have any axes to grind, my mother looked at this testament of affection and regard from old friends and neighbors and perfect strangers and said, "This *almost* makes it all worth while!" That struck me as the understatement of the century.

My mother has criticized my late hours, tendency to procrastinate, inability to get off my thank-you notes promptly, and sometimes my taste in friends. She can put a sardonic inflection into her voice which jerks me up. When the papers recently made a thing of my dancing several times at El Morocco with a gentleman who has a vivid record of marriages and inamoratas, she called me on the telephone about something else. In the course of the conversation she remarked guilelessly, "How did you happen to be dancing with So-and-So the other evening?"

"He asked me," I said. "I couldn't be rude."

"I should think once would be enough to take care of manners," she said.

"He was such a good dancer," I said.

"Do you have to do it again?" she asked.

Since the gentleman in question had been calling every hour on the hour all day and I was about worn down sufficiently to take the call, this conversation came at a good time for me. Although I already knew that I shouldn't take the call (my conscience is a good compass), without giving any orders, she strengthened my resistance.

The fact is, I love my parents and enjoy their company, not from a sense of filial duty, but because they are friends and good companions.

I am sensible of the contributions made to my days by those who have been close to me, in and out of the family circle. These people have been blessed with integrity, humor, and common sense, and these are the qualities that have most attracted me in human beings. I find it difficult to string along on a personal basis with anybody who does not have such equipment. My fiancé, Clifton Daniel, has all of these things. Cliff has wavy, prematurely gray hair, fine brown eyes and a thin, almost ascetic face. Though he is remarkably handsome (some people may say I'm prejudiced but I'm not!), I first fell in love with his marvelous sense of humor. I met him at the home of old friends of mine, Mr. and Mrs. George Backer. I had dropped in there after dinner with another man. Cliff started right in to tease me. Since I had grown up in a teasing family, this made me feel as if I had known him always. Our friendship started on a note of mutual laughter.

Nobody can doubt, after reading this book, that all faintly romantic occasions in my life have been conducted in the glare of publicity. Because I valued my friendship with Cliff so seriously, I especially didn't want our dates to be photographed or chatted and speculated about in the newspapers. While we certainly did not go into seclusion or make it a point to meet in out-of-way places, we were fortunate enough to have many mutual friends and had the good luck to meet in the homes of friends and to go to private parties together. Occasionally we dined out together. Mother and Cliff and I had dinner together one Saturday night in January at the Pavillon in New York, but nobody seemed to notice. We had dinner at 21 occasionally. Maybe the press had given me up as far as romance went, or maybe my prayers were answered. Not more than a half-dozen people, including my parents and Cliff's, knew that we were engaged until my father and mother announced my engagement at noon on March 12, as I had always proposed they should.

The keeper of this secret who found the burden most difficult was Mother! I really think she almost burst. We originally intended to announce our engagement on March 15, but Mother telephoned me ten days before and said piteously that she was entertaining her famous bridge club on March 13, and couldn't she just tell *them!* We had been having a few normal mother-daughter disagreements on the details of the wedding, which Dad had been mediating like a diplomat (Dad as mediator usually persuades me that Mother knows best, which she obviously *does*), but I couldn't resist her wistful plea. So we changed the date of the announcement so Mother and the Bridge Club could talk it over.

My wedding is scheduled at Trinity Church, in Independence,

Missouri, where my father and mother were married, and where I attended Sunday school and sang in the choir since I was a little girl. Dear old Trinity—it has witnessed many happy occasions of my life, and what occasion can ever be happier than this? Only members of our families will attend the ceremony, which will be followed by a small reception at 219 North Delaware for old and dear friends. I feel that marriage vows are sacred and I hope that mine will be spared the hurly-burly of a news event.

I do not think that fancy trappings make a wedding, or much of anything else. The people make a wedding and I feel fortunate that my fiancé is a man of character—a good man—whose integrity is unassailable, whose powers of decision are well known and whose humor is a sheer delight. Cliff is a Southerner—he hails from the small town of Zebulon, North Carolina—was educated at the University of North Carolina at Chapel Hill and is a Baptist! What else? My father is delighted and looks forward to having an ally completely in his corner. Though Mother is an Episcopalian, I think she is already in Cliff's corner. I'm surrounded! As a newspaperman, foreign correspondent, and now assistant to the Foreign News Editor of *The New York Times*, Cliff is accustomed to making the decisions —and I'm learning to abide by them.

I'm awfully glad I waited until he came along.

I am also deeply grateful to the American people for the opportunities and experiences I have had as a result of their generosity. I feel obligated to them above and beyond the call of duty. While my residence in the White House may have been an inadvertent result of their decision at the polls, they have treated me with warmth and affection when I have appeared before them on my own. I can never repay this gift of interest, but I hope never to bring sorrow or disillusionment on them through any act of mine and to comport myself with the dignity and honor they deserve.

When I think of the tremendous proportions of my days in the White House, I know that I never permitted myself to realize what was happening to me, or I should have been lost. It was always like a dream from which one might awaken at any given moment. Too much happened to be entirely taken in or assimilated. It will take me many more years to sort it out or see it in the proper perspective. If I had been older or younger I might have taken it in my stride, but I was of an age when fantasy and fact were already intermingled, and impressions fell so thick and fast that it was difficult to settle on one or the other.

I did what I could to keep my head, and in this I was ably abetted by my mother, who looks on spoiling the child as one of the more cardinal sins. I do not think I became spoiled in the specific sense of the word, but one of the inescapable results of such an experience is a kind of spoiling through sheer force of circumstance. While I believe I can honestly say that my character, formed by inheritance, early training, and constant exposure to the horse-sense attitudes of wise and careful people, changed very little, the opportunity of meeting some of the great figures of our time sophisticated me beyond my years and my nature. I use the word sophisticated timorously, for anybody who has read thus far must know that I have never ceased to be naïve and that I am incapable of being blasé. Maybe I should have said *matured*. But I have been in the company of so many men who were already standing at the pinnacles of great careers that my vision may have become blurred where people my own age were concerned. When I am with them, I feel that I have been there before. Such spoiling is a mixed blessing. If my fabulous dinner partners have sophisticated me, they have also beckoned me out of my own age group, so that I always seem to be standing between generations and unable to involve myself wholly with either, like the child who has skipped a grade at school.

There was also the matter of convenience and mere creature comforts to connive at reducing resistance. While my mother strove mightily to maintain the Spartan outposts, such as doing one's personal laundry and washing one's own hair, the lack of time and the spreading involvement in what seemed requisite affairs made it necessary for someone else to keep the dresses pressed and the wardrobe in order. When we traveled, there was no way to gainsay the red carpet or the red roses. Long black cars with drivers are habit-forming, no matter how you fight against it. The White House has a large staff of servants. One becomes inured to flashbulbs and reading one's own name in the paper, so that after a while the limelight seems more important than it is. Deep in the shamed subconscious, the Little Princess rears her ugly head, and has to be dealt with.

Needless to say, such advantages must be paid for with physical exhaustion, with the sacrifice of privacy, with the eternal neces-

362

sity of offending no one, with the warm smile and the gracious word and the nice gesture and genuine interest, even if your feet or your head or some other portion of your anatomy is killing you. They must be paid for with the guarded tongue, the unspoken opinion, the smiling façade, the congenial parry to the rude question, with the importance of being forever nice, with the assumption of a dignity which the young can only find difficult. They must be paid for with the burden of becoming, in a sense, public property, available to mean gibes, the subject of ridiculous rumor, a sitting pigeon for critics and busybodies—and without recourse. They must be paid for with the soft answer.

These too become habit-forming. One finds oneself secretive or unable to express a spontaneous opinion, no matter what the conviction, or incapable of involving oneself entirely. One becomes wary, because one has discovered that people are not above making use of one. One becomes suspicious. One finds oneself being *nice*, because it is politic or because of what people will say, and not for its own sweet sake. But these are minor disadvantages, which have to be controlled, and they disappear in the glory of the recollection.

I do not go along with the people who say to me, "What can happen to you now that can possibly compare to what has already happened?" Plenty can happen to me. Life has touched me as lightly as a curled feather, and I know that I must be prepared for anything. I am an explorer on a new continent, already a little past the average age for such adventure because of my long sojourn in Arcady. At long last, I must seek and find and prove myself.

While I can never be anything but grateful for being identified as a portion of a family group, and I hope always to be thus associated, I know that to make a contribution, the individual must stand alone. No matter what surrounds us, we are alone, and sometimes when I sit staring into the unknowable future I have a driving urge to express myself, to make some original and personal gift to the world that has given me so much. I still do not know how this can be done. I do not know whether it can best be done by submerging oneself in another personality and contributing through the thoughts and hopes and dreams of a husband. I have a feeling that if one feels deeply in love it would be the only way.

Since I can remember, it has seemed to me that what I wanted most to do was to make other people happy, to take them out of themselves and make them forget their cares for a little while. When I was given my first comedy lines to read on a broadcast, the studio audience burst into prolonged laughter. How can I make you know what that sound meant to me? Talk about music to the ears! I understood then why a comedian wants to hog the center of the stage and can scarcely be dragged off into the wings, even when his stint is over. He wants to hear the people laugh again. There is no sound like it, not even applause.

It is not easy to know oneself. The real self hides behind a hundred subterfuges and deludes one with acquired mannerisms and superficial trappings. It was especially not very easy for me to know myself because I never had time. When I look back over the strenuous program which has made up my first thirty-one years, I wonder how I survived. Being forever at the mercy of the calendar and the clock and leaping from one spectacular event to another gives little time for inviting the soul. Then it gets to be a habit not to invite it but to fill one's days with fripperies and to submit to footless events just to put it off, as one will go to a dull movie to keep from writing the pressing thank-you notes or balancing the checkbook.

Along with my wish to share, I think this prompted me to undertake this book, for an inspection of the past may give some inkling to the present and the future. It is not easy to try to turn oneself and one's life into words to be read casually by any passer-by. Along with a natural bent for privacy I have had a lifelong education in circumspect utterance. To suddenly switch to the opposite extreme has had its moments of agony. While I have never been a victim of shyness, I have had normal qualms about a few hitherto unpublished incidents and intimacies which appear here. Having produced this book at considerable pains, I have had moments when I wondered whether I could bear to have anybody read it. But out of the exercise has come clarification and an improved understanding of myself.

Well, the diaries have run out and it is time to fold the clippings and gather up the invitations, the place cards, the letters, the scrawled notes, the photographs and snapshots and menus, the corsage ribbons and the mementos, the pressed flowers and the scraps of silk and lace, the luck pieces and the talismans, the battered old chalice that christened the USS *Missouri*—all the bits and pieces of the past —and put them back in the old trunk, turn the key, and run joyfully to meet whatever lies in store.

Our divertissement is finished, and I say with Prospero, liberally excerpted:

> Now my charms are all o'erthrown
> And what strength I have's mine own,—
> Which is most faint . . .
> But release me from my bands
> With the help of your good hands.
> Gentle breath of yours my sails
> Must fill, or else my project fails,
> Which was to please.